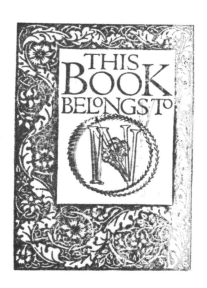

THIS BOOK BELONGS TO

KINGFISHER REFERENCE

CHILDREN'S
CONCISE
ENCYCLOPEDIA

KINGFISHER  REFERENCE

CHILDREN'S CONCISE ENCYCLOPEDIA

GENERAL EDITOR: JOHN PATON

Kingfisher Books

Contributors

Jacqui Bailey Ian Graham Marie Greenwood Ann Kay David Lambert Keith Lye
Christopher Maynard Isabelle Paton

Editorial and Educational Advisors

Brian Williams J.M.B. Tritton, Head Teacher, Star Primary School, Newham
Nigel Cox, Framlingham College Junior School, Woodbridge

Editorial and Design

John Paton (General Editor)

Jim Miles Jennifer Justice Yvonne Ibazebo Terry Woodley Michele Arron Elaine Willis

Concise Edition

John Paton (General Editor) Jim Miles Jennifer Justice Catherine Headlam Cynthia O'Neill
Louise Jervis Terry Jeavons TBI Ltd Matthew Gore

Kingfisher Books, Grisewood & Dempsey Ltd,
Elsley House, 24–30 Great Titchfield Street, London W1P 7AD

This Concise edition published in 1992 by Kingfisher Books.
Reprinted 1993

Originally published in 1989 as *The Kingfisher Children's Encyclopedia* by Kingfisher Books and
revised in 1991 and 1992.

Copyright © Grisewood & Dempsey Ltd 1989, 1991, 1992

British Library Cataloguing-in-Publication Data
A catalogue record for this book is available from the British Library

IBSN 0 86272 964 5

Printed in Hong Kong by South China Printing Co (1988) Ltd

ABOUT *your* ENCYCLOPEDIA

This encyclopedia is very easy to use. All the entries are arranged in alphabetical order. You should find most of the information you want by first looking up the main entry word. If the subject you are looking for does not have its own entry, look in the Index at the back. Usually you will find some information about your subject in another article.

•

Throughout the encyclopedia you will find words printed in small capitals, like this: MAMMALS. These words are cross-references. When you see one, you will know that there is a separate entry on the subject in your encyclopedia. That entry may have more information about the subject you are looking up.

•

Subject symbols appear next to each heading. These are helpful when you are browsing through the encyclopedia and want to find entries on Transport ▪, for instance, or History ▪, or Countries and Places ▪ – there are 16 symbols in all.

•

In addition to the main text there are occasional See-it-Yourself panels which show in a practical way how you can find out more about the subject.

•

There are Fact Panels, containing at-a-glance information on the biggest, highest, longest, etc. And the outside column has a host of fascinating snippets of additional and often surprising information.

•

By using your encyclopedia you will discover a wealth of information about people, ideas, events, and the world around you.

THE SUBJECT SYMBOLS

Each entry in this encyclopedia has its own easily-recognized symbol opposite the heading. This symbol tells you at a glance which area of interest the entry falls into – is it animals, history, or science? Below are the 16 subject areas we have used.

 PLANTS AND FOOD From microscopic plants to gigantic trees – what they are, how they grow, the food they provide.

 THE ARTS Drawing, painting, sculpture, crafts, ballet, modern dance, drama, theatre, TV, cinema, etc., plus the great artists.

 PEOPLES AND GOVERNMENT Descriptions of peoples of the world, the things they do and the way they govern their countries.

 LANGUAGE AND LITERATURE How language is constructed, plus descriptions of great playwrights, novelists, poets, etc.

 SPORTS AND PASTIMES Competitive sports, great athletes and sporting stars, plus descriptions of many hobbies.

 ASTRONOMY AND SPACE Birth of the universe, the solar system, galaxies, space exploration, etc.

 **SCIENCE** How science is applied in everyday life, the elements, sources of energy, important scientists, etc.

RELIGION, PHILOSOPHY, AND MYTH How these have changed through history and the ones that have survived.

 ANIMALS Descriptions of behaviour, homes, and individual species; mammals, birds, reptiles, fishes, insects, etc.

 MACHINES AND MECHANISMS Explanations of everything from simple machines to jet engines, plus descriptions of their inventors.

 TRAVEL AND TRANSPORT The history and development of aircraft, ships, railways, cars, motorcycles, etc.

 HUMAN BODY How the body works, the process of birth, ageing, diseases, immunity, genetics, etc.

 BUILDINGS The history and development of architecture, modern construction and design, famous buildings and architects etc.

 OUR EARTH How the Earth was formed, and how it is still changing; its deserts, mountains, oceans, rivers, etc.

HISTORY Great events and great figures from ancient civilizations up t the present day.

COUNTRIES AND PLACES Descriptions, flags, maps, essential statistics, etc. for all countries, plus places o interest.

Aardvark

The aardvark is an animal that eats TERMITES. When it has broken open a termites' nest with its powerful claws, it pokes in its long, sticky tongue and pulls it out covered with the insects. The aardvark lives in central and southern Africa. It has large ears like a donkey and is an expert burrower. If caught away from its home it can dig a hole for itself at astonishing speed. The word 'aardvark' is Dutch for 'earth pig'. These shy animals can be 2 metres long and nearly a metre high.

◀ *Aardvarks are shy animals that come out mostly during the night.*

▼ *The abacus here shows what each bead counts when it is pushed toward the centre bar. The top abacus reads 7—two 1 beads pushed to the bar and one 5 bead. If we want to add 171 to the 7, we push one more 1 bead to the bar, add a 50 and two 10s for the 70, and one 100 bead—178.*

Abacus

The abacus is a simple counting machine first used by the ancient Greeks and Romans. It consists of rows of beads strung on wires; those on the first wire count as ones, those on the second wire count as tens, on the third wire they count as hundreds, and so on. The abacus is still used in some Eastern countries. The Romans sometimes used small stones as counters. They called these counters *calculi* and it is from this that we get our word 'calculate'.

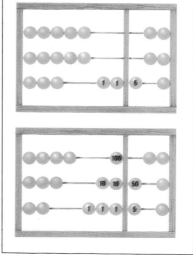

▼ When a ball is dropped, it
accelerates—goes faster and faster. In
the first second it travels 4.9m, in the
next second 14.6m, and so on. A
cricket ball and a tennis ball would fall
at the same speed.

Starting
point

After 1
second

After 2
seconds

Aborigine

The word 'aborigine' really means the first people
who lived in any country. But it is now used when
we talk about the natives of AUSTRALIA. These are
slim black people with broad noses and black wavy
hair. They came to Australia thousands of years ago
from south-eastern Asia. In Australia they had no
permanent homes but wandered about the desert
hunting or gathering their food. Their weapons
were the boomerang and the throwing spear.

The Aborigines were very badly treated by the
white men who came to Australia. Today Aborigines have rights as Australian citizens.

Acceleration

When a car increases speed, it accelerates. If it is
travelling at 40 miles an hour and increases speed to
50 miles an hour after 1 minute, it has accelerated at a
rate of 10 miles per hour per minute.

If you drop a ball from the top of a tall building it
accelerates—goes faster and faster—as it falls. It
reaches a velocity of 9.8m per second after one
second. After two seconds it reaches a velocity of
19.6m per second. Every second that it falls, it
increases its speed by 9.8m per second. The ball
accelerates as it falls because it is being pulled down
by the force of GRAVITY. The strange thing is that the
force of gravity pulls everything down at the same
speed. If there was no air and you dropped a feather
and a cricket ball from the top of a building at the
same time, they would hit the ground together. Of
course, air holds up the feather much more than the
ball. The feather's shape makes the difference.

Acid

An acid is a liquid chemical compound that is often
poisonous. Some acids, such as sulphuric acid, nitric
acid and hydrochloric acid, are very strong and can
corrode, or eat away, even the strongest metals.
Other acids are harmless. These include the citric
acid that gives lemons and oranges their sharp taste,
and the acetic acid in vinegar. Lactic acid is produced when milk goes sour. All acids turn a special
sort of paper called *litmus* red.

Acid Rain

All rain is very slightly ACID. The weak acid in rainwater can eat away the limestone in buildings and statues. Limestone is an alkali.

Rain can also react with the waste gases sent out by power stations, factories and cars. Such gases can be carried great distances by the wind. Then they fall as weak sulphuric acid and nitric acid, so they are called acid rain. After a time, lakes and streams are slowly poisoned by the acid rain, threatening plants and wildlife. People are trying to reduce the waste gases poured out by industrial nations.

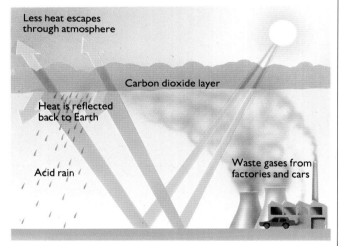

Less heat escapes through atmosphere

Carbon dioxide layer

Heat is reflected back to Earth

Acid rain

Waste gases from factories and cars

ACID

SEE IT YOURSELF
Cut half a red cabbage into strips. Put the strips into a pan of hot water and let the mixture cool. Strain the liquid and pour into clean glasses. Add a few drops of water. This shows the neutral colour. Now add a few drops of lemon juice to one glass to show its acid colour, and some washing soda to the other glass to show its alkaline colour.

▲ *Two of the main threats to our atmosphere are acid rain and the 'greenhouse effect'. They are both caused by gases sent out by power stations, factories and cars. The greenhouse effect is caused by a 'blanket' of carbon dioxide gas in the air which traps the Sun's heat and prevents some of it escaping into space. The Earth can become warmer and warmer over the years.*
▶ *Scientists are not in agreement on how much damage is done by acid rain. The trees in this picture have been damaged severely.*

Africa

Africa is the world's second largest continent. It covers an area of 30,319,000 square km, one-fifth of the world's land. Africa stretches from the Mediterranean Sea in the north to the Cape of Good Hope at its tip in the south. Large parts of Africa are empty wasteland. The scorching SAHARA Desert

AFRICA

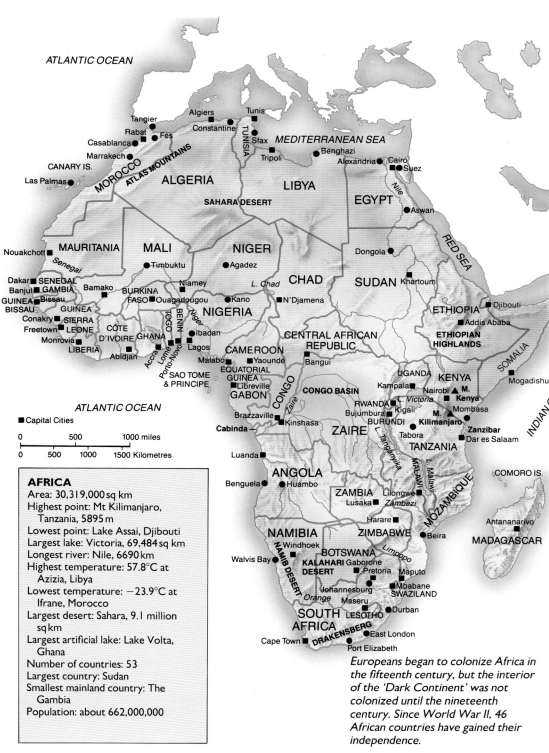

ATLANTIC OCEAN

Tangier
Algiers
Tunis
Rabat
Constantine
Fès
Casablanca
TUNISIA
Sfax
MEDITERRANEAN SEA
Marrakech
Benghazi
Tripoli
Alexandria
Cairo
CANARY IS.
Suez
Las Palmas
MOROCCO
ATLAS MOUNTAINS
ALGERIA
LIBYA
EGYPT
SAHARA DESERT
Aswan
Nile
RED SEA
Nouakchott
MAURITANIA
MALI
NIGER
Dongola
SENEGAL
Timbuktu
Agadez
CHAD
SUDAN
Khartoum
Dakar
SENEGAL
Bamako
Niamey
L. Chad
Banjul
GAMBIA
BURKINA
Ouagadougou
Kano
N'Djamena
ETHIOPIA
Djibouti
GUINEA
Bissau
FASO
Niger
Addis Ababa
BISSAU
GUINEA
NIGERIA
ETHIOPIAN
Conakry
SIERRA
TOGO
BENIN
CENTRAL AFRICAN
HIGHLANDS
Freetown
LEONE
CÔTE
Ibadan
REPUBLIC
Monrovia
D'IVOIRE
GHANA
Lagos
SOMALIA
LIBERIA
Abidjan
Accra
Lomé
Porto-Novo
CAMEROON
Mogadishu
Malabo
Yaoundé
Bangui
SAO TOME
EQUATORIAL
UGANDA
KENYA
& PRINCIPE
GUINEA
Libreville
Kampala
Nairobi
M.
GABON
CONGO
Zaire
CONGO BASIN
L. Victoria
Kenya
RWANDA
Mombasa
Brazzaville
Bujumbura
Kigali
M.
Cabinda
Kinshasa
BURUNDI
Kilimanjaro
Zanzibar
ZAIRE
Tabora
Dar es Salaam
TANZANIA
Luanda
L. Tanganyika
MALAWI
ANGOLA
COMORO IS.
Benguela
Huambo
ZAMBIA
Lilongwe
L. Malawi
Antananarivo
Lusaka
Zambezi
MOZAMBIQUE
Harare
MADAGASCAR
NAMIBIA
ZIMBABWE
Beira
Windhoek
BOTSWANA
Limpopo
Walvis Bay
KALAHARI
Gaborone
NAMIB DESERT
DESERT
Pretoria
Maputo
Johannesburg
Mbabane
Orange
Maseru
SWAZILAND
SOUTH
LESOTHO
Durban
AFRICA
East London
Cape Town
DRAKENSBERG
Port Elizabeth

ATLANTIC OCEAN

INDIAN OCEAN

■ Capital Cities

0	500	1000 miles
0	500	1000	1500 Kilometres

AFRICA
Area: 30,319,000 sq km
Highest point: Mt Kilimanjaro,
  Tanzania, 5895 m
Lowest point: Lake Assai, Djibouti
Largest lake: Victoria, 69,484 sq km
Longest river: Nile, 6690 km
Highest temperature: 57.8°C at
  Azizia, Libya
Lowest temperature: −23.9°C at
  Ifrane, Morocco
Largest desert: Sahara, 9.1 million
  sq km
Largest artificial lake: Lake Volta,
  Ghana
Number of countries: 53
Largest country: Sudan
Smallest mainland country: The
  Gambia
Population: about 662,000,000

*Europeans began to colonize Africa in
the fifteenth century, but the interior
of the 'Dark Continent' was not
colonized until the nineteenth
century. Since World War II, 46
African countries have gained their
independence.*

spreads over much of the northern part of the continent. Near the EQUATOR, which runs through the centre of Africa, are thick rain forests. There the trees grow so close together that their leaves blot out the sunlight.

More than a third of Africa is a high, flat plain, or plateau. Grassland called *savanna* covers much of the plateau region. Great herds of grazing animals roam the savanna. They include zebras, giraffes, wildebeest and impala. Other animals, such as lions, cheetahs and hyenas, prey upon the grazing animals. In the past, many animals were killed by hunters, but today special reserves have been set up to protect them.

Mt Kilimanjaro, the highest mountain in Africa, rises 5895 metres in Tanzania. Africa's largest lake, Lake Victoria, lies between Kenya and Tanzania. The continent's great rivers are the NILE, Zaire (formerly called Congo), Niger and Zambezi.

Many different types of people live in Africa. In North Africa are ARABS and Berbers, who mostly follow the Muslim religion. So-called 'black Africa' lies south of the Sahara Desert. The Negroid peoples who live there make up three-quarters of Africa's population. People with European and Asian ancestors make up the rest of the population.

Most Africans are farmers, growing crops such as cocoa, coffee, cotton, sisal and tea. Africa produces nearly three-quarters of the world's palm oil and palm kernels, which are used to make items like soap and margarine.

For centuries Africa was called the 'Dark Continent' because Europeans knew little about it or its people. The first people to learn more were the Portuguese, who found a sea route to India by sailing around the southern tip of Africa. From the 1400s, European sailors began to ship slaves from Africa. About 14 million slaves were taken to the Americas between 1500 and the 1800s.

By the 1800s the countries of Europe were becoming interested in setting up colonies in Africa and soon the continent had been carved up between them. The Europeans brought new ways of life to Africa and, after some years, many Africans began to resent being ruled by foreigners. During the 1950s and 1960s most former colonies became independent African countries.

▲ Africa is a huge continent. It is more than 120 times as big as the British Isles. The great Sahara Desert covers most of northern Africa. It separates the Arab countries along the Mediterranean from the Negro countries of central Africa. Most of the rest of Africa is grassland, or savanna.

▲ This beautifully carved ivory mask was worn as an ornament by the king of the West African kingdom of Benin. Great empires grew up in Africa before the white people came.

▼ *When the AIDS virus enters a white blood cell, the core of the virus breaks open and releases DNA. The virus DNA takes over the white blood cell which begins to make copies of the virus and then dies.*

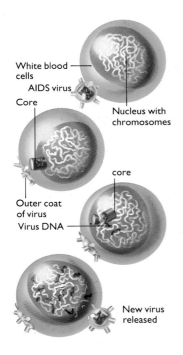

White blood cells

AIDS virus

Core

Nucleus with chromosomes

core

Outer coat of virus

Virus DNA

New virus released

HIV Human Immunodeficiency Virus.
AIDS Acquired Immune Deficiency Syndrome.
Syndrome A combination of symptoms/signs showing that a condition/illness exists.

AIDS

AIDS (Acquired Immune Deficiency Syndrome) is caused by a VIRUS named HIV. The AIDS virus attacks white BLOOD cells that fight off viruses and BACTERIA when they enter the body. When these white blood cells are destroyed, the patient can become very ill with a disease that would not be serious to a healthy person. Because the body of a person with AIDS has lost its means of fighting disease, the patient can often die.

AIDS is passed from person to person in three main ways: by intimate sexual contact, by exposure to blood infected with HIV, and by transmission to a baby in an infected mother's womb. One common way for people to catch the disease is by sharng hypodermic needles. People who have been infected with HIV may not become seriously ill until years later. AIDS is a serious world problem.

Air

Air is all around us—it surrounds the Earth in a layer we call the *atmosphere*. All living things must have air in order to live. Air is colourless and has no smell. Yet it is really a mixture of a number of different gases. We can feel air when the wind blows, and we know air has weight. Air carries sound—without it we would not be able to hear, because sounds cannot travel in a VACUUM.

The chief gas in air is nitrogen, which makes up nearly four-fifths of the air. About one-fifth of the air is made up of OXYGEN. Air also holds some water in very fine particles called *vapour*. When we talk about the degree of HUMIDITY in the air, it is the amount of water in the air we are measuring.

The air that surrounds the Earth gets thinner the higher you go. All high-flying aircraft have to keep the air in their cabins at ground-level pressure so that passengers can breathe normally. In the same way mountaineers carry their own air supply beause the air at the top of high mountains is too thin to breathe properly.

Warm air expands and becomes lighter. The air around a heater becomes lighter and rises. Cool air moves into its place. This too warms and rises, so the entire room is heated.

Aircraft

From earliest times people dreamed of being able to fly like the birds. Myths and legends are filled with tales of supermen who could fly. Brave but foolhardy inventors leaped from high towers wearing wings, but all such attempts ended in failure. In the 1500s Leonardo da Vinci drew plans for a helicopter but such a machine could not have been built in his day.

The conquest of the air by people began with the first BALLOON flight in 1783. Later, AIRSHIPS, steerable balloons with engines and propellers, took to the sky. Inventors built gliders, proving that flight was also possible using winged aeroplanes that were heavier than air.

It was the development of the petrol engine in the 1880s that made powered aeroplanes a practical possibility. On 17 December 1903 the Wright brothers made the first controlled and powered manned flight in their flimsy aeroplane, the *Flyer*.

Since that historic flight progress in aviation has been amazingly rapid. Today we live in a world where people take air travel for granted. Jumbo jets like the Boeing 747 can carry up to 500 passengers. Supersonic jet aircraft, such as *Concorde*, can fly the Atlantic Ocean in three hours. Space shuttles can fly into space and return to land on a runway, like an airliner.

▼ A selection of aircraft throughout the ages.

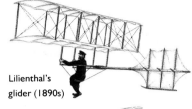

Lilienthal's glider (1890s)

Seaplane (1920s)

Spitfire fighter (1940s)

Bell X-I (1947)

Concorde (1970s)

Dash 8 (1970s)

Albania

Albania is a small, rugged country that lies between Yugoslavia and Greece on the eastern shore of the Adriatic Sea. Most Albanians live in small, remote mountain villages. Albanian farmers grow wheat, barley, tobacco and cotton. Beneath the ground there are mineral deposits, oil and natural gas. Albania was ruled by Turkey for over 400 years. After World War II Albania became a communist state, but by 1991 it was moving away from communism.

ALBANIA

Government: Communist
Capital: Tirana
Area: 28,748 sq km
Population: 3,250,000
Language: Albanian
Currency: Lek

Alexander the Great

Alexander the Great (356–323 BC) was a ruler of GREECE and one of the greatest generals who ever lived. The son of Philip of Macedon, the young Alexander was taught by Aristotle, the famous Greek philosopher. His father taught him to plan and win battles.

Alexander conquered the Greek city-states after he became king when Philip died in 336 BC. He then marched east to conquer Persia, which was at that time the greatest empire in the world. By 327 Alexander's empire stretched from Greece to India. When his armies reached India they were worn out from marching and fighting. Alexander had to turn back. When he reached Babylon he became ill with a fever and died. He was still only 33. Alexander's body was carried back to Alexandria, the great city he had founded in EGYPT. There it was placed in a magnificent tomb.

▲ The above picture of Alexander is part of a mosaic found at Pompeii in Italy.

Alligator and Crocodile

The alligator is a large reptile that belongs to the same family as the crocodile. There are two species: one is the American alligator of the south-eastern USA; the other is the smaller Chinese alligator that lives in the YANGTZE RIVER. Alligators look very like crocodiles, but have broader, flatter heads with rounded snouts. When they close their mouths, the lower jaw cannot be seen.

Crocodiles are clumsy on land, but in the water they move swiftly without a sound. They hunt fish, turtles and water mammals. Crocodiles and alligators lay their eggs in nests or holes in the ground.

▲ When the crocodile (top) closes its jaws, the fourth tooth in its lower jaw sticks out. The alligator (centre) has heavier jaws than its relative the gharial (bottom).

Alloy

An alloy is a mixture of two or more METALS. The mixture is usually more useful than each metal on its own. For example, a soft metal such as COPPER can be strengthened by adding zinc to it to form *brass*, or tin to form *bronze*, both of which are strong metals. An alloy which is said to have *high tensile strength* can resist great pressure without breaking; some alloys can withstand very high temperatures, other alloys are very light.

USEFUL ALLOYS		
Alloy	**Made mostly of**	**Some uses**
Steel	Iron, carbon and other elements	Cars, beams, tools etc.
Brass	Copper and zinc	Gears, propellers, scientific instruments etc.
Bronze	Copper and tin	Scientific instruments, bells etc.
Pewter	Tin, antimony, lead and copper	Household utensils
Dentist's amalgam	Mercury and copper	Teeth fillings
Cupronickel	Nickel and copper	'Silver' coins
Invar	Nickel and iron	Precision instruments, watch balance wheels
Sterling silver	Silver and copper	Tableware

18% chromium
8% nickel
1% carbon
73% iron

▲ *Pure iron is not very strong and rusts easily. It is mixed with chromium, nickel and carbon to make stainless steel, the alloy used for cutlery.*

Amazon, River

The Amazon is the mightiest river in South America, and, at a length of 6437 km, is the second longest in the world, after the Nile. It flows from Peru through Brazil to the Atlantic Ocean. Almost the whole of the Amazon basin is dense tropical forest. In the 1540s a Spanish explorer saw female Indian warriors on the Amazon's banks, so the river was named after the Amazons (female warriors) of Greek legends.

American Indians

American Indians are the native peoples of the Americas—that is, the first people to live there. They are known as Indians because when Christopher COLUMBUS reached America in 1492 he thought he had arrived in India.

The Indians of the Americas (also known as native Americans) are thought to have crossed to the North American continent from Asia about 20,000 years ago. Very gradually, over the centuries, they spread through North America and down into what is now Central and South America. They developed different ways of life according to where they lived.

When Europeans began to settle in North America, conflict broke out as they invaded the Indians' hunting grounds. Many Indians were killed or forced to move farther west. By the late 1800s almost all the tribes had been sent to live on special reservations by the US government. Today many Indians are working to gain equal opportunities.

The greatest American Indian contribution to our way of life has been the hundreds of plant species that were unknown in Europe before the time of Columbus. Among the strange plants being grown by the Indians when white people first set foot in America were potatoes, beans, maize (Indian corn), tomatoes, cacao (for chocolate), pineapples and Jerusalem artichokes.

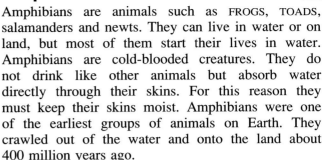

Amphibian

Amphibians are animals such as FROGS, TOADS, salamanders and newts. They can live in water or on land, but most of them start their lives in water. Amphibians are cold-blooded creatures. They do not drink like other animals but absorb water directly through their skins. For this reason they must keep their skins moist. Amphibians were one of the earliest groups of animals on Earth. They crawled out of the water and onto the land about 400 million years ago.

All amphibians have backbones. Nearly all of them lay their eggs in water, in a layer of jelly which protects them. When the young amphibians hatch, they feed on algae (tiny water plants). A young frog at this stage is called a tadpole. It breathes the oxygen dissolved in water through gills. After two or three months the tadpole begins to change into an adult. Its tail gradually disappears, and its gills turn into LUNGS. Hind legs and then front legs appear. The little frog leaves the water and spends the rest of its life as an air-breathing adult. But it must return to the water to mate and lay its eggs.

▲ Amphibians such as the toad and newt are creatures that are at home both on dry land and in the water. All amphibians have tails when they are babies. Some kinds, such as toads, lose their tails as they grow, but others, such as newts, keep them all their lives. The toad has stubbier legs than a frog, and its body is usually wider and flatter. It also has a rougher skin than a frog.

▼ Millions of years ago, amphibians such as these developed on earth. The top two are named Diadactes, the lower one Seymouria.

Andes

The Andes mountain range is the longest in the world. It stretches for more than 7000 km down the west side of South America, running the whole length of the continent. Several peaks are more than 6000 m high, and Aconcagua, on the border beween Argentina and Chile, is the highest mountain in the Americas at 6960 m. Many of the peaks are active volcanoes. The Andes are rich in minerals such as copper, silver and gold.

Anglo-Saxons

Anglo-Saxon is the name given to the group of Germanic tribes who settled in Britain during the AD 400s and 500s. These tribes were the Angles, Saxons and Jutes. They gradually occupied all of England, driving the original Celtic people of Britain into Wales and Cornwall. By the 700s there were seven main Anglo-Saxon kingdoms—Wessex, Sussex, Kent, Essex, East Anglia, Mercia and Northumbria. About half the words we use today come from Anglo-Saxon.

Life was hard for Anglo-Saxon peasants. The tribes were farming people who lived in the countryside in groups of about fifty. Each group was made up of the family and relations of one man. Their houses were very simple and crude.

◄ Many Anglo-Saxon peasants lived in very simple houses like the ones shown here. Note the 'chimney hole' in the straw roof!

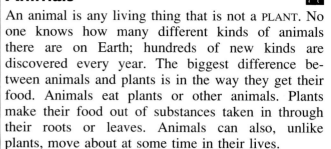

The biggest land animal so far discovered is a dinosaur called Ultrasaurus. The fossil remains of this huge creature were found in 1979 in Colorado, USA. It stood about 8 metres high at the shoulder—four times the height of a tall man—and must have weighed about 130 tonnes. Ultrasaurus was about 30 metres long—the length of 1½ cricket pitches!

Animals

An animal is any living thing that is not a PLANT. No one knows how many different kinds of animals there are on Earth; hundreds of new kinds are discovered every year. The biggest difference between animals and plants is in the way they get their food. Animals eat plants or other animals. Plants make their food out of substances taken in through their roots or leaves. Animals can also, unlike plants, move about at some time in their lives.

Some animals such as the tiny amoeba reproduce by just splitting in two. In most other animals the female produces eggs that are fertilized by the male. Creatures such as the cod produce millions of eggs, of which only a very few ever hatch and even fewer reach maturity. These animals never see or care for their young.

Ant

Ants are 'social' insects—they live together in colonies. Some colonies are in heaps of twigs; others are in chambers deep in the ground. Still others are hills of earth or sand. There are three types of ant: males, queens which lay eggs, and workers or females that do not mate or lay eggs.

Antarctic

The Antarctic is the continent that surrounds the SOUTH POLE. It is a vast cold region, with very little animal or plant life on land. Nearly all of the Antarctic is covered by an ice cap, broken only by a few mountain ranges. This ice cap averages 2500 metres in thickness, but is as much as 4700 metres thick in places.

Anteater

The anteater of South America is a curious creature with a long, tapering snout. This snout is specially shaped to winkle ants, termites and grubs from their nests. It catches the insects with its long, whip-like tongue. An anteater may measure over 2 metres from the tip of its tail to its snout. It uses its strong front claws to tear open ant and termite nests.

▲ *Anteaters live in the tropical forests and swamps of South America. They are active only at night.*

Antibiotics

Antibiotics are substances, produced by living things, that are poisonous to harmful bacteria. For a long time it was thought that any medicine that was able to kill a particular microbe would also kill the patient. Then, early in this century, scientists began to discover drugs that would kill bacteria but do the patient no harm. The most important of these drugs was penicillin, a drug produced by a mould. Penicillin was a 'wonder drug' that saved many lives. It was especially useful against pneumonia. The antibiotic streptomycin has almost got rid of the disease tuberculosis. Scientists have found many more useful antibiotics that can fight diseases such as whooping cough and typhus.

Antibiotics do not work against viruses, organsms that cause the common cold, flu, mumps, measles, AIDS and other diseases.

Ape

Apes are our closest animal relatives. We share the same kind of skeleton and have the same kind of blood and catch many similar diseases. Apes have large brains, but even the gorilla's brain is only half the size of a person's. Unlike monkeys, apes have no tails. There are four kinds of ape: the GORILLA and CHIMPANZEE are African; ORANG-UTANS live in Borneo; gibbons live in South-East Asia.

Arabs

Arabs were originally those people who lived in Arabia. But from the AD 600s Arabian Arabs, inspired by their new faith, ISLAM, swept through western Asia and North Africa, conquering and settling a huge area. They taught the inhabitants the Arabic language and their Islamic religion. Today an Arab is anyone whose mother tongue is Arabic. This includes Arabic-speaking peoples from countries such as Algeria, Syria, Iraq and Libya. Musims in Iran, India and Pakistan pray in Arabic, but do not use it in everyday speech, so they are not considered Arabs.

After World War II many Arab countries became extremely rich from the production of OIL.

▼ Apes have highly developed hands and fingers and enjoy swinging from branches.

Gibbon

Chimpanzee

Gorilla

Orang-utan

Archimedes is supposed to have played a part in the construction of one of the Seven Wonders of the Ancient World. It was the Pharos of Alexandria, a lighthouse designed by Ptolemy I of Egypt. The lighthouse was about 122 metres high, and at the top fires were kept burning. The fires were reflected by mirrors designed by Archimedes so that they could be seen 50 km away at night.

Archaeology

Archaeology is the study of history through the things that people have made and built. They may include tools, pottery, houses, temples, or graves. Even a garbage pit can help to reveal how people lived. Archaeologists study all these things, from the greatest of monuments to the tiniest pin. Modern archaeology began during the RENAISSANCE, when people became interested in the culture of ancient GREECE and ROME. At first archaeological sites were ransacked for the treasures they contained. But by the early 1800s archaeologists had begun to uncover sites carefully, noting all they found and where they found it. Many exciting and important discoveries were made, including the tomb of the pharaoh Tutankhamun (1922).

Archimedes

Archimedes (282–212 BC) was a famous Greek scientist who lived in Sicily. Among many other things, he discovered Archimedes' Principle which tells us that if we weigh an object in the air and then weigh it again submerged in a liquid, it will lose weight equal to the weight of the liquid it displaces. Archimedes is supposed to have discovered this when he stepped into a bath full to the brim, and water spilled onto the floor.

GREEK CAPITALS

These are the three main styles of ancient Greek capital (the decorated top of columns used in their buildings).

Doric

Ionic

Corinthian

Architecture

Architecture is the art of designing buildings. If we look at old buildings still standing we can learn a great deal about the people who built them.

Architecture as we know it began about 5000 years ago in ancient EGYPT. The Egyptians built huge PYRAMIDS as tombs for their kings, and many of these pyramids still stand.

Greek architecture began to take shape about 600 BC and developed into the beautiful styles we can see today on the Acropolis at Athens.

When the Romans conquered GREECE they copied Greek architecture. But they soon discovered how to make an arch, so they could build larger, stronger buildings. They also began to make domes for the first time.

About AD 800 the Romanesque period of architecture began in Europe. Romanesque architecture at first imitated the style of ancient Rome, but soon took on a style of its own—a style that was strong and heavy. This style was followed by the Gothic. Most of the fine old cathedrals are in the Gothic style. They have graceful pointed arches over doors, windows, and often in the roof as well. The roof of a Gothic cathedral is usually made of a series of criss-cross arches which take the weight of the ceiling. Roofs like this are called *vaulted* roofs.

In about 1400 a new style of architecture began in Italy. This was during the RENAISSANCE (the word means re-birth) and it spread all over Europe. Renaissance architects paid almost as much attention to public buildings and people's houses as they did to churches.

Later, many famous architects changed the building styles to fit the times in which they lived.

▲ *An example of modern architecture. This building is in Munich in Germany.*

Arctic

The Arctic is the region around the North Pole. At the North Pole itself there is no land, only a huge area of frozen sea. The land in the Arctic region is frozen solid for most of the year. In the short summer the surface soil thaws and some plants can grow, even brightly coloured flowers. There are now more people in the Arctic than there used to be. This is because valuable minerals and oil have been found there. You can find the Arctic Circle at 66½ degrees north on a map.

Argentina

Argentina is the second largest country in SOUTH AMERICA. Most of the country's 32,322,000 people are farmers and ranchers, for much of Argentina's wealth comes from livestock and crops. Argentina is one of the world's top producers of beef and veal, fruit, wheat, millet and sorghum, and wool. The chief farming region is on the *pampas*, a Spanish word meaning 'plains'. The pampas lie to the north-west and south of Argentina's capital, Buenos Aires. Here, vast farms raise millions of cattle and sheep which graze on the rich pasture. Northern Argentina is an area of tropical forests, and is little

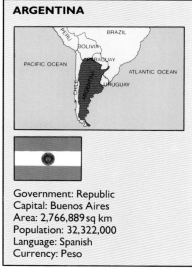

ARGENTINA

Government: Republic
Capital: Buenos Aires
Area: 2,766,889 sq km
Population: 32,322,000
Language: Spanish
Currency: Peso

developed. In the far south, near the tip of South America, is Patagonia, a desert waste. The western part of the country is dry, and the land rises to the ANDES MOUNTAINS, including Aconcagua, at 6960 metres the highest peak in South America.

Armada

Armada is a Spanish word for a great fleet of armed ships. The most famous armada was the Spanish fleet that tried to invade England in 1588. The 130 Spanish ships were large, clumsy and heavily armed. The English ships were faster and easier to manoeuvre, and were manned by more skilful seamen. The English sent fire ships towards the Spanish fleet, which retreated out to sea. Later, several Spanish ships were sunk and many damaged in battle. The Armada was forced to flee around the northern tip of Britain. Only 67 of the original 130 ships reached Spain.

> The Spanish called the Armada the 'Great Enterprise', and indeed it was. Enough food had to be taken on board for six months: 5 million kg of biscuit, 300,000 kg of salt pork, 180,000 litres of olive oil, 14,000 barrels of wine were but a part of the necessities for a force of over 30,000 men. With the great fleet were 6 surgeons, 6 physicians, 180 priests, 19 justices and 50 administrators.

Armadillo

Armadillos are strange animals that live in Central and South America. Their backs are covered with an armour of bony plates. Some kinds of armadillo can roll themselves into a ball when attacked, giving them complete protection. They have strong claws which they use for digging burrows and tearing open termite nests to find food. There are ten different kinds of armadillo, the biggest being about 1.2 metres long.

▲ The armadillo is able to protect itself by rolling into a tight ball when under threat of attack.

Armour

Armour is covering used to protect the body in battle. It was first worn at least 5000 years ago and was originally made of tough leather. Then men made metal breast-plates, helmets and shields. But the rest of the body was still protected by leather or chain mail, many small iron rings linked together to form a flexible metal coat. In the MIDDLE AGES, knights rode into battle encased from head to toe in plate armour which weighed up to 30kg. When firearms were invented, armour was no longer worn, except for the helmet. The weight of metal needed to stop a bullet was too great.

▲ Monet's Spring.
◄ Raphael's The School of Athens, a sixteenth century fresco.

Art

Since the very earliest times people have painted and made sculptured objects. We can still admire cave paintings that were drawn over 20,000 years ago. Beautiful wall paintings and sculptures from ancient EGYPT, GREECE and ROME still survive.

The Christian religion has had a great influence on art. During the MIDDLE AGES painters worked on religious scenes, often in a rather stiff way. But when the RENAISSANCE came in the 1400s art began to flower and artists became famous for their work. Painters such as LEONARDO DA VINCI and MICHELANGELO began to make their subjects more life-like. Great Dutch painters such as Rembrandt painted everyday scenes. In the 1700s and 1800s many artists went back to making their work look something like early Greek and Roman art.

Later, painting became more real looking, but by the 1870s a new style called Impressionism was starting. Artists such as Monet (1840–1926) and Renoir (1841–1919) painted with little dabs of colour, making soft, misty outlines. Painting in the 1900s became even freer. Styles included Abstract Art and Cubism, with famous painters such as Cézanne (1839–1906) and PICASSO.

The oldest pieces of sculpture we know were made by STONE AGE artists about 30,000 years ago. The ancient Egyptians made very fine sculptures between 2000 and 4000 years ago. Some of the world's most beautiful carving was done by the sculptors of ancient Greece and Rome, in what is known as the Classical period. During the Renaissance, especially in Italy, the art of sculpture advanced by leaps and bounds.

▲ This sculpture of Tutankhamun, the boy pharaoh, was found in his tomb.

▲ Picasso's Weeping Woman.

Scientists have produced machines that easily recognize and read printed words. The pattern of each character is scanned with a laser and compared with patterns that have already been programmed into the machine.

Artificial intelligence

Artificial intelligence is the performance by COMPUTERS of tasks that seem to require INTELLIGENCE. It is as if the computer can think for itself. In fact, we know that any computer can only follow a series of operations laid down in instructions called programs. These are written by computer programmers. Research in this area concentrates on getting computers to solve problems. This has led to the development of computers that can, for example, work out where best to drill for oil, how to diagnose medical conditions and even how to fly aircraft. In order to make these decisions, the computer has to be given vast amounts of information.

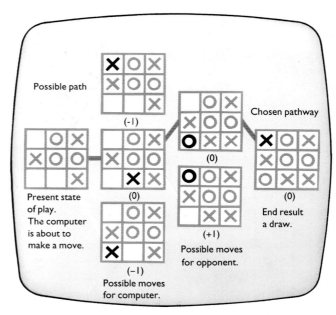

▶ When playing noughts and crosses a computer weighs up all possible moves at each stage. It gives each move a value; +1 for a win, 0 for a draw and -1 for a loss. Each move is then tried out and the one that gives the best score is taken. The computer's moves (X) are shown right.

Experiments are under way to link cameras with computers so that they can identify shapes. Sound links will enable computers to recognize human speech so that instructions can be spoken to a computer instead of entering them through a keyboard. The whole area of 'expert systems', where computers can help us to make important decisions by analysing masses of information quickly and accurately, will form the basis for future computer research. Scientists have also produced machines that can easily recognize and read printed words. The pattern of each character is scanned with a laser and compared with patterns that have already been programmed into the machine.

Asia

Asia is the largest of all the continents. It also has more people (3,172,000,000) than any other continent. Places such as the Ganges-Brahmaputra delta, the river valleys of CHINA and the island of Java are among the most thickly-populated places in the world.

Northern Asia is a cold, desolate tundra region. In contrast, the islands of INDONESIA are in the steamy tropics. The world's highest mountain range, the HIMALAYAS, is in Asia, and so is the lowest point on land, the shores of the Dead Sea. Asia's people belong to the three main races: Caucasoids live in the south-west and northern INDIA; Mongoloids, including the Chinese and Japanese, live in the east. A few Negroids are found in the south-east. And all the world's great religions began in Asia—JUDAISM, Christianity, ISLAM, HINDUISM, BUDDHISM, Confucianism and Shinto.

Most Asians are farmers, and many are very poor. The chief food crops are wheat and rice. Other crops are exported: they include tea, cotton, jute, rubber, citrus fruits and tobacco. Many nations such as China are developing their industries, but JAPAN is the only truly industrialized nation.

Asia was the birthplace of civilization, and was the home of many great civilizations, including those of Mesopotamia, Babylon, China and the Indus Valley in what is now PAKISTAN. Europeans began to visit Asia in the 1400s and trade quickly grew up. Later, for several centuries, China and Japan closed their doors to trade with Europe.

▲ Tokyo, the capital of Japan, today resembles many Western cities.

Asia has the deepest lake in the world—Lake Baikal in Siberia, Russia. It has a maximum depth of 1,620m—more than three times the height of the world's tallest building. Lake Baikal also contains more fresh water than any other freshwater lake —a fifth of all the fresh water on the Earth's surface.

◄ Asiatic elephants are used in the logging industry in several Asian countries. Elephants are very intelligent and can be trained to carry heavy loads.

ASIA

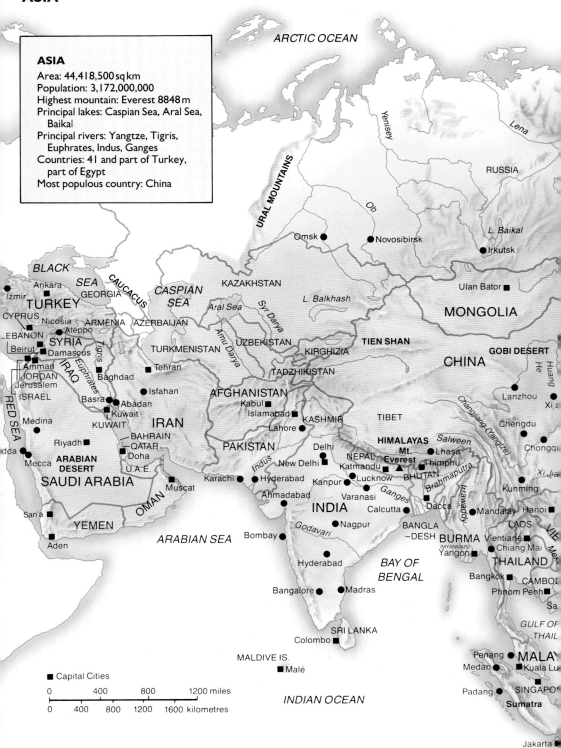

ASIA

Area: 44,418,500 sq km
Population: 3,172,000,000
Highest mountain: Everest 8848 m
Principal lakes: Caspian Sea, Aral Sea,
  Baikal
Principal rivers: Yangtze, Tigris,
  Euphrates, Indus, Ganges
Countries: 41 and part of Turkey,
  part of Egypt
Most populous country: China

ARCTIC OCEAN

RUSSIA

Yenisey

Lena

Ob

L. Baikal

Omsk

Novosibirsk

Irkutsk

URAL MOUNTAINS

KAZAKHSTAN

L. Balkhash

Ulan Bator

MONGOLIA

BLACK
SEA

CAUCACUS

Ankara

Izmir

TURKEY

GEORGIA

CYPRUS

Nicosia

ARMENIA

AZERBAIJAN

CASPIAN
SEA

Aral Sea

Syr Darya

TIEN SHAN

GOBI DESERT

CHINA

LEBANON

SYRIA

Aleppo

TURKMENISTAN

UZBEKISTAN

KIRGHIZIA

He

Huang

Beirut

Damascus

Amu Darya

TADZHIKISTAN

Lanzhou

Xi a

Amman

JORDAN

IRAQ

Tehran

AFGHANISTAN

Chengdu

Jerusalem

Baghdad

Isfahan

Kabul

KASHMIR

TIBET

Chongqu

ISRAEL

Basra

Abadan

Islamabad

Lahore

HIMALAYAS

Salween

Changjiang (Yangtze)

Medina

Kuwait

KUWAIT

IRAN

Lhasa

Xi Jia

RED SEA

Riyadh

BAHRAIN

QATAR

PAKISTAN

Delhi

NEPAL

Mt.
Everest

Thimphu

Kunming

dda

Doha

Katmandu

BHUTAN

Brahmaputra

Mecca

ARABIAN
DESERT

U.A.E.

Karachi

New Delhi

Kanpur

Lucknow

Irrawaddy

Mandalay

Hanoi

SAUDI ARABIA

Muscat

Hyderabad

Ahmadabad

Varanasi

Ganges

Dacca

LAOS

VI E

San'a

OMAN

Godavari

Nagpur

INDIA

Calcutta

BANGLA
-DESH

BURMA

Vientiane

Me

YEMEN

ARABIAN SEA

Bombay

(MYANMAR)

Yangon

Chiang Mai

Aden

Hyderabad

BAY OF
BENGAL

THAILAND

Bangalore

Madras

Bangkok

CAMBOL

Phnom Penh

Sa

SRI LANKA

GULF OF
THAIL

Colombo

MALDIVE IS.

Malé

Penang

MALA

Medan

Kuala Lu

INDIAN OCEAN

Padang

SINGAPO

Sumatra

Jakarta

■ Capital Cities

| 0 | 400 | 800 | 1200 miles |

| 0 | 400 | 800 | 1200 | 1600 kilometres |

26

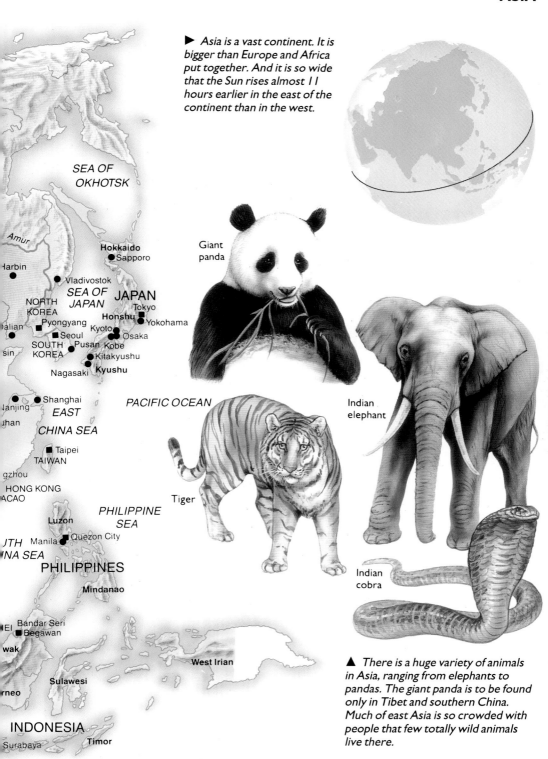

► Asia is a vast continent. It is bigger than Europe and Africa put together. And it is so wide that the Sun rises almost 11 hours earlier in the east of the continent than in the west.

SEA OF OKHOTSK

Amur

Harbin

Hokkaido
● Sapporo

● Vladivostok

SEA OF JAPAN

JAPAN

NORTH KOREA

Pyongyang

Dalian

■ Seoul

SOUTH KOREA

Pusan

Kobe

sin

● Kitakyushu

Nagasaki

Kyushu

Honshu

Tokyo

Kyoto ● Yokohama

Osaka

Giant panda

Nanjing

Shanghai

EAST CHINA SEA

han

■ Taipei

TAIWAN

gzhou

HONG KONG
ACAO

PACIFIC OCEAN

Indian elephant

Luzon

Manila ● Quezon City

PHILIPPINE SEA

JTH NA SEA

PHILIPPINES

Mindanao

Tiger

EI ■ Bandar Seri
Begawan

wak

West Irian

rneo

Sulawesi

Indian cobra

INDONESIA

Surabaya   Timor

▲ There is a huge variety of animals in Asia, ranging from elephants to pandas. The giant panda is to be found only in Tibet and southern China. Much of east Asia is so crowded with people that few totally wild animals live there.

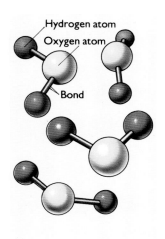

▲ *During the Middle Ages, the Arabs were very interested in astronomy, studying the planets and stars.*

Hydrogen atom
Oxygen atom
Bond

▲ *Water is made up of tiny molecules. Each molecule contains two atoms of hydrogen and one of oxygen. One of the hydrogen atoms in the picture is cut away to show its central proton and the single electron spinning round about it.*

Asteroid

Asteroids are countless thousands of tiny planets left over from the time when the Sun and planets were being formed. Most of them can be found in the wide gap between the orbits of MARS and JUPITER. Asteroid collisions formed the craters that can be seen on the MOON and MERCURY.

The largest asteroid is Ceres, about 1000 km across, but most of the 30,000 asteroids big enough to be photographed are less than a tenth of this size.

Astronomy

Astronomy is the scientific study of the heavenly bodies, and is the oldest science in existence. Early observations of the heavens enabled people to divide the year into months, weeks, and days, based on the movements of the SUN, EARTH and MOON. The development of the CALENDAR helped early astronomers to forecast the appearance of COMETS and the dates of ECLIPSES. For many centuries people believed that the Earth was the centre of the UNIVERSE, until, in the 1540s, Nicolaus COPERNICUS revived the idea that the Sun was at the centre of the SOLAR SYSTEM.

Atom

Everything is made of atoms. Things you can see, like the wood in a table; things you cannot see, like the air, are all made of atoms. You are made of atoms, too. If the atoms in something are packed closely together, that something is a solid. If the atoms in something are not so tightly packed—if they move about more—that something is a liquid, like water. And if the atoms move about a great deal, we have a gas, like air.

It is very difficult to imagine how small an atom is. We cannot see them—they are far too small. Look at the full stop at the end of this sentence. It has in it about 250,000 *million* atoms! But even atoms are made up of smaller pieces. The simplest atom is that of the light gas HYDROGEN. The centre is a tiny body called a *proton*. Around it spins an even smaller *electron*. Other atoms, such as the carbon atom, are more complicated than the hydrogen atom.

Australia

Australia is the world's smallest CONTINENT. Even so it is a huge landmass, more than 30 times as big as the United Kingdom. Australia was the last continent to be discovered and settled by Europeans. Its first inhabitants were the ABORIGINES, who wandered its wilderness hunting and gathering food.

Much of Australia is dry, flat desert. Most of its people live along the coasts, and more than half of all Australians live in the four largest cities (Sydney, Melbourne, Brisbane and Perth). Farming is an important activity. Cattle are raised on the inland pastures, and in the east and south-east green grassy highlands provide pasture for vast numbers of sheep. One-third of all the wool used in the world comes from Australia. Mining and manufacturing are also important.

Australia's first European settlers came from Britain, but today the population includes people whose families came originally from other parts of Europe and South-East Asia. The country is a member of the Commonwealth of Nations and its head of state is Queen Elizabeth. Each state has its own government, but national affairs are looked after by the Federal government headed by the prime minister.

Government: Democratic, federal state system
Capital: Canberra
Area: 7,686,849 sq km
Population: 17,086,000
Language: English
Currency: Australian dollar

STATES and TERRITORIES	CAPITAL
New South Wales	Sydney
Victoria	Melbourne
Queensland	Brisbane
South Aust.	Adelaide
Western Aust.	Perth
Tasmania	Hobart
Aust. Capital Territory	Canberra
Northern Territory	Darwin

AUSTRIA

POLAND
GERMANY
CZECHOSLOVAKIA
FRANCE
U.S.S.R.
SWITZERLAND
AUSTRIA
HUNGARY
ITALY
ROMANIA
FORMER
YUGOSLAVIA
ADRIATIC SEA
MEDITERRANEAN SEA

Government: Parliamentary
democracy
Capital: Vienna
Area: 83,849 sq km
Population: 7,712,000
Language: German
Currency: Schilling

Austria

Today, this small country is hardly much bigger than Ireland. But once it was one of the largest and most powerful nations in Europe.

For almost 700 years, from 1278 to 1918, Austria was ruled by a dynasty of kings and queens called the Hapsburgs. Their lands covered most of Central Europe. They included Hungary, Czechoslovakia, large parts of Italy, Yugoslavia, Poland, Germany, Spain and the Netherlands.

The Austrian Empire collapsed after World War I. But there are many relics of the rich court life of the Hapsburg emperors. Vienna, the capital city where over 1½ million Austrians live, is filled with castles, beautiful buildings and churches, statues and parks.

55 ## Aztecs

The empire of the Aztecs was a great Indian civilization in Mexico and Central America when Spanish soldiers discovered it. A Spanish commander by the name of Hernando Cortés landed with 600 men on their shores in 1519. Within two years he had smashed the Aztec empire for ever.

Montezuma was the last ruler of the Aztecs. He was captured by Spanish soldiers soon after a small army of them arrived in his capital city. By holding him hostage, they were able to control his subjects even though they were greatly outnumbered.

The Aztecs were famous for their grim religious practices. One of their gods regularly had human beings sacrificed to him in front of his temple.

▶ The Aztecs built great pyramids with broad stairways leading to a temple at the top. They sacrificed many people there, usually by cutting out their heart. The Aztecs were expert craftsmen. They fashioned fine sculptures and masks, like those shown here.

Bach, Johann Sebastian

Johann Sebastian Bach (1685–1750) was one of the greatest composers of all time. He was born at Eisenach in Germany, and all his family were musical. In fact, there were more than sixty musical Bachs before the family died out in the 1800s. From an early age Bach played the violin and the viola.

When Bach died, his music was almost at once forgotten. No one even put up a monument to him. Almost a hundred years passed by before people began to realize what a genius Johann Sebastian Bach had been.

Bacteria

Bacteria are tiny living things—so tiny that they cannot be seen by your naked eye. They are some of the simplest kinds of life.

Bacteria are more like plants than animals. They come in various shapes and sizes. Under a good MICROSCOPE it is possible to see that some are rod-like, some spiralled and others round in shape.

There are thousands of different kinds of bacteria. They are found in huge numbers almost everywhere you care to look. Some live in the soil. They help to break down animal and vegetable matter and thus make the soil rich. Bacteria also take the gas nitrogen from the air and turn it into forms that help plants to grow. Some bacteria even live inside our bodies. They help with the digestion of our food.

Although most bacteria are quite harmless, some can cause diseases. These kinds are known as germs. Pimples and boils are caused by bacteria. A few are deadly once they get inside the human body.

Bacteria multiply very quickly. Some of them can divide into two every 20 minutes. From a single bacterium there can be millions of bacteria in only a few hours.

We now have drugs which kill bacteria. *Sulphona-mides* are chemicals which stop bacteria growing. Antibiotics such as penicillin destroy bacteria. But because bacteria multiply so quickly, they soon develop new kinds that are not affected by the drugs that used to kill them. Then new drugs have to be made to kill the new kinds of bacteria.

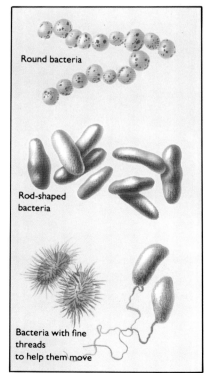

Round bacteria

Rod-shaped bacteria

Bacteria with fine threads to help them move

▲ *There are many different kinds of bacteria. A few of them are shown here. There are now drugs, such as penicillin, which destroy bacteria, but because they multiply so quickly, new kinds soon develop which are not affected by the drugs.*

Balkans

The Balkan peninsula is a mountainous region of south-eastern EUROPE. It includes the countries of GREECE, ALBANIA, YUGOSLAVIA, ROMANIA, BULGARIA and the European part of TURKEY.

The Turks ruled much of this region for 500 years, from the 1300s to the 1800s.

It was in the Balkans that Archduke Ferdinand of Austria was assassinated in 1914. This event triggered off WORLD WAR I.

Ballet

Ballet is a precise and beautiful form of dancing that is performed in a theatre. A kind of ballet first appeared in Italy in the 1400s, but ballet as it is danced today began in France. During the reign of King LOUIS XIV, in the 1600s, it was officially recognized as a form of art. The French Royal Academy of Dance was founded in 1661 to promote ballet.

Traditional, or *classical*, ballet follows strict rules and traditions. There are standard positions for the arms, legs and hands, and special movements that make the dance flow smoothly.

Classical ballet uses orchestras, elaborate scenery and splendid costumes. Many ballets tell a story, but the dancers do not speak any words. They mime (act out) the story, using their bodies. The person who arranges the dance movements is called the *choreographer*.

Modern ballets often look very different from classical ones. They include freer, more modern dance steps.

▲ *Modern ballet often uses striking costumes and poses like this one to achieve a stunning effect.*

▼ Swan Lake, *by the Russian composer Tchaikovsky, is a favourite ballet of many people.*

Balloons and Airships

Balloons and airships use lighter-than-air gases to fly. Balloons can only drift in the wind, but airships can be flown and steered.

The first manned balloon was a hot-air craft launched in 1783. It was built by two French brothers, the Montgolfiers. Their balloon was an open-ended bag. A fire was burned under the opening to fill it with hot air. In the same year, the first gas-filled balloon took to the air. The gas used was HYDROGEN, and it was a simpler craft to fly.

In the 1800s, manned balloons were used by the military for observations. Today, balloons are used to study the weather.

Most airships are bigger than balloons. The simplest sort looks like a cigar-shaped bag under which is slung a cabin and engines. More advanced airships have a rigid skeleton covered with fabric.

The first successful airship flew in 1852. It was powered by a steam engine and could manage a speed of 8 km/h. In 1929 the famous *Graf Zeppelin* of Germany flew round the world. But a series of disasters brought the building of airships to an end. They were simply not safe enough for regular passenger use because they were filled with dangerous, highly flammable hydrogen gas.

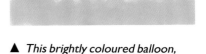

▲ *This brightly coloured balloon, built by the Montgolfier brothers, was the first one to carry passengers.*

▼ *Airships like this one were popular in the 1920s but they were slow, clumsy and often dangerous—many people lost their lives in airship accidents.*

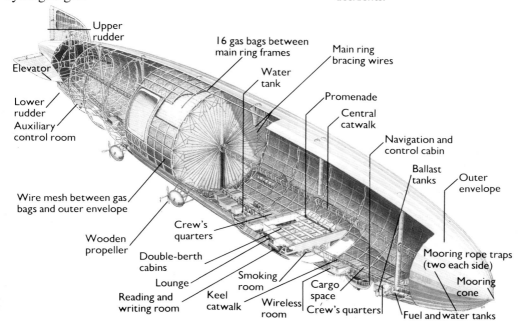

Upper rudder

Elevator

Lower rudder
Auxiliary control room

16 gas bags between main ring frames

Water tank

Main ring bracing wires

Promenade

Central catwalk

Navigation and control cabin

Ballast tanks

Outer envelope

Wire mesh between gas bags and outer envelope

Wooden propeller

Crew's quarters

Double-berth cabins

Lounge

Reading and writing room

Smoking room

Keel catwalk

Wireless room

Cargo space

Crew's quarters

Mooring rope traps (two each side)

Mooring cone

Fuel and water tanks

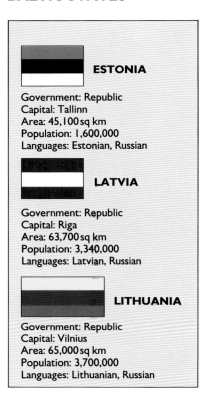

ESTONIA

Government: Republic
Capital: Tallinn
Area: 45,100 sq km
Population: 1,600,000
Languages: Estonian, Russian

LATVIA

Government: Republic
Capital: Riga
Area: 63,700 sq km
Population: 3,340,000
Languages: Latvian, Russian

LITHUANIA

Government: Republic
Capital: Vilnius
Area: 65,000 sq km
Population: 3,700,000
Languages: Lithuanian, Russian

Baltic States

The Baltic States, Estonia, Latvia and Lithuania, are situated north of Poland, on the Baltic Sea. Formerly part of the Russian Empire, they became independent countries in 1918. In 1940 during World War II, they were seized by the SOVIET UNION and became Soviet republics. German troops invaded and controlled the Baltic States until they were driven out by the Soviet army at the end of the war. In 1991 while the Soviet Union was in a state of turmoil, Estonia, Latvia and Lithuania declared their independence. These three States are once more free of Soviet control.

The Baltic States have kept their own languages, literature and traditions. Estonia has textile, ship-building and mining equipment industries. Latvia is an important producer of railway passenger coaches and telephone exchanges. Lithuania produces cattle, pigs and electrical appliances.

Barometer

Put simply, high air pressure is a sign of good weather. Low air pressure is a sign of changing and bad weather. The barometer is used to measure such changes and in this way we can use them to help forecast the weather.

There are two kinds of barometer, the aneroid and the mercury. The aneroid is more widely used. Inside it is a flat metal box. The air inside the box is at very low pressure. The metal walls of the box are so thin they will bend very easily. They do not collapse because a spring keeps them apart.

As air pressure drops, the spring pushes the sides of the box apart. As it rises, the sides of the box are squeezed together. These movements are picked up by levers and gears that move a pointer around.

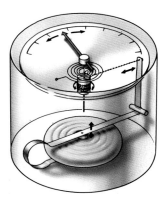

▲ If you have a barometer at home it is probably an aneroid barometer. If the air pressure rises, it pushes in the sides of the thin metal (yellow) box. This moves the pointer around.

Baseball

Baseball is the American national game. It began in 1845 when Alexander Cartwright organized a club in New York. Cartwright's rules said the game would consist of 9 innings, that each team would have 9 players and that the 'diamond' playing area would have four bases 90 feet apart.

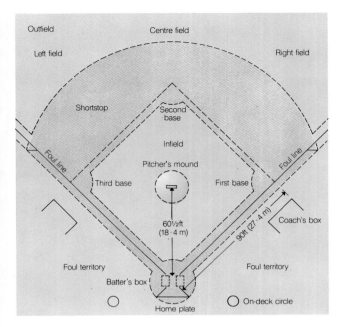

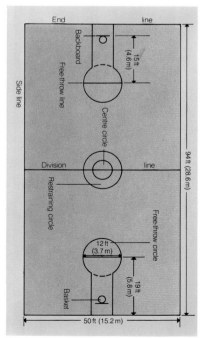

◄ Baseball is played on a large field on which is marked a square. The square, known as the 'diamond', has sides 27.4 metres long. At the base of the diamond is the home plate where the batter stands.

In the game, each batter tries to advance around the bases safely and score a run. A team bats until three players are out. The pitcher throws a *ball* when the batter does not swing and the umpire says the ball does not cross the home plate at a height between the batter's knees and his armpits. A *strike* is a pitch that crosses the plate correctly. When the batter swings at a pitch and misses or if he hits a foul ball, it is a strike. Three strikes and the batter is out. A batter can also be caught out, or he is out if a fielder picks up and throws the ball to a base before the batter reaches it.

Basketball

Basketball is an American game that has won popularity all over the world. It has been an Olympic sport since 1936. Professional basketball is played by two teams of five players each. Each team tries to score points by shooting a ball into a net, or basket. The basket is 10 feet (3 metres) from the floor and 18 inches (46 cm) in diameter at the top. The ball can be advanced by bouncing it along the floor (dribbling) or by passing it to a teammate. A player cannot take more than one step while holding the ball. The opposing players try to block him or her without making physical contact.

▲ Professional basketball is played on a court measuring 94 ft (28.6 m) long by 50 ft (15.2 m) wide. A match consists of two 20-minute halves, with a ten-minute interval at half time.

▼ *The greater horseshoe bat gets its name from the shape of its nose. It is the largest bat in Europe, being about 70 mm long.*

Bat

Bats fly like birds, yet in fact they are MAMMALS. They are the only mammals that can truly be said to fly. Their wings do not have feathers, but are made of a thin sheet of skin stretched between the long 'finger' bones. In most bats the wings are also joined to the legs and tail.

There are more than 2000 different kinds of bat. Most live in the tropics and warm parts of the world.

The biggest of all bats are the fruit-eaters or flying foxes. One, the kalong, has a wing-span of 1·5 metres. The insect-eaters are usually smaller. Their wing-span is rarely as much as 30 cm.

Most bats are nocturnal—they sleep in the day and fly at night. Scientists have shown in experiments that bats do not need good eyesight for flying. They find their way in the dark by using a 'sonar' system. They make high-pitched shrieks that few human ears can hear, and use the echoes bouncing off objects to tell where they are.

▶ *Dry batteries are useful for supplying small quantities of electricity for torches, transistor radios and electric bells. In dry batteries, a pastelike chemical mixture is packed round a carbon rod. When the chemicals are used up the battery cannot be recharged.*

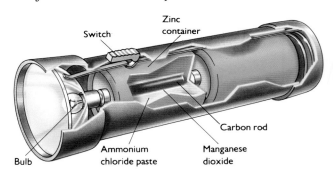

Switch

Zinc container

Carbon rod

Bulb

Ammonium chloride paste

Manganese dioxide

Battery

Batteries make electricity from chemicals stored inside them. Dry batteries such as those used in some transistor radios, torches and calculators make electricity for only a limited time. Car batteries can be recharged with electricity and used again and again. They contain pairs of lead and lead oxide plates bathed in dilute sulphuric acid. As the battery is used, the chemicals in the plates change until no more electricity is produced. But feeding an electric current into the battery changes the chemicals in the plates back to their original state. When the battery's positive and negative terminals are joined by a conductor a current flows once more.

Battles

Wars and battles are as old as mankind. It was in the Middle East more than 3500 years ago that the first effective armies appeared. In the ancient world the warriors of Egypt, Assyria, Greece and Rome were feared by their enemies. Until modern times infantry (foot soldiers) made up the bulk of most armies. The armoured corps of the armies of the past were knights on horseback, protected by metal and leather armour.

The invention of gunpowder and cannon made warfare more destructive. The Chinese used gunpowder rockets before AD 1000; in Europe, cannon were in use on the battlefield by the 1300s. Later, after the INDUSTRIAL REVOLUTION of the 1800s, came mechanised warfare-battles between war machines. Modern weapons such as missiles, aircraft and tanks have made the battlefield even more terrible than in ancient times when armies met in hand-to-hand combat.

Battles have been fought on land, in the air, and both on and beneath the sea. The most successful military commander is not always the person leading the largest force. Many famous victories have been won against seemingly hopeless odds. Some battles have decided the course of history and the destiny of nations. One example is the Battle of Yorktown in 1781, where the Americans defeated the British to gain independence.

SOME FAMOUS BATTLES

Marathon 490 BC 10,000 Greeks defeated 60,000 Persians

Tours AD 732 Franks defeated Arabs

Hastings 1066 Normans led by William defeated Saxons and conquered England

Agincourt 1415 English led by Henry V defeated much larger French army

Constantinople 1453 Turks overran Byzantine Empire

Armada 1588 English fleet defeated Spanish invasion

Trafalgar 1805 Nelson's British fleet defeated combined French-Spanish fleet

Waterloo 1815 Napoleon's final defeat by Allies, led by Wellington

Alamo 1836 Heroic defence by Texans against Mexicans

Little Big Horn 1876 Sioux Indians defeated US cavalry

Somme 1916 Bloodiest battle of World War I

Alamein 1942 Montgomery's British army drove Rommel's German army out of North Africa: World War II

Stalingrad 1942–43 Germans failed to capture city from Russians

▼ The Battle of Gettysburg, fought in 1863 in the American Civil War, was a turning point in the war.

▲ *The sloth bear, also called the honey bear, lives in the forests of India and Sri Lanka.*

▲ *The brown bear once lived in Britain. Now it is only seen in zoos or performing tricks in circuses.*

▲ *The polar bear lives in the Arctic. It is one of the biggest bears.*

Bear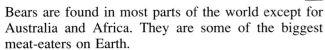

Bears are found in most parts of the world except for Australia and Africa. They are some of the biggest meat-eaters on Earth.

The largest of all bears are the brown bears of Alaska. These can reach a weight of over 750 kg. Other giants include the polar bear of the Arctic and the grizzly of western North America.

The only bear that lives in South America is the small spectacled bear. Its name comes from the ring-like markings around its eyes.

The smallest bear in the world is the sun bear of the jungles of South-East Asia. It weighs no more than 65kg.

Bears can be slow, lumbering beasts. They have short, powerful limbs and heavy, broad heads with powerful jaws. They also have long, dangerous claws for digging and tearing.

Bears do not have very sharp eyesight, but their sense of smell is very good. Although they look clumsy, all but the biggest bears can climb trees.

Beaver

Beavers are big RODENTS more than a metre long, including the tail, and weigh more than 25 kg. They live in woods by the side of lakes and rivers and are good swimmers. Beavers are able to stay under water for up to 15 minutes. They have a broad, flat tail covered in scaly skin. This is used for steering when they swim.

Beavers need pools to build their homes in, and often block up, or dam, streams with mud and sticks to make one. They cut down small trees with their sharp teeth and use them to strengthen the dam.

Bee

There are many different kinds of bee, but the best known kind is the honey bee. Honey bees live in hives or colonies of about 50,000 worker bees. Worker bees are female but they do not breed. Each colony also has a queen bee which breeds, and a few hundred stingless drones which are male.

The worker bee's life is very short, usually about four weeks, so the queen has to lay many eggs to pro-

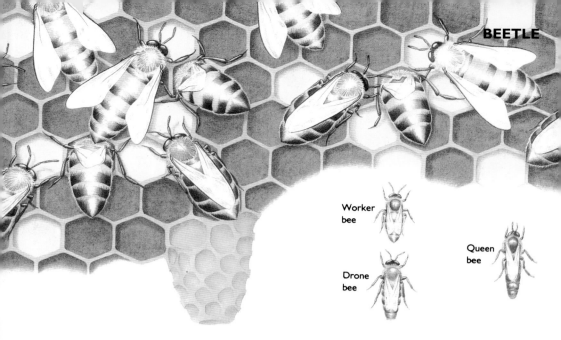

Worker
bee

Drone
bee

Queen
bee

vide enough bees. She can lay up to 1500 eggs in one day. From time to time a new queen is born. The old queen then leaves the hive with a *swarm* of about half the workers to seek another home.

The workers collect *pollen* and nectar from flowers. The nectar is made into honey. It is stored in the hive to feed the bees in winter. Beekeepers carefully remove the honey from the hive. They give the bees sugar syrup to replace the honey they take.

▲ Inside the hive of the honey bee are cells made of wax. The queen lays eggs in the cells. Larvae hatch out of the eggs and are fed by the workers. Worker bees collect nectar and pollen from flowers. The nectar is made into honey, which is stored in the hive for food.

Beethoven, Ludwig Van

Ludwig van Beethoven (1770–1827) was a German musician who composed some of the greatest music ever known. This included symphonies, concertos, choral and chamber music. When he was young, Beethoven was well-known as a pianist and was admired by many famous people. He began to go deaf at the age of 30 but continued to compose music even when he was totally deaf.

Beetle

There are over 300,000 species of beetle known. In prehistoric times all beetles had two pairs of wings. But over millions of years the front pair changed, or *evolved*, into hard, close-fitting coverings for the second pair underneath. All beetles used to be flying insects but now many of them live on the ground.

▲ When Beethoven was young he studied under Mozart and Haydn.

▲ *The Colorado beetle is a pest that ruins potato crops.*

Beetles start their lives as eggs which hatch into grubs, or larvae. The larvae then turn into chrysalises, or pupae, before the adult beetles emerge.

Many beetles and their larvae are destructive pests. Woodworms, weevils, wireworms, cockroaches, Colorado and flea beetles do great damage to crops, trees and buildings.

Some beetles can be very useful. Ladybirds are small beetles which eat harmful insects such as greenflies. Dung beetles clear away dung.

▶ *Burying beetles bury the corpses of small birds and mammals by digging soil from under them. They lay their eggs on the buried animal and the grubs feed on it.*

Belgium

Belgium is a small country sandwiched between France, Germany and Holland. Its capital is Brussels. Belgium's population is made up of two main groups: the Germanic Flemings of the north, and the French-speaking Walloons of the south. Because of its central and strategic position, Belgium has been invaded and fought over throughout the course of European history. Today Belgium is an international centre. The headquarters of the EUROPEAN COMMUNITY (EC) and NATO are both in Brussels.

Bell, Alexander Graham

Alexander Graham Bell (1847–1922) is remembered as the inventor of the TELEPHONE. Bell was the son of a Scottish teacher who went to Canada with his family in 1870. Two years later Alexander set up a school for teachers of the deaf in Boston, in America. Through his work with devices to help the deaf, Bell became interested in sending voices over long distances. On March 10, 1876, the first sentence was transmitted by telephone. The historic words were spoken by Bell to his assistant: 'Mr Watson, come here; I want you'.

BELGIUM

Government: Parliamentary democracy under a constitutional monarch
Capital: Brussels
Area: 30,513 sq km
Population: 9,845,000
Languages: Flemish; French
Currency: Belgian franc

Bible

The Bible is the sacred book of the Judaeo-Christian religion. It is in two parts. The first is called the Old Testament and records the history of the Jewish people and the teachings of their prophets before the birth of JESUS. The second part, the New Testament, records the life and sayings of Jesus and his disciples.

> The Bible has always been the best-selling book. More than 2½ billion copies have been sold since 1816. It has been translated into more than 1500 languages.

Bicycle

The bicycle is a two-wheeled vehicle powered by its rider, who turns two pedals by foot. The earliest bicycles, called 'dandy-horses', were invented in the 1700s. They were simply two wheels joined by a rod, with a seat on top. The rider pushed it along the ground by foot.

The first bicycle with pedals did not appear until 1865. These machines were known as 'bone-shakers' because the seats had no springs. The next important development was the 'penny farthing', which had an enormous front wheel and a tiny rear wheel. The modern style of bicycle appeared in the 1880s. It had a chain-driven rear wheel and air-filled tyres, and this basic style has changed very little since then.

Riding a bicycle is difficult but most people manage it with practice. It is more difficult to keep your balance at a slow speed. This is because the wheels of a bicycle have a *gyroscopic* effect—like a spinning top. The bicycle is steadier at fast speeds.

▲ *In 1817 Karl von Drais built his 'dandyhorse', or 'draisine'. It had no pedals, and the rider pushed it along by foot.*

Big Bang Theory

The Big Bang theory is today's most popular explanation of the origin of the UNIVERSE. It suggests there was a 'big bang' that caused the GALAXIES to start moving apart at great speeds 17,000 million years ago. There would have been an unbelievably hot, dense cloud of atomic particles. Physicists have calculated that in just *three minutes* these particles had turned into all the hydrogen ATOMS that now make up 90 percent of the Universe. As the hydrogen cloud expanded, it began to break up into separate clouds. These eventually became galaxies of stars like our own Milky Way galaxy, still moving apart from the Big Bang.

▲ *The Matchless ordinary bicycle, produced in 1883, was a 'penny farthing'. It had solid tyres and a step to help the rider get on.*

The Universe may expand for ever, or it may eventually stop expanding and then collapse inwards, in what some people call the Big Crunch. Gravity will pull the galaxies together until they collide. At this point there would be another big explosion, which would probably result in another Universe similar to the existing one.

▲ Some scientists believe that the Universe was created about 15 billion years ago in an explosion called the Big Bang. Matter was formed in the tremendous heat that followed and galaxies were created.

0	Ø	Ø	Ø	Ø
1	Ø	Ø	Ø	1
2	Ø	Ø	1	Ø
3	Ø	Ø	1	1
4	Ø	1	Ø	Ø
5	Ø	1	Ø	1
6	Ø	1	1	Ø
7	Ø	1	1	1
8	1	Ø	Ø	Ø

▲ A diagram of the binary system, in which the numerals 1 and 0 are used to represent all numbers.

Binary System

The binary system is a number system that uses only two numerals—0 and 1. Our everyday *decimal system* uses ten numerals—0 to 9. In the decimal system you multiply a number by 10 by moving it one place to the left—2, 20, 200 etc. In the binary system, when you move a numeral one place to the left you multiply its value by two. A 1 by itself is 1. Move it a place to the left and it becomes 1 times 2, or 2. It is written 10. Move it another place to the left and it becomes 1 times 2 times 2, or 4. It is written 100. The binary for 93 is 1011101—one 1, no 2s, one 4, one 8, one 16, no 32s, and one 64.

Biochemistry

Biochemistry is the study of the chemical reactions that take place inside tiny cells that make up all living things. Biochemists find out about the food people must eat to be healthy. They help fight disease by making chemicals that kill harmful bacteria. They also help farmers by finding out what foods are needed by plants and animals.

Biochemists also study special molecules in living things called *nucleic acids*. One kind of nucleic acid—DNA (deoxyribonucleic acid)—is found in the nucleus of cells. It carries and passes on the plan of a living thing from one generation to the next. It is the substance that makes each human being different from any other person that has ever lived. Biochemists are finding out more and more about the chemistry that makes us what we are.

> Biochemistry is a vast subject. Some biochemists are busy designing new drugs. Others are searching in the muscles to find molecules that expand and contract like tiny rubber bands. Still others are trying to find out which chemicals existed in the oceans when the Earth was new. They want to find out how life first began.

Biology

Biology is the study of living things, from the tiniest amoeba, which consists of just one CELL, to a mighty oak tree or a human being. The part of biology that deals with the PLANT world is called BOTANY. The study of ANIMALS is called zoology. One of the earliest biologists was the ancient Greek thinker Aristotle, who was the first to dissect, or cut open, and classify animals.

There was little interest in biology for more than a thousand years, until the RENAISSANCE, when scholars and artists such as LEONARDO DA VINCI tried to discover how living things grew and worked. At first the study of the human body by dissection was frowned upon by the Church. But this changed after the 1500s, and William HARVEY was able to show how the BLOOD travels around the body, and other people were able to compare the structure of various animals with that of man.

The invention of the MICROSCOPE in the 1600s opened up whole new areas of study for biologists. They were able to learn more about the animal and plant cells that are the building blocks of life.

In the 1800s the English naturalist Charles DARWIN revolutionized biology with his theory of EVOLUTION. Today biology is divided into dozens of separate sciences.

▲ Darwin's theory of evolution stirred up much controversy. Here he is mocked in a cartoon of the time.

▲ *A bird skeleton, with hollow and lightweight bones. The breastbone is deep and large.*

▼ *There are many different kinds of bird. Tropical birds, such as the macaw and the bird of paradise, are often brightly coloured. The emperor penguin is a flightless bird but an excellent swimmer. It finds its food under water, as does the flamingo, a wading bird.*

Gold and blue macaw

Lesser bird of Paradise

Bird

Birds come in all shapes and sizes, but they all have wings and feathers. Some birds can fly thousands of kilometres. Others, such as the OSTRICH and the PENGUIN, cannot fly at all. The ostrich is the largest bird. It can weigh more than 150 kg. The smallest bird, a HUMMINGBIRD, weighs less than 2 grams.

Birds developed from scaly REPTILES that lived about 180,000,000 years ago. Their scales changed over millions of years into feathers, and their front legs became wings. Birds have hollow bones for lightness in the air and strong breast muscles for working their wings. Large birds can flap their wings slowly and float, or hover, on air currents. Small birds need to flap their wings fast to stay in the air.

All birds lay EGGS. Most birds are busy parents who work hard to rear their young. Some, like the CUCKOO, lay their eggs in other birds' nests for foster parents to rear. Other birds bury their eggs in warm places and leave them. Most birds are wild but some, such as chickens, pigeons and canaries, have been tamed or *domesticated*. Some birds are bred on farms for their eggs and meat.

Birds' beaks have many different shapes. Sparrowhawks have hooked beaks for tearing up their prey. Blue tits have short beaks for eating small nuts, seeds and insects. The nuthatch has a powerful, pointed beak for breaking open nuts.

Green woodpecker
Robin
Long–tailed tit
Hoopoe
Magpie
Wren
Emperor penguin
Rosy flamingo

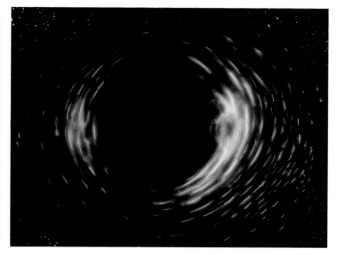

◀ A close-up view of a black hole might appear like this – a pattern of bright light around its edge. The light, coming from distant stars behind the black hole, has been 'bent' by the extra strong gravitational force around the hole.

Black Hole

Stars are made up mostly of hydrogen. It is the turning of this hydrogen into helium that makes stars like our Sun shine and give out heat. When a massive star uses up all its hydrogen fuel, it collapses. This collapse is called a *supernova* explosion. All that is left after such an explosion is a tiny star only a few kilometres across—a *neutron star*. The material in a neutron star is so squashed together— so dense—that a pinhead-sized piece of it would weigh as much as a large building! The GRAVITY of some neutron stars is so great that even light waves find it impossible to escape from them. As the light waves cannot get out, we call them *black holes*. Because these strange objects are entirely black, astronomers have never actually seen one, but they have found stars that could have an invisible black hole nearby. There could be a huge black hole at the centre of our Milky Way Galaxy.

A black hole turns space inside out. From outside it might appear to be a round black object only a few kilometres across. But if you were inside it, it would seem as big as a universe. You could not see anything outside it.

Blériot, Louis

Louis Blériot (1872–1936) was a famous French airman. He was a pioneer of aviation and designed and built a number of early aeroplanes. On July 25, 1909, he took off from Calais in one of his own AIRCRAFT. Twenty-seven minutes later he touched down at Dover, becoming the first man to fly the English Channel. In doing so he won a prize of £1000 offered by the London *Daily Mail* newspaper.

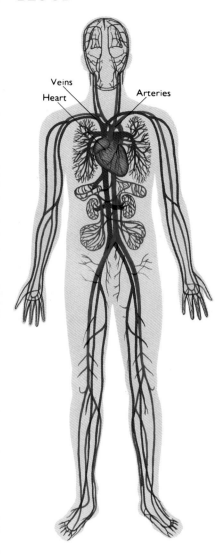

The heart pumps blood round the body, through a system of arteries, veins and capillaries.

Blood

Blood is the fluid that nourishes our bodies and removes waste products. It takes in food from the digestive system, and OXYGEN from the LUNGS, and carries them to all the CELLS in the body. Each cell takes exactly what it needs from the blood and the blood carries away cell waste, including water and carbon dioxide. Blood also carries special body chemicals to where they are needed. And it kills germs and keeps the body at the right temperature.

Blood is made in the marrow of the bones. The adult human body contains about five litres of blood. This blood is made up of a pale liquid called *plasma*, and millions of cells, or *corpuscles*. Corpuscles are tiny red discs that give the blood its colour. The blood also contains white corpuscles. There are about 5 million red corpuscles and between 5000 and 10,000 white corpuscles in every tiny cubic millimetre of blood.

White corpuscles attack germs that enter the body by absorbing them. Often many white corpuscles are killed in the fight against disease or infection. Large numbers of dead white corpuscles collect as *pus*. Other blood particles, called *platelets*, help our blood to clot when we bleed. This helps scratches and other wounds to heal more quickly.

We can all be classified into blood groups A, B, AB, or O, according to the type of blood we have.

Body Scanner

A body scanner is a machine used in MEDICINE to produce pictures of the inside of the body. There are two basic types of scanner. The first uses a process called *computerized tomography* (CT). A thin beam of X-RAYS is fired through the body at different angles. The results registered by X-ray detectors are analysed by a COMPUTER. This adds each result together to make a picture of a slice through the body. The second type of scanner uses a process called *magnetic resonance* (MR). Hydrogen particles in the body move a very small amount in a magnetic field and then give out a field of their own. Sensors in the MR scanner detect these tiny magnetic fields which, as in a CT scanner, can be looked at by a computer to produce a picture of a slice through the patient's body.

Bolivia

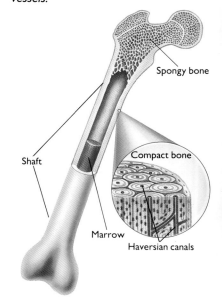

Bolivia is a land-locked country in central SOUTH AMERICA, west of Brazil. Most of Bolivia is an enormous plain stretching from the Brazilian border to the eastern foothills of the Andes Mountains. High in the Andes lies the great Bolivian plateau, over 4000 metres high. Two-thirds of Bolivia's people live here. The capital is La Paz, the highest capital in the world, and Lake Titicaca, at 3812 metres above sea level, is one of the highest lakes in the world.

Spain ruled Bolivia from 1532 until 1825. It gained freedom from Spain with the help of Simón Bolívar, a Venezuelan general, after whom Bolivia is named.

Government: Republic
Capitals: La Paz (seat of government)
Sucre (legal capital)
Area: 1,093,581 sq km
Population: 7,400,000
Language: Spanish
Currency: Peso

Bone

Bones make up the hard framework that supports the flesh and organs of all vertebrates (animals with backbones). All bones are made up of the same thing, mostly calcium. Bones are hard on the outside but soft on the inside. Bone *marrow*, in the hollow centre of the bone, is where new red BLOOD cells are made.

The human skeleton has four kinds of bones: long bones, such as arm and leg bones; flat bones such as the skull; short bones, including ankle and wrist bones; and irregular bones, such as those that make up the backbone. If bones are broken they will knit together again if they are rejoined or *set* properly. The cells in the broken ends of the bone produce a substance that helps the ends to grow together again so that the mended bone is as strong as it ever was. But as human beings get older their bones become more brittle and will break more easily.

▼ *Bones may look lifeless, but they are a mass of living cells. The Haversian canals contain blood vessels.*

Spongy bone

Compact bone

Shaft

Marrow

Haversian canals

Botany

Botany is the study of PLANTS and how they grow. There are more than 300,000 different kinds of plants. They vary from tiny *algae* that can be seen only with a microscope, to giant redwood trees nearly 100 metres high. New kinds of plants are being discovered all the time.

Without plants there would be no animals, because animals depend on plants for all their food. There would be no cattle for us to eat if there was no grass for the cattle to eat. Animals also breathe the gas OXYGEN that plants give out.

By studying the way in which the qualities of one generation of plants are passed on to the next generation, scientists are able to grow bigger and better crops. They can breed varieties that are better at fighting plant disease.

In 1753 Carl von Linné (known as Linnaeus), a Swedish botanist, invented the first real system for naming plants. He gave every plant a name made up of two Latin words.

► *Plants are classified, or grouped, into four main divisions, which are further subdivided. For example, the flowering plants, or angiosperms, are divided into two groups – dicotyledons and monocotyledons – according to the number of seed leaves they have.*

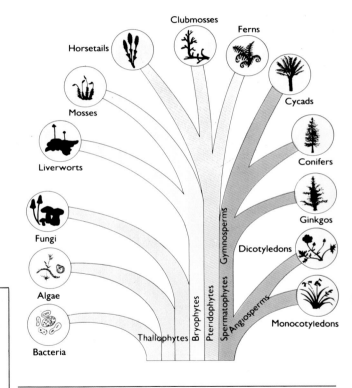

The size and weight of our brains are in proportion to our body size and weight. Men have slightly heavier brains than women. Tall people have heavier brains than short people, but it has been found that there is very little connection between a large head and intelligence. Doctors have discovered that the average man's brain has increased in weight from 1370 grams in 1860 to 1420 grams today. The average woman's brain has increased from 1245 grams to 1270 grams.

Brain

The brain controls all the other parts of the body. In some tiny insects it is no bigger than a speck of dust. Even in some mighty dinosaurs it was no bigger than a walnut. But MAMMALS have big brains in relation to their size, and a human has the biggest brain of all. The human brain is largely made up of grey and white matter. Grey matter contains NERVE cells, and white matter contains the nerve fibres that carry messages from the nerve cells to the body. These

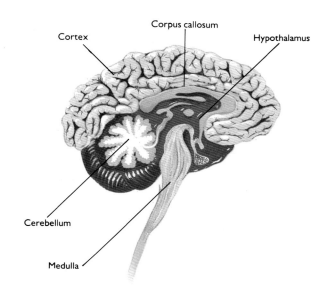

Cortex
Corpus callosum
Hypothalamus
Cerebellum
Medulla

◀ *The brain is the body's control centre. It uses a fifth of all the energy produced in the body. The* medulla *and* hypothalamus *control involuntary activities such as breathing and blood pressure. The* cerebellum *controls muscles and organs of balance. The* cortex, *the largest area, controls conscious feeling and voluntary movements such as writing and running. The* corpus callosum *is a band of nerves linking the two halves of the cortex.*

nerve fibres leave the brain in large bundles and reach out to all parts of the body. Messages from the body are travelling back along the fibres to the brain all the time.

Different parts of the brain control different parts of the body. For example, most thinking is done in the front part. Sight, on the other hand, is controlled from the back of the brain.

Brazil

Brazil is by far the largest country in SOUTH AMERICA and the fifth largest country in the world. Much of Brazil is low-lying, and contains the huge basin of the AMAZON river and the world's largest rain forest. Until recently, only tribes of Indians lived here. Today, the government is trying to open up the Amazon region but some scientists fear that this will destroy the fragile balance of the great forest.

Over half of Brazil's people live in cities that include Rio de Janeiro, São Paulo, Belo Horizonte and Recife. Brasilia, a specially built modern city, has been the capital of Brazil since 1960.

Brazil was ruled by Portugal from the early 1500s until 1822, and most people still speak Portuguese. About three-quarters of the people are descended from Europeans; most of the rest are of mixed European, Indian and African ancestry. Most Brazilians work on

BRAZIL

Government: Federal republic
Capital: Brasilia
Area: 8,511,965 sq km
Population: 150,368,000
Language: Portuguese
Currency: Cruzeiro

▲ *Rio de Janeiro is a beautiful city lying among bays, islands and rounded hills.*

farms. The country leads the world in producing coffee, and oil is becoming a more important product. Brazil is also one of the biggest producers of beef, cocoa, cotton, maize, sugar cane and tobacco. Most of Brazil's great mineral wealth is still undeveloped.

Breathing

Breathing is something we rarely have to think about. As soon as a baby is born, it starts to breathe, and we go on breathing all our lives. It is the OXY-GEN in the air that we need. Like all other animals, we must have oxygen to stay alive. This oxygen is used with the food we eat to give us energy to move about and keep our bodies going.

We draw air into our LUNGS. From there it goes through tiny tubes which allow the oxygen to pass into the BLOOD vessels. So oxygen goes all round our bodies in the blood. We breathe out another type of gas called carbon dioxide. An adult normally breathes in and out about 20 times a minute (children usually breathe faster than this). However, not all animals need air to breathe. A fish breathes in water, by means of gills either side of its head. It takes in water through its mouth and, as the water passes over the gills, the gills extract oxygen from the water.

Inhaling

Exhaling

Diaphragm

Lungs

Rib cage

▲ *When you breathe in, your rib cage is pulled upwards and the diaphragm is lowered. Air is sucked into your lungs. These actions happen in reverse when you breathe out.*

Bridge

Bridges are used to take roads, paths and railways over rivers, valleys or other obstacles. People have been building bridges for thousands of years.

The first simple bridges were probably fallen tree trunks placed across a river or small valley. Later, they may have been supported underneath by stones or logs. Another kind of simple bridge is the rope bridge made from long pieces of rope slung across a river.

The Romans were among the first great bridge builders. Some of their stone bridges are still standing today. In the MIDDLE AGES bridges in towns often had shops and houses built on top of them.

▼ *The Firth of Forth Bridge, opened in 1890, had two arches either side of Inchgarvie Island. About 55,000 tonnes of steel were cast in foundries set up on shore to build the bridge.*

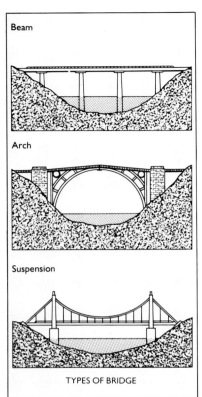

Beam

Arch

Suspension

TYPES OF BRIDGE

Today there is a great variety of bridges. They have to be carefully planned and built. The weight of the bridge must be balanced so that it does not fall down. It must also be strong enough to carry traffic and stand up to the force of the wind.

There are three main kinds of bridge. These are the *beam*, the *arch* and the *suspension* bridge. Some are fixed and others can be moved.

Different kinds of bridge

A modern beam bridge works in the same way as a simple tree trunk bridge. It is made of strong girders, or beams, which stretch from one bank to the other. Sometimes the middle of the bridge rests on pillars. Railway bridges are often girder bridges.

An arch bridge may have one arch or more. In the past, it was usually built from stone, but today some are made of steel, like the Sydney Harbour Bridge in Australia. It has a span (the distance from one side to the other) of 503 metres. Others, such as Waterloo Bridge in London, are made of concrete.

LONGEST BRIDGE SPANS	
Akashi-Kaikyo, Japan (suspension)	1780m
Humber Estuary, England (suspension)	1410m
Verrazano Narrows, USA (suspension)	1298m
Golden Gate, USA (suspension)	1280m
Mackinac Straits, USA (suspension)	1158m
Second Bosporus, Turkey (suspension)	1090m
First Bosporus, Turkey (suspension)	1074m
George Washington, USA (suspension)	1067m
Tagus river, Portugal (suspension)	1013m
Forth Road, Scotland (suspension)	1006m
Severn, England–Wales (suspension)	988m
Tacoma Narrows, USA (suspension)	853m
Kanmon Strait, Japan (suspension)	712m
Transbay, USA (suspension)	704m

▲ *Tower Bridge across the river Thames in London has a roadway carried on* bascules, *or arms, which are pivoted and lift to allow ships to pass beneath it.*

Suspension bridges are hung by strong steel cables from tall towers. The towers also have cables fixed to the ground.

Some beam bridges over rivers can be moved to let ships pass through. Tower Bridge in London is a *bascule* bridge. Both sides of the bridge can be lifted up in the middle, like drawbridges. *Swing* bridges are on pivots and can be swung sideways.

Modern bridge building began with IRON bridges in the 1700s. Later, many of these were built for the railways. The first modern suspension bridge was built by Thomas Telford at Menai in North Wales.

By the end of the 1800s steel was being used. Brooklyn Bridge in New York, finished in 1883, was one of the first steel suspension bridges. It has a span of 486 metres. The longest suspension bridge in Britain is the Humber Estuary bridge. It has a span of 1410 metres. The Akashi-Kaikyo bridge in Japan is even longer at 1780 metres.

British Isles

The British Isles are made up of two main islands, Britain and IRELAND, and more than 5000 smaller ones. These range from large islands such as the Isle of Man, Shetland, the Orkneys and the Channel Islands, to bare rocks sticking out of the sea.

Britain is divided into ENGLAND, SCOTLAND and WALES. Ireland is divided into Eire (the Republic of Ireland) and Northern Ireland.

The British Isles are part of EUROPE. They are on the European CONTINENTAL SHELF. During the last ICE AGE Britain was joined to Europe by a wide land bridge across what is now the English Channel.

The climate of the British Isles is mild and quite wet. Most of the country is low-lying. There are some mountains and high ground in Scotland, Wales, the north of England and parts of Ireland. Much of the country used to be covered in forests or bog but most of this has been cleared or drained.

> The British Isles are rather rainy. But the west coast has much more rain than the east. The hilly west coast has an average of 2540 mm of rain a year, while low areas in the east have only between 500 and 750 mm. The London area is the driest.

◀ The discovery of oil in the North Sea brought a new source of wealth to the British Isles. Here, an oil rig temporarily out of service lies offshore of the city of Dundee in Scotland.

Buddha

The word Buddha means 'Enlightened One'. This name is given to great teachers of the Buddhist religion.

The first Buddha was Siddhartha Gautama. He was born about 563 BC in northern India. For most of his life he travelled around India teaching people. Buddha taught his followers that the only way to true happiness was to be peaceful and kind to other people and animals, and to avoid evil.

Like the HINDUS, Buddhists believe that after they die they are born again as an animal or human being. If they are very good, they are not born again but live in a kind of heaven called *Nirvana*.

▲ *Buddha in a characteristic pose, with legs folded. His restful expression reflects the Buddhist ideal state of complete happiness and peace.*

▲ *Early shelters were made from the most available materials – in this case animal bones and hide.*

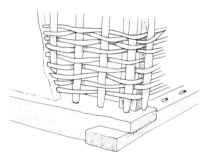

▲ *Early houses in Europe had walls of woven branches, or wattle, filled in with hardened lumps of mud, or daub.*

▶ *Modern buildings are constructed using reinforced concrete and prefabricated sections. Towering cranes make the job of moving building materials fast and efficient.*

Building

Early people built with the materials they found around them—stones, branches, mud and turf. In Europe, poor people usually lived in houses made of wattle and daub. Wattle was a wickerwork of branches, and this was plastered over with a 'daub' of wet mud. When this hardened it made quite a strong wall.

Because in some areas certain materials were easily available, buildings look quite different in different places. Where there was plenty of clay, people built with bricks; where there was plenty of limestone or sandstone, people built their houses with those.

Today, houses being built everywhere look very much the same. Large buildings have a framework of steel girders or reinforced *concrete* which takes all the

weight of the building. The walls can be light and there can be plenty of windows.

All buildings, especially high ones, have to be built on firm foundations. If they are not they may collapse or sink into the ground like the Leaning Tower of Pisa in Italy.

Bulgaria

Bulgaria is a country in Eastern EUROPE. Like several of its European neighbours, it has had a communist government, with restrictions on personal freedom. However, since the late 1980s, the government has become more democratic.

Bulgaria has 9,000,000 people and covers 110,912 sq km. Its capital city is Sofia.

In the north are the Balkan Mountains. To the east is the Black Sea where many people spend their holidays. In the centre of Bulgaria is a big valley with many farms. The farmers grow fruit, flowers, vegetables, grain and tobacco. There are also many factories and mines in Bulgaria.

BULGARIA

Government: Multi-party system
Capital: Sofia
Area: 110,912 sq km
Population: 9,011,000
Language: Bulgarian
Currency: Lev

Burma (Myanmar)

Burma is a country in SOUTH-EAST ASIA. It has mountains, forests and rivers. The biggest river is the Irrawaddy which is 2080 km long.

Burma has over 40,000,000 people and covers 676,552 sq km. The capital city is Rangoon on the Rangoon River. Most of the people are farmers. They grow rice, teak, rubber and jute. Nearly all of the Burmese follow the Buddhist religion.

Butterfly and Moth

Butterflies are flying INSECTS. There are about 17,000 kinds of butterfly. They are related to moths, and live in most parts of the world, even as far north as the Arctic circle.

Butterflies have many colours and sizes. One of the smallest, the dwarf blue of South Africa, has a wing-span of only 14 mm. The largest, the Queen Alexandra birdwing, has a wing-span of 28 cm.

All butterflies begin their lives as CATERPILLARS which hatch from eggs. The caterpillars spend their lives eating the plant they were hatched on. They

BURMA (MYANMAR)

Government: Military
Capital: Rangoon
Area: 676,552 sq km
Population: 41,675,000
Language: Burmese
Currency: Kyat

BUTTERFLY AND MOTH

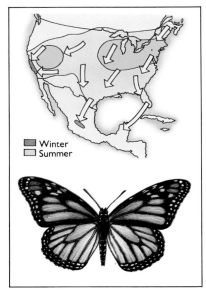

■ Winter
□ Summer

▲ The monarch butterfly of North America travels thousands of miles to winter in Mexico and southern California. Sometimes huge clusters of them are spotted 'resting' in trees en route.

▼ There is a great variety in the appearance of moths and their caterpillars.

change their skins several times as they grow. When a caterpillar is fully grown it changes into a chrysalis with a hard skin. Inside this the chrysalis changes into an adult butterfly. When it is ready, the butterfly breaks out and flies away to find a mate and lay eggs of its own.

Some butterflies *migrate*. They fly from one part of the world to another at certain times of the year. One of the most famous migrating butterflies is the monarch butterfly in North America. In the summer it lives all over the United States, Canada and Alaska. In the autumn, the butterflies gather together in groups. They fly south to Mexico, Florida and southern California for the winter. Sometimes thousands of monarchs are seen flying together. In spring, they fly north again.

It can be hard to tell moths and butterflies apart. These are the signs to look out for. Moths usually fly in the evening and at night, while butterflies can be seen in the daytime. Moths have plumper bodies than butterflies. Moths' antennae are like tiny combs, or have feathery hairs on them. Butterfly antennae end in tiny knobs. When butterflies rest on a plant, they hold their wings upright. Moths spread their wings out flat.

Moths belong to one of the biggest insect groups. There are over 100,000 kinds of moth and they are found all over the world. The smallest scarcely measure 3mm across. The largest may be bigger than a person's hand. Some moths have very striking colours that warn their enemies that they are poisonous or bad tasting. Moths hatch from eggs.

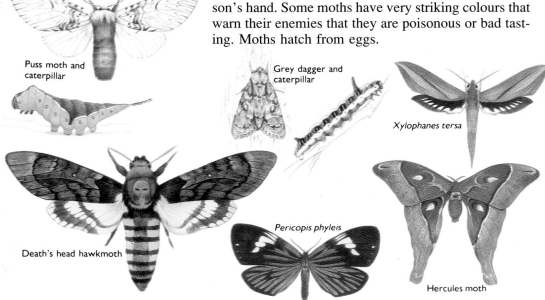

Puss moth and caterpillar

Grey dagger and caterpillar

Xylophanes tersa

Death's head hawkmoth

Pericopis phyleis

Hercules moth

◀ *Cacti come in all shapes and sizes, from small pincushion-sized specimens to the giant saguaro cactus that may reach 15 metres in height.*

▼ *Julius Caesar was a military genius. During his nine years campaigning in Gaul, he lost only two of the battles in which he took part.*

Cactus

There are hundreds of different cacti, but they all have one thing in common. They are able to grow in hot DESERT climates. Cacti can do this because they store water in their fleshy stems. They are covered with prickly spines instead of leaves. The spines protect the plant's store of water from the desert animals.

Caesar, Julius

Julius Caesar (*c*. 102–44 BC) was a great leader of the ROMAN EMPIRE. He is most famous for his part in turning the Roman Republic into an empire ruled by one man.

He first became powerful when he commanded an army that conquered what is today France, the Netherlands and Germany. In 55 BC, he crossed the Channel and invaded Britain. He rebelled against the Roman Senate (the government), when he led his victorious armies into Italy itself. He captured Rome without a struggle, and in 48 BC he defeated

A 13-month year is one of the proposals for the reform of the present calendar. Each month would be exactly 4 weeks long. An extra month called Sol would be placed between June and July. A 'Year Day' at the end of the year would not belong to a week or month, and every 4 years a 'Leap-Year Day' would be added before 1 July.

Pompey, his main rival for power. Caesar became the sole ruler of Rome.

But Caesar made enemies, who hated what he was doing to the Republic. A group of them plotted to kill him. On the 'Ides of March' (the 15th of the month), 44 BC, they stabbed him to death in the Roman Forum.

Calendar

Calendars are used to measure and record the passage of TIME. For thousands of years most calendars were based on either the observation of the phases of the MOON or the Earth's orbit round the Sun. A year is the amount of time it takes for the EIME to travel once around the SUN. A day is the time required for the Earth to rotate once on its axis – almost exactly twenty-four hours.

Julius Caesar introduced the Julian calendar in 46 BC. This is the basis of the one we use today. It had a 365-day year, with one extra day added every fourth, or leap year. This was found to be inaccurate. The calendar year was about 11 minutes longer than the solar year, the time the Earth takes to go round the Sun, about 365¼ days. The difference soon became noticeable and by 1582 the calendar was 10 days shorter than the solar year. Pope Gregory decided that October 5 should become October 15. He said leap years should not occur on centenary years except for multiples of 400, which is why the year 2000, unlike 1900 and 1800, will be a leap year.

The first people to measure the length of a year were the ancient Egyptians. They noticed that when the brightest star in the sky – Sirius the dog-star – rose just before sunrise, the Nile always overflowed its banks. They counted the days that went by before this happened again and found that it came to 365 days – a year.

▶ The 20 days in the Aztec month are represented in the inner ring of this calendar stone.

Cambodia

Cambodia is a country in South-east Asia. It changed its name from Cambodia to Kampuchea in 1976 and back to Cambodia in 1988. Most of Cambodia's people live in small villages and grow rice, fruit and vegetables. The country was formerly part of the French colony of Indochina. It became independent in 1955. Since then Cambodia has seen bitter CIVIL WAR and starvation. In 1991 the country's warring factions signed a peace treaty.

CAMBODIA

Government: Coalition
Capital: Phnom Penh
Area: 181,035 sq km
Population 8,246,000
Language: Khmer
Currency: Riel

Camel

With their wide splayed feet, gangly legs, humped body and long thick neck, camels look as if they have been made up from the parts of half a dozen other animals. But if it were not for these beasts of burden, life in some desert regions would have been almost impossible.

The camel is one of the few creatures that can stand up to extreme heat and still do work carrying heavy loads. They are ideally suited for the job of making long journeys across deserts. Their wide padded feet grip well on loose sandy ground. They are powerful and swift and can go for days without eating or drinking, living off the fat stored in their humps. Camels will eat almost anything, including the thorny shrubs and thistles found in the desert. They will chew their way through tent cloth, mats and even baskets.

Camera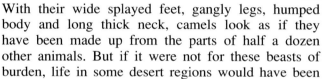

Modern cameras work in much the same way as those of a hundred years ago. A shutter opens to let light from the scene being photographed pass through a glass lens to fall on the film. The amount of light that gets through can be varied by adjusting the size of the hole through which the light passes – the 'aperture'. Apertures are measured in 'f-numbers'. A high f-number such as 16 or 22 means a small aperture. With a low f-number such as 2 or 2.8 the aperture is large. The light forms an upside- down image of the scene on the film. The film is then treated with chemicals (developed). The image on the developed film is printed onto a special type of paper. The result is a photograph.

Taking pictures with the early cameras was a slow process. The first real camera, invented by the Frenchman Louis Daguerre at the beginning of the 19th century, needed a very long exposure time. The subject had to sit motionless for as much as ten minutes, usually with his or her head in a clamp to keep it still. Some modern cameras have shutter speeds as fast as one thousandth of a second to take pictures of fast-moving objects.

CANADA

▶ *To take a picture, the shutter opens and light passes through a lens into a small aperture – the iris. From there it is focused onto the film by a second set of lenses. The image formed is upside down.*

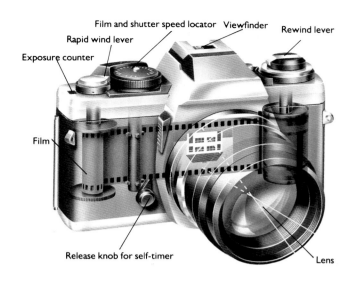

Film and shutter speed locator Viewfinder Rewind lever
Rapid wind lever
Exposure counter
Film
Release knob for self-timer
Lens

Today, most cameras have a lot of different parts to help us to take photographs in many kinds of light and from close up or from far away.

Canada

The second biggest country in the world, Canada covers an area of some ten million square km.

In the ARCTIC, Canada reaches almost as far north as Greenland. To the south, it extends to the same LATITUDE as southern France. The distance from the Pacific coast in the west to the Atlantic in the east is further than from North America to Europe. But in spite of its size, two-thirds of the population of Canada lives in a narrow belt of land no more than 200 km from the U.S. border.

In the east are the GREAT LAKES that lie on the border with the United States. These huge inland seas empty into the St Lawrence River, which links them with the Atlantic Ocean. The centre of government and finance is in Ontario, as are many of Canada's industries.

Britain and France each governed Canada in the past. Today, 18 per cent of Canadians still speak only French.

Canada is often called 'a land of the future'. The country's enormous oil and mineral resources have hardly been touched. Canada is among the ten leading industrial nations of the world.

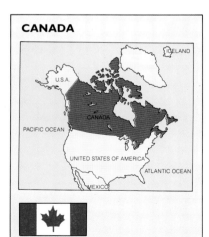

CANADA

ICELAND
U.S.A.
CANADA
PACIFIC OCEAN
UNITED STATES OF AMERICA
ATLANTIC OCEAN
MEXICO

Government: Confederation with parliamentary democracy
Capital: Ottawa
Area: 9,976,130 sq km
Population: 26,522,000
Languages: English, French
Currency: Canadian dollar

Canal

A canal is a man-made waterway built to carry water traffic. Until the 1500s, canals could be built only across flat country. With the invention of canal locks they could be built across high ground too.

Early canals could only be used by narrow, shallow-bottomed boats. These boats were pulled along by horses that walked on tow paths running alongside the canal. Some canals, like the SUEZ CANAL and the PANAMA Canal, are big enough to let ocean liners pass through them.

Cancer

Cancer is a disease of the body CELLS. Their functioning and REPRODUCTION become uncontrolled. When a cell turns cancerous or malignant, it will not work properly. It divides rapidly to produce more cells. A collection of cancerous cells is called a tumour. These cells are able to break away and are carried in the blood to other parts of the body, where they continue to grow.

Usually cells are replaced as they become old and inefficient. The development of these new cells is controlled so that the right amount of replacements are formed. However, with cancer, so many abnormal cells are produced that they interfere with normal body functions. If they are not treated they may cause very severe illness or death.

We do not know what causes cancer, but chemicals such as tar from cigarette smoke, and many other substances are known to change normal cells into cancer cells. Cancer can be treated by surgery, or by very powerful drugs or radiation which damage the cancerous cells. Though people still die from cancer, modern treatments are helping more to survive.

Car

In about a hundred years the motor car has changed the world. The car itself has changed too. The clumsy 'horseless carriage' has become the fast, comfortable and reliable car of today.

Most cars have petrol engines. If petrol is mixed with air and a spark takes place in the mixture, it explodes. The power from this explosion, repeated

▼ *How a canal lock works. Before the ship can enter, the level of water in the lock must be the same as that in the lower pool.*

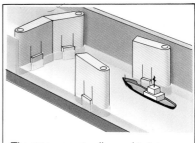

The gates open to allow a ship into the lock before closing again.

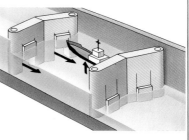

Openings in the upper gates release water into the lock.

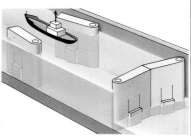

When the water level inside the lock is the same as that above the gates, they are opened to allow the ship to pass through.

again and again, is made to turn the wheels of the car. (You can read more about this in the article on the INTERNAL COMBUSTION ENGINE.) The driver can make the car go faster by pressing the *accelerator* pedal. This makes more petrol go into the engine.

Cars are pushed along by either their front or back wheels. The engine is usually at the front. As the engine's *pistons* go up and down, they turn the *crankshaft*. The crankshaft is joined to the *clutch* and the *gearbox*, as you can see in the picture. The clutch cuts off the engine from the gearbox. When the driver presses the clutch pedal, the crankshaft is separated from the GEARS. Then the driver can safely change into another gear. If the driver wants maximum power he or she uses a low gear – first gear. The car needs plenty of power for starting or going up a steep hill. When the driver travels along a clear road at speed he or she uses top gear.

Cars today are put together on assembly lines. They are built in huge numbers, which makes them cheap enough for most people to afford. The pioneer of the assembly line was Henry Ford in the United States. By building his cars out of standard parts his factories were able to turn out hundreds a day. His cars were so cheap that many people could afford to buy them. Ford's biggest success was the Model T.

▼ *A cutaway of a modern motor car showing the main parts. Power produced by the engine is transmitted to the driving wheels. For most cars these are the rear wheels, although some cars use the front or all four as driving wheels.*

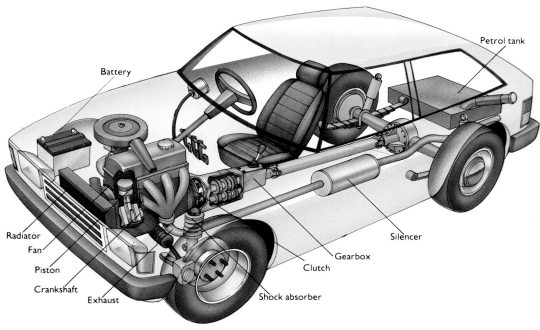

Carbon

Carbon is an important ELEMENT that is found in every living thing—both plant and animal. Many of the things we use every day have carbon in them, such as sugar and paper. Forms of carbon also exist as COAL, OIL, graphite (the 'lead' in our pencils is graphite) and DIAMONDS.

Carbon dating

Carbon dating is a way of discovering the age of any object that was once alive. Recent fossils are dated by this method. It is also called radio-carbon or carbon-14 dating.

Not all carbon atoms are the same. Most contain 12 particles but some have 13 or 14. Carbon-14 is RADIO-ACTIVE because it is unstable and breaks down, or decays, very slowly into other ELEMENTS. Carbon-14 in the atmosphere is taken in by plants which are eaten by animals. When the plants or animals die, the carbon-14 inside them begins to decay at a constant rate. So we can discover the age of any once-living object by measuring the amount of carbon-14 it still contains. In this way carbon dating confirms archaeological finds. Parts of a skull and jawbone thought to be over 250,000 years old were found in Sussex, England between 1908 and 1912. Carbon dating showed the bones to be a hoax.

For more than 40 years many scientists believed that the "missing link" between modern humans and apes had been found. Parts of a skull and jawbone thought to be more than 250,000 years old were found at Piltdown in Sussex, England between 1908 and 1912. Carbon dating of the skull in 1955 showed that the Piltdown Man was a hoax.

Carnivore

Carnivores are a group of MAMMALS that feed mainly on the flesh of other animals.

Although carnivores mostly live on meat, they will sometimes eat insects and plants. But what they all have in common is a set of very powerful jaws for chopping up their food, deadly curved claws for tearing, and long sharp teeth for seizing, stabbing and killing their victims.

Carnivores include CATS, DOGS, FOXES, RACCOONS, weasels and hyenas. All have good eyesight, smell and hearing and are fast, intelligent and skilled at hunting down other animals. Some carnivores, like wild dogs and hyenas, hunt in packs. In this way they can kill animals much larger than themselves. Other carnivores, like the LEOPARD and the JAGUAR, hunt alone.

▼ Foxes, along with badgers, are Britain's largest carnivores. They like eating rabbits and often scatter bones and feathers around their dens.

▲ *This castle in southern Germany, built with tall, rounded towers, is much like the castle of fairy tale and fable.*

Cartoon

Most people think of short, funny films with talking creatures and plants when they speak of cartoons. But originally, cartoons were rough sketches of the design for a PAINTING or a tapestry. These sketches were drawn to the same size as the finished work. Comic strips in newspapers are called strip cartoons.

Cartoon films are made by joining together a series of drawings. Each drawing is a little different from the one before. When they are shown one after another at a very fast speed it looks as if the scene is moving.

Castle

One of the few places where kings and lords in the MIDDLE AGES could feel safe was behind the thick stone walls of their castles. There, they and their men could fight off attacks by roving bandits and sit out long sieges by invading armies.

As castles developed they became larger and more comfortable. Instead of having all the living quarters crowded into the main keep, small 'villages' of huts and buildings sprang up inside the castle walls.

Castles had high, thick stone walls. A wall-walk ran right around the top, and through each tower. Soldiers could run from one point of attack to another without ever showing themselves to their enemies.

Rounded towers could stand up to battering rams and hurled rocks much better than square towers. The towers jutted out from the main wall. This gave the defenders a better chance to fire on the attackers and stop them from reaching the castle walls.

What do the cat, the camel and the giraffe have in common? Very little, except one surprising fact. Other animals move their front leg on one side at the same time as the back leg on the other side. The cat, the camel and the giraffe move their front and back legs on the same side at the same time, then the front and back legs on the other side.

Cat

A cat belongs to the group of MAMMALS called the feline family. Although the cat family ranges in size from domestic breeds to TIGERS, they all have many things in common. Cats have short, rounded heads, long face whiskers, sharp teeth that serve as deadly weapons for grabbing and biting their prey to death, and powerful claws. All cats except the cheetah can pull their claws back into a sheath of skin when they are not in use. Their long tails help them balance and make them superb at jumping and climbing. *Lions* and cheetahs live in families. All other cats live mostly alone.

Catalyst

A catalyst is a substance that speeds up a reaction between two other substances. However, it is not used up or changed itself by the reaction. Catalysts are very important in making some chemical substances for industries. The process by which they work is known as catalysis. In most chemical reactions there are several possible sequences of steps through which the reactions can proceed. Catalysts take part in some or all of these steps. They help reactions to take place more quickly and more efficiently than they otherwise would. For example, heated IRON is used to speeds up the combination of hydrogen and nitrogen in the industrial manufacture of ammonia. Chemicals called enzymes are catalysts that speed up complicated chemical reactions in all animals and plants.

It is easy to see an example of a physical catalyst when a sugar cube is put in a glass of lemonade or other fizzy drink. The fizzy drink fizzes up violently.

> Catalysts in plants and animals are called enzymes. They are protein molecules which speed up the chemical reactions without which life would be impossible. Enzymes break down substances into simpler substances. A single enzyme molecule can perform its entire function a million times a minute. The human body has over 1000 kinds of enzyme. Enzymes in the digestive system, for example, break down food for the body.

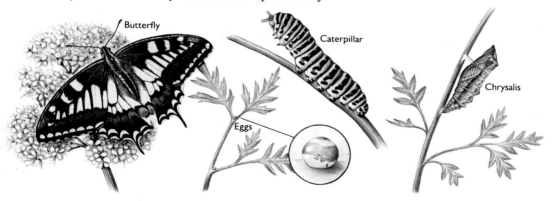

Caterpillar

The middle or 'adolescent' stage in the lives of BUTTERFLIES AND MOTHS is when they are called caterpillars.

Butterflies and moths usually lay their eggs on plants. After they hatch, small, soft, worm-like creatures—the caterpillars—emerge. Some are smooth-skinned. Others are spiny or hairy.

▲ *From egg to winged beauty – the life cycle of a butterfly. In very cold regions, some species take two or three years to pass from the egg to the butterfly stage.*

Caterpillars spend their whole time feeding. Their only purpose in life is to eat and grow and prepare for the change into adulthood. For this reason they have powerful jaws for chewing up plants. Many feed on crops and can cause great damage.

As caterpillars grow, they become too big for their skins. After a while the skin stretches and splits and they emerge with a new one. This happens several times. The last 'skin' is quite different from the others. It forms a hard layer which makes it impossible for the caterpillar to move. In this state it is called a *chrysalis*. Inside the chrysalis, the caterpillar changes into a butterfly. A moth caterpillar will spin a cocoon around itself before turning into a chrysalis. Caterpillars take almost a year to grow to full size.

Cathode ray tube

A cathode ray tube is a tube, usually made of glass. Most of the air has been removed from it, and inside a beam of electrons (*see* ATOM) is produced. The beam comes from an electron gun made of a piece of heated METAL. The electrons are emitted from the surface and accelerate to a high speed. The piece of hot metal is known as the cathode. The tube gives out a glow because the electrons collide with the air molecules

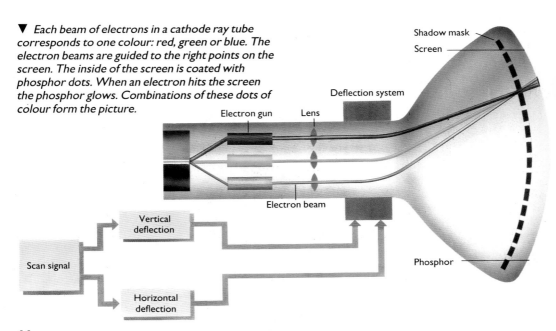

▼ Each beam of electrons in a cathode ray tube corresponds to one colour: red, green or blue. The electron beams are guided to the right points on the screen. The inside of the screen is coated with phosphor dots. When an electron hits the screen the phosphor glows. Combinations of these dots of colour form the picture.

Shadow mask
Screen
Deflection system
Electron gun
Lens
Electron beam
Vertical deflection
Scan signal
Horizontal deflection
Phosphor

producing light ENERGY. Very narrow beams of electrons can now be produced. If the far end of the tube is covered with luminescent paint, the beam then produces a small spot of light. The beam can be bent so the spot traces an image. After the spot of light has moved on the paint continues to glow for a while. Because of this, our eyes do not see the movement of the light. This is how pictures are produced by a TELEVISION or an oscilloscope. Colour pictures can be made by using luminescent paints which glow different colours. The first cathode ray tube was made by Sir William Crookes.

Cave Dweller

Anybody who lives in a cave could be called a cave dweller. But what we usually mean are people who were the ancestors of modern man. Caves are natural places to shelter from the weather and from wild animals. They were some of the first dwelling places used by human beings.

The mouth of a cave is often dry and it is possible to build a fire inside when the weather is cold. In hot weather, caves give shelter from the sun. Also, with walls all around them, the cave people could fight off dangerous animals from the cave mouth. The

▼ Many cave dwellers built their shelters in the entrances to caves. The dark interiors were often only used for ceremonies and rituals.

remains of ancient cave dwellers have been found in sites all around the world—in China, southern Asia, Europe and Africa. Here, bits and pieces of their tools and weapons have been dug up, along with bones of the animals they hunted. Remains of their fires have also been found. Deep toward the back of the caves, graves of cave people have been unearthed. On the walls of some caves, paintings of animals have been found.

Cell

Cells are the smallest living parts of plants and animals. Single cells can only be seen under a MICROSCOPE. Even a tiny bit of human skin contains millions of them.

Cells are usually round in shape. A few are spiralled and some, like nerve cells, have sprawling tree-like branches.

In 1665, a scientist called Robert Hooke looked at a piece of cork under a microscope and saw that it was made up of tiny compartments. He named them cells and this term has been used ever since.

▼ *Every living thing – plant or animal – is made up of cells. They differ in shape, size and function. The diagrams below are 'typical' cells only in that they show the characteristics of plant and animal cells. The nucleus is the control centre of the cell. Plant cells have a* cell wall *containing cellulose, a stiffening substance. They also have* chloroplasts, *which contain the green substance* chlorophyll *used in photosynthesis.*

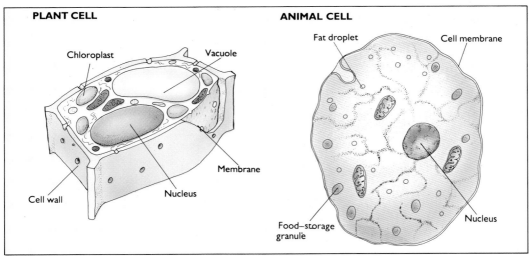

PLANT CELL

Chloroplast
Vacuole
Membrane
Nucleus
Cell wall

ANIMAL CELL

Fat droplet
Cell membrane
Food–storage granule
Nucleus

Charlemagne

Charlemagne (AD 742–814) was a great military leader. In the AD 700s he founded an empire that covered most of western Europe.

In the year 768, Charlemagne became the king of the Franks, a people who lived in the country we now call France. Through his skill in war he soon took over northern Spain, Italy and Germany. He fought for the Church in Rome, and in return, the POPE crowned him Holy Roman Emperor on Christmas Day in the year AD 800.

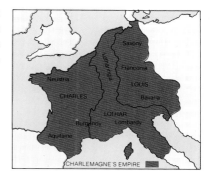

▲ This map shows the extent of Charlemagne's empire at its height. When he died, his sons fought among themselves. Eventually Charlemagne's empire was divided between his grandsons, Charles, Louis, and Lothar.

Charles I

Charles I (1600–1649) is known in history as the only British king to have caused his people to rebel and execute him. He came to the throne in 1625, but he was such a bad king he made enemies almost everywhere and in 1642 the country was split by CIVIL WAR.

Charles II

As King of Britain, Charles II (1630–1685) was liked as much as his father was disliked. He spent most of his youth in exile in Europe, while CHARLES I fought to save his crown and his life, and lost both.

In 1660, after being ruled by Oliver CROMWELL for ten years, the English invited Charles II to return and take back the crown. He was a wise ruler

▲ Charles I defied Parliament and was ultimately convicted of treason and beheaded.

▲ *After the stark years of Puritan rule under Cromwell, Charles II won the hearts of the people with his great personal charm.*

and he was very careful in the way in which he treated his people and PARLIAMENT. His court was very lively and gay and his personal charm won him many friends. His subjects called him the 'merry monarch'.

Chaucer, Geoffrey

Geoffrey Chaucer (1345–1400) was a great English poet. He was one of the first people to write in the English language rather than in Latin. His best known work is *The Canterbury Tales*. It is a collection of stories told by an imaginary group of pilgrims as they travelled to Canterbury Cathedral. The tales were still unfinished when he died.

▶ *A detail from an early illustration from* The Canterbury Tales. *Chaucer wrote the work in Middle English, the form of English used from about 1100 to 1450.*

Chemistry

Chemistry is the study of materials—solids, liquids and gases. A chemist finds out what things are made of and how they are joined together. If a piece of wood is burned in a fire, this is a *chemical reaction*. The wood turns to ash and, at the same time, heat and light are given off. It took chemists a long time to find out that burning is the joining together of the wood with the gas oxygen from the air. There are lots and lots of chemical reactions.

The true science of chemistry as we know it began only in the 1600s. Chemists at this time began to find out how chemicals really work. Then they discovered the ELEMENTS, simple substances which make up all the millions of different substances on Earth. There are only about a hundred elements, each of them made up of tiny ATOMS. The atoms of elements often join together to make different substances. The salt you put on your food is made up of atoms of the elements sodium and chlorine. An atom of sodium joins with an atom of chlorine to make a molecule of salt.

Our bodies contain many different chemicals. More than half the atoms in the body are hydrogen. Next in abundance comes oxygen. Then there is carbon, making up one-tenth of the body's weight. That is enough carbon, if it were pure, to fill 3000 pencils!

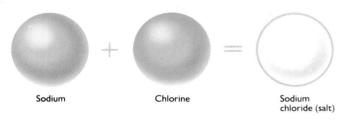

Sodium   Chlorine   Sodium chloride (salt)

Chemistry is today a very important science, and chemists are employed in a vast number of industries researching and developing new ideas.

▼ Research into cancer at a biochemistry laboratory in the United States. Growth, genetics and reproduction are all of great interest to biochemists.

Chimpanzees are among the noisiest of all animals. They scream and shriek, drum on trees, slap the ground and keep up an almost constant hooting and muttering. But when a human appears they usually fall silent and disappear into the forest.

Chimpanzee

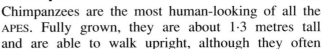

Chimpanzees are the most human-looking of all the APES. Fully grown, they are about 1·3 metres tall and are able to walk upright, although they often

▶ A chimpanzee infant watches as an adult probes a termite nest with a stick. Chimpanzees are intelligent animals capable of using simple tools.

use their hands to help push themselves along the ground. Chimpanzees come from the jungles of Africa. They live in family groups and are very fond of their young and take good care of them. They are playful and intelligent animals. Tame chimpanzees have been taught to behave like humans in many ways. They can even learn to talk in simple sign language.

China

China is the third largest country on Earth, and the nation with the greatest population. There are more than 1 billion Chinese – a fifth of the Earth's people. China has the oldest continuous civilization of any country.

Natural barriers, including the Himalaya Mountains and great deserts, cut off China from its neighbours on the Asian mainland. In the east are great plains and rivers, including China's longest river, the Chang Jiang (or Yangtze Kiang) and the slightly shorter Huang Ho or Yellow River. It is here that most of the people live. Many Chinese are citydwellers, working in factories. The capital, Beijing, is a centre of industry and

CHINA

Government: People's republic
Capital: Beijing (Peking)
Area: 9,596,961 sq km
Population: 1,100,000,000
Language: Mandarin Chinese
Currency: Yuan

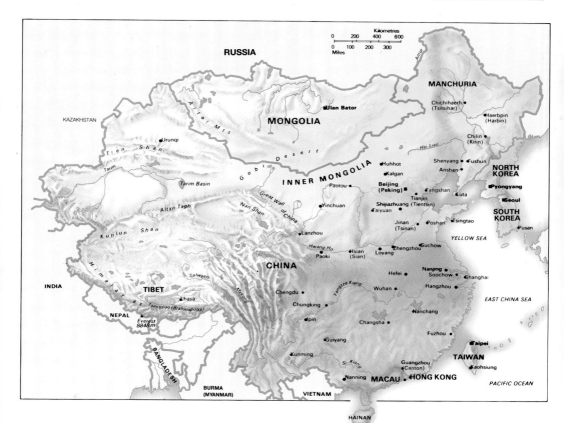

learning. More than 10 million people live there. Others till the soil, as their forefathers have done for centuries.

For more than 3000 years China was an empire. Chinese inventions included paper, printing, silk, porcelain and gunpowder – all discovered long before such things were known in Europe. Since 1912 the country has been a republic. A bitter civil war between Nationalists and Communists ended in 1949 with the Communists victorious. Under Mao Tse-tung Communist rule was often harsh, and China became isolated from the rest of the world. Later leaders have 'opened up' China to new ideas and Western trade.

Chlorophyll

This is a chemical substance that is found in the leaves and stems of almost all PLANTS. It gives them their green colour. Chlorophyll is found inside plant CELLS in tiny bodies called *chloroplasts*.

Plants need chlorophyll to make their food.

我宴马上找医生
我这里痛上
请别理得太短

THE CHINESE LANGUAGE

More people speak Chinese than any other language. Chinese is written in picture-signs or characters. A Chinese person can manage perfectly well using about 5000 characters. But there are many more: a dictionary of 1716 listed more than 40,000! To spell the sounds of Chinese in the Western alphabet, the Chinese use a system known as Pinyin. In Pinyin, the old name for the capital of China, Peking, becomes Beijing. Another city, Canton, becomes Guangzhou, and so on. Pinyin is based on Mandarin, the standard form of the language taught in China.

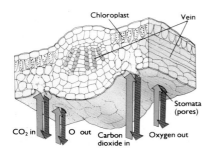

Chloroplast Vein

Stomata (pores)

CO_2 in   O out Carbon dioxide in   Oxygen out

▲ *In most plants, photosynthesis happens in the upper part of the leaf. Water and nutrients are carried to the food-producing cells by a network of veins, while gases such as carbon dioxide (CO_2) pass in and out of the leaf by tiny pores called 'stomata'. The leaf gives out oxygen (O) which we breathe.*

Sunlight, falling on the leaves, acts with the chlorophyll to turn carbon dioxide from the air, and water, which the plant's roots suck up from the soil, into food made up of SUGARS and STARCHES. At the same time, the plant's leaves give out OXYGEN. This whole process is called *photosynthesis*. It is a very important part of life on our Earth, as all living things need oxygen in order to breathe.

Plants can only produce chlorophyll when they are grown in the light. Plants kept in darkness often turn white or yellow because they lack chlorophyll.

Chromosomes and genes

Inside the nucleus of every living CELL there are a number of microscopic threads called chromosomes. These chromosomes carry all the information necessary for the cells, and the whole body, to develop properly. Each kind of plant or animal has its own particular number of chromosomes and they come in pairs. Humans have 22 pairs in each normal cell plus two extra chromosomes, sex chromosomes, which decide the body's sex.

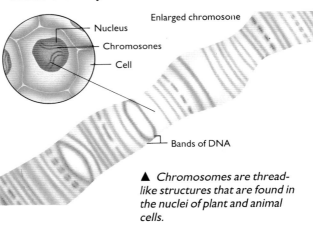

Enlarged chromosone

Nucleus

Chromosones

Cell

Bands of DNA

▲ *Chromosomes are thread-like structures that are found in the nuclei of plant and animal cells.*

▼ *Humans have 23 pairs of chromosomes in most of their cells. Males and females differ only in the sex chromosome of the 23rd pair. A female's chromosomes would look like XX, instead of XY.*

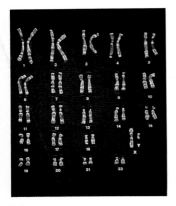

The chromosomes are made largely of chains of DNA molecules. Areas of these chains are genes, and there may be hundreds of them on a chromosome. Each one controls one or more features in the body by determining what proteins are made in the cells. Proteins are the major materials of living cells.

Although we all have the same number of chromosomes in our cells, we have slightly different genes, and so we look different.

Cinema

The art of making moving pictures came from an invention called the *kinetoscope*, built by an American, Thomas EDISON, in 1891. Soon after Edison's machine became known, two French brothers, Auguste and Louis Lumière, built a similar machine of their own called a *cinématographe*. This machine projected pictures from a piece of film onto a screen. The pictures were shown one after the other, so quickly that the images on the screen appeared to move. In 1896, in Paris, the Lumière brothers gave the world's first public film show. Soon, people all over Europe and North America were making films.

These early films did not look much like the ones we are used to seeing today. They were only in black and white, the movements were very jerky and they had no sound. At first, films were made to show news and real events, but by 1902 film-makers began to make up their own stories, using actors to play the parts of imaginary people. These films were very popular in France and the United States, and Hollywood in California became the film-making centre of the world. The first 'talkie', or moving picture with sound, was shown in America in 1927. It was called *The Jazz Singer*.

America remained the leader in the film world. Huge amounts of money were spent on films that used hundreds of actors, singers and dancers, lavish costumes and specially designed 'sets' or backgrounds. But Europe too produced many important films, and after World War II, a more realistic type of film became popular, telling stories of everyday life. Nearly all films were made in colour.

▲ King Kong *was perhaps the most famous of the early special effects films. At the time, amazed audiences didn't know how he had been brought to life.*

◀ Gone with the Wind, *made in 1939, was an American Civil War epic that became one of the most popular films ever.*

Today, films are made all over the world, although the United States still produces most of the big feature films, using modern technology to create fantastic visual effects. Television has been a threat to the film industry since the 1960s, and there have been many experiments in recent years to develop new kinds of films.

Which story character has been a film hero more often than any other? The answer is Sherlock Holmes, Conan Doyle's famous detective. There have been 187 films about him between 1900 and the present time. And no doubt there will be lots more!

Civil War (English)

Civil war happens when a whole country is divided into two or more groups who fight each other over their different political or religious beliefs. In England, the last civil war lasted from 1642 to 1649 and was fought between the king, CHARLES I, and PARLIAMENT.

By this time it was agreed that although the King ruled the country he could tax money from the people only if Parliament agreed. Charles believed that God had given him the right to do this alone. So in 1629 he got rid of Parliament and ruled without it, taxing the people whenever he needed money.

People became very unwilling to pay their taxes to Charles. In 1640 Charles was forced to recall Parliament because he needed more money. Instead of giving him money, Parliament argued with the King and said he could not rule or tax the people on his own. Charles angrily dismissed Parliament and later tried to arrest some of its leaders.

▼ *Royalist forces clash with Cromwell's troops at the Battle of Naseby. Cromwell's sweeping victory actually decided the war, though fighting went on for some time in the west of England.*

In 1642 the King called his friends to arm themselves. They were called Royalists. Parliament had its own army. They were called Roundheads because they had short hair. The Roundheads had a great general called Oliver CROMWELL. He was very strict and trained his army carefully.

After several battles the Royalist forces lost the war and the King was captured. Charles was put on trial and in 1649 he was executed. For some years, Parliament ruled without a king, led by Cromwell.

▼ The Earth can be roughly divided into five climatic zones. Within each zone there are variations because climate is determined by altitude as well as by latitude.

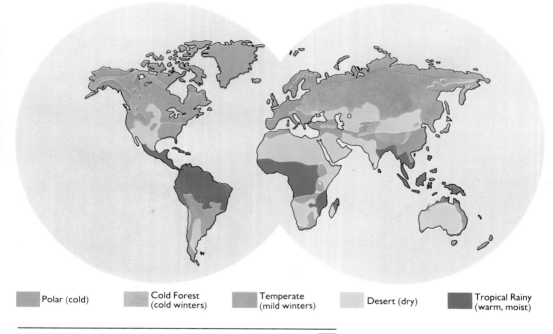

Polar (cold)	Cold Forest (cold winters)	Temperate (mild winters)	Desert (dry)	Tropical Rainy (warm, moist)

Climate

Climate is the usual WEATHER of a place over a long period of time. The weather can change from day to day but the climate stays the same.

The Sun has the greatest influence on the climate. It heats the land, the seas and the air. Countries near the equator get more of the Sun's rays and usually have a hotter climate than places further north or south. The Sun's rays do not get to the Arctic and the Antarctic easily. They have very cold climates.

When the Sun heats the air it causes winds which can make the climate hotter or colder. The winds may also carry rain or dry air which can make the climate wet or dry.

▼ The Poles get less heat than the equator because the Sun's rays have to travel farther through the Earth's atmosphere. The rays also reach the Poles at a slant because the Earth is round.

▲ Early mechanical clocks in Europe were driven by a weight on the end of a cord wound round a drum. As the drum rotated, it turned the hands of the clock.

▼ One of the most famous clocks in the world is at the Houses of Parliament in London. It is often mistakenly called Big Ben – this is actually the name of its biggest bell.

Together with the winds, the Sun's heat makes ocean currents. The Gulf Stream is a current which travels from Mexico to north-western Europe. In winter the warmth from its water makes the climate of Britain milder than other places so far north.

Mountains also affect the climate. On a mountain top the air is thinner. It does not soak up the heat of the Sun as much as air at the bottom of mountains or in valleys.

Clock

Long ago people measured TIME by putting a stick in the ground and watching its shadow move with the Sun. Sundials work in the same way. Sun clocks work only when the Sun is shining, so people began to measure time by watching how long it took a candle to burn or a tank of water to empty.

The first mechanical clocks were made in Europe in the 1200s, although the Chinese probably had clocks as early as the 600s. European clocks were first used in churches to mark the time of services. A clock in Salisbury Cathedral dates from 1386.

Early clocks like these were bad time-keepers and could lose or gain an hour a day. In 1581 the great astronomer Galileo discovered that the pendulum could be used to measure time. This helped people to make much more accurate clocks. Ordinary clocks are now accurate to within a few minutes a year.

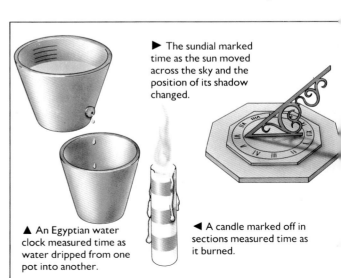

▶ The sundial marked time as the sun moved across the sky and the position of its shadow changed.

▲ An Egyptian water clock measured time as water dripped from one pot into another.

◀ A candle marked off in sections measured time as it burned.

Today's scientists need very accurate clocks. They invented first the electric and then the quartz crystal clock. The most accurate clock today is at the United States Naval Research Laboratory in Washington, D.C. It is an atomic hydrogen maser clock and is accurate to one second in 1,700,000 years.

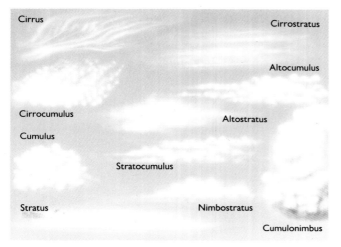

Cirrus
Cirrostratus
Altocumulus
Cirrocumulus
Altostratus
Cumulus
Stratocumulus
Stratus
Nimbostratus
Cumulonimbus

◀ *Different types of cloud bring different weather. The high cirrus clouds are made of ice, and are sometimes called 'mares' tails'. Puffy cumulus clouds often mean fine weather. Low, grey, stratus clouds bring rain and the towering cumulonimbus are thunder clouds.*

Cloud

Clouds are great clusters of tiny water droplets or ice crystals in the air. A cloud may float more than 10,000 metres up, or drift so low that it touches the ground, when it is known as mist or fog.

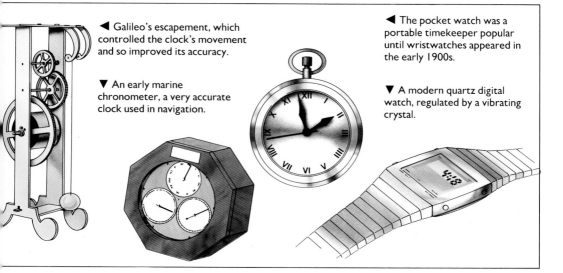

◀ Galileo's escapement, which controlled the clock's movement and so improved its accuracy.

▼ An early marine chronometer, a very accurate clock used in navigation.

◀ The pocket watch was a portable timekeeper popular until wristwatches appeared in the early 1900s.

▼ A modern quartz digital watch, regulated by a vibrating crystal.

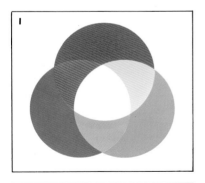

▼ Most coal is now cut by machines. The workings of a coal mine may stretch for miles underground.

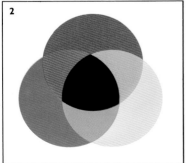

▼ Coloured light behaves differently from coloured pigments (the substances that give inks and paints their colour). All the colours in light (1) combine to make white light, but mixing coloured pigments (2) results in black.

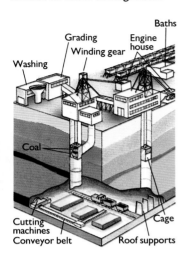

There is always a certain amount of water *vapour* in the air. It is made up of tiny specks of water. Warm air that contains water vapour often rises and cools. Since cool air cannot hold as much water as warm air, the vapour particles start to form droplets (condense) around bits of dust, pollen and salt.

As more water vapour condenses, the droplets grow in size and clouds begin to form. At first they are white and gauzy. As they become heavy with water they become thick and grey. Finally the droplets become so heavy that they clump together and fall to the earth. If the temperature is high enough they come down as rain. Otherwise they land as hail or snow.

Most clouds form along the boundaries between cold and warm air masses. By watching how they build and move it is possible to tell what sort of weather is coming. Different types of clouds tell weather forecasters different things. Clouds are one of the best ways we have of predicting the WEATHER.

Coal

Coal is a fuel which is found in layers, or *seams*, under the ground. It is known as a FOSSIL FUEL because it was made millions of years ago from dead plants. Coal is used for heating and in making electricity, gas and chemicals. It is also made into another fuel called coke. It was the most important fuel of the INDUSTRIAL REVOLUTION.

Colour

The first man to find out about coloured light was Isaac NEWTON. He shone sunlight through a piece of glass called a *prism*. The light that came out of the prism was broken up into all the colours of the rainbow—red, orange, yellow, green, blue and violet. Newton had found out that ordinary white light is made up of many colours added together.

When sunlight falls on rain or spray from a garden hose, we sometimes see a rainbow. Rainbows are caused by the drops of water behaving like tiny prisms. They break up the Sun's light into a *spectrum* of colours. The colours are always in the same order. They are red, orange, yellow, green, blue, indigo and violet.

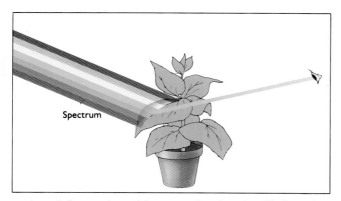

◀ *Why we see colour: a green plant looks green to us because it absorbs all the colours in light apart from green, which it reflects back to our eyes.*

A red flower is red because it takes in all the other colours and throws back only red. A white flower gives back to our eyes all the colours of light. We know that all the colours added together make white.

Columbus, Christopher

Christopher Columbus (1451–1506) was a sailor and explorer. He discovered America for Spain in 1492. Although Columbus returned to America three more times, he died believing that the land he had reached was Asia.

Like many people of his time, Columbus knew that the Earth was not flat but round. Sailors from Europe used to sail east to the 'Indies' (Asia). They brought back rich cargoes of gold, spices and treasure. Columbus thought that if he sailed west instead he could reach the Indies quicker. The Queen and King of Spain gave him ships and money to make this voyage.

In 1492 Columbus sailed west with three small ships, the *Santa Maria*, the *Pinta* and the *Niña*. The ships sailed for three weeks without seeing any land and the crews became afraid. Then, on 12 October, they reached an island in the Americas. Columbus named it San Salvador – an island in the Bahamas. When he returned to Spain, Columbus had a hero's welcome.

Colombus made further voyages, but it was not until his third expedition in 1498 that he found mainland America. He thought he had sailed to the Indies. This is why the people he met in America were called Indians. The islands he first reached are still known as the West Indies.

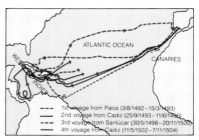

ATLANTIC OCEAN

CANARIES

WEST INDIES

--- 1st voyage from Palos (3/8/1492–15/3/1493)
——— 2nd voyage from Cadiz (25/9/1493–11/6/1496)
——— 3rd voyage from Sanlúcar (30/5/1498–20/11/1500)
---- 4th voyage from Cadiz (11/5/1502–7/11/1504)

▲ *Christopher Columbus made four voyages to the Americas, first landing in San Salvador. His flagship on the first voyage, the 100-tonne caravel Santa Maria, ran aground and had to be abandoned.*

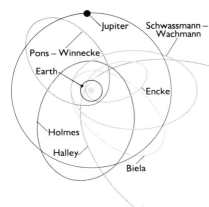

Comet

Comets travel round the SOLAR SYSTEM in paths, or orbits. Sometimes they pass close to the Sun. At other times they move far beyond the path of Pluto, the outermost planet. A complete orbit by a comet is called its period. Encke's Comet has the shortest period of all. It lasts for three years and four months. Others have periods of centuries or even thousands of years. Comet West, which was visible in daylight in 1976, will not return to the Sun for about a million years.

Comets are clouds of frozen gases, ice, dust and rock. The biggest are only a few kilometres across, but their bright tails may be millions of kilometres long.

Most of the time comets cannot be seen, even through the biggest telescopes. But whenever their orbits bring them back into the middle of the solar system they flare up and look very bright.

As a comet travels towards the Sun, the Sun's rays knock particles out of the comet and push them away to make a long tail. The tail is made of glowing gas and dust. But the tail is so fine that a rocket passing through it would not be harmed. The Earth has passed through the tails of several comets. One of the most famous comets is named after the astronomer Edmond HALLEY. In 1682 he studied the path of a bright comet and accurately forecast when it would return.

▲ Some of the comets that return regularly to the Sun every few years. Part of the much bigger orbit of Halley's Comet is also shown. Encke's Comet has the smallest period and it passes close to the Sun every three years and four months, although it cannot be seen without a telescope. Comets are usually named after those who discovered them. They were once thought to foretell the coming of evil events, since they appeared so unexpectedly and dramatically.

▶ Comet West, photographed on March 9, 1976, showing its dust tail (white) and its gas tail (blue).

Commonwealth of Nations

A commonwealth is a group of countries or people who are friendly and help each other. The Commonwealth of Nations is made up from most of the countries that were once ruled by Britain. Most of these countries now have their own governments and laws but many of them still have the queen or king of Britain as their monarch.

The Commonwealth came into being at a meeting held in 1926. Commonwealth countries share some of the same beliefs and trade with each other. The heads of Commonwealth countries that have their own governments meet together often. They talk about their problems and try to help each other.

Communication

Communication is the exchange of ideas – through words, pictures and numbers. We learn by communication with other people. And it is by means of communication that civilization has grown. Imagine a world without any way of storing and recording information (such as a printed book). Each new generation would have to reinvent the wheel, relying on word of mouth and memory alone to pass on knowledge.

Communication began with the first human languages, and with the cave paintings of Stone Age people. The first writing, using picture-signs, was invented more than 5000 years ago. But it is in the last 500 years that the communication 'explosion' has taken place. The invention of printing made books available to everyone who could read. Since the INDUSTRIAL REVOLUTION of the 1800s communications science has changed our lives, bringing amazing new ways of message-sending and message-storing. Inventions such as PHOTOGRAPHY, sound RECORDING, RADIO, TELEPHONES, TELEVISION and COMPUTERS have brought about the modern communications revolution.

The communications revolution is very obvious in the home. Small portable cassette players make it possible for us to listen to sound recordings almost anywhere. Home video recorders allow us to view recorded programmes. The telephone allows us to talk to friends and family anywhere in the world. And small portable computers mean more and more people can work from home, rather than in an office.

MEMBERS OF THE COMMONWEALTH

Antigua and Barbuda	New Zealand
Australia	Nigeria
Bahamas	Papua New Guinea
Bangladesh	Western Samoa
Belize	Seychelles
Botswana	Sierra Leone
Brunei	Singapore
Canada	Solomon Islands
Cyprus	Sri Lanka
Dominica	St Kitts-Nevis
The Gambia	St Lucia
Ghana	St Vincent and the Grenadines
Grenada	
Guyana	Swaziland
India	Tanzania
Jamaica	Tonga
Kiribati	Trinidad and Tobago
Lesotho	
Malawi	Tuvalu
Malaysia	Uganda
The Maldives	United Kingdom
Malta	Vanuatu
Mauritius	Zambia
Nauru	Zimbabwe

THE ELECTRONIC REVOLUTION

▲ The first radio signals were sent across the Atlantic Ocean by Guglielmo Marconi in 1901.

► The desktop microcomputer can be a useful educational tool.

► Large dish aerials are used to send TV signals up to a satellite, from where they are directed to a dish in the receiving country and transmitted to TV receivers.

Advances in communication in this century include the first transatlantic radio signal, sent by Marconi in 1901. And the electronic computer, which plays a bigger and bigger part in all our lives, first appeared in 1946. It was the result of combined effort from many scientists.

Communism

Communism is a set of ideas about the way a country should be run. The main idea of communism is that people should share wealth and property. This makes people more equal because nobody is very rich or very poor. In most communist countries the people own the factories and farms but it is usually the government that runs them. The government controls almost everything, and personal freedoms are restricted. However, during the late 1980s, the USSR and most eastern European countries adopted a freer form of Communism and obtained more democratic government.

Many countries became communist in the early part of the twentieth century. They included the Soviet Union, China and Cuba, and some countries in Eastern Europe and the Far East. LENIN and Mao Tse-Tung were among the great communist leaders of the twentieth century.

Compass

A compass is an instrument for finding the way. A magnetic compass always points to the Earth's magnetic poles, which are close to the North and South Poles. The magnetic compass has been used for centuries by sailors and explorers to find the right direction.

A magnetic compass works by MAGNETISM. It has a magnetic needle fixed to a pivot so that it is free to swing round. The needle always points north and south when it is at rest. With a compass showing where north and south are, it is easy to travel in a straight line in any direction you wish to go.

The needle always points north and south because the Earth itself is a big magnet. The compass needle lines up parallel with the Earth's magnetic field.

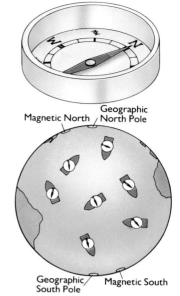

Magnetic North / Geographic North Pole

Geographic South Pole / Magnetic South

Computer

Computers are playing a bigger and bigger part in all our lives. They can play a game of chess with you, guide a spacecraft, check fingerprints and draw a map of Australia. They can do all these things and many more merely because they can add, subtract and compare one number with another. Computers are special because they can do millions of calculations in a second.

▲ A compass does not point directly at the North Pole. This is because the Earth's magnetic field does not line up with the geographic Poles. The difference between the geographic and magnetic poles is called the 'magnetic variation'.

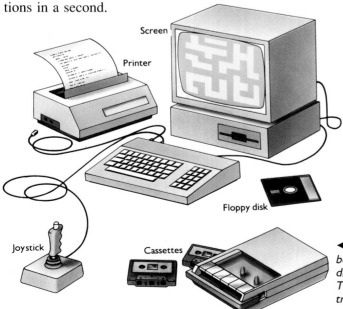

Screen

Printer

Floppy disk

Joystick

Cassettes

◄ Computer programs and data can be stored on a cassette or on a floppy disk. Floppy disks are more efficient. They store information in concentric tracks that enable data to be located quickly.

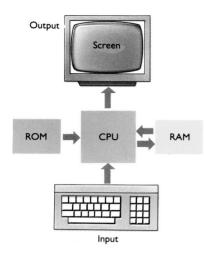

Output · Screen

ROM → CPU ⇄ RAM

Input

▲ *A computer has four basic parts, the 'input' (keyboard), memory (RAM and ROM), central processing unit (CPU), and the 'output', a screen or printer.*

Although the computer works with numbers, the information it uses does not have to start off as numbers. We can feed almost anything into it, but the first thing the computer does is to turn everything into numbers. But the numbers it uses are not quite the same as ours. We use the numbers 0 to 9. All the computer needs is 0 and 1. In fact, it can only count up to 1! This is called the BINARY SYSTEM. The computer uses the binary system because it has been designed to work with electrical currents. It can recognize the difference between a big current and a small current flow. If there is a big current, it registers 1; if there is a small current, it registers 0. When we type on the keys of a computer keyboard, we are making little electrical currents flow through tiny circuits in microchips. It is these tiny currents that give us the answers we need.

Congo

The Congo is a country in the west of central AFRICA. It was formerly part of a huge French colony and became independent in 1960. It has an area of 342,000 sq km.

The Congo is a hot, wet country. It has great forests and swamps, and a low grassy plain on the coast. The capital is called Brazzaville. The Congo produces a lot of timber, but it also has diamonds, sugar, oil, cocoa and coffee.

Along the Congo's border with its larger neighbour, Zaire, runs a great river. This river used to be called the Congo, but is now called the Zaire River. It is 4667 km long, one of the longest in the world.

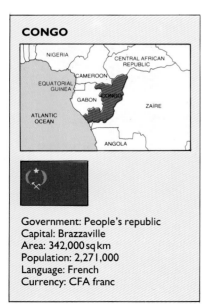

CONGO

NIGERIA · CENTRAL AFRICAN REPUBLIC · CAMEROON · EQUATORIAL GUINEA · GABON · CONGO · ZAIRE · ATLANTIC OCEAN · ANGOLA

Government: People's republic
Capital: Brazzaville
Area: 342,000 sq km
Population: 2,271,000
Language: French
Currency: CFA franc

Conservation

Human beings use plants, animals, soil, water and minerals for nearly everything they make. Often they waste and destroy those natural resources. Conservation means using these resources wisely and protecting them. It also means preserving areas of natural beauty.

Today the need to conserve wildlife and natural resources is a world problem. It involves the study of ECOLOGY, the branch of BIOLOGY that deals with the relationship between all living things and their surroundings. People must avoid upsetting Nature's balance.

Continental Shelf

Continents do not end where their coasts meet the sea. Their true edge lies far out under the sea. Each continent is ringed by a gently sloping shelf of land under the sea called the continental shelf. This shelf sometimes stretches for hundreds of kilometres from the shore. Beyond the continental shelf is the deep ocean floor.

In the past, the sea level was lower and much of the continental shelf was dry land. Rivers flowed through it to the sea and made valleys or canyons.

▲ *Felling trees to meet the world demand for paper and wood has laid bare thousands of acres of forest land. Conservation means careful use of such resources.*

◄ *Most of the continental shelf lies under about 140 metres of water. At its edge, the seabed falls steeply to the deep ocean floor.*

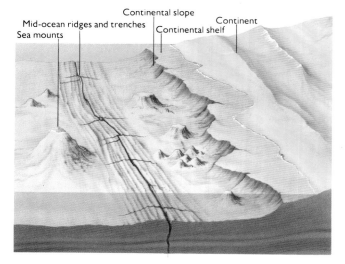

Continental slope
Continent
Mid-ocean ridges and trenches
Continental shelf
Sea mounts

These canyons are still there, but today they are under the sea.

Most sea life is found on the continental shelf. Sunlight shines through the water, helping plants, fish and other animals to grow.

Continent

A continent is a large area of land. The Earth has seven continents: Africa, Antarctica, Asia, Australia, Europe, North America and South America. Some people say that because Europe and Asia are joined, they are one big continent called Eurasia.

The continents are not fixed. They are made of lighter rock than the rock on the ocean floor. The great heat in the centre of the Earth has made the surface rocks break into huge pieces called *plates*. When the plates move they move the continents with them. This movement is very slow. A continent moves only a few centimetres in one century.

A few hundred years ago some people saw that the shapes of America, Europe and Africa looked like jigsaw pieces that would fit closely if they were

▼ *Continental drift at various stages in the Earth's history. Over millions of years, the single continent we call Pangaea broke up to produce the pattern of continents we know today.*

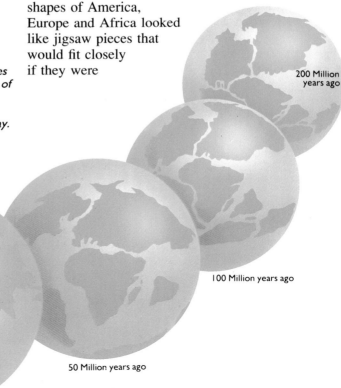

200 Million years ago

100 Million years ago

50 Million years ago

Today

pushed together. This gave them the idea that the continents used to be one big piece of land which broke up. This idea is called continental drift. Continental drift was first suggested in 1912 by Alfred Wegener. He found evidence to show that America was once in contact with Africa. Today, people who study GEOLOGY believe this idea is true.

Geologists think that the movements of the continents pushed up some pieces of land to make mountains such as the Alps and the Himalayas.

> During the Ice Age, the northern and southern parts of the world were covered by great ice-caps. So much water became ice that the sea-level dropped by as much as 150 metres. This meant that vast areas of the shallow continental shelf became dry land. It has been estimated that a total area of about 30 million square km of sea became dry land – an area bigger than the Soviet Union, the biggest country in the world.

Cook, James

James Cook (1728–1779) was a famous British sea captain and explorer. His expeditions took him round the world and all over the Pacific Ocean. Cook's discoveries led to Australia, New Zealand and many South Pacific islands becoming British colonies.

After serving in the Royal Navy for 13 years, Cook was put in command of an expedition to Tahiti in 1768. After Tahiti, Cook carried on to New Zealand. He sailed around both North and South Islands, and then went on to Australia. Cook landed in Botany Bay in 1770 to claim the continent for Britain.

On his second voyage (1772–1775), Cook set off to look for the 'southern continent', which many people believed lay south of Australia. He crossed the Antarctic Circle and explored the edges of Antarctica. He also charted many unknown Pacific islands.

> In 1934, the cottage in which James Cook lived as a boy at Great Ayton in Yorkshire was presented to the government of Victoria in Australia. It was carefully taken apart and re-erected in Fitzroy Gardens, Melbourne.

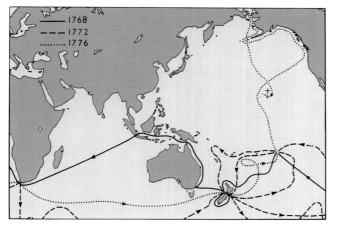

◄ *The routes followed by Captain Cook on his three voyages. On his first voyage in 1768 he was in command of the* Endeavour, *with a crew of 80 and 3 scientists on board. Many of the places Cook discovered are named after him. His detailed surveys and observations set new standards for the explorers that followed him.*

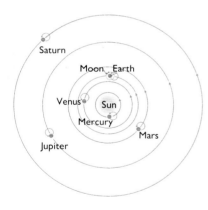

▲ In New Zealand Cook met the Maoris, a warlike people who were skilful craftsmen. They often carved clubs and charms from a green stone. Their houses were made of wood, and finely carved.

Cook's third and last voyage began in 1776. He left England with two ships—the *Resolution* and *Discovery*—to try to find a route around North America. Again he sailed to the Pacific. In early 1778 he discovered the Hawaiian Islands. From there Cook sailed north along the west coast of America. He got as far as the Bering Strait off Alaska before being forced back by ice. Returning to Hawaii, he was killed in a scuffle with natives over a stolen boat. Today Cook is remembered as a skilled navigator and a great explorer.

Copernicus, Nicolaus

Nicolaus Copernicus (1473–1543) was a Polish scientist. He is sometimes called the father of modern ASTRONOMY.

Copernicus showed that the Earth is not the centre of the UNIVERSE, as people used to believe. Instead, the Earth and PLANETS revolve round the Sun. Copernicus also showed that the Earth itself moves round, or *rotates*, each day.

Copernicus' theory was dangerous at a time when the Bible was believed to prove that the Earth is the central and most important body of all in the Universe. It made him unpopular. He published his theory in a book which very few people bought or read. However, the fact that the book existed was enough to start others discussing his ideas.

▲ Copernicus realized that the Earth-centred universe theory was not supported by the actual movements of the planets. He correctly showed that all the planets revolved round the Sun. But he wrongly thought that all the planets move in small circles as well.

Copper

Copper is a reddish-brown METAL. It was probably one of the first metals that people used. About 7000 years ago the ancient Egyptians and people in Iraq began to use copper for their tools and weapons. They also made copper ornaments. At first they used pure copper which they found in the ground. But most copper is found with other metals and minerals in a mixture called ore. People began to heat, or *smelt*, copper ores so that the pure copper melted and flowed out.

Copper is very soft when it is pure. But if it is mixed with other metals it makes ALLOYS such as brass and bronze, which are harder and better for making tools. If copper is exposed to the air for a long time it turns green.

◄ *Nearly three-quarters of the world's copper is mined in only six countries: the USA, Russia, Zambia, Chile, Canada and Zaire. Copper is the world's second most widely used metal after iron.*

Copper can be beaten into sheets or pulled out into wire. It lets heat and electricity pass through it very easily, so it is often used for making pots and pans and electric wires.

Coral

Coral is a kind of limestone found mostly in warm, shallow seas. It is made by tiny animals, called coral polyps, that build limestone 'shells' around themselves for protection. Most coral polyps live in groups, or colonies. These may take many shapes, from lacy fans to stubby branches, all in beautiful colours. Other colonies form thick underwater walls known as reefs.

At the beginning of the 19th century Swansea in south Wales was the centre of the world's copper industry. Three-quarters of world production of the metal was smelted in the Swansea valley. There were about 600 furnaces in the valley, chiefly smelting copper, and the 'copper smoke' did great damage to the countryside.

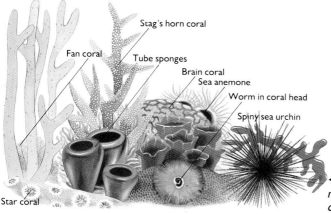

Stag's horn coral
Fan coral
Tube sponges
Brain coral
Sea anemone
Worm in coral head
Spiny sea urchin
Star coral

◄ *Coral reefs provide homes for many sea animals which find shelter in crevices or burrow into the soft coral.*

HOW AN ATOLL IS FORMED

Coral grows in the warm waters surrounding an island; in this illustration an island that has been formed by volcanic action.

Coral continues to grow on the reefs as the island sinks or the sea rises.

Once the island has completely disappeared, the coral reefs remain, forming a typical atoll.

▼ Cortés founded the town of Veracruz on the coast of Mexico. There he dismantled his ships and set out to explore the country, arriving in the Aztec capital, Tenochtitlán, in November 1519.

Along some reefs waves may throw up bits of sand and coral which gradually build up on top of the reef until it is above water. The reef then becomes an island. One kind of coral island is the atoll, a ringed reef that encloses a central lagoon.

Cork

The cork that is used to make bottle stoppers comes from the smooth bark of the cork oak tree of the Mediterranean. It is a light, spongy material that forms a thick layer about 3 cm deep around the trunk of the tree.

Cork is stripped from cork oaks once every nine or ten years until the trees are about 150 years old.

Cortés, Hernando

Hernando Cortés (1485–1547) was a Spanish soldier and explorer who in 1519 landed on the coast of Mexico. With a force of only 600 men and a handful of horses he conquered the great AZTEC empire. His horses and guns helped convince the Aztecs he was a god. Cortés marched on their capital, captured the Aztec emperor Montezuma, and by 1521 had taken control of Mexico.

Cotton

Cotton grows in warm and tropical places all round the world. It is one of the most important plants grown by people; its fibres and seeds are both used. The fibres are made into cloth and the seeds are used for oil and cattle food. The oil is used in soaps, paints and cosmetics.

Cotton has green fruits called bolls. When they are ripe, the bolls split open. Inside them is a mass of white fibres and seeds. The bolls are harvested and the fibres are separated from the seeds. The fibres are spun into yarn and then woven into cloth.

Cow

The cow that gives us milk is a member of the cattle family. Cattle are large grass-eating animals. Grass is difficult to digest, and all cattle have four stomachs to make it easier. During digestion the food is returned to the mouth to be chewed and swallowed again. When a cow does this we say it is 'chewing the cud'. The farm cow is descended from an extinct wild cow called an *aurochs*, and has been tamed by people for about 6000 years.

▲ *The Swiss Simmental is bred for both milk and meat.*

◄ *The Hereford is a popular beef breed in North America and Australia.*

Crab

Most people think that crabs live only in the sea, but there are some kinds that live in fresh water (rivers or lakes) and some tropical kinds that make their home on land.

Crabs belong to a group of animals called CRUSTACEANS. They have hard, thick shells that cover their flat bodies. They also have long, spidery legs for walking underwater, swimming and burrowing. The first pair of legs have pincers which are used for attacking and holding prey. Crabs have their eyes on the end of short stalks. These can be pulled into the shell for safety.

▲ *The Jersey is a small cow that produces very rich milk and cream.*

▲ *Nearly two-thirds of all cows in Britain are Frisians.*

Crimean War

The Crimean War (1854–56) was a struggle between Russia on one side and Turkey, France and Britain on the other. At that time the Turkish Empire was very weak. Russia hoped to make its power greater in the eastern Mediterranean by taking Constantinople (now called Istanbul).

The British, French and Turks pushed the Russian army back into the Crimean peninsula, where the war was fought. There was much misery and suffering.

▲ *The dairy shorthorn, bred for meat, is red, white or roan.*

▼ The British light cavalry rode to their deaths at the battle of Balaclava in the Crimea. The poet Tennyson commemorated the battle in his poem 'The Charge of the Light Brigade'.

For the first time, newspaper reporters and photographers went to the battle-grounds. They reported the terrible conditions of the soldiers to the newspapers.

▼ Oliver Cromwell's cavalry forces were called Ironsides.

Cromwell, Oliver

Oliver Cromwell (1599–1658) was the only ruler of Britain never to have been a king or queen. He came to power after the CIVIL WAR of the 1640s. Cromwell was a member of PARLIAMENT. He fought against CHARLES I with the army of Parliament and became its leader.

After Charles I was executed, Cromwell became the head of the country but he never made himself king. From 1653 he was called the 'Lord Protector'. Cromwell held strict views about religion and behaviour, but he was devoted to literature and music.

After Cromwell died, CHARLES II became king.

Crusades

The Crusades were wars between Christians and Muslims in the MIDDLE AGES. They took place in Palestine, the Holy Land. In 1071, Turkish Muslims captured the city of Jerusalem in Palestine. The Muslims stopped Christians from visiting the holy places in Palestine.

The Christian rulers in Europe were very angry about this. A few years later, the Byzantine emperor in Constantinople asked the Pope to help him drive the Turks from the Holy Land. The Pope started the first Crusade. He said he would forgive the sins of all the people who went and fought in the Holy Land.

The armies of the first Crusade were successful. They took Jerusalem from the Muslims in 1099. The Crusaders set up Christian kingdoms along the coast of Palestine and Syria and built strong fortresses to defend their new lands.

There were seven more Crusades after the first one. Many of them failed because the Crusaders quarrelled with each other. The Muslims took back much of the Holy Land from the Christians. When the Muslims took Jerusalem in 1187, the third Crusade set off from Europe. When they got to the Holy Land, the Crusaders were defeated by the Muslims who had a new general called Saladin.

▼ To attack the strong walls of cities and castles, the Crusaders used catapults and battering rams. They built tall towers from which they could fire arrows and climb over the walls.

Later, the Crusaders forgot that they were fighting for their religion. Many of them went to Palestine hoping to take the land and become rich. By 1291, the Muslims had taken the last remaining Christian city at Acre.

During the Crusades, European people learnt more about the eastern parts of the world. When they returned to Europe they took back with them many new things including foods, spices, silk clothes and paper. They learnt about medicine, mathematics and astronomy from the Arabs of the east, and trade between east and west began to grow.

Crustacean

Crustaceans are a large group of about 10,000 animals. They include sandhoppers, wood-lice, waterfleas, barnacles, crayfish, shrimps, prawns, CRABS and lobsters. All have hard, jointed bodies and jointed legs. Most crustaceans live in the sea.

Crustaceans are *invertebrates* (animals with no backbones). Most have SHELLS around their bodies.

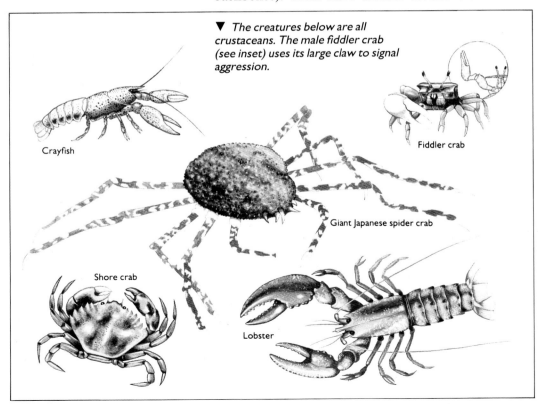

▼ The creatures below are all crustaceans. The male fiddler crab (see inset) uses its large claw to signal aggression.

Crayfish

Fiddler crab

Giant Japanese spider crab

Shore crab

Lobster

This keeps their soft bodies safe. Many have a set of claws, or pincers, on their front legs. They use these to defend themselves and to grab their prey.

Crustaceans began life as *eggs*. These hatch into tiny *larvae* which make up much of the floating *plankton* which other sea animals eat. As each larva grows, it sheds its shell and grows a new one which is bigger. This is called *moulting*. When the larva becomes an adult, it continues to grow and moult.

The best-known crustaceans are the large shellfish such as lobsters, shrimps, crabs and crayfish. They all have ten jointed legs, including the pair with pincers. They are known as decapods (ten legs). Shrimps and prawns are swimming crustaceans. Crabs and lobsters use their legs for walking and have large pincers. Except for crayfish, they all live in the sea. Many of them are very good to eat.

Barnacles live on rocks, on pieces of wood and often on the bottom of boats. They open their shells and put out long, feathery hairs which trap food floating in the water. They do this as the tide comes in. When the tide goes out the barnacles bring the feathery hairs in with the trapped food.

The heaviest crustacean is the North Atlantic lobster. Specimens weighing more than 20 kg and over a metre long have been caught. This lobster is also the longest-lived crustacean. Some may be 50 years old.

Crystal

If you look closely at sugar through a magnifying glass, you will see that it is made up of thousands of tiny glassy pieces with flat sides. They are sugar crystals. Snow is made up of tiny crystals of frozen water. So are the beautiful patterns on a frosty window. Some crystals are so small they can be seen only through a microscope. Others can grow to be as big as a person.

All crystals have a definite shape. They have smooth, flat sides that meet in sharp edges. The shape of any one type of crystal never changes, but there are many different crystal shapes. The differences between them are caused by the ATOMS in the crystals arranging themselves in different ways.

For example, the salt you eat is made up of two different kinds of atoms—sodium atoms and chlorine atoms. The tiny sodium and chlorine atoms are arranged in cube patterns. If you look at salt grains through a magnifying glass, you will see that most of them are little CUBES. All salt crystals are built in the same way.

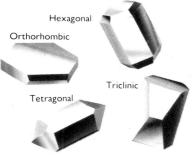

▼ Crystals can be many different shapes. Some are combinations of two or more patterns, making complicated designs.

Hexagonal

Orthorhombic

Triclinic

Tetragonal

SEE IT YOURSELF
You can grow crystals yourself, using minerals such as salt or washing soda. Pour hot water into a bowl and add the mineral little by little, stirring all the time. Eventually no more mineral will dissolve. Now let the solution cool. Hang a thread in the solution and crystals will form on the end.

CUBA

Government: Communist state
Capital: Havana
Area: 114,524 sq km
Population: 10,609,000
Language: Spanish
Currency: Peso

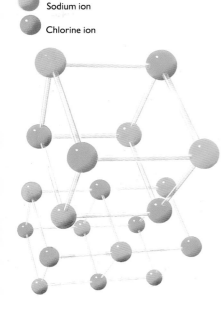

Sodium ion

Chlorine ion

▲ *The atoms in a crystal of salt are all arranged in cube patterns. Thousands and thousands of these tiny cubes join together to make one grain of salt, which is also a cube.*

Cuba

Cuba is an island country in the Caribbean Sea. It is part of the WEST INDIES. Cuba has 10,600,000 people and covers an area of 114,524 sq km. The capital city is Havana.

Part of the island is hilly, with high mountains in the south-east. In the centre are large cedar and mahogany forests. Cuba has big sugar cane plantations and tobacco farms.

The climate is warm and pleasant, but Cuba lies in the path of HURRICANES which come blowing through the West Indies every year. Hurricanes are very strong winds which travel fast and often damage buildings and farms.

Cuba was ruled by Spain after Christopher COLUMBUS went there in 1492. The United States took Cuba from Spain in 1898. In 1902 the island became independent. Cuba became a communist country in 1959 under its leader Fidel Castro.

Cube

A cube is an object with six square sides. All the edges are the same length. Sugar and ice are often made in cubes.

The space a cube fills is called its volume. You can find the volume of a cube by multiplying the length of a side by itself and then by itself again. If the length of a side is 3 cm, the volume of the cube is $3 \times 3 \times 3 = 27$ cubic cm.

Many kinds of CRYSTAL have a cube shape. This is because of the way their ATOMS are arranged.

Cuckoo

Cuckoos are a family of birds. There are many kinds of cuckoo. They are found in a lot of countries, but most live in the warm parts of the world. Cuckoos that live in cool countries fly to warm places for the winter.

The European cuckoo is a large bird about 30 cm long. It is blue-grey in colour with stripes underneath. It eats mainly insects. The call of the European cuckoo sounds just like its name. The birds can be heard calling in spring when they return from Africa.

◄ *Young cuckoos grow quite large before they leave the nest. This young cuckoo is already much bigger than its foster parent, a willow warbler.*

European cuckoos do not build nests. They lay their eggs in the nests of other birds such as warblers and sparrows. The female cuckoo watches while the other birds build their nests and lay their eggs. When they leave the nest to find food the cuckoo pulls one of the eggs out of the nest with her beak. Then she lays her own egg in its place and flies away. When the other birds return they do not notice the strange egg.

After about two weeks the young cuckoo hatches. It pushes the other eggs or baby birds out of the nest. The foster parents feed and take care of the cuckoo until it is ready to fly away. Young cuckoos are greedy and usually grow much bigger than their foster parents.

Curie, Marie and Pierre

Marie Curie (1867–1934) and Pierre Curie (1859–1906) were scientists who worked together. She was Polish, he was French. They studied RADIOACTIVITY and discovered the elements radium and polonium. They married each other in 1895.

For their work on radioactivity and their discovery of radium in 1898, they were given the NOBEL PRIZE for physics in 1903. When Pierre was killed three years later, Marie took over his job as professor at the Sorbonne University in Paris. In 1911 she was given a second Nobel Prize, this time for chemistry.

▲ *Pierre and Marie Curie devoted their lives to their research, spending their money on equipment and often living in conditions of hardship.*

CZECHOSLOVAKIA

Government: Multi-party system
Capital: Prague
Area: 127,869 sq km
Population: 15,662,000
Languages: Czech and Slovak
Currency: Koruna

Cyclone *See* Hurricane

Czechoslovakia

Czechoslovakia is a country in eastern EUROPE. It is surrounded by Germany, Poland, the former USSR, Hungary and Austria. The country covers an area of 127,869 sq km. The highest point is Gerlachovsky peak, which is 2655 metres tall.

Much of Czechoslovakia is covered in hills and mountains, and there are some big forests. Many of the people are farmers. Czechoslovakia also has coal and iron and an important steel industry.

Czechoslovakia was formed in 1918 when the Czech and the Slovak people came together to found an independent nation. The Czechs live in the west, and the Slovaks live in the east of the country.

The capital of Czechoslovakia is Prague. It is a medieval city with many fine churches and old buildings. Most of the people speak either Czech or Slovak. In 1989 the people obtained more freedom from the Communist government. Now, the Czechs are governed by a multi-party democracy.

▼ *Prague, the capital of Czechoslovakia, is steeped in history and has many beautiful old buildings.*

Dam

A dam is a barrier built across a river or stream to control its flow. There are many reasons for building dams. The most common is to make a *reservoir*. A reservoir is a man-made lake in which water is stored and sent across the country in pipes so that people can use it for drinking, washing and cooking.

Another reason for building dams is to store water for irrigating fields in the dry season. People have been doing this in hot countries for hundreds of years.

Whenever water is at a height from which it can fall it can be made to do work. Dams are built to harness this power. In the past, small dams were built to force streams of water into narrow channels. The rushing stream turned water wheels that drove machinery. Today, huge dams build up an enormous pressure of water that falls through big pipes. The rushing water hits the blades of turbines, making them spin and turn generators. From the generators comes ELECTRICITY.

Dance

Dance is one of the most ancient human arts. Thousands of years ago people acted out stories in dance. Dance became part of religion; people danced to bring rain to make crops grow and to guarantee good hunting. Warriors danced war dances to make themselves feel brave before a battle.

People all over the world dance. Dancing is usually done to a rhythmic beat, and some music is written especially for dancing. Every country has its own folk dances, with traditional steps. Morris dancing is a form of English folk dance.

Ballet developed in the 1600s from court dancing in Europe. Ballroom dancing became popular in the 1800s, with popular dances such as the waltz and, later, the tango which was borrowed from a South American folk dance. Today, in the theatre, on film and television, and in the disco dance is enjoyed in different styles.

Dancing is excellent exercise. Everyone can enjoy dance; through moving your body in time to music you can express your feelings, and have fun. What's more, in today's disco, you can dance either with a partner, in a group, or on your own.

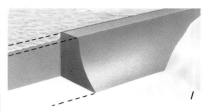

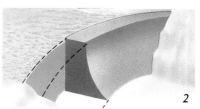

▲ A gravity dam (1) made of stone or concrete blocks that take the whole weight of the water. An arch dam (2) is curved so that the weight of water pushes against the sides of the canyon instead of against the dam wall. An embankment dam (3) is just a heap of rocks and earth, with an outside layer of concrete.

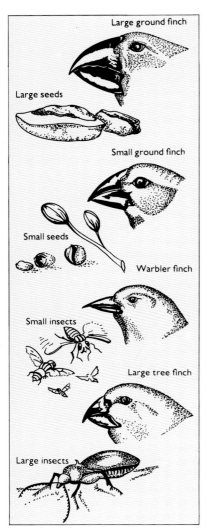

Large ground finch

Large seeds

Small ground finch

Small seeds

Warbler finch

Small insects

Large tree finch

Large insects

▲ *Darwin discovered a variety of finches on the Galapagos Islands, each species of which had evolved different beaks suited for eating different foods. All had originally come from a South American finch that had reached the islands long before.*

Darwin, Charles

Charles Darwin (1809–1882) was an English biologist. In 1859 he published his great book *On the Origin of Species*. Before this, almost everyone believed that the world was created by God exactly as the Bible described. Darwin put forward the theory that all living things *evolved* from earlier forms. They were alive because they had won the struggle to survive.

Within any species of living thing there would be small variations in shape, size or habit. Some of these variations would increase the living thing's chance of survival. For example, a giraffe with a long neck could reach leaves a giraffe with a shorter neck could not. In times of famine, the taller giraffe would survive while the shorter one would die. The taller giraffe that survived would, in time, replace the variety with the shorter neck.

This theory outraged many people. They thought it was against the teachings of the Bible. But today most people accept Darwin's theory, and many churches have decided that it does not conflict with their teachings or threaten religious beliefs.

Day and Night

The Earth turns on its own axis as it moves around the Sun. So the part of the Earth facing the Sun is light while the part facing away from the Sun is dark. The lighted part is 'day' and the dark part 'night'. Because the Earth turns around, day and night follow each other continually.

Scientists have another way of describing a 'day'. They say it is the time the Earth takes to complete one full turn on its axis. If you measure how long it takes from one sunrise or one sunset to the next you will find that it takes almost exactly 24 hours.

The length of time that any particular part of the Earth is in daylight varies depending on where it is on the globe. This is because the axis of the Earth is tilted at an angle to its path around the Sun. This also means that some parts of the Earth have different amounts of day and night at certain times of the year. For instance, in June in the Arctic it is always daylight. In the Antarctic, it is always night. In December it is the other way round—dark all the

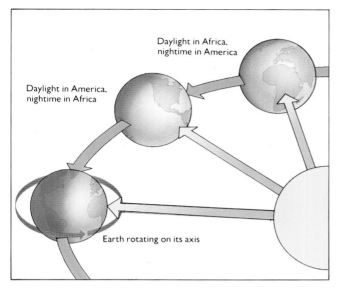

◀ Day and night happen because the Earth spins like a top as it circles the Sun. Only one half of the Earth faces the Sun at any one time.

▼ Deer antlers develop each year from tender stumps covered in a layer of soft, hair-covered skin to fully grown branches. The four stages cover the period from spring to autumn.

time in the Arctic and light all the time in the Antarctic.

Because the Earth turns all the time it is always day in one place when it is night somewhere else. The world is divided into 'time zones'. There is no single time, such as 'noon', for the whole world. When it is noon in London it is midnight in New Zealand.

To make a clear difference between one day and the next, an imaginary line was drawn from the North to the South Pole. On one side it is one day, and on the other side, the day following. This line, known as the 'dateline', runs through the Pacific Ocean. It has a strange effect: if you cross the dateline going eastwards you gain a day, while those travelling westwards miss a day.

Deer

Deer are animals related to cattle and antelopes. They are different from their relatives because they have antlers rather than permanent horns. Male deer grow new antlers every year. Female deer, except for reindeer, do not grow antlers.

Every year in early spring, a lot of blood starts to flow into two bony lumps on the male deer's forehead. The blood carries a bony substance that makes the antlers grow quite rapidly. At first they are covered with a soft, hairy skin known as velvet.

DEER

Deer have a common origin with giraffes. They became separated from the giraffes about 20 million years ago. Fossil bones show that prehistoric people often dined on deer meat. Deer hides were used for clothing, and antlers were made into weapons and tools.

In early summer the antlers are fully grown. The blood supply is then cut off and the velvet dies. The male deer rubs off the velvet until his antlers are hard and shiny. Some antlers can be very big indeed. One red deer's antlers weighed as much as 35 kg. A moose's antlers have measured 2 metres across.

Deer are mainly found in the Northern Hemisphere. But there are some species in South America and Asia.

In autumn, male deer become very aggressive. They fight each other for the right to mate with groups of females which they guard very jealously.

Deer vary enormously in size. The biggest is the Alaskan moose which stands up to 2·3 metres at the shoulder and weighs over 800 kg. The smallest is the Pudu of Chile which can measure as little as 33 cm at the shoulder and weigh as little as 8 kg.

Reindeer can be tamed to pull sledges, and their meat and hides are valued by the Lapp people of Scandinavia. Red deer can be kept on farms, for their meat (called venison). Deer are naturally wild animals but some of them, such as reindeer, have been successfully domesticated.

▼ The moose is the largest of all deer. The reindeer is well adapted to life in northern latitudes, while the fallow deer is often found in parks. The red deer is the most important British species. The little muntjac is about 45 cm high and barks like a dog.

Red Deer

Moose

Fallow Deer

Muntjac

Reindeer

Democracy

Democracy is a type of government, organized by the people, for the people. In a democracy people elect their own government. Representatives of different political parties stand for election and people vote for the one they prefer. The people can also dismiss their government if they want to. In a democracy people can say and read what they like – they have a right to 'freedom of speech'. They cannot be put into prison without a proper trial.

The great American president Abraham Lincoln described democracy as 'government *of* the people, *by* the people and *for* the people'. He meant that in a democracy everyone takes part in making the laws that everyone has to obey.

◄ *The Statue of Liberty stands at the entrance to New York Harbor as a symbol of freedom under American democracy.*

There are many different kinds of democracy. The British form is a monarchy with an elected PARLIAMENT. The American form is a republic with an elected president and an elected congress.

Denmark

Denmark is a small Scandinavian country in the north of EUROPE. It consists mainly of a peninsula called Jutland surrounded by 600 islands. In the west is the North Sea, to the east is the Baltic Sea, and to the south is Germany. The capital is Copenhagen. Denmark is a flat country whose soil and climate are ideal for agriculture. Dairy and pig farming are especially important. Denmark is a member of the EUROPEAN COMMUNITY. It exports a great deal of butter and bacon to Britain. The Danes also make and export lager beer. There is little heavy industry. The Danes prefer to concentrate on high-quality goods like china and furniture.

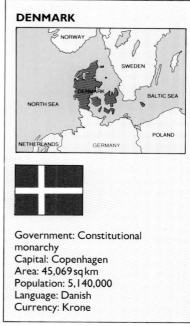

DENMARK

Government: Constitutional monarchy
Capital: Copenhagen
Area: 45,069 sq km
Population: 5,140,000
Language: Danish
Currency: Krone

▼ *Many animals keep cool in the desert by hiding away during the daytime, coming out after the Sun sets. To conserve water, desert animals sweat very little.*

Desert

Not all deserts are hot and sandy. Some are cold, and some are rocky. But all are very dry. Some scientists say that a desert is any area where less than 8 cm of rain falls in a year. Other scientists call a place a desert when there is more rain than this but where it evaporates quickly in the sun or sinks rapidly into the ground.

Many big deserts are in the tropics, often inland on large continents where rainbearing winds cannot reach them.

◄ The peregrine falcon preys on small desert animals. It is one of the fastest flying birds.

There are three main types of desert. The first is rocky, where any soil is blown away by the wind. The second has large areas of gravel. The third is made up of great sand dunes, burning hot by day and bitterly cold at night.

It is difficult for plants and animals to live in such conditions. Some plants, like the CACTUS, store moisture in their fleshy stems. Others have seeds that lie apparently lifeless in the ground for long periods.

▼ There are two types of camel, the Bactrian (two-humped) of the Gobi desert and the Arabian (one-humped).

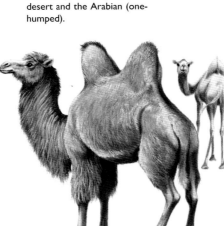

▲ Dingoes are wild dogs, descended from dogs brought to Australia by the first people to arrive there.

▲ The Gila monster is a poisonous lizard. Its poison travels along grooves in its teeth while it is biting its victim.

► The frilled lizard opens its jaws with a hiss and unfolds its frill to frighten intruders.

▼ The sand grouse soaks its feathers in a waterhole and takes the water to its thirsty young.

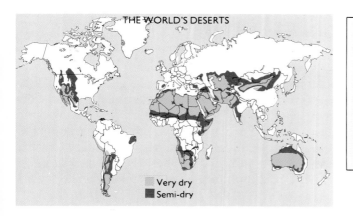

THE WORLD'S DESERTS

Very dry
Semi-dry

LARGEST DESERTS	
Sahara	9,065,000 sq km
Gt. Australian	3,885,000 sq km
Libyan	1,295,000 sq km
Gobi	777,000 sq km
Rub' al Khali	647,500 sq km
Kalahari	310,000 sq km
Kara Kum	284,900 sq km
Atacama	64,750 sq km
Mohave	38,850 sq km

When a shower of rain falls they burst into life and can flower and produce new seeds within weeks. Many desert animals shelter from the sun by day and come out only at night. Some never drink, but get all the moisture they need from their food.

The world's largest desert is the SAHARA in Africa. The driest desert is the Atacama in South America, where it may not rain for several years. There are also cold deserts. These include Antarctica and a large part of the Arctic.

Detergent

The word *detergent* means any substance that will clean things. *Soap* is a detergent. But today the word detergent usually means synthetic, or man-made, detergents such as most washing powders. Detergents are similar to soaps, but soaps leave behind filmy deposits, such as the familiar bath-tub ring. Detergents can reach soiled areas better than soaps and do not leave deposits.

Diamond

Diamonds are CRYSTALS. They are harder than anything else in the world. They are formed by great heat and pressure deep beneath the surface of the earth. Diamonds are made of pure CARBON, the same mineral that is found in ordinary coal. They are usually colourless and have to be cut in a special way to catch the light and 'sparkle'. A diamond cutter is very skilled and uses tools tipped with diamonds, for only another diamond is hard enough to cut a diamond.

The Cullinan diamond, named after its finder, Thomas Cullinan, was the largest ever found. It was discovered in 1905 at Pretoria in South Africa. The great uncut stone was about 13 cm across and weighed nearly three-quarters of a kilogram. In 1908, the diamond was cut by expert diamond cutters in Amsterdam and finished up as 105 separate stones. One big diamond cut from the Cullinan is called the Star of Africa. It is in the royal sceptre. Another is in the State Crown, and others are in jewellery worn by the Queen.

The world's most famous coloured diamond is the large Hope diamond. It is deep blue and came originally from India. The Hope is now in the gem collection of the Smithsonian Institution in Washington, D.C. Although diamonds are usually colourless, they are found in a variety of colours in shades of blue, yellow, pink and champagne.

▲ Dickens, the famous novelist.

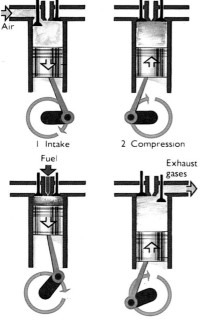

1 Intake	2 Compression

Fuel

Exhaust gases

3 Injection and power	4 Exhaust

▲ How a diesel engine works. As the piston goes down (1), air is drawn into the cylinder. When the piston goes up, the air is squeezed and becomes very hot (2). When the piston gets to the top, oil is squirted in and bursts into flame. The hot gases expand and push the piston down (3). When the piston goes up again it pushes the spent gases out through the exhaust valve (4).

Dickens, Charles

Charles Dickens (1812–1870) was a great English writer. His books give us a vivid picture of life in Victorian England in the middle 1800s. Several of his stories are about children, especially poor children and orphans. Dickens tried to improve the lives of the poor by making their suffering more widely known through his books. He also created some of the liveliest and best-known characters in English literature. Some of his most famous books are *Oliver Twist*, *David Copperfield*, *Great Expectations* and *A Christmas Carol*.

Dictionary

A dictionary is a book that tells us what words mean. The words are arranged in alphabetical order from A to Z. Often the meanings, or definitions, include the history of the words and how they are used and pronounced. Dictionaries may vary in size from many volumes to dictionaries small enough to slip into your pocket. Dr Samuel Johnson (1709–84) made one of the first large dictionaries of English words. This was published in 1755.

Diesel Engine

Diesel engines are a type of INTERNAL-COMBUSTION ENGINE in which fuel is burned inside the engine. Diesel engines are named after their inventor, Rudolf Diesel, who built his first successful engine in 1897 to replace the steam engine. Diesel engines use a cruder, heavier fuel oil than petrol. They are cheaper to run than petrol engines, but they are heavier and more difficult to start, so until recently they were not widely used in cars. They are used to drive heavy machines such as trains, tractors, ships, buses and trucks. A properly-working diesel causes less pollution than a petrol engine.

A diesel engine is similar to a petrol engine. But instead of using a spark from a sparkplug to ignite the fuel, the diesel engine uses heat that is made by a piston squeezing air inside a cylinder. When air is very tightly compressed, or pushed into a much smaller space than it filled before, it gets very hot. This heat sets fire to the diesel oil, which burns instantly, like a small explosion. The burning oil heats the air and forces it to extend again to push the piston downwards and thus drive the engine.

Many RAILWAYS began using diesel engines after World War II. Railways badly damaged in the war took the opportunity to modernize their engines and replaced the old steam locomotives with diesel engines. Diesel engines were first used regularly on the railroads of the United States in the 1930s. Today, diesel-electric engines are in use all over the world. In these engines the diesel motor is used to make electricity. The electricity then drives the train.

Digestion

Digestion is the way in which the food we eat is broken down into substances that can be used by the body. It takes place in the digestive tract, or *alimentary canal*, a long tube that runs from the mouth to the anus. Digestion starts in the mouth, where the teeth and special chemicals in the saliva help to break down the food. The food then passes down a tube called the *oesophagus*. Muscles in the oesophagus push and squeeze the food down into the STOMACH. There, acids and more chemicals help to turn the food into a creamy liquid. Then a muscle at the lower end of the stomach opens from time to time to release food into the small intestine.

Inside the small intestine, bile from the LIVER and juice from the pancreas help to break down the food

▲ *London taxis are driven by diesel engines, which are cheaper to fuel and cause less pollution.*

◄ *The human digestive tract. The alimentary canal in an adult is eight to ten metres long.*

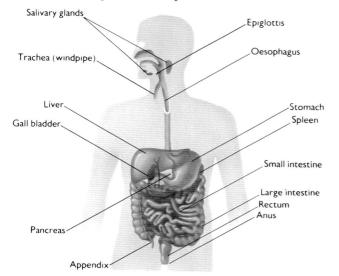

Salivary glands

Epiglottis

Oesophagus

Trachea (windpipe)

Liver

Stomach

Gall bladder

Spleen

Small intestine

Large intestine

Rectum

Anus

Pancreas

Appendix

During the age of the dinosaurs, 200 million years ago, the continents were all joined together in one great land mass. This is why dinosaurs have been found in every continent except Antarctica. About 300 different species of dinosaurs have been found, but some of these are known only from a single tooth or a small bone fragment.

still further. Much of it passes through the thin walls of the intestine into the bloodstream. The remainder goes into the large intestine. There, liquids and salts are absorbed until only solid waste material is left. Bacteria in the large intestine digest any remaining food products. The final waste product is passed out of the body as *faeces*.

Dinosaur

The word *dinosaur* means 'enormous lizard'. These creatures lived between 65 and 225 million years ago, long before there were any people on earth. They developed from primitive REPTILES.

There were two main groups of dinosaurs – the *saurischians* and the *ornithischians*. The ornithischian dinosaurs were all plant-eaters and most of them went around on all fours. Some of these, like *Stegosaurus* and *Triceratops*, were large and lumbering but had bony armour to protect them from the teeth and claws of the great meat-eating dinosaurs. *Triceratops*, for instance, had three horns.

▼ *Many of the dinosaurs of the late Cretaceous Period could survive an attack from great meat-eaters such as* Tyrannosaurus. *The ostrich dinosaurs such as* Struthiomimus *could run very fast, while the ceratopsian* Triceratops *and the ankylosaur* Ankylosaurus *had strong armour.*

Ankylosaurus

Struthiomimus

The saurischian group contained both plant-eaters and meat-eaters. The plant-eaters included the largest dinosaurs, the biggest of which scientists are calling '*Ultrasaurus*'. The remains of this creature are incomplete, but they include a huge arm and shoulder girdle which show that it was about 8 metres high at the shoulder – four times the height of a tall man! It probably weighed as much as 130 tonnes, even heavier than the blue whale. But these great beasts were harmless plant-eaters.

Perhaps the most famous of the dinosaurs are the great carnivores, or meat-eaters. *Tyrannosaurus*, which was up to 14 metres from snout to tail, stood on its hind legs. Its toes had claws as long as carving knives. Sabre-like teeth – some nearly the length of a man's hand – lined the jaws. No flesh-eating beasts that ever lived on land were larger or more menacing than these monsters.

No one knows why all the dinosaurs, great and small, died out about 65 million years ago.

> The largest flying creature that we know about was a pterosaur that glided over parts of North America about 70 million years ago. Scientists calculate from its fossil remains that it had a wingspan of about 11 metres – more than half the length of a cricket pitch!

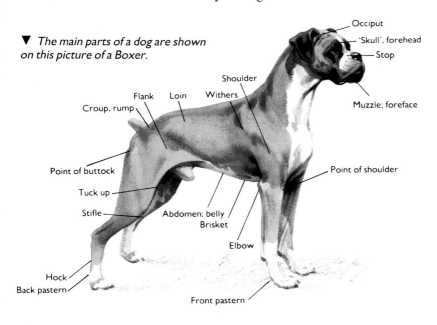

▼ *The main parts of a dog are shown on this picture of a Boxer.*

Occiput
'Skull', forehead
Stop
Shoulder
Flank
Loin
Withers
Croup, rump
Muzzle; foreface
Point of buttock
Point of shoulder
Tuck up
Stifle
Abdomen; belly
Brisket
Elbow
Hock
Back pastern
Front pastern

Dog

People have been keeping dogs for perhaps 10,000 years. Most dogs are kept as pets but some do useful work like herding sheep or guarding buildings.

The first dog was probably descended from a WOLF and looked much like a wolf. Today there are

Dogs see a world that is blurred and has no colour. They are shortsighted and see only shades of grey. But a dog's sense of smell is thousands of times better than ours. Customs officers use specially trained dogs for sniffing out illegal drugs. It is not necessary to open cases or crates – one sniff is enough for a dog, even if the drugs are packed in tins.

more than 100 breeds of dog of many colours, shapes, and sizes. The St Bernard is the largest breed. A St Bernard may weigh nearly twice as much as a man. The Yorkshire terrier is one of the smallest dogs. A fully grown Yorkshire terrier may weigh less than a small pot of jam.

Most of the modern breeds of dog were developed to be good at special kinds of work. Airedales and other terriers make fine rat hunters. Labrador retrievers bring back ducks shot by hunters and also make excellent guide dogs. Collies round up sheep. Dachshunds were once used for hunting badgers. Dobermanns are ferocious guard dogs, first bred in the 19th century.

All puppies are born blind and helpless, and at first only feed on their mother's milk. But small dogs are fully grown in a year or so. Most kinds of dog live for about 12 years.

Dolphin and Porpoise

Dolphins are small whales. Although they never leave the sea, they are mammals. They breathe air and are warm-blooded. They have sharp teeth and their heads end in beaklike mouths. Porpoises, close relatives of the dolphins, have no beak and the front of the head is rounded. Because the dolphin is a friendly creature, it has been well-known since ancient times. Dolphins are intelligent and communicate with each other by means of whistles and clicks. Tame dolphins can learn many tricks.

▼ *Dolphins and porpoises are small whales. The bottle-nosed dolphin has a shorter, more up-turned beak than the common dolphin.*

Bottle-nosed dolphin

Common porpoise

Common dolphin

Drake, Francis

Sir Francis Drake (about 1540–1596) was a sea captain who helped to make England a great sea power. In the 1570s he led sea raids against Spanish ships and ports in the Caribbean Sea. He also became ' the first Englishman to sail around the world. In 1588 he helped to destroy the Spanish ARMADA.

When we read about Drake's exploits, it is hard to imagine how small his ships were. When he set out to pillage Spanish possessions in the West Indies, his two ships weighed just 71 tonnes and 25 tonnes.

▲ Sir Francis Drake got his first command as captain of a ship at the age of 24.

Dream

Dreams occur when our brains are active while we are asleep. Some dreams are of everyday occurrences. Others may be just a series of jumbled images. On waking, we may or may not remember what we have dreamed.

We do not know exactly why people dream. Dreams may be sparked off by indigestion or a similar physical cause, such as a cramped sleeping position. External noises may also cause dreams. Some dreams are very common. These include dreams of falling, or being chased, of lakes, or water.

Drug

Drugs are chemicals that affect the way the body works. Doctors give drugs to patients to help them fight disease. Antibiotics attack certain kinds of germs. These drugs help to cure people suffering from pneumonia and other illnesses. Drugs like aspirin help to deaden pain. The strongest pain-killers are called anaesthetics. Some people need drugs containing VITAMINS or other substances their bodies must have.

Certain drugs come from plants or animals. For instance, the foxglove gives us a drug called digitalis. This makes weak hearts beat more strongly. Many other drugs are made from MINERALS.

Some people take drugs such as cocaine, cannabis or alcohol just because these give a pleasant feeling. Some of these drugs can be addictive (habit-forming), cause illness and even death.

▲ Foxgloves are still cultivated for the drug digitalis that is used in the treatment of heart disease.

Duck

These web-footed water birds are related to swans and geese. Ducks look rather like small geese with short necks.

The two main groups of ducks are dabbling ducks and diving ducks. Dabbling ducks feed at the surface of the water. They may put most of their body under the water, but they do not dive. Dabbling ducks include the mallards that swim on pools and rivers in the northern half of the world. (Farmyard ducks were bred from mallards.) Other dabbling ducks include teal and widgeon, and the pretty mandarin and Carolina ducks.

Diving ducks dive completely underwater in their hunt for food. Most diving ducks live out at sea. These ducks include the eider duck from which we get eiderdown. Sawbills are also diving ducks. Their long beaks have inside edges like the teeth of a saw.

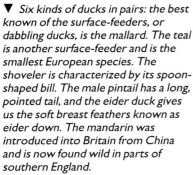

▼ Six kinds of ducks in pairs: the best known of the surface-feeders, or dabbling ducks, is the mallard. The teal is another surface-feeder and is the smallest European species. The shoveler is characterized by its spoon-shaped bill. The male pintail has a long, pointed tail, and the eider duck gives us the soft breast feathers known as eider down. The mandarin was introduced into Britain from China and is now found wild in parts of southern England.

114

Eagle

Eagles are large birds of prey. Most hunt small mammals and birds. Some catch fish or reptiles. The harpy eagle and the monkey-eating eagle catch monkeys. Each of these great birds measures more than 2 metres across its outspread wings. These eagles are the largest in the world.

Many eagles soar high above the ground. Others perch on a tree or rock. When an eagle sees its prey it swoops suddenly and pounces. It seizes its prey with its sharp claws and tears off pieces of flesh with its strong, hooked beak.

Ear

Our ears help us to hear and to keep our balance. Each ear has three main parts. These are the outer ear, middle ear and inner ear.

The outer ear is the part we can see, and the tube leading from it into the head. Sounds reach the outer ear as vibrations, or waves, in the air. The cup-like shape of the ear collects these sound waves and sends them into the tube.

Next, the sound waves reach the middle ear. Here, the waves make the *eardrum* move to and fro. This is a thin 'skin' across the entrance of the middle ear. The moving eardrum sets tiny bones vibrating in the middle ear.

The vibrations travel on into the inner ear. Here they set liquid moving in the *cochlea*. This looks like

If you spin round quickly and stop suddenly, the liquid in the hollow loops in your inner ear keeps on spinning for a while. The nerve cells in your ear send confusing messages to your brain, and you feel dizzy. The dizziness ends when the liquid in the loops stops moving.

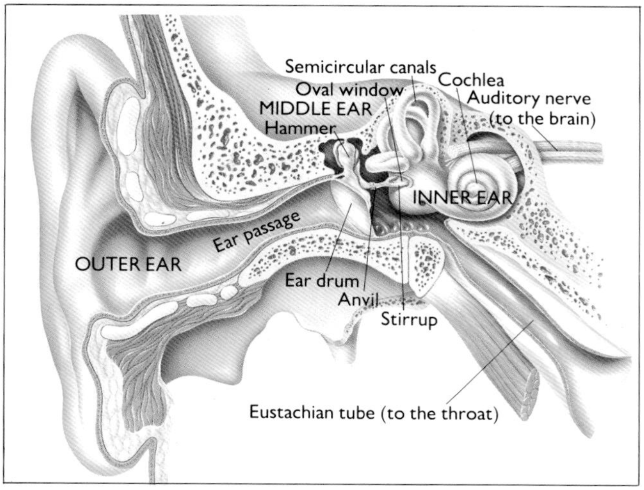

Semicircular canals Cochlea
Oval window
MIDDLE EAR
Hammer
Auditory nerve (to the brain)

INNER EAR

Ear passage

OUTER EAR

Ear drum
Anvil
Stirrup

Eustachian tube (to the throat)

◀ This picture shows the main parts of the outer, middle and inner ear. The eustachian tube helps to keep air pressure the same on both sides of the eardrum.

a snail's shell. The nerves inside it turn vibrations into messages that travel to your brain. The inner ear also has three hollow loops containing liquid. These loops send signals to the brain to help you keep your balance.

Ears are easily damaged. Hitting or poking into an ear can cause injury and may lead to deafness.

The Earth

Our Earth is the fifth largest of the PLANETS that move around the SUN. Seen from Space the Earth looks like a giant ball. Land and WATER cover the surface, and AIR surrounds the Earth.

So far as we know, the Earth is the only planet that supports life. Our world is a medium-sized planet, orbiting a star (the Sun) along with eight other planets. What makes our Earth unique are its atmosphere and its water. Together these make possible a rich variety of animal and plant life. Seen from space, Earth appears to be mostly covered by ocean, wreathed in swirling clouds. Land covers only about one quarter of the planet's surface. Beneath the surface is an intensely hot, dense core.

If the Earth was the size of a football, the highest land masses such as the Himalayas would be no higher than a coat of paint on a ball. The deepest ocean trenches would be almost invisible scratches in the paint's surface.

Although the Earth is between 4 and 5 billion years old, no rocks as old as this have ever been found. It is thought that the Earth's original rocks have all been worn away. Rocks found in the USA have been dated at about 3.8 billion years old.

◄ *The Earth photographed from space. Cloud 'swirls' are depressions – areas of low atmospheric pressure where warm tropical air meets cold polar air. Such views help weather experts to plot the paths of hurricanes and so give warning of dangerous storms. Astronauts see the Earth outlined by a black sky.*

HOW MOUNTAINS ARE FORMED

Fold mountains (below right) are thrown up when huge forces buckle rock layers into giant wrinkles. The Rocky Mountains and the Andes were formed in this way when the Earth's crustal plates collided. Some rocks were folded over onto others, and over millions of years a new mountain range was born. Other kinds of mountains are formed when faults (breaks) in the Earth's crust take place.

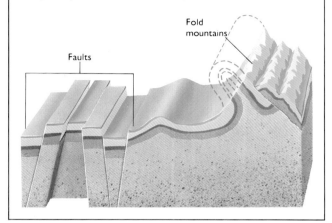

Faults

Fold mountains

FAMOUS EARTHQUAKES

Shensi Province, China, 1556: Over 800,000 people perished – more than in any other earthquake.
San Francisco, USA, 1906: An earthquake and the fires it caused destroyed the city.
Kwanto Plain, Japan, 1923: Some 570,000 buildings collapsed. This was the costliest earthquake ever as measured by damage to property.
Lebu, Chile, 1977: The strongest earthquake shock ever recorded.
Armenia, USSR, 1988: About 25,000 people died and several towns and villages were buried.

Earthquake

People often use the saying 'safe as houses'. But in certain lands houses sometimes topple over because the ground starts trembling. This trembling is called an earthquake. About half a million earthquakes happen every year. Most are so weak that only special instruments called *seismographs* show that they have happened. Only one earthquake in 500 does any damage. But some earthquakes can cause terrible damage and suffering. Three-quarters of a million people are thought to have died when an earthquake hit the Chinese city of Tangshan in 1976.

Small tremors can happen when VOLCANOES erupt, when there is a landslide, or when the roof of an underground cave falls in. The largest earthquakes occur when one huge piece of the Earth's crust slips suddenly against another piece. This slipping may take place deep underground. But the shock travels up through the crust and sets the surface quaking.

A seabed earthquake may set off a huge ocean wave called a *tsunami*. These can rise higher than a house and travel faster than the fastest train.

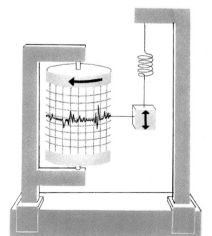

▲ *A seismograph shows earth tremors as wiggles in a line traced on a turning drum. A tremor vibrates the weight that holds the tracer.*

▲ *When you hear an echo, you hear the sound twice or more. This is because the sound waves that reach your ears also bounce off nearby cliffs or walls. These waves reach your ears a second or two later, and you hear an echo.*

Echo

An echo is a SOUND bounced back from a wall or some other object. Sound travels at a known, fixed speed, so we can use echoes to find how far off some objects are. A ship's sonar uses echoes to find the depth of the sea. Echoes help BATS to fly in the dark. RADAR depends on echoes from radio signals.

Eclipse

An eclipse happens when the shadow of one planet or moon falls on another. If the shadow hides all of the planet or moon there is a total eclipse. If the shadow hides only a part there is a partial eclipse.

The only eclipses you can easily see without a telescope take place when the Sun, Moon and Earth are in line. When the Earth lies between the Sun and the Moon, the Earth's shadow falls on the

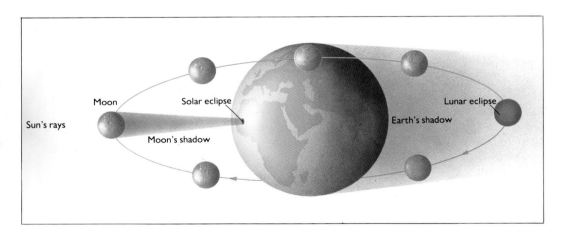

Sun's rays | Moon | Solar eclipse | Moon's shadow | Earth's shadow | Lunar eclipse

▲ *A solar eclipse is caused as the Moon's shadow falls on the Earth, and a lunar eclipse as the Earth's shadow falls on the Moon. Only the* umbra – *the dark middle part of the Moon's shadow – is shown for the solar eclipse.*

Moon. This is an eclipse of the Moon. When the Moon lies between the Earth and the Sun, the Moon's shadow falls on a part of the Earth. An eclipse of the Sun, or solar eclipse, can be seen from that part. Two or three of each kind of eclipse happen every year.

The centre of the shadow of a solar eclipse is called the *umbra*. It is a dark circle only about 270 km across. Inside the umbra, the eclipse is complete – the Moon completely hides the Sun. Around the umbra is a lighter shadow about 3000 km across, in which part of the Sun can be seen.

Ecology

Ecology is the study of living things and their surroundings. Scientists called ecologists try to find out how living things and their surroundings affect each other. Ecology shows us that most plants and animals can live only in a special set of surroundings such as a pond, field, forest or desert. Within each place live plants that are suited to a certain soil, temperature, and so on. All the animals living there eat the plants or one another. So the plants and animals are linked in what ecologists call a food web. If some kinds die out, those that eat them lose their food and may die too.

Everything in the world changes. Human inventions and discoveries are causing rapid changes. Sometimes the air is being filled with poisons; waterways are being polluted. Ecologists can help us to use the inventions and discoveries without making the world sick.

The introduction of animals from foreign lands can have harmful effects on the balanced ecology of a place. In 1850, three pairs of European rabbits were turned loose in Australia. With no natural enemies, the rabbits multiplied so quickly that they became a plague to farmers. Only the introduction of a disease that was fatal to rabbits halted the plague.

Edison, Thomas

Thomas Alva Edison (1847–1931) was an American inventor. As a boy he spent only three months at school, and his teacher thought him stupid. But he went on to produce over 100 inventions. The most famous were the electric light and the phonograph for RECORDING and playing back sounds. The first recording ever made was of Edison himself.

Edward (Kings)

Nine kings of England were called Edward. Edward 'The Confessor' (about 1002–1066) founded Westminster Abbey. Edward I (1239–1307) brought Wales under English rule. Edward II (1248–1327) was the first English Prince of Wales. Edward III (1312–1337) began the Hundred Years' War. Edward IV (1442–1483) took the crown from Henry VI in the Wars of the Roses. Edward V (1470–1483) was murdered in the Tower of London. Edward VI (1537–1553) reigned as a boy king for only six years. Edward VII (1841–1910) was Prince of Wales for 60 years. Edward VIII (1894–1972) gave up the throne to marry Mrs Simpson, a divorced American.

▲ Two English kings called Edward: Edward the Confessor (top) ruled from 1042–1066, before the Norman conquest. Edward VII was the eldest son of Queen Victoria.

119

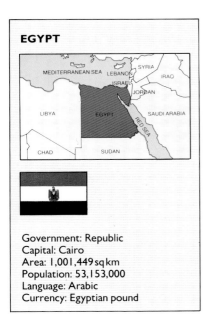

EGYPT

Government: Republic
Capital: Cairo
Area: 1,001,449 sq km
Population: 53,153,000
Language: Arabic
Currency: Egyptian pound

Egg

An egg is a female CELL that will grow into a new young plant or animal. Most eggs only grow if they are joined with, or fertilized by, male cells. In most MAMMALS the fertilized eggs grow inside the mother's body, but birds and most reptiles and fish lay eggs that contain enough food to help the developing young grow inside the egg.

Egypt

Modern Egypt dates from AD 642 when Egypt was conquered by Muslim soldiers from Arabia. Egypt is now a Muslim, mainly Arab, country. It has over 50 million people, more than any other nation in Africa. No other African city is as large as Cairo, Egypt's capital. But Egyptians still depend upon the waters of the river NILE that made Egypt great.

In 1979 Egypt signed a peace treaty with ISRAEL. This agreement was disliked by other Arab states, leaving Egypt isolated from its Arab neighbours.

Egypt, Ancient

About 5000 years ago the ancient Egyptians began to build one of the world's first great civilizations. For the next 2500 years, ancient Egypt was one of the strongest, richest nations on Earth.

The people who made Egypt great were short, slim, dark-skinned men and women with black hair. They probably numbered no more than six million. Scarcely any of them lived in the hot sand and rock deserts that cover most of Egypt. Almost all the people settled by the river NILE that runs from south to north across the land.

Each year the river overflowed and left rich mud on nearby fields. Farmers learnt to dig and plough the fields. They could grow two crops a year in the warm, fertile soil. The farmers grew more than enough grain, fruit and vegetables to feed themselves. The rest of the food helped to feed Egyptian craftsmen, miners, merchants, priests, noble families, and the PHARAOHS who ruled over the entire land.

Most Egyptians were poor and lived in mud-brick huts with palm-leaf roofs. Rich Egyptians lived in

Several times during the Twentieth Egyptian Dynasty the workmen building a tomb for the pharaoh were not paid their food and other goods on time. The men went on strike. They marched to the temple where supplies were kept, and sat down outside calling for bread. They soon got what they wanted because it was unthinkable that the pharaoh's tomb should not be finished on time.

large, well-furnished houses and had meat and cakes to eat. They wore fine clothes and jewels.

The most splendid buildings in the land were tombs and temples. Thousands of workers toiled for years to build the mighty PYRAMIDS. In each such tomb, Egyptians would place the mummy (preserved body) of a pharaoh. They believed the dead went on living, so they buried food and furniture beside each mummy. Thieves later emptied almost all the tombs. But the boy pharaoh Tutankhamun's tomb shows us what royal burials were like.

The dry Egyptian air has preserved hieroglyphics written on fragile paper made from the papyrus plant. Paintings and hieroglyphics tell us a great deal about how the ancient Egyptians lived. The ancient Egyptians also left many fine statues.

In time, foreign armies using iron weapons defeated the Egyptians. Their land fell under foreign rule after 525 BC.

▲ *Albert Einstein helped to develop the first atomic bomb, but he was also passionately concerned about the control of nuclear weapons after World War II.*

Einstein, Albert

Albert Einstein (1879–1955) was a great scientist who was born in Germany. His theory of relativity was a new way of looking at time, space, matter and ENERGY. Einstein showed that a small amount of matter could be changed into a vast amount of energy. This made it possible for people to use NUCLEAR ENERGY.

Elasticity

When you pull a rubber band it stretches. When you let it go, it springs back to its original size. It is elastic – it has elasticity. If you drop a rubber ball, the part of the ball that hits the ground is flattened. Then the ball springs back into its original round shape. As this happens, the ball pushes on the ground and springs up. The ball has elasticity.

Elasticity happens because the molecules that make up the elastic material like to stay at a certain distance from each other. If they are squeezed more tightly together they immediately push apart. If they are pulled apart, they want to get together again. All solids and liquids have some elasticity. Even a steel ball will bounce a little when it hits a concrete floor.

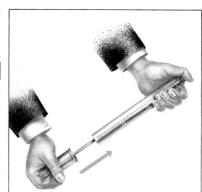

SEE IT YOURSELF
Air has elasticity too. It can be squeezed into a container and the energy stored in it can be used to drive machines such as pneumatic drills and hammers. You can feel the elasticity of air by putting your thumb over the end of a bicycle pump and pushing the pump handle.

In 1752, the American scientist and statesman Benjamin Franklin wondered whether lightning and thunder were caused by electricity. During a thunderstorm he flew a kite with a metal tip joined to a silk string. He attached a key to the string at a point near the ground. In a few seconds Franklin had the answer to his question. When he touched the key there was a spark. He could *feel* the electricity. But don't try this; it is very dangerous.

Election

Most countries and local areas hold elections from time to time. Elections give people the chance to elect, or choose, a new government or council. They do this by voting. In Britain each voter goes to a certain building on election, or polling, day. He or she is given a paper, or ballot, printed with the names of several candidates. The voter marks a cross against the name of the person he wants to represent him in PARLIAMENT or on the local council. Each area has its own candidates. Those who win the most votes are elected.

In some countries anyone may be a candidate. In others the government chooses candidates. Teams and clubs also hold elections to choose leaders.

Electricity

Electricity is the kind of ENERGY that powers electric trains, vacuum cleaners, radios, television sets and many more devices.

The electricity that we use flows through wires as electric current. Current flows when tiny particles called electrons jump between the ATOMS that make up the metal in the wire. Current can flow only if a

▼ *Portable radios and cassette players are just two devices that are electronic. Television sets, home computers, pocket calculators, digital watches, video recorders and many other things we use every day work electronically.*

wire makes a complete loop called a circuit. If a gap is made in the circuit, the current stops flowing. Switches are simply devices that open and close gaps in circuits.

BATTERIES produce electric current that can be used to start cars, light torch bulbs and work radios. But most of the electricity we use is produced in power stations. In a power station GENERATOR, coils of wire are made to rotate between powerful magnets. This makes electric current flow through the coils in wire. This current then flows through other long wires to our homes.

> The unit of electric current is the amp, short for ampere. The current in one of our nerves to make us raise an arm is about one hundred thousandth of an amp. A 100-watt light bulb carries one amp. A lightning flash can peak at about 20,000 amps. A nuclear power station can deliver 10 million amps.

Electronics

Electronics is an important part of the study of ELECTRICITY. It deals with the way in which tiny particles called electrons flow through certain CRYSTALS, GASES or a VACUUM. Electronic devices like TRANSISTORS and SILICON CHIPS are used in such things as COMPUTERS, RADAR, television sets and radios. Electronics helps us to see the smallest living things, to guide planes, and to do difficult sums instantly. Without electronics, space travel would be impossible.

Element

Your own body and everything you see around you is composed (made up) of chemical ingredients called elements. In each element all the ATOMS are of the same kind. You can join different elements to make more complicated substances called compounds, but you cannot break an element into a simpler kind of substance.

Chemists have found more than 100 different elements. Ninety-two of these occur naturally. Scientists have produced other elements in laboratories. At ordinary temperatures, some elements are GASES, some LIQUIDS, and some solids.

Elements fall into several groups that are alike. The first person to realise this was a Russian scientist called Dmitri Mendeleyev. In 1869 he published the Periodic Table, showing the groups.

OXYGEN is the most plentiful element on Earth. Half of the Earth's crust and most of your body is made of oxygen.

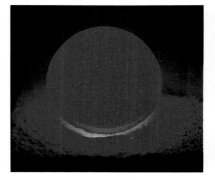

▲ *This pellet of the element plutonium shines from the glow of its own radioactivity. Plutonium (Pu) does not occur in nature except in tiny quantities from the decay of Uranium-238.*

▲ *The African elephant has larger ears and tusks than the Indian, or Asiatic, elephant.*

Queen Elizabeth I was vain of her good looks, especially her long hands. She wore extravagant clothes and ornate wigs. It is also said that she wore makeup so thick that sometimes she found it difficult to smile.

Elephant

Elephants are the largest living land animals. A big bull (male) elephant may stand twice as high as a man and weigh as much as seven family cars. An elephant has larger ears, thicker legs, a longer nose and longer teeth than any other creature. Its skin is nearly as thick as the heel of a man's shoe.

Baby elephants stand no taller than big dogs. Elephants are fully grown after 20 years. They live almost as long as people.

Indian elephants can be trained to move heavy loads. African elephants are harder to tame. Many thousands have been killed just for the ivory of their tusks. Today, most are protected by law.

Elizabeth I

Elizabeth I (1533–1603) was a famous English queen. She never married, but she reigned for 45 years with the help of wise advisers. She worked for peace between quarrelling religious groups but had her rival MARY QUEEN OF SCOTS put to death. Elizabeth's seamen crushed the Spanish ARMADA and made England powerful at sea. Great English playwrights, poets and scholars lived in her reign. People often call it 'the Elizabethan Age'.

Elizabeth II

Elizabeth II (1926–   ) is Queen of the United Kingdom of Great Britain and Northern Ireland and head of the COMMONWEALTH. Her husband is the Duke of Edinburgh. Her eldest son, and heir to the throne, is Charles, Prince of Wales.

Energy

Having energy means being able to do work. MUSCLES and machines have mechanical energy – they can move loads. Energy exists in several forms. There are two main kinds – *potential energy* and *kinetic energy*. Potential energy is the energy of position – stored energy. For example, the water in a high dam has potential energy. Then, when the water falls through pipes and works turbines to make electricity, it has kinetic energy – energy of movement. Other forms of energy are electrical, heat, chemical, sound, radiant and nuclear. These forms can be changed into each other. For example, the chemical energy of petrol is turned into kinetic energy as it moves a car's pistons; to electrical energy in the car's generator; to light in the headlamps; to sound in the car's horn, and so on. At every stage some energy is turned into heat.

Radiant energy from the Sun gives us most of our energy on Earth. Coal, oil and natural gas – the FOSSIL FUELS – were formed from plants and animals that depended for their life on the Sun's light and warmth.

> The ancient Egyptians were the first real engineers. When the pyramids were being built about 2500 BC, Egyptian workmen were already using tools such as the lathe. They smelted and cast metals. Their quarrying and stoneworking techniques were so advanced that they could fit blocks of stone 12 metres long so closely together that a hair couldn't be passed between them.

Engineering

Engineers do a great many different types of jobs. Mining engineers find useful MINERALS and take them from the ground. Metallurgical engineers separate METALS from unwanted substances and make them usable. Chemical engineers use chemicals to make such things as explosives, paint, plastics, and soap. Civil engineers build bridges, tunnels, roads, railways, ports, airports and so on. Mechanical

▼ *Engineers design big machines such as this excavator to save time, labour and cost. One such machine can do more work in an hour than a hundred men using hand tools could do in a day.*

ENGLAND

Area 131,756 sq km
Population: 49,000,000
Highest point: Scafell Pike 977 m
Greatest width: 515 km
North to south: 570 km
Longest rivers: Thames 346 km
                Severn 338 km
Largest lake: Windermere

▼ As an island nation, the English have had a long association with the sea. This small village in Yorkshire was once a thriving fishing community, but the fishing declined as long ago as the early 1900s.

engineers make and use machines. They design JET ENGINES and factory machinery. Electrical engineers work with devices that produce and use electricity. Some specialize in building a particular type of GENERATOR. Others, such as those who design and build computers, are known as electronic engineers. Electronic engineers form the newest branch of electrical engineering. Power engineers maintain machinery in power stations. Most kinds of engineering fall into one or other of these groups.

England

England is the largest country in the United Kingdom of Great Britain and Northern Ireland. If Great Britain were divided into five equal parts, England would fill three of them. England's neighbours are Scotland and Wales, but most of England is surrounded by sea. Green fields spread over the plains and low hills that cover most of the country. In the north and west there are mountains with moors and forests. Most English people live and work in big cities like London, Birmingham, Liverpool and Manchester.

England gets its name from the Angles, a group of the ANGLO-SAXONS who sailed to this island and settled down about 1500 years ago. Today, England and the rest of the United Kingdom is a multi-racial society. Since the early 1960s many black and Asian people have moved here from the Commonwealth.

Equator

The equator is an imaginary line around the world, halfway between the North and South Poles. The word 'equator' comes from an old Latin word meaning 'equalizer'. The equator divides the world into two equal halves, the Northern Hemisphere and the Southern Hemisphere. Distances north and south of the equator are measured in degrees of *latitude*. The equator itself has a latitude of 0 degrees. A journey round the equator covers 40,076 km.

Eskimo

Eskimos are hardy people who live in the cold, ARCTIC lands of Greenland, North America and north-east Asia. They have slanting eyes, a wide, flat face, and a short, thick body with short arms and legs. This shape helps to keep them warm in the cold, Arctic climate.

Eskimos once wore only fur clothes. Some lived in tents in summer and built snow homes called igloos for the winter. They made bows and arrows and harpoons, and hunted seals, whales, fish, seabirds and deer. Eskimos paddled skin boats and canoes called kayaks. Dogs pulled their sledges overland.

Many Eskimos no longer lead this kind of life. They now live and work in towns.

▲ *On winter hunting expeditions Eskimos wear jackets with hoods, called* anoraks *or* parkas.

Europe

Europe is a peninsula sticking out from the western end of Asia. Other small peninsulas jut from the main one and there are many offshore islands. Australia is the only continent smaller than Europe, but Europe holds more people than any continent except Asia.

European people have settled in the Americas, Australia, New Zealand, South Africa, and Siberia. European ideas and inventions helped shape the way of life of many people all around the world.

Mountains cross the countries of southern Europe. From west to east there are the Pyrenees, Alps, Apennines, Balkans, Carpathians, Caucasus and other ranges. The Caucasus has Mount Elbrus, Europe's highest peak.

▲ *Europe has more advantages for people than any other continent. It has scarcely any desert and a greater proportion of the land can be farmed than in any other continent. It is rich in coal and iron, essential for industry. Its climate is seldom either too hot or too cold.*

127

EUROPE

ARCTIC OCEAN

NORWEGIAN SEA

Murmansk

Narvik

■ ICELAND
Reykjavik

FAROE IS.

Arkhangelsk

SHETLAND IS.

KJØLEN MOUNTAINS

Trondheim

SWEDEN

FINLAND

L. Onega

Tampere

NORWAY

Sundsvall

Vyborg

L. Ladoga

Helsinki

St Petersburg

ORKNEY IS.

Bergen

Oslo

Stockholm

Aberdeen

Stavanger

Vänern

ESTONIA

Novgorod

RUSSIA

Yaroslavl

NORTH SEA

Vättern

Gothenburg

BALTIC SEA

LATVIA

Riga

Moscow

Glasgow

Edinburgh

DENMARK

LITHUANIA

Dvina

Smolensk

Belfast

UNITED

Copenhagen

Malmö

Kaliningrad

IRELAND

KINGDOM

Dublin

Manchester

Hamburg

Gdańsk

Minsk

Cork

NETHER-

Poznań

BYELORUSSIA

Birmingham

LANDS

Elbe

Berlin

Warsaw

Cardiff

London

Amster-dam

Rhine

GERMANY

Kharkov

English Channel

Thames

Brussels

Bonn

Prague

Kiev

Le Havre

BELGIUM

Frankfurt

POLAND

UKRAINE

Dnepr

Brest

Paris

LUX-EMBOURG

Kraków

Nantes

Loire

Seine

Stuttgart

CZECHOSLOVAKIA

CARPATHIANS

Dnepropetrovsk

Saône

ALPS

Munich

Vienna

Dnestr

Odessa

FRANCE

Bern

SWITZ-ERLAND

Budapest

Prut

MOLDOVA

Bordeaux

Geneva

LIECHTENSTEIN

AUSTRIA

HUNGARY

ROMANIA

La Coruña

Lyon

Rhône

Turin

Po

Milan

SLOVENIA

Zagreb

Bucharest

BLACK SEA

Santander

Bilbao

Toulouse

MONACO

Venice

Trieste

Belgrade

Danube

Oporto

Valladolid

PYRENEES

Marseille

Nice

SAN MARINO

CROATIA

YUGOSLAVIA

BULGARIA

Lisbon

PORTUGAL

ANDORRA

Florence

Dubrovnik

Sofia

Istanbul

Tagus

Madrid

Barcelona

Corsica

ITALY

Rome

ADRIATIC SEA

ALBANIA

TURKEY

Guadiana

Ebro

Ajaccio

Douro

Valencia

Naples

Bari

Tirana

Thessaloniki

Seville

SPAIN

BALEARIC IS.

Sardinia

Taranto

Cádiz

Málaga

Cagliari

GREECE

GIBRALTAR

Palermo

Messina

Athens

Sicily

Crete

MALTA

MEDITERRANEAN SEA

■ Capital Cities

0   100   200   300   400 miles

0   200   400   600 Kilometres

ATLANTIC OCEAN

In northern Europe low mountains cover much of Iceland, Ireland, Scotland, Wales, Norway, and Sweden. Between the mountains of the north and south lies a great plain. Here flow Europe's longest rivers. The Volga in the former Soviet Union is the longest of them all.

All Europe lies north of the hot tropics and most of it lies south of the cold Arctic. So most of Europe does not have extremes of temperature. But Mediterranean lands have hot summers and countries in the north and east have long, cold winters.

Shrubs and flowering plants grow in the far north. Next come the great northern forests of conifers. Farther south lie most of Europe's farms and cities.

Much of Europe's wealth comes from its factories, farms and mines. Europe's richest nations include Germany and Switzerland. The largest European country is Russia. The smallest European country is Vatican City in Rome. There are 34 countries in Europe.

EUROPE
Area: 10,531,623 sq km, 7 per cent of the world's land area
Population: 500,000,000 (9.3 per cent of world total)
Highest point: Mount Elbrus, 5633 m
Lowest point: Caspian Sea, 28 m below sea level
Longest river: Volga, 3700 km long
Biggest lake: Lake Ladoga in Russia, 18,388 sq km
Northernmost point: North Cape, Norway
Southernmost point: Cape Tarifa, Spain
Westernmost point: Dunmore Head, Ireland
Easternmost point: Ural Mountains

European Community

This is a group of western European nations that work together to help goods, people, and money travel between countries in the Community. Its members are Belgium, Denmark, France, Ireland, Italy, United Kingdom, Greece, Luxembourg, the Netherlands, Portugal, Spain and Germany. The 12 nations aim to unite their economies and bring about political union of the democratic states.

Everest, Mount

Mount Everest is the world's highest peak. It rises 8848 metres above sea level. The mountain stands in the HIMALAYAS on the borders of Nepal and Tibet. Gales and falling masses of rock and snow sweep the steep, cold slopes. Many climbers tried to reach the top before two finally succeeded in 1953. They were the New Zealander Edmund Hillary and Tenzing Norgay, a Nepalese Sherpa tribesman.

Evolution

The theory of evolution states that today's plants and animals are descended from other forms that lived long ago. This slow process of change has been

▲ The modern horse evolved from an animal no bigger than a dog, with four toes on its front feet and three on its hind feet.

EVOLUTION

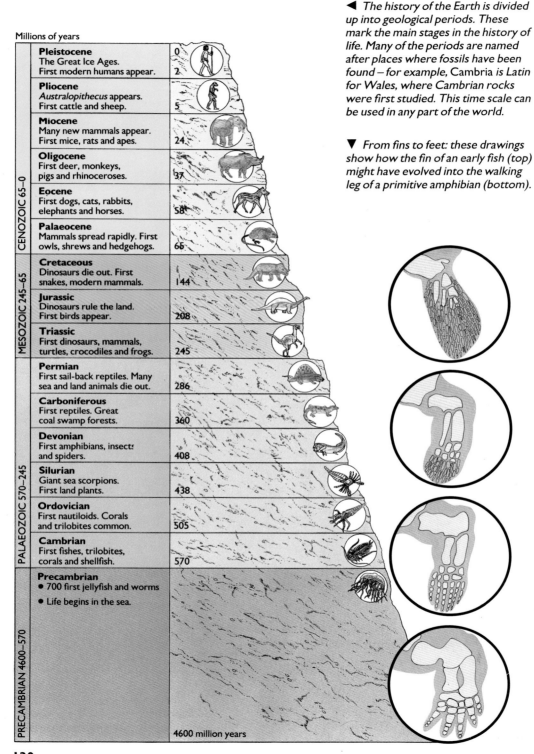

◀ The history of the Earth is divided up into geological periods. These mark the main stages in the history of life. Many of the periods are named after places where fossils have been found – for example, Cambria is Latin for Wales, where Cambrian rocks were first studied. This time scale can be used in any part of the world.

▼ From fins to feet: these drawings show how the fin of an early fish (top) might have evolved into the walking leg of a primitive amphibian (bottom).

Millions of years

CENOZOIC 65–0	**Pleistocene** The Great Ice Ages. First modern humans appear.	0 – 2
	Pliocene *Australopithecus* appears. First cattle and sheep.	5
	Miocene Many new mammals appear. First mice, rats and apes.	24
	Oligocene First deer, monkeys, pigs and rhinoceroses.	37
	Eocene First dogs, cats, rabbits, elephants and horses.	58
	Palaeocene Mammals spread rapidly. First owls, shrews and hedgehogs.	65
MESOZOIC 245–65	**Cretaceous** Dinosaurs die out. First snakes, modern mammals.	144
	Jurassic Dinosaurs rule the land. First birds appear.	208
	Triassic First dinosaurs, mammals, turtles, crocodiles and frogs.	245
PALAEOZOIC 570–245	**Permian** First sail-back reptiles. Many sea and land animals die out.	286
	Carboniferous First reptiles. Great coal swamp forests.	360
	Devonian First amphibians, insects and spiders.	408
	Silurian Giant sea scorpions. First land plants.	438
	Ordovician First nautiloids. Corals and trilobites common.	505
	Cambrian First fishes, trilobites, corals and shellfish.	570
PRECAMBRIAN 4600–570	**Precambrian** • 700 first jellyfish and worms • Life begins in the sea.	

4600 million years

going on for millions and millions of years—ever since life first appeared on earth—and is still happening. Much of the evidence for evolution comes from FOSSILS. Rocks contain the remains of extinct plants and animals and so help to build up a family tree for species now living.

The theory of evolution says that plants and animals must adapt to their surroundings if they are to survive. Those which adapt best are most likely to survive.

Charles DARWIN, an English naturalist, first put forward the theory of evolution in 1859, in a book entitled *On the Origin of Species.*

On April 30, 1978, Neomi Uemura, a Japanese explorer, became the first person to reach the North Pole alone. During his 54-day dogsled trek over the ice, Uemura survived several attacks by a polar bear.

Explorer

Explorers are people who travel to find out about unknown places. There have always been explorers. The Stone Age men and women who wandered across continents were in a way explorers. Phoenician seamen sailed the Mediterranean about 2600 years ago. ALEXANDER THE GREAT, in the 300s BC, explored and conquered all of the Middle East as far as India. In the Middle Ages, MARCO POLO reached China from Europe.

But the great age of exploration began in the 1400s. Sailors like Vasco da GAMA, Christopher COLUMBUS, Ferdinand Magellan and James COOK discovered the shape, size and position of continents and oceans. Later, David Livingstone, Roald Amundsen and others explored wild, untamed continents. The world's highest peak, Mount Everest, was climbed by Edmund Hillary and Tenzing Norgay in 1953. SPACE EXPLORATION now takes people beyond the Earth, and the explorations of the next century will probably make all past discoveries seem minor by comparison.

Explosive

Explosions happen when people heat or strike certain solid or liquid substances. These suddenly turn into hot GASES. The gases fill more space than the solids or liquids, so they rush violently outward. High explosives like dynamite explode faster and do more damage than low explosives like gunpowder. Engineers use explosives to break up rocks and old buildings.

▲ *Robert Peary, the American naval officer who reached the North Pole in 1909.*

Human eyes have a better sense of colour than those of any other animal. We can distinguish 250 different pure colours, from red to violet, and about 17,000 mixed colours. We are also able to distinguish about 300 shades of grey between black and white.

The animal with the largest eye is the giant squid. One big specimen has eyes nearly 40 cm in diameter. The biggest whales have eyes about 10 cm across.

Eye

Our eyes show us the size, shape and colour of objects in the world around us. Our eyes can see something as small and near as a tiny insect crawling on this page, or as far off as the Moon or stars.

A human eye is much larger than the part you can see. The eye is a ball bigger than a marble. It works much like a camera. Both bend LIGHT rays to form a picture of the object that the rays are reflected from.

Light rays enter the eye through a layer of transparent skin called the *conjunctiva*. The rays pass through a hard, transparent layer called the *cornea*. This bends the rays. The LENS brings them into focus on the *retina* at the back of the eye. But you do not 'see' the picture formed here until light-sensitive nerve endings on the retina send the brain a message along the *optic nerve*.

To see properly, all the parts of the eye have to work correctly. For example, the *iris* (the eye's coloured part) can open and close to let more or less light through the *pupil*.

Our tear glands protect our eyes against outside infection. Tears are wiped over the eye regularly by blinking. They are mildly antiseptic and contain a substance that kills bacteria.

▼ Inside the eye the image on the retina is upside down, but the brain turns it over so that we see things the right way up.

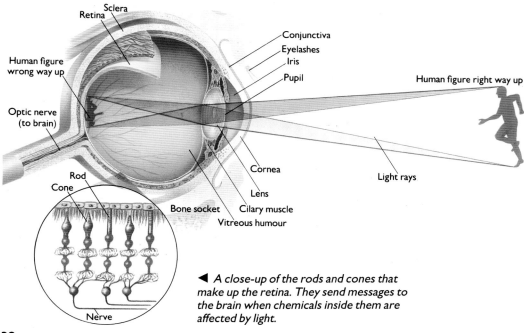

Sclera
Retina
Conjunctiva
Eyelashes
Iris
Pupil
Human figure wrong way up
Human figure right way up
Optic nerve (to brain)
Cornea
Light rays
Rod
Cone
Lens
Bone socket
Cilary muscle
Vitreous humour
Nerve

◄ A close-up of the rods and cones that make up the retina. They send messages to the brain when chemicals inside them are affected by light.

Falcon

Falcons are a group of birds of prey that are found all over the world. They can be recognized by the dark markings around their eyes and by their pointed wings. Falcons use their large, hooked beaks for tearing flesh, but they kill their prey with their sharp claws. Falcons swoop down on their victims from above, hitting them with their claws. This act is called 'stooping'. It is used to kill smaller birds in mid-flight and also to take RODENTS and other small animals on the ground.

The biggest of all falcons is the gyrfalcon of the Arctic. It may reach over 60 cm in size. The smallest is the pygmy falcon of southern Asia. It is less than 15 cm long and feeds mainly on insects.

The peregrine falcon is one of the fastest flyers in the world. In a fast dive, it can reach 280 km/h.

Faraday, Michael

Michael Faraday (1791–1867) was a brilliant English scientist. His studies of chemistry and physics made him world famous. Faraday is best known for his experiments with ELECTRICITY. He showed that it could be made to flow in a wire when the wire was passed between the poles of a magnet. Today this is how most electricity is produced in big generators.

▲ *The merlin is one of the smallest of the falcons. It flies low and fast as it chases smaller birds.*

Farming

Farming began somewhere in the Middle East around 9000 years ago. Today about half the world's people are farmers. Many are *subsistence* farmers, growing just enough to feed themselves. Others grow *cash* crops, to sell.

Farming has become more and more scientific. In the 1600s turnips and clover were introduced to winter-feed farm animals, which had always been killed as winter approached. Now breeders could keep good stock longer, and so develop larger, fatter breeds of cattle, sheep and pigs. New plants, such as potatoes and tomatoes, came from the New World. In the 1800s came steam engines and motor tractors to replace horses and oxen.

Today, most farms in developed countries are mechanized. Few people are needed to work on them.

▲ *For many years Michael Faraday gave science lectures for children. One of the best-known lectures is called 'The Chemical History of a Candle'.*

▲ *In some parts of the world old farming methods are still used. Modern machinery is slowly taking over.*

THE HISTORY OF FARMING

7000 BC Farming begins when people discover how to grow grain and rear domestic animals.

4000 BC Irrigation of crops in Mesopotamia and Egypt.

500 BC Iron tools and heavy ox-drawn ploughs in use.

AD 600 Open-field system common in northern Europe. Peasants share fields, growing crops in narrow strips.

1400s Enclosure (fencing) of open fields. Sheep-rearing important.

1500s New plants brought to Europe from America.

1600s Improved breeds of farm animals are developed in Europe.

1700s New machinery, such as Eli Whitney's cotton gin (1793).

1800s Steam power, threshing and reaping machines, new fertilizers; North America and Australia become important farming regions.

1900s Wide use of chemicals as fertilizers and pest-killers; new strains of plants able to resist disease; factory farming and the 'green revolution' improve food production.

Only 3 percent of Americans are farmers. Poultry and calves are often reared indoors, as if in a factory. The rich countries produce more food than they need. But despite the success of the "green revolution" which has brought new crops and new farm methods to the Third World, many people in poor countries still starve. In Africa, Asia and South America most farms are small and the work is done mostly by hand.

Fat

Fat is an important food for both animals and plants. The tissue of these living things contain fat. Fat in a pure state can take the form of a liquid, such as vegetable oil, or a solid such as butter or lard.

Fat is a store of ENERGY. A unit of fat contains twice as much energy as the same amount of PROTEIN or STARCH. Fats play an important part in our diet. We get most vegetable fat from the seeds and fruits of plants, where it is stored. In animals and human beings fat is stored in tiny 'droplets' in a layer under the skin and in the CELLS of the body.

Feather

The only animals with an outer layer of feathers are BIRDS. Feathers protect birds and keep them warm. They give their bodies a smooth, streamlined shape. Feathers also form the broad surface area of the wings that allows birds to fly.

Feathers are replaced once or twice a year. This process is called moulting. Old feathers that are worn and broken fall out. New ones grow in their place.

SEE IT YOURSELF
Collect feathers in the woods and look at them with a magnifying glass to see how they are made. 'Unzip' part of the flat vane to see the tiny hooked branches that fit neatly together to form it. Fix your feathers in a notebook and label them with the birds' names if you know them.

Fibre Optics

An optical fibre is a flexible glass strand thinner than a human hair. Along this fine fibre a beam of light can travel very easily. The light can be used to carry telephone conversations and television pictures or to allow doctors to see inside our bodies. The fibres are made of specially pure glass designed to reflect the light in towards the centre of the strand. Using LASER light, signals can be sent for more than 50 km before they have to be amplified. This means that optical fibres are much more efficient than copper cables and much thinner and lighter. A pair of fibres can carry hundreds of telephone conversations at the same time.

Fingerprint

Fingerprints are marks we leave behind whenever we touch something. You can see them by pressing your fingertips into an ink pad and then onto a sheet of white paper. Everybody has patterns of lines and swirls on their fingers. But each person's fingerprints are different from everybody else's. Because of this, police officers use fingerprints to help identify criminals. They keep files of thousands of different prints. By comparing those on file with those found at the scene of a crime they can often trace the guilty person. Computers can now hold details of the fingerprints of half a million people. In a few seconds the computer will match any of these prints with those of a suspect.

In many hospitals the footprints of babies are taken after birth. Footprints, like fingerprints, never change so the baby will always be known by these prints.

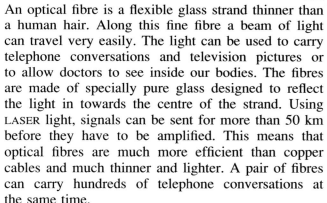

Arch

Whorl

Loop

Composite

▲ *All fingerprints can be divided into four main types – the arch, the whorl, the loop and the composite.*

FINLAND

Government: Constitutional republic
Capital: Helsinki
Area: 337,009 sq km
Population: 4,986,000
Languages: Finnish and Swedish
Currency: Markka

▲ *In ancient times people found that two flints struck sharply together produced a spark. Later, a flint was struck against a piece of steel to make a spark which could be used to light an easily-burnt material called tinder.*

Finland

Finland is a country in northern EUROPE tucked between Scandinavia and Russia. Northern Finland stretches north of the Arctic Circle.

The thousands of lakes and rivers that dot the Finnish landscape form a great inland waterway. About 75 percent of the land is covered by thick forests of spruce, pine and larch trees. The main industries of Finland are logging and the making of wood products, such as paper.

Five million people live in Finland. The capital, Helsinki, has a population of about 487,000.

Fiord

Along the coasts of NORWAY and Greenland are a series of steep-sided valleys called fiords. Here the sea has invaded the land. Narrow tongues of water wind inland in narrow mountain gorges.

Fiords were formed when the great glaciers of the ICE AGES gouged out valleys as they flowed to the sea. When the ice melted, the sea flooded the valleys. Fiords are very deep and make perfect shelters for large ocean-going ships.

Fire

The ability to make and use fire is one of the great advantages people have over animals. Primitive people found fire frightening, just as animals do. But once they learned to make and control fire, it became a necessary part of life. It kept out the cold, lit up the dark, cooked food, kept people warm, and scared away animals. But even today fires that get out of control cause terrible damage and suffering.

Fish

Fish were the first animals with backbones (vertebrates) to develop on Earth. They are the animals best adapted to life in the water. They breathe by means of gills, and they swim by beating their tails from side to side. They use their fins for steering and balance. Fish are found in salt and fresh water, from the cold polar seas to the warm tropics.

Scientists divide fish into three groups. The *carti-*

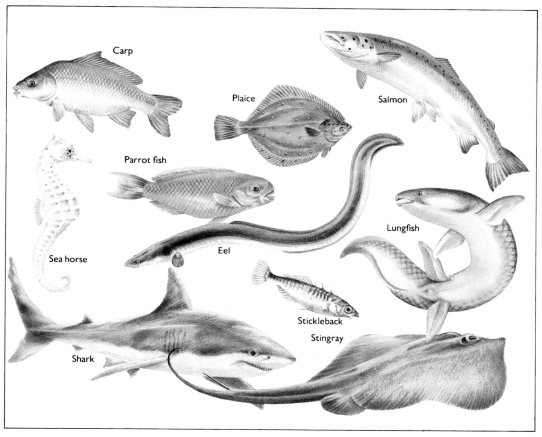

Carp

Salmon

Plaice

Parrot fish

Lungfish

Sea horse

Eel

Stickleback

Stingray

Shark

laginous fish have gristly, rather than bony, skeletons, and leathery skins, not scales. They include the sharks and rays. The *bony* fish make up the next and largest group. All these fish have bony scales covering their body. The third and smallest group are the *lungfishes*, which are unusual in being able to come out on land and breathe air.

▲ *The three fish groups include fish of a wide variety of shapes and sizes.*

People have eaten fish since earliest times. Today the world's fishing fleets catch millions of tonnes of fish every year.

Fishing

Fishing is one of the world's most important activities. In one year, about 60 million tonnes of fish are taken from the seas, rivers and lakes.

Although fish are a good source of food, much of the catch ends up as animal feed or FERTILIZER. Oil from fish is used to make SOAPS for tanning–turning animal skins into leather.

The United States flag, or 'Stars and Stripes', has had the same basic design since 1777, during the War of Independence. It has 13 horizontal stripes which represent the original 13 colonies that rebelled against British rule. Fifty white five-pointed stars, representing the 50 states of the Union, appear on a dark blue field in the *canton*, the rectangular area in the top corner near the staff.

Often the catch is made far from the home port. The fish must be preserved or they will quickly spoil. In the past fish were often dried, smoked or salted, because there were no refrigerators. Today they are packed in ice or frozen. Some fishing fleets include large factory ships. These take fresh fish straight from the other ships, and can them or package them on the spot.

The best places to fish at sea are where the sloping sea bottom is no more than 180 metres deep. Here, fish can be found feeding in huge numbers. The Grand Banks off the coast of Newfoundland is one such region. It has been fished for hundreds of years.

Flag

Flags are pieces of coloured cloth, often decorated with bold markings. They have special fastenings so that they can be flown from masts and poles. Flags are used by countries, armies and groups such as marching bands and sports teams.

Flags have been used as emblems since the time of the ancient Egyptians. Their flags were flown on long poles as battle standards, held by 'standard-bearers'. Flying high in the air, flags helped soldiers to find their companions as they plunged into battle. And they showed which soldiers belonged to which king or general.

Today, national flags are flown as a symbol of a country's history, its power and its importance, or *prestige*. They are also a symbol of people's loyalty to one nation and one government.

Flags are also used for signalling. Since 1857 there has been an international code for flag signals. It is used by ships. A yellow flag, for example, means that a ship is in quarantine because of illness on board. For thousands of years flags have been important as a way of identifying ships at sea.

▼ *The World Scout flag (1) and the flag of the Red Cross (4) both represent organizations. The Japanese naval ensign (2), flown from the stern of a ship, is a recognized flag of nationality. The personal standard of Queen Elizabeth (3) is just one of the royal standards.*

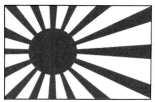

1   2   3   4

Other well known signals are a white flag—a sign of truce—and a flag raised to half-mast—a sign that people are mourning someone's death.

Fleming, Alexander

Sir Alexander Fleming (1881–1955) was a British doctor who discovered the antibiotic drug penicillin. It is one of the most important drugs known. Penicillin fights infections caused by many kinds of GERMS and BACTERIA. Although the drug fights the infection it does not usually harm the body. Penicillin has saved thousands of lives.

Fleming discovered the drug by accident in 1928. He found an unknown kind of mould growing in his laboratory. From this he was able to make penicillin. For his work, Fleming shared the 1945 Nobel Prize in medicine with Howard W. Florey and Ernst B. Chain, the doctors who found a way to produce penicillin in large quantities.

▲ *Sir Alexander Fleming, the British bacteriologist who discovered penicillin.*

Flight

The first human flights were made by balloon. They were based on the idea that a bag full of warm air floats upwards. The next development was the airship, a rigid container full of hydrogen gas, propelled by engines. Specially shaped wings in modern aircraft mean that when the craft is forwards, the difference in airflow above and below these wings creates an upward force called lift. This is the same principle that enables birds to fly and is the same principle which the Wright brothers used when they made the first flight in a heavier-than-air machine in 1903.

Flint

Flint is a glassy MINERAL that is a form of QUARTZ. It is found in beds of chalk and limestone. A lump of flint is dull white on the outside and shiny grey to black on the inside.

Flint is very hard, but it can be easily chipped into sharp-edged flakes. Stone Age people made tools and weapons out of flint. Because it will give off a spark when struck against iron, it can be used for starting a FIRE. A spark from a flint also ignited the powder in a flintlock GUN.

▲ *A pointed flint tool and a tool for scraping, both made by Neanderthal people about 50,000 years ago.*

▼ *The parts of a flowering plant.*

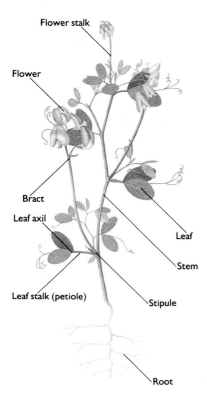

Flower stalk

Flower

Bract

Leaf axil

Leaf

Stem

Leaf stalk (petiole)

Stipule

Root

Flower

There are about 250,000 different kinds of flowering plants in the world. Their flowers come in a dazzling array of colours, sizes and shapes. Some grow singly. Some grow in tight clusters. Many have showy colours, a strong scent and produce a sweet nectar. Others are quite drab and unscented.

Whatever they look like, flowers all have the same part to play in the life of the plant. Flowers help plants to reproduce themselves. Inside a flower are male parts, called *stamens*, and female parts known as *pistils*. The stamens contain hundreds of powdery grains of pollen. These fertilize the pistil. Then a FRUIT begins to form and grow. Inside the fruit are the SEEDS for a new generation of plants. The seeds are scattered in different ways. They may be blown by the wind, or carried off by birds and animals. From them new plants will grow.

Fly

Flies are winged insects. They are one of the largest groups of insects in the world. There are more than 750,000 different kinds of flies. They have two pairs of wings, one pair for flying and a smaller set behind the main pair to help them to balance in flight.

Many flies are dangerous. They spread deadly diseases such as cholera and dysentery. They pick up germs from manure and rotting food and carry them into homes where they leave them on our fresh food.

Some flies bite and feed on the blood of animals. Horseflies and gadflies attack cattle and horses in great swarms. Tsetse flies, which live in the tropics, spread sleeping sickness among humans. Blowflies lay their eggs in open wounds on the skin of animals.

▼ *Houseflies lay their eggs in decaying matter. The life cycle can be complete in a week in warm weather. The sponge-like mouth is drawn in the circle.*

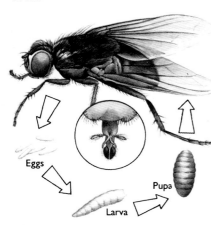

Eggs

Pupa

Larva

Food Chain

When you eat a piece of fish, such as cod, you are taking part in a food chain that began somewhere in the sea. There the tiny floating plants and animals called plankton were eaten by tiny fish. The tiny fish were eaten by bigger fish, and these bigger fish were eaten by even bigger fish such as your cod.

Every living thing has its place in one or many food chains. The chain begins with green plants. They make their own food from water, chemicals in the soil and air, and sunlight. Animals cannot make their own food as plants can. Instead, they eat plants or other animals. When animals or plants die, tiny BACTERIA that live in the soil break down the animal or plant tissues. The chemicals that make up the animals or plants are released into the soil. These chemicals act as fertilizers to enrich the soil and help the green plants to grow. And so the food chain begins all over again.

At each stage in any food chain, energy is lost. This is why food chains seldom extend beyond four or five links. In overpopulated countries, people often increase the total food supply by cutting out a step in the food chain. Instead of eating cows that eat plants, the people themselves eat the plants. Because the food chain is made shorter, the total amount of energy available to the people is increased.

Football

There are several kinds of football games. They differ in the shape of the ball, the size of the teams and the rules. Soccer is played all over the world. The ball is round, the field, or 'pitch', can be from 90 to 118 metres long, and each team has 11 players. Teams score by kicking the ball into the goal at the opposite end of the field. The ball may not be touched by the hand or arm, except by the goal-keeper within his goal area.

American football uses an oval ball. The game consists mostly of tackling, passing and running, with very little kicking. The players—11 on each side—are protected by helmets and pads.

Rugby football is played in Britain, the Commonwealth and parts of Europe. The ball may be kicked or carried. Australian Rules football has 18 players to a side. All players can kick and catch the ball.

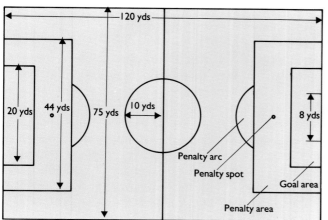

▲ *Soccer is called football in most countries of the world. In this game the ball must not be handled, and the players rely on agility and speed.*

◄ *The dimensions of a football pitch.*

Forest

Forests are large areas of tree-covered land. Tropical rain forests are found near the EQUATOR. In this hot and steamy climate many kinds of trees and plants grow very quickly.

Coniferous forests are nearly always found in cold northern lands. These forests are mostly made up of one kind of tree, such as spruce, fir or pine. Few other plants grow there. In temperate lands like Europe and the cooler parts of Africa, there are deciduous forests with trees like oak and beech. Most Australian forest trees are eucalyptus.

▼ *Acres of forest can be laid waste through the careless use of fire by people.*

Fossil

Fossils are the hardened remains or impressions of animals and plants that lived a very long time ago.

Most fossils have been found in areas that were once in or near the sea. When the plant or creature died its body sank to the seabed. The soft parts rotted away but the hard skeleton became buried in the mud. Over millions of years more and more mud settled on top of the skeleton. Eventually these layers of mud hardened into rock, and the skeleton became part of that rock. Water seeping through the rock slowly dissolved away the original skeleton.

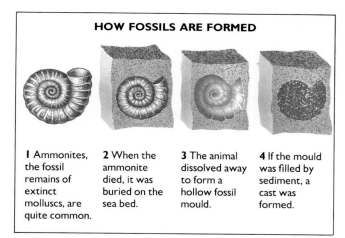

HOW FOSSILS ARE FORMED

1 Ammonites, the fossil remains of extinct molluscs, are quite common.

2 When the ammonite died, it was buried on the sea bed.

3 The animal dissolved away to form a hollow fossil mould.

4 If the mould was filled by sediment, a cast was formed.

It was replaced by stony MINERALS which formed exactly the same shape.

Fossil fuels

Petroleum, COAL and natural gas are all fossil fuels. They are extracted from the rocks of the Earth's crust and used to provide the fuel for heating and the generation of ELECTRICITY. Many chemicals are also derived from petroleum. These fuels are made from the animal and plant remains which have formed FOSSILS and so they are called fossil fuels. Natural gas and oil are often found together. The gas is found in tiny spaces in the rocks, at a higher level than the oil. Petroleum also occupies spaces in permeable rocks (rocks that allow liquids to pass through them). They are often capped by an impermeable layer such as clay.

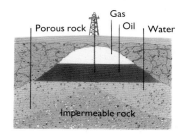

Porous rock | Gas | Oil | Water

Impermeable rock

▲ Oil-bearing rock holds drops of oil between its grains. It seeps up through porous rock, such as sandstone, until it is stopped by impermeable rock, such as granite.

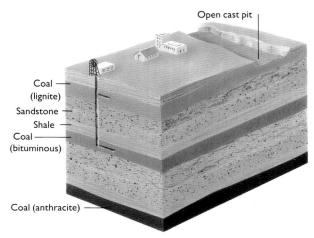

Open cast pit

Coal (lignite)

Sandstone

Shale

Coal (bituminous)

Coal (anthracite)

◄ Coal can be extracted from seams that lie near the surface by removing topsoil to make an open-cast pit. Deeper seams are reached by shafts and tunnels. Anthracite, the hardest and best coal, is usually the deepest.

FOX

▼ *The fennec fox (below) is the smallest of the foxes. The bat-eared fox (bottom) looks more like a jackal than a fox. Both these animals have very large ears because they live in open desert country and their ears help to get rid of excess heat from their bodies. Their big ears also give them acute hearing.*

Fox

Foxes belong to the same animal family as dogs. The most common kind is the red fox, which is found in Europe, North Africa, North America and parts of Asia. It eats small birds, animals and insects, and occasionally poultry or lambs.

Foxes live in holes called 'earths' which they either dig themselves or take over from rabbits or badgers. Recently, more and more foxes have been found in cities. They live under the floors of buildings or in any hidden place they can find. They eat scraps from dustbins.

Foxes are very cunning animals. Sometimes they catch rabbits and other prey by chasing their own tails very fast. This fascinates the rabbit who watches without realizing that the fox is gradually getting nearer and nearer. When the fox gets close enough it straightens out and grabs its dinner.

France

France is the largest country in western EUROPE. It has a population of 55,800,000. In ancient times France was inhabited by Celts, but Julius CAESAR conquered it and for 500 years it was part of the Roman Empire. The Franks, from whom the country got its name, invaded in the AD 400s. France was once divided into hundreds of small parts. There was no standard language until the founding of the French Academy in the 1630s.

France is a very varied and beautiful country. It has a temperate climate and is very fertile. Farmland covers about half the country and many of the people are employed in farming, fishing or forestry. France produces a lot of grain, fruit, and vegetables, and it is famous for its wines.

The history of France is long and turbulent. For centuries the French and English were enemies and fought many wars. The French people suffered under the rule of greedy kings and nobles. Then in 1789 the people started the FRENCH REVOLUTION. They made France a republic.

But the country was soon taken over by NAPO-LEON, who made himself Emperor. He went to war and conquered most of Europe before he was finally defeated at Waterloo in 1815.

FRANCE

Government: Republic
Capital: Paris
Area: 547,026 sq km
Population: 55,800,000
Language: French
Currency: French franc

Today France is one of the wealthiest nations in Europe. It was one of the first members of the EUROPEAN COMMUNITY. The capital city is PARIS on the river Seine.

Francis of Assisi

St Francis (1182–1226) was born in Assisi in central Italy. When he was 22 he suffered a severe illness. Afterwards he decided to devote his life to the service of God. He lived in poverty and gathered around him a band of monks who became known as the Franciscans. St Francis was very fond of birds and animals whom he called his brothers and sisters.

Franklin, Benjamin

Benjamin Franklin (1706–1790) was a gifted American politician and scientist. He was born in Boston, the youngest of 17 children. Franklin became a printer and then went on to publish a yearly almanac which made him his fortune.

He became involved in the Revolutionary War, which brought America freedom from British rule. He was one of the men who signed the Declaration of Independence and helped draw up the peace treaty at the end of the war.

His scientific inventions include bifocal eyeglasses, and the lightning conductor, a rod that protects buildings from lightning.

French Revolution

In the 1700s the poor people of FRANCE suffered under the rule of their kings and nobles. Rich people built themselves lavish palaces and mansions while many others starved in misery. French kings forced the peasants and shopkeepers to pay taxes to support their extravagant way of life, and to finance the wars they were always fighting.

There was no parliament to stop the king from treating his subjects badly, and eventually, in 1789, the French people's anger exploded into revolution. King LOUIS XVI was imprisoned but tried to escape. Violent leaders like Danton, Robespierre and Marat directed the Revolution, and the king and queen and many nobles were beheaded.

▼ Three well-known French monuments – from top to bottom, the Eiffel Tower, Sacré Coeur and the Arc de Triomphe. The Arc de Triomphe, in Paris, was built by Napoleon. The white-domed church of Sacré Coeur is a landmark on Montmartre, the tallest hill in Paris. The Eiffel Tower was erected for the Paris Exhibition of 1889.

Then followed the 'Reign of Terror', when the Revolutionary leaders began to quarrel among themselves, and many of them were beheaded too. The people tired of bloodshed and in 1795 they set up a government called 'The Directory'. But it ruled the country badly, and in 1799 it was overthrown by NAPOLEON.

> Without friction the world would be a strange place. We could not walk because our shoes would not grip the ground. Cars would stand still no matter how fast their wheels turned. Nails and screws would not hold.

Friction

When two things rub together it causes friction. Friction makes it hard to move something across a surface. Smooth objects cause much less friction than rough objects, so when things need to go fast we try to reduce friction. This is why the wheels of a train and the rails of the track are smooth. When we want things to slow down we add friction; for example, putting on the brakes in our cars. If two things rub together at great speed the friction produces HEAT. If you rub your hand very fast against your leg you can feel the heat made by the friction.

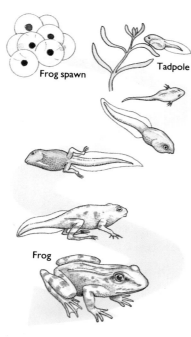

Frog and Toad

Frogs and toads are AMPHIBIANS. This means that they can live both on land and in water. Frogs and toads are found all over the world except in very cold lands that are always frozen. There are hundreds of different kinds. The biggest is the Goliath frog of Central Africa. This frog can be over 30 cm long and weigh over 3 kg. The smallest is a tree frog from the United States, which is less than 2 cm long.

Frogs and toads breathe through their skins as well as their LUNGS. It is important that they keep their skins wet, because if the skin became too dry they could not breathe and would die. This is why you will never find a frog very far away from water.

Common frogs feed on insects, grubs and slugs. They catch their food with a long sticky tongue which is attached to the front of the mouth. A frog can flick its tongue in and out in a fraction of a second. Really big frogs eat snakes, small animals and other frogs, as well as insects.

Toads' skins are rough, dry and lumpy. They can live in drier places than can frogs.

▲ The life cycle of a frog: The jelly-like eggs, or spawn, are laid in a pond and hatch into tadpoles. The tadpoles gradually develop legs and their tails shrink. They develop lungs instead of gills. They become adult frogs in about 3 years.

Green tree frog
(North America)

Midwife toad
(Europe)

Gliding frog
(Malaysia)

Common toad
(Europe)

Arrow-poison frog
(South America)

Spadefoot toad
(North America)

Fruit

To most of us 'fruit' means juicy foods which grow on certain plants and trees. Apples, oranges and pears are three examples. These fruits taste good and are important in our diet. They give us mineral salts, sugar and VITAMINS. The water, skins and seeds of fruit help our DIGESTION.

To scientists who study plants, fruits are the ripe SEED cases of any flowering plant. The fruits protect the seeds as they develop and help spread them when they are ripe. Some fruits scatter seeds. Others are eaten by birds and animals that spread the seeds.

▲ These are just a few of the world's 2500 different species of frogs and toads. The brightly-coloured arrow-poison frogs of South America are among the most poisonous of all. Indians of the Amazon basin use their poison to tip hunting arrows. Tree frogs have pads on their fingers and toes which help them to climb trees. Gliding frogs have webs on their feet which they use as 'wings'. The male midwife toad carries the eggs laid by the female on his legs and back. After three weeks he takes them into the water and the baby tadpoles hatch.

Fungus

A fungus is a simple PLANT with no true roots, stems, or leaves. Fungi do not have the chlorophyll that helps green plants to make food. So fungi have to find a ready-made supply of food. Some feed as parasites on living plants or animals. Others feed on animal and plant remains. These kinds of fungi are called *saprophytes*. They will feed on the leave, twig and plant remains that end up lying on the ground.

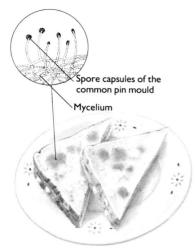

Spore capsules of the common pin mould

Mycelium

▲ *The fungus family includes moulds. Uncovered food offers a perfect place for moulds to grow. The tiny, thread-like growths (inset) spread quickly.*

There are more than 50,000 kinds of fungus. Some have only one *cell*. Other fungi are chains of cells. These produce tiny, thread-like growths that spread through the substance they feed on. Many fungi grow a large fruiting body that sheds spores to produce new fungus plants. The *mushrooms* we eat are the fruiting bodies of a fungus. Some fungi are useful. Penicillin, the *antibiotic* drug, and *yeast* are both fungi.

Furniture

Furniture is used for resting things on and for storing things in. Beds, chairs and tables all support some kind of load. Chests and cupboards hold such things as sheets and china.

The first pieces of furniture were simple slabs of stone and chunks of wood. In time, people tried to make furniture that was beautiful as well as useful.

Wealthy Egyptians had carved and painted beds, chairs and tables 4000 years ago. The Romans used bronze and marble, and made tables with legs carved in animal shapes. From the end of the MIDDLE AGES onwards many different styles of furniture have been made.

More recently, people have tried using new materials and machines to make furniture with clean, simple shapes.

Furniture was so scarce in Europe during the Middle Ages that it was quite common for a visitor to bring along his or her bed and other pieces of furniture.

In England until the 17th century, the three-legged stool was still widely used. People thought that a proper chair should only be used by the lord of the manor.

Fuse

This word has two meanings. One kind of fuse is a safety device in an electric circuit. Fuse wire is made so that it will melt at a low temperature. If too much ELECTRICITY flows through the circuit the wire 'fuses', or melts. This breaks the circuit.

In this way, an electric fuse stops the wire in the circuit from becoming too hot and possibly setting fire to nearby objects. Electric current must pass through fuse wire to get from the main power line to the electric wiring in a house. Inside the house, each electric plug also has a fuse.

The other kind of fuse is a device that sets off EXPLOSIVES. A safety fuse burns slowly until the flame reaches the explosive. A detonating fuse explodes itself and this explosion sets off a much larger amount of dynamite or other explosive.

▲ *A cartridge fuse (left) is fitted inside ordinary household plugs. Too large a current will cause the wire inside it to melt, thus breaking the circuit (right).*

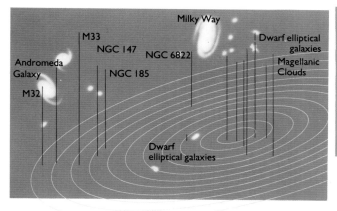

Galaxy

Someone once called galaxies 'star islands' in space. A galaxy is made up of a huge group of STARS. Our SUN is just one star of about 100,000 million stars that belong to the Milky Way galaxy. A beam of light would take about 100,000 years to shine from one side of the Milky Way to the other. Yet the Milky Way is only a middle-sized galaxy.

Beyond our galaxy there may be as many as 10,000 million more. The nearest large galaxy is called Andromeda. The light we see it by took more than two million years to reach us.

Some galaxies have no special shape. Others have spiral arms made up of many millions of stars. The Milky Way and Andromeda galaxies both look like this. There are also galaxies that look like saucers or balls. Astronomers used to think that these changed

◀ Our galaxy belongs to what we call the Local Group – a collection of about 30 galaxies. This diagram of the Local Group shows the galaxies so far discovered at their correct distances apart, although their sizes are not to scale.

▼ Edge on, our Milky Way galaxy looks like a flat disc with a swollen middle – the nucleus. From above, it looks like a whirlpool of stars. The position of our solar system is marked by the red arrows.

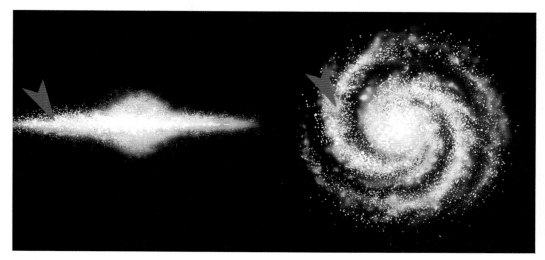

into galaxies with spiral arms. Now some astronomers believe instead that the spiral galaxies shrink into the other kind.

RADIO ASTRONOMY has shown that radio waves are sent out from many galaxies. Strong radio waves also come from strange starlike objects known as QUASARS. Quasars are very powerful energy sources. Some people think that a quasar may be the beginning of a new galaxy. Scientists think that galaxies may form where GRAVITY pulls huge clouds of gas together.

Galileo

Galileo Galilei (1564–1642) was an Italian mathematics teacher and one of the first true scientists. Instead of believing old ideas about the way the world worked, Galileo made careful experiments to find out for himself. He learnt that a PENDULUM took the same time to make a long swing as it did to make a short one. He showed that light objects fell as fast as heavy ones when pulled towards the Earth by what we know as GRAVITY. He built a TELESCOPE and became the first man to use this tool for studying the Moon and PLANETS. What he saw made Galileo believe COPERNICUS's idea that the Earth was not the centre of the UNIVERSE. The Church punished him for his belief in this idea. But later scientists like Isaac NEWTON built new knowledge on Galileo's discoveries.

▲ Galileo was a mathematician, astronomer and physicist, and one of the first true scientists.

Gama, Vasco da

Vasco da Gama (about 1469–1524) discovered how to sail by sea from Europe to India by way of southern Africa. This Portuguese navigator left Lisbon with four ships in July, 1497. In East Africa he found a guide who showed him how to sail across the Indian Ocean. Da Gama reached Calicut in southern India in May, 1498. But Arab traders who were jealous of the Portuguese tried to stop him from trading with the Indians. On the journey home, 30 of his 90 crewmen died of scurvy, and only two of the four ships got back to Lisbon.

But da Gama had found a way to reach the spice-rich lands of the East. In 1502 he made a second voyage to India, this time with nineteen ships.

Gandhi

Mohandas Karamchand Gandhi (1869–1948) is sometimes called the 'father of modern India'. This frail-looking Hindu lawyer helped to free INDIA from British rule by peacefully disobeying British laws. In 1920 he told the Indians to spin cloth for their own clothes instead of buying it from Britain.

Gandhi led the campaign by personal example. People admired his beliefs, his kindness, and his simple way of life. He was called the Mahatma, meaning 'Great Soul'. In 1947 Britain gave India independence. Soon after, one of his fellow HINDUS shot Gandhi for preaching peace between Hindus and Muslims (followers of ISLAM).

▼ Gandhi was called the Mahatma by his followers, which means 'Great Soul'.

Gas

Gases are substances with no special shape or size. They take up the size and shape of any container that holds them. This can happen because a gas is made of ATOMS moving freely in space. When a gas becomes cold enough it turns into a liquid. Liquids have a fixed size but no fixed shape. If that liquid becomes much colder still it turns into a solid. Solids have a fixed shape and size.

The gas we use to cook with and heat our homes is called natural gas. This gas is found beneath the Earth's surface in many parts of the world.

Generator

Generators produce electric current. Huge generators in power stations provide ELECTRICITY for homes and factories. The largest generators can light 20 million 100-watt electric lamps. But there are tiny generators too. A bicycle dynamo is a generator you can hold in one hand.

If a loop of wire is turned between the ends of a horseshoe-shaped magnet, an electric current flows in the wire. Generators work much like this. They change the ENERGY of motion into electrical energy. The energy to work a generator's moving parts can come from wind, flowing water, or steam produced by heat from fuels such as oil or coal. Big generators have thousands of coils of wire which are made to turn very quickly between powerful magnets.

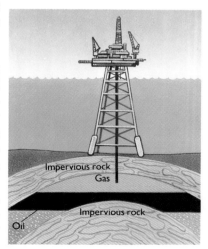

▲ Oil and natural gas collect in porous rocks (rocks that allow liquids to soak through). They are trapped between impervious rocks (which will not allow liquids to pass through).

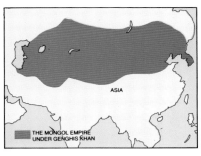

▼ *At its height, the Mongol empire under Genghis Khan stretched from China in the east right across Asia.*

ASIA

THE MONGOL EMPIRE
UNDER GENGHIS KHAN

Ptolemy of Alexandria was the most famous ancient geographer—he lived about AD 150. Ptolemy drew a map of the then-known world that is remarkably accurate, considering what was known about the Earth in those days. His eight-volume *Guide to Geography* consisted of a list of all known places, each with its latitude and longitude, a system Ptolemy devised.

Genetics

Each animal or plant passes on certain characteristics to its offspring. For example, we say that someone has 'his father's eyes' or 'her mother's hair'. The science of genetics explains why living things look and behave as they do.

Heredity works in an amazing way. Each individual produces sex cells. If a male and a female cell join, the female cell grows into a new individual. Inside every cell there are tiny chromosomes, largely made of a chemical called DNA. Different parts of each chromosome carry different coded messages. Each of these parts is called a *gene*. The genes carry all the information needed to make a new plant or animal look and behave as it does. They decide its sex and also every other characteristic it inherits from its parents.

Genghis Khan

Genghis Khan (1167–1227) was a Mongol chief who cruelly attacked many Asian peoples and won a mighty empire. His real name was Temujin ('iron-smith').

At 13 he took his dead father's place as chief of a small Mongol tribe of nomads. He soon won power over nearby tribes as well. In 1206 he became known as Genghis Khan, 'Very Mighty King'. Genghis Khan formed a huge army of tough, hard-riding nomads on the great grasslands of central Asia. Then he set off to conquer the lands around him. His troops pushed south-east to Beijing in China, and south into Tibet and what are now Pakistan and Afghanistan. In the south-west they invaded Persia (Iran) and southern Russia.

After he died, other Mongol rulers won more land and made the empire even larger.

Geography

Geography is the subject we study when we want to learn about the surface of the Earth. Geographers study everything on the Earth—the land, sea, air, plants, animals and people. They explain where different things are found, how they got there, and how they affect one another.

There are many different areas, or branches, of geography. For instance, physical geography describes things like mountains, valleys, lakes and rivers. Meteorology describes weather. Economic geography deals with farming, mining, manufacturing and trade. Human geography divides the peoples of the world into *cultures*.

MAPS AND CHARTS are the geographer's most useful tools.

For a long time, people have tried to work out the age of the Earth. In the 1600s, an Irish archbishop named Ussher decided from reading the Scriptures that the world was created in 4004 BC. It was not long, however, before geologists realized by examining the rocks that this date was very wrong. We now know that the Earth was formed about 4500 million years ago.

Geology

Geology is the study of the Earth itself. Geologists discover what things the Earth is made of, where they are found, and how they got there. Geologists study the chemicals in ROCKS and MINERALS. They also try to find out how rocks are formed, and how they are changed by movements beneath the surface of the Earth. VOLCANOES and EARTHQUAKES give us useful clues about movements deep down underground.

Geologists also study the history of the Earth. They have found rocks 3800 million years old, and FOSSILS showing that EVOLUTION began over 3400 million years ago.

Geologists help engineers to choose where to build a road or tunnel. They help miners to find coal, oil or gas beneath the ground. By studying rocks brought back by astronauts they were able to tell us what the Moon is made of.

◀ *Geologists study rocks, which tell them about the Earth's structure. There are three kinds of rock: igneous, formed when molten rock is pushed up from deep inside the Earth; sedimentary, which is hardened layers of sediment; and metamorphic, which is igneous or sedimentary rock that has been changed by heat and pressure inside the Earth. Of the rocks shown here, obsidian (1) and granite (2) are igneous rocks, marble (3) and slate (4) are metamorphic rocks, and coal (5), limestone (6) and sandstone (7) are sedimentary rocks. Conglomerate (8) is made up of stone stuck together in a sedimentary 'concrete'.*

▲ *George V, who reigned during World War I, changed the family name to Windsor, giving up all German titles.*

George (Kings)

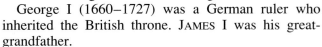

Six British kings were called George.

George I (1660–1727) was a German ruler who inherited the British throne. JAMES I was his great-grandfather.

George II (1683–1760) was the last British King to lead troops into battle. He reigned when Britain was winning Canada and India.

George III (1738–1820) ruled as the INDUSTRIAL REVOLUTION began. He lost what became the UNITED STATES. In old age he went mad.

George IV (1762–1830) was a spendthrift who loved to be in fashion. As Prince Regent he took his mad father's place from 1811.

George V (1865–1936) was a naval officer before he was king. He reigned during WORLD WAR I.

George VI (1895–1952) reigned during WORLD WAR II. He was the father of ELIZABETH II.

Germ *See* Bacteria; Virus

Germany

Before WORLD WAR II Germany was one great nation, but after the war the land was divided into two countries: West Germany and East Germany. East Germany was a Communist country, closely allied to the Soviet Union. The two Germanys remained separate until 1990, when they were finally reunited under a federal government.

Germany lies in the middle of Europe and has the largest population of any western European nation. Farms and cities stand on a low, flat plain to the north; the south is a region of wooded mountains. In the far south the tall peaks of the Alps rise thousands of metres above sea level. Germany's major rivers are the Rhine, the Elbe and the Oder. They flow north towards the North Sea and the Baltic Sea.

Before reunification, West Germany was the richest nation in Europe. Its mines and factories produced more coal, steel, cars and television sets than any other western European nation. East Germany, less than half the size of West Germany, had mines and factories, too, but much of its

GERMANY

NORTH SEA • DENMARK • BALTIC SEA
NETHERLANDS • POLAND
BELGIUM
LUX • GERMANY • CZECHOSLOVAKIA
FRANCE • AUSTRIA
SWITZERLAND

Government: Republic
Capital: Berlin
Area: 356,755 sq km
Population: 79,070,000
Language: German
Currency: Mark

industry was old-fashioned and unproductive. Now that the rich West and the poorer East are united there are problems to be faced, but the German people are working together to overcome them.

Geyser

Geysers are hot springs that now and then squirt out steam and scalding water. They work like this. Water fills a deep crack in the ground, often near VOLCANOES. Hot rock heats the water deep underground, but the weight of the water above it stops the hot water from boiling until it is much hotter still. Then it turns to steam that forces the water upward, emptying the crack. The next eruption happens when the crack is full again.

There are many geysers in some parts of Iceland, the United States and New Zealand. The tallest geyser ever known was the Waimangu geyser in New Zealand. In 1904 this squirted steam and water nearly 460 metres into the sky.

▲ A geyser seems to work in a similar way to a pressure cooker. The higher the pressure, the hotter the water has to be to boil. The super-heated steam and water is pushed out as a powerful jet. When enough water has seeped back and heated up, the process starts again.

Ghana

Ghana is a nation in West AFRICA. It is a bit smaller than the United Kingdom. The country is hot, with plenty of rain in the south where Ghana meets the Atlantic Ocean. The land here is low, with tropical forests and farms. The north is drier and grassy.

Most of Ghana's people are farmers. They grow cocoa and mine diamonds and gold. Lake Volta provides water power to make electricity. It is the biggest man-made lake in the world.

Gibraltar

This small British colony is a rocky peninsula that juts out from southern Spain. Most of Gibraltar is a mountain called the Rock. Britain won Gibraltar from Spain in 1704. Gibraltar guards the western end of the Mediterranean Sea.

Giraffe

Giraffes are the tallest animals. An adult male may stand three times taller than a tall man. They have long legs and a long neck. Yet this neck has only

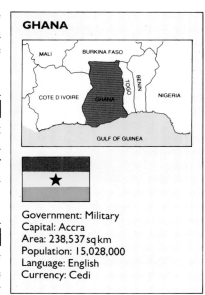

GHANA

Government: Military
Capital: Accra
Area: 238,537 sq km
Population: 15,028,000
Language: English
Currency: Cedi

▼ *Endocrine glands produce hormones that control such things as growth and reproduction.*

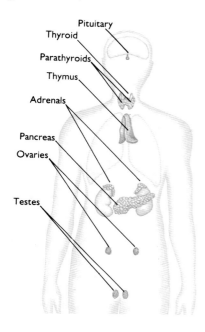

Pituitary
Thyroid
Parathyroids
Thymus
Adrenals
Pancreas
Ovaries
Testes

seven bones, the same as any other MAMMAL. Giraffes live in the hot grasslands of Africa and feed on leaves from shrubs and trees.

Gland

Glands are organs that produce special substances needed by the body. There are two kinds—*endocrine* and *exocrine* glands. Endocrine glands send their substances, called *hormones*, directly into the bloodstream. One main endocrine gland is the

THE ENDOCRINE GLANDS	
Pituitary gland	The small 'master gland' that produces at least nine hormones, including those that control growth and reproduction
Thyroid gland	Controls the rate at which food is converted into energy. The tiny **parathyroids** regulate the amount of calcium in your bones and blood
Ovaries	Produce oestrogen and progesterone, which control female characteristics. Also produce the *ova*, or egg cells
Testes	Produce testosterone, which controls the production of sperm cells and male characteristics
Pancreas	Produces insulin, which controls the level of glucose, a source of energy
Adrenal glands	Produce adrenaline, the 'emergency' hormone that speeds up heartbeat and breathing rate when danger threatens

thyroid. Its hormone controls the rate at which the body uses energy.

Exocrine glands release their substances through tubes, either into the intestines or onto the skin. Sweat, tears and saliva come from exocrine glands.

▲ *Some of the most magnificent decorative stained glass was made in Europe during the Middle Ages. You can see examples in many churches and cathedrals, especially in Britain, France, Germany and Italy.*

Glass

Glass is one of our most useful materials because it is easy to shape and cheap to make. It can be made as flat sheets, thick castings, or delicate wafers. It can be made into curved lenses for cameras, microscopes, and other optical instruments. It can be blown into bottles, or drawn out into tubes, wires and very thin fibres.

Glass is made from mixing and heating sand, limestone and soda ash. When these ingredients are melted in a furnace, they become glass. Special ingredients can be added to make glass that is heatproof, extra-tough or coloured. Although glass looks like a solid, it is really a 'supercooled' liquid. Glass is a good electrical insulator as it does not conduct current easily. It also resists common chemicals. Glass which contains a high amount of lead has been found to provide a good shield against radiation and is used in nuclear energy plants.

> The biggest gold nugget ever found weighed about 214 kg. It was discovered in New South Wales, Australia, in 1872. When refined, it yielded about 85 kg of pure gold.

Gold

This is a lovely yellow metal that never goes rusty. It is so soft that you can beat it into thin sheets, or pull it out into a wire.

People find thin veins of gold in cracks in certain rocks. It was formed long ago by hot gases and liquids rising from deep underground. If water washes out the gold, lumps called nuggets may collect in the beds of streams and rivers. Half of the world's gold is mined in one part of South Africa.

Because gold is beautiful and scarce, it is also very valuable. Most of the world's gold is kept in brick-shaped bars (called ingots) in banks. People make jewellery from gold mixed with other substances to make it harder. But gold is useful, too. Dentists sometimes put gold fillings in people's teeth.

> Gorillas in zoos are normally heavier than those in their natural surroundings. It is not unusual for male gorillas in captivity to weigh as much as 260 kg, four times the weight of a man. They can reach a height of 1.8 m. Females are shorter and weigh about half as much as the males.

▼ *Gorillas live in family groups. The leading male defends the group if danger threatens and takes charge of nest building.*

Gorilla

Gorillas are the largest of the APES. A big male may be as tall as a man. Gorillas live in family groups in the warm forests of central Africa. They eat fruit, roots, tree bark and leaves. Every night they make beds of twigs in the low branches of trees.

> A noun is a word that names. The name of everything is a noun, whether it is a person (Mary); a place (China); a thing (book); a quality (kindness) or anything else.

Grammar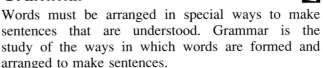

Words must be arranged in special ways to make sentences that are understood. Grammar is the study of the ways in which words are formed and arranged to make sentences.

Words are usually classified as *parts of speech*, according to what they do in a sentence. There are four main kinds of words: verbs (action words), nouns and pronouns (naming words), adjectives (describing words for nouns or pronouns) and adverbs (describing words for verbs and adjectives). Words can change from one part of speech to another. 'Clean' can be a verb or an adjective. 'Tin' can be a noun or an adjective.

If someone says 'I see the cat', he or she is speaking of something happening now. If they say 'I saw the cat', it happened in the past. The word 'see' changes to 'saw'. Changes like this are called *inflexions*.

The order of words in a sentence is very important. 'The dog bites the girl' means something quite different from 'The girl bites the dog', but exactly the same words are used. It is usual in English for the subject of a sentence – 'dog' in the first example, 'girl' in the second – to come before the verb – 'bites'. Exceptions to this rule are called *idioms* – 'There goes the boy.'

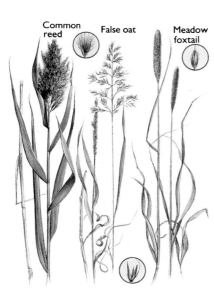

Common reed   False oat   Meadow foxtail

▲ *Three of the more than 10,000 species of grass. The flowers, and later the grains, are contained in scaly spikelets (inset).*

Grass

Grasses are flowering plants with long, thin, leaves growing from hollow stems. Bamboo is as tall as a tree but most grasses are short. Sheep and cattle eat grass. We eat the seeds of cultivated cereal grasses like wheat and rice.

Gravity

Gravity is the pull that tries to tug everything towards the middle of the EARTH. It is gravity that makes objects tend to fall, stops us flying off into space, and keeps the MOON circling the Earth. When we weigh something, we are measuring the force with which gravity pulls that object down. The more closely packed the substances in an object are, the heavier it seems.

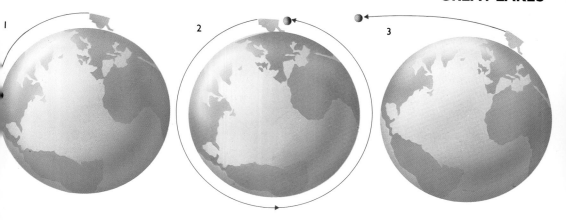

Not just the Earth, but all PLANETS and STARS exert a pulling force. Scientists call this gravitation. The larger and denser a star or a planet is and the nearer it is to other objects, the more strongly it pulls them towards it. The SUN is far from the planets, but it is so huge that its gravitation keeps the planets circling around it. The Moon is small and its gravitation is weak, only about one-sixth as strong as on Earth. An astronaut on the Moon weighs far less than he weighs on Earth, although his *mass* stays the same.

▲ *A small body, such as this cannonball, orbiting a large one balances its speed against the gravitational pull. The speed in this path is too low, and it falls to the ground (1). When it is fired at a greater speed it is attracted towards the surface at the same rate as the surface curves away, and will go into orbit (2). If its speed it too fast gravity cannot hold it, and it escapes into space (3).*

Great Britain *See* England etc.

Great Lakes

This is the world's largest group of freshwater lakes. They are larger than the whole of Great Britain. Lake Michigan lies in the UNITED STATES. Lakes Superior, Erie, Huron and Ontario are shared by

Eight states of the United States touch the Great Lakes. These eight states make more than half of the country's manufactured goods. Two-thirds of Canada's population and most of its factories lie on the Great Lakes or on the St Lawrence River. A ship can go from the Atlantic up the St Lawrence River and through the lakes to the western end of Lake Superior, halfway across the continent of North America.

◄ *Lakes Erie and Ontario are at two different levels, linked by the 50-metre Niagara Falls and the Niagara River. Ships avoid this route by using the Welland Canal.*

GREECE

Government: Presidential
   parliamentary republic
Capital: Athens
Area: 131,944 sq km
Population: 10,048,000
Language: Greek
Currency: Drachma

the United States and CANADA. The largest lake of all is Superior. The lakes were formed when a huge sheet of ice melted 18,000 years ago.

Rivers and canals connect the lakes to each other and to the Atlantic Ocean. Ships can reach the sea from lake ports that lie 1600 km inland. Lots of factories are built around the lakes. Most of the goods that the factories produce are taken to other parts of the country by boat.

Great Wall of China

More than 2000 years ago the first emperor of CHINA, Shih Huang Ti, built this wall to keep out China's enemies from the north. The Great Wall is the longest wall in the world. It stretches for 2400 km from western China to the Yellow Sea.

The wall is made from earth and stone. Watchtowers were built every 200 metres along it. Chinese sentries sent warning signals from the towers if anyone attacked the wall. The signal was smoke by day and a fire at night.

Greece

Greece is a country that lies in south-east EUROPE. Mountains cover most of the land, and peninsulas poke out into the sea like giant fingers. Greece includes the island of Crete and many smaller islands in the Aegean and Ionian seas. Greek summers are hot and dry. Winters are mild and wet.

About ten million people live in Greece. Many work in the capital city, Athens. Greek farmers produce crops of lemons, grapes, wheat and olives. Millions of tourists visit Greece every year.

▲ *The sun-baked buildings of this town on the Greek island of Santorini, also known as Thera, perch on the remains of an exploded volcano.*

Greece, Ancient

The first great people in Greece were the Minoans and the Mycenaeans. The Minoans lived in Crete. They had rich cities and farms and led a peaceful life. The Mycenaeans lived on the mainland of Greece. They were warriors and sailors. The heroes of Homer's poems were probably Mycenaean. Both these civilizations ended in about 1200 BC.

Around this time, new groups of people began to move into Greece. They came from the north, but spoke Greek. Instead of making Greece one kingdom, they built separate cities. They often fought wars with each other. Sometimes they joined together to fight enemies, such as the Persians. Two of the strongest cities were Athens and Sparta. In the 400s BC Athens was ruled by a *democracy*. It became very powerful.

The Greeks loved the theatre, art and poetry. They had many great thinkers, or *philosophers*, including Aristotle, Plato and Socrates. Greek cities had many graceful buildings. They were decorated with beautiful SCULPTURE. The Greeks also started the first OLYMPIC GAMES. In 339 BC Greece was conquered by Philip, the father of ALEXANDER THE GREAT.

▲ The marketplace, or agora, of a Greek town was an open area surrounded by temples and public buildings. Storage jars such as the one at the top of the picture were often decorated with figures or scenes.

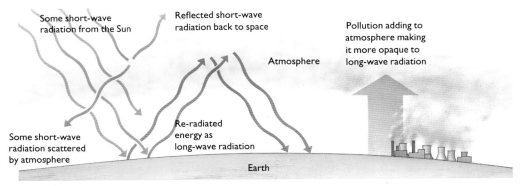

Some short-wave radiation from the Sun

Reflected short-wave radiation back to space

Atmosphere

Pollution adding to atmosphere making it more opaque to long-wave radiation

Some short-wave radiation scattered by atmosphere

Re-radiated energy as long-wave radiation

Earth

▲ *Pollution pumped into the atmosphere produces an increase in carbon dioxide, which makes it more opaque to radiation from the Earth's surface. This means that radiation is absorbed rather than passing through into space. Much of this absorbed radiation is reflected back to Earth. This may cause a gradual increase in temperature at the Earth's surface.*

Greenhouse effect

When FOSSIL FUELS, or other fuels such as wood or peat, which contain CARBON are burned, carbon dioxide is released into the atmostphere. This is made when the carbon in the fuel mixes with oxygen during burning. Vehicles, including those running on unleaded fuel, are major contributors to the increase in carbon dioxide in the atmosphere.

Carbon dioxide occurs naturally in the atmosphere and absorbs long-wave radiation which forms part of the ENERGY sent out by the SUN. This causes the atmosphere to warm up and we call this the greenhouse effect. Many scientists think that the greenhouse effect may change the CLIMATE over the next 100 years or so. One effect of so-called 'global warming' resulting from the greenhouse effect could be melting of the polar ice. This, in turn, could lead to a potentially disastrous rise in sea level. Large areas of coastal land, where many people live, could be flooded.

If carbon dioxide proves to be harmful as thought, we would need to reduce carbon dioxide levels. This would mean reducing the use of fuels which give off a lot of carbon dioxide when burned.

▲ *The Gatling gun was the first successful machine gun. Invented in 1861 and used during the American Civil War, it had up to 10 barrels rotated by a hand crank.*

Gun

Guns are weapons that fire bullets or other missiles from a tube open at one end.

Guns were probably invented in the 1200s. By the 1300s guns were firing missiles that could pierce armour and break down castle walls.

Early guns were large weapons, far too heavy for one man to carry. The first gun was a big bucket with a small hole in the bottom. Soldiers put gunpowder into the bucket. Then they piled stones on top. They lit the gunpowder through the hole. When the gunpowder exploded, the stones flew out. The large, long guns called cannons were first used about 1350. Cannons fired big metal cannonballs. In the 1800s came guns which fired pointed shells that exploded when they hit their target. A spiral groove cut in the gun barrel made the shells spin as they flew through the air. Soldiers could fire such shells farther and hit their targets more often than with cannonballs.

Troops first used small arms in the 1300s. Small arms are guns that one man can carry. Inventors developed short-barrelled pistols and revolvers for firing at nearby targets. They developed muskets, rifles and machine guns for long-distance shooting. In modern guns a hammer sets off an explosion that drives a shell or bullet from the barrel.

▲ This modern anti-aircraft gun can destroy attacking aircraft from the ground.

◀ This breech-loading cannon of the 1400s fired solid balls which could knock down the thickest castle walls.

Gutenberg, Johannes

Johannes Gutenberg (about 1395 to about 1468) was a German goldsmith sometimes called the father of PRINTING. In his day, people slowly copied books by hand or printed them from wooden blocks where each letter of every page had to be carved separately. About 1440, Gutenberg learned to make metal letters called type. He could pick them up and place them in rows to build pages of type. Each page was held together by a frame. Gutenberg fixed the frame to a press, and quickly pressed the inky surface of his type onto sheets of paper. Gutenberg's movable type helped him to make copies of a book faster and more cheaply than ever before.

Printing meant that new, cheaper books helped the spread of learning during THE RENAISSANCE.

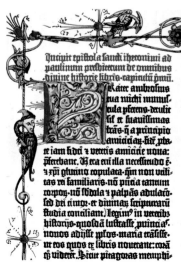

▲ One of Gutenberg's first books was a Bible printed in Latin in 1455.

Asymmetrical bars

Rings

Parallel bars

Beam

Pommel horse

Floor

Vault

▲ *Modern competitive gymnastics developed from German and Swedish systems of exercise.*

▼ *This spinning toy gyroscope is tilted, yet it balances on the tip of a pencil. It seems to defy gravity. As it slows down it will wobble and fall.*

Gymnastics

Gymnastics are exercises that help to make and keep the body fit. The OLYMPIC GAMES have separate gymnastic exercises for men and women. Women perform graceful steps, runs, jumps, turns and somersaults on a narrow wooden beam. They hang from a high bar and swing to and fro between it and a lower one. They leap over a vaulting horse. Women also perform floor exercises to music.

Men hang from a high bar and from rings, swinging up and down, to and fro, and over and over in giant circles. Using two parallel bars, they swing, vault, and do handstands.

Gyroscope

A gyroscope is a wheel that spins in a special frame. No matter how the frame tilts, the wheel's axle points in the same direction. Even GRAVITY and the Earth's MAGNETISM do not affect the axle.

On a ship or aircraft, a COMPASS made from a gyroscope always points north. Gyroscopes can also keep an aircraft on course without the pilot steering.

Hair

Hair grows like living threads from the skins of MAMMALS. It has the same ingredients that make nails, claws, hooves, feathers, and reptiles' scales. Hair helps to keep the body warm, and protects the skin. There are several kinds of hair. Cats have plenty of soft, thick fur. Porcupines are protected by sharp, stiff hairs called quills.

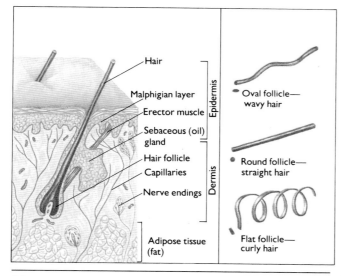

◄ Each hair root is enclosed in its own follicle, which has a blood supply, a tiny erector muscle and a gland. The type of hair you have depends partly on the shape of your hair follicles.

Halley, Edmond

Edmond Halley (1657–1742) was an English astronomer who is best known for his study of comets. In 1676, at the age of 20, he went to the island of St Helena to catalogue the stars of the Southern Hemisphere, something that had never been done before. He became interested in comets and noticed

Edmond Halley was a friend of Isaac Newton, the great scientist. He encouraged Newton and helped him with money to publish his most famous work, *Mathematical Principles of Natural Philosophy*.

◄ When Halley's Comet passed near the Earth in 1985, its nucleus was discovered to be a peanut-shaped mixture of rock, dust and ice about 2 km long. Each return to the Sun leaves the nucleus with a smaller store of ice and dust, and eventually the comet will 'die'.

165

▲ *Handel was born in Germany but made England his home. He became a British subject in 1726.*

that the path followed by a comet he had seen in 1682 was very much like those reported in 1607 and 1531. He decided that these sightings must be of the same comet and predicted that it would return in 1758. On Christmas Day, 1758, it did, and Halley's Comet reappears regularly every 76 years.

Handel, George Frideric

George Frideric Handel (1685–1759) was a German-born British composer, famous for the oratorio *Messiah* and the orchestral *Fireworks Music* and *Water Music*. He wrote about 21 oratorios and a number of operas.

Hannibal

Hannibal (247–183 BC) was a Carthaginian general who invaded Italy. In 218 BC he left Spain and marched an army over the Alps into Italy. The army included many elephants, brought along to carry equipment. Hannibal won a number of battles. But though he fought the Romans for 15 years he never managed to conquer them. In the end he killed himself.

Harp

The harp is the oldest of all stringed instruments. The early harp was little more than a bow with strings of different lengths stretched across it. Harps have been played in Wales and Ireland for many centuries. The modern harp has a wooden frame with strings attached between the hollow sounding board and the top of the instrument. There are seven foot pedals that can change the pitch of the strings. The harpist plucks the strings with his or her fingers and thumbs.

Flat   Natural   Sharp
Pins
Discs
String
Pedals

▲ *To change the pitch of a string on the harp, pedals turn small discs with pins that grip the string, thus shortening or lengthening them to produce flat or sharp notes.*

Harvey, William

William Harvey (1578–1657) was an English doctor who showed that BLOOD flows around the body in an endless stream. Harvey proved that a beating heart squeezes blood through arteries and flaps in the heart, and that blood returns to the heart through veins. He worked out that the amount of blood pumped by a heart in an hour weighs three times more than a man.

Hastings, Battle of

In 1066 this battle made Norman invaders the masters of England.

WILLIAM THE CONQUEROR sailed with 7000 Norman troops and some war horses from France to England in about 450 open boats. Meanwhile, the English (ANGLO-SAXONS) under King Harold were defeating Norse invaders in northern England.

Harold quickly marched south. He fought William at Senlac near Hastings. The Anglo-Saxons defended a hilltop with axes, spears, swords and shields. The Normans attacked with arrows, lances, spiked clubs and swords. The battle lasted all day. Then the Normans pretended to run away. When some Anglo-Saxons followed, Norman cavalry cut them down. Then the Normans showered arrows on the rest and attacked once more. By evening, Harold was dead and his army was beaten.

By 1071, William the Conqueror had subdued all of England. Since then, no foreign army has landed and won a battle on English soil.

Much of what we know about William the Conqueror's invasion and the Battle of Hastings comes from the Bayeux Tapestry. It is this tapestry that seems to show Harold being killed in the battle when an arrow pierces his eye. Many historians now think that the soldier with the arrow in his eye is not Harold. A French account of the battle written in 1068 says that Harold was attacked by four French knights. One of them pierced Harold with his lance, while another 'hacked off his leg and hurled it far away'!

Heart

The heart is a muscle in the body. It pumps BLOOD around the body through VEINS and arteries. In an adult person, the heart goes on working at between 70 and 80 beats a minute until death. It was the English doctor William HARVEY (1578–1657) who discovered how the heart works.

▼ The English, armed with spears, slings and battle axes, fought fiercely against the heavily armoured Norman cavalry, but the Normans eventually wore them down.

► *Your heart is about the same size as your clenched fist and is made of strong cardiac muscle. It constantly pumps blood around your body, so that each cell gets the food and oxygen it needs. The areas shown in red in the illustration indicate where oxygen-rich blood travels. The areas shown in blue show where blood low in oxygen travels back to the lungs. The* atria *(plural of* atrium) *collect the blood flowing into the heart. The* ventricles *are strong muscles that pump blood into the arteries.*

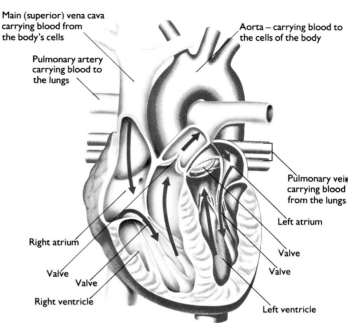

Main (superior) vena cava carrying blood from the body's cells

Pulmonary artery carrying blood to the lungs

Aorta – carrying blood to the cells of the body

Pulmonary vein carrying blood from the lungs

Left atrium

Valve

Valve

Left ventricle

Right atrium

Valve

Valve

Right ventricle

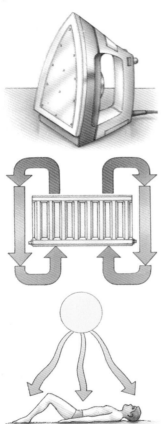

▲ *Heat travels in three ways – by conduction, convection and radiation. A conductor, such as a metal iron, allows heat to pass through it. When heat is carried from a radiator by convection, molecules in the air move, taking the heat with them. Heat from the Sun travels by radiation in the form of electromagnetic waves.*

The blood carries *oxygen* from the *lungs* and energy from the food we eat. Arteries carry this rich red blood to feed the body. Veins carry away waste products and return the dark 'tired' blood to the heart to be 'recharged' with oxygen from the lungs.

When the heart stops beating, the body is starved of oxygen and quickly dies. But doctors can sometimes massage a stopped heart back to life. People with diseased hearts can be given 'spare parts' to repair them and even a new heart, transplanted from someone who has just died.

Heat

Heat is a form of ENERGY. We can feel it but we cannot see it. We feel heat from the SUN, or when we sit in front of a fire. When something burns, heat is produced. The Sun gives out enormous amounts of heat, which is produced by atoms joining together, or 'fusing', inside the Sun. This same kind of energy can be released by a hydrogen bomb on Earth. It is because we get just the right amount of heat from the Sun that our Earth and ourselves are what they are. A few degrees less heat from the Sun and our world would be a lifeless waste much like the cold, dark side of the moon. A few degrees more heat and life could not exist.

◄ *The energy in heat can be used in many different ways. This picture shows a solar-powered car that converts the Sun's energy and uses it to drive along.*

Most of the heat we use comes from burning fuels. But heat can also be made by FRICTION, or rubbing. Heat is also produced when electricity travels through a coil of wire. This is what makes the coils inside a toaster glow red.

We can measure how hot a thing is by finding its temperature. This is done with a THERMOMETER. When a substance gets hot, the molecules, or tiny particles, of which it is made move around more quickly. Often the substance expands as this happens.

We need fuel to keep our body warm. This fuel is the food we eat. The human body contains a surprising amount of heat. It gives out about 100 calories of heat an hour. This is about the same as a 120-watt electric bulb. You can see, therefore, why it can become quite hot if a lot of people are gathered in a room!

Helicopter

The helicopter is an unusual and useful aircraft. It was invented in the 1930s and today is used for all kinds of jobs, especially sea- and mountain-rescue.

▼ *The UH-1* Iroquois *was used by the United States army in the Vietnam war. A similar type is still being made today. The Ka-26* Kamov Hoodlum *is mainly used for farming purposes, although it is also used as an air ambulance. It has two sets of main rotors rotating in opposite directions.*

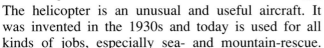

Ka-26 Hoodlum

UH-1 Iroquois

▲ *Henry VIII came to the throne in 1509, when he was only 17 years old. When young he was handsome, slim and athletic.*

▼ *Henry VI was a quiet and religious king, very different from his strong-willed wife, Margaret of Anjou. The Wars of the Roses were fought during his reign.*

This is because helicopters can take off and land vertically and can therefore work in areas too small for ordinary aircraft. Helicopters can fly in any direction and hover in mid-air. Instead of fixed wings they have a moving wing called a rotor which acts as a wing and a propeller. The pilot controls the craft by changing the angle, or 'pitch', at which the blades of the rotor go through the air. A smaller rotor on the tail keeps the helicopter from spinning around. Helicopters are also used for carrying passengers over short distances and for transporting troops to remote areas.

Henry (kings)

Eight English kings have been named Henry. Henry I (1069–1135) was the youngest son of WILLIAM THE CONQUEROR. Henry II (1133–1189) was the first of the Plantagenet line of kings. He quarrelled with Thomas à Becket, Archbishop of Canterbury, who was then murdered by the king's knights. His grandson, Henry III (1207–1272), was a weak king who was ruled by the powerful barons.

During the Wars of the Roses, the families of York and Lancaster fought for the English throne. Three Lancastrian kings were called Henry: Henry IV, or Henry Bolingbroke (1367–1413), Henry V

(1387–1422), and Henry VI (1421–1471). Henry V was a brilliant soldier. He is famous for leading his army to victory against the French at the battle of Agincourt.

The first Tudor king was Henry VII (1457–1509), who restored peace. His son, Henry VIII (1491–1547), was clever and popular, but also ruthless. He was married six times and broke away from the Roman Catholic Church to divorce his first wife, Catherine of Aragon. Three of his children reigned after him: EDWARD VI, Mary I and ELIZABETH I.

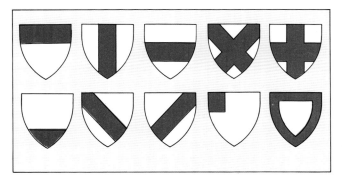

◄ These simple designs found on old heraldic shields are called charges or ordinaries. The designs of many modern flags are based on these shapes.

Heraldry

In the MIDDLE AGES, a knight in full ARMOUR was hard to recognize, for his face was hidden by his helmet. So knights began to use special designs worn on their surcoats and shields. These designs became special family emblems which no-one else could wear. They were called coats-of-arms.

Heralds were officials who kept records of coats-of-arms and awarded new ones. The College of Heralds in London still does this. There are special names for the colours and patterns used in heraldry.

Hibernation

When an animal hibernates, it goes to sleep for the winter. It does this because in winter food is scarce. Going to sleep during the cold weather saves certain animals from starving to death.

Before hibernating, animals eat as much food as they can find. The dormouse, for example, stuffs itself until it is fat and round. As autumn approaches, it makes a snug nest, curls into a ball, and falls into a sound sleep. In fact, its heart beats so

A hibernating marmot may slow down its breathing from 16 to 2 breaths a minute, and its heartbeats from 88 to 15 per minute. In a test, the temperature of a hibernating ground squirrel fell to almost freezing. The creature later woke up unharmed.

▼ *Hibernating animals have to find a warm, safe place to spend the winter. They need to reserve their energy until the weather warms up.*

Newt

Adders

Natterjack toad

Green toad

Common toad

Tortoise

Woodchuck

slowly, the dormouse looks dead. Its body uses hardly any energy while in hibernation, in order to make its store of fat last as long as possible. In spring, a thin and hungry dormouse wakes up and comes out of its nest to look for food.

In cold countries many animals hibernate. Not all sleep right through the winter. Squirrels wake up on mild days and eat food they had hidden away in the summer. But all hibernating animals find a warm, dry place to sleep, safe from hungry enemies.

Hieroglyphics

Hieroglyphics were an ancient form of writing. Our alphabet has 26 letters. However 5000 years ago the ancient Egyptians used picture-signs instead of letters. Later these signs became hieroglyphics—marks which stood for things, people, and ideas. Egyptian hieroglyphics were sometimes written from right to left, and sometimes from left to right.

Hieroglyphic writing was very difficult and only a few people could do it. When the Egyptian empire died out, the secret of reading it was lost. No one could understand the hieroglyphics carved on stones and written on papyrus scrolls. Then, in 1799, a Frenchman found the Rosetta Stone, which is now in the British Museum in London. On it was

▲ *Many examples of hieroglyphic writing carved in stone have survived over thousands of years, and can now be understood.*

something written in two known languages, and also in hieroglyphics. By comparing the known languages with the hieroglyphics, experts were at last able to understand and translate the signs.

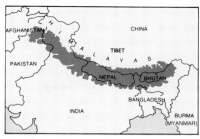

◀ *The Himalayas form a great natural barrier between India and the large plateau of Tibet. The passes that run through the Himalayas are among the highest in the world. Few are lower than 5000 metres.*

Himalayas

The highest range of mountains in the world is the mighty Himalayas. The name means 'land of snow'. The Himalayas form a great barrier range across Asia, dividing India in the south from TIBET (part of China) in the north. Many of Asia's greatest rivers rise among the Himalayas.

Until aircraft were invented few outsiders had ever been into the Himalayas. There are no roads or railways. The only way to travel is on foot, over steep mountain tracks. Horses, yaks, goats, and even sheep are used to carry heavy loads.

The highest mountain in the world lies in the Himalayas. This is EVEREST, 8,848 metres high.

▼ *Hindus believe in many gods, all with different characters. Four-armed Kali, often shown dancing, is the wife of Shiva. Ganesh, Shiva's son, has the head of an elephant and is believed to bring success if prayed to.*

Kali

Shiva

Ganesh

Hinduism

Hinduism is one of the world's great religions. Most Hindus live in Asia, and particularly in INDIA. Their religion has grown over a period of 4000 years.

Hindus believe that God is present in all things. Only priests (Brahmins) can worship the supreme God. Ordinary people worship other gods, such as Vishnu, God of Life. The most important holy books of the Hindus are the *Vedas*. Hindus believe that certain animals, such as the cow, are sacred.

▲ Hippopotamuses have eyes on the tops of their heads so they can stand under water and peep out without being seen. They can stay submerged for almost ten minutes without coming up for breath.

Hippopotamus

The name hippopotamus means 'river horse', but in fact the hippo is related to the pig, not the horse. It is a huge, heavy animal and lives in Africa. Of all land animals, only the elephant is bigger.

Hippopotamuses live near rivers and lakes. They spend most of their time in the water and are good swimmers. In spite of their fearsome-looking jaws, hippopotamuses eat only plant food. They browse on water weeds and grasses, and at night often come ashore to feed.

These animals are not usually dangerous if left alone, but they can inflict serious wounds with slashes from the tusks in their lower jaws.

▼ The history of ancient civilizations has to be pieced together from clues that have come to us over the years. This bronze head is of a king who lived almost 4500 years ago.

History

History is the story of the past. The people who write down the history are called historians. They usually write about important events such as wars, revolutions and governments, because these affect nations. However, historians are also interested in the lives of ordinary people and in what they did and thought about.

Nowadays, we think of history as being written down in history books. But in earlier times, before books and printing, history was passed on by word of mouth. People told stories about their kings, their wars, their adventures, and also about their own families. It was in this way that the stories of ancient Greece were collected by the poet Homer to form the *Iliad* and the *Odyssey*. Some early stories such as these were made up in verse, and sung to music. This made it easier for people to remember the stories correctly.

In ancient Egypt, scholars recorded the reigns of the PHARAOHS, and listed the victories they won in battle. Often these accounts were written in HIERO-GLYPHICS on stone tablets. The Chinese, Greeks and Romans were also very interested in history. It was they who first took the writing of history seriously, and they wrote of how their civilizations rose to power. During the MIDDLE AGES in Europe, many people could not read or write, and printing had not been invented. It was the priests and monks who preserved ancient books and kept the official records and documents. These records include the *Domesday Book* (1086), which tells us much of what we know about Norman England. History became an important branch of study in the 1700s and 1800s. Famous historians were Edward Gibbon (1737–1794) and Lord Macaulay (1800–1859).

Historians get their information from hidden remains such as things found buried in old graves, as well as from old books. The study of hidden remains is called ARCHAEOLOGY. But history is not just concerned with the long distant past. After all, history is *our* story. What is news today will be history tomorrow. So modern historians are also interested in recording the present. They talk to old people about the things they remember, and they keep records on film and tape. For a table of events in history, see pages 176–177.

▲ *We know a great deal about the history of Europe, even in the Middle Ages. This type of ship, called a caravel, was used in the 15th century for voyages of discovery.*

Hitler, Adolf

Adolf Hitler (1889–1945) was the 'Fuhrer', or leader, of GERMANY during WORLD WAR II. An ex-soldier, born in Austria, he became leader of the Nazi Party which took over Germany in 1933.

Germany was still weak after its defeat in WORLD WAR I. The Nazis promised to avenge this defeat and create a new German empire. In 1939 Hitler led Germany into World War II and conquered most of Europe. Millions of people were killed in Nazi death camps. But by 1945 Germany had lost the war. Hitler killed himself in the ruins of Berlin to avoid capture. After his death, many surviving Nazis were put on trial as war criminals.

It is sometimes said, 'Those who fail to learn the lessons of history are destined to repeat them.' One of the best-known and most incorrect statements about history came from the famous American car manufacturer Henry Ford. He said: 'History is bunk'. But Ford was in the habit of doing silly things. He sent a peace ship to Europe in 1915, hoping to persuade Germany and the Allies to stop World War I! He also for years financed anti-Jewish propaganda.

HISTORY

AFRICA

BC

3,000,000	Australopithecus is early ancestor of modern man
30,000	Human hunters in Africa
5000	Stone Age craftworkers in Nile Valley
4500	Metal-working in Egypt
2780	First pyramid in Egypt
1400	Golden age of Egypt's power
500	Kushite kingdom in Africa
146	Romans destroy power of Carthage, a great North African city-state

AD

500	Kingdom of Ghana
850	Building of citadel at Great Zimbabwe
980	Arabs begin to settle on east coast
1000	Muslims control all of North Africa; Ife bronze art at its peak in West Africa
1307	Empire of Mali in central Africa reaches its height under Munsa Mali
1498	Vasco da Gama begins Portuguese trade along east coast
1500	Empire of Gao
1591	Fall of Songhai empire (which had succeeded Mali)
1652	Europeans led by Jan van Riebeeck settle at Cape of Good Hope
1713	Height of slave trade between West Africa and the New World
1818	Chaka founds the Zulu empire
1821	Liberia (West Africa) founded as free state for ex-slaves from USA
1835–37	Great Trek by Boers to found Transvaal
1869	Opening of Suez Canal creates shorter sea route from Europe to Asia.
1884	Berlin Conference allows European powers to divide Africa between them
1899–1902	Boer War; Britain defeats Boers
1936	Italy conquers Ethiopia, Africa's oldest independent African nation
1949	South Africa adopts policy of apartheid (separation of the races)
1956	President Nasser of Egypt nationalizes the Suez Canal; this leads to a brief war with Britain and France
1960	Civil war in Congo
1960s	Many former European-ruled states become self-governing
1963	Formation of Organization of African Unity
1967	Civil war in Nigeria after Biafra breaks away
1974	Portugal gives up its last African colonies
1980	Zimbabwe (Rhodesia) becomes independent
1980s	Apartheid eases in South Africa; civil war in parts of the continent; drought and famine are serious problems

ASIA

BC

9000	Beginnings of agriculture in 'fertile crescent'
7000	Jericho is world's first town
3500	Copper working in Thailand
3100	Earliest known writing, cuneiform script from Sumer
2300	Mohenjo-daro civilization in the Indus River valley (modern Pakistan)
2100	Abraham migrates from Ur
1500	Chinese master the skills of bronze-working
1230	Peak of Assyrian power
565	Birth of Buddha
551	Birth of Confucius
221–210	Reign of Chinese emperor Shihuangdi, builder of the Great Wall: China is the world's largest empire

AD

4?	Birth of Jesus Christ
570	Birth of Muhammad
1000	Perfection of gunpowder in China
1100	Temples of Angkor Wat in Cambodia
1190	Genghis Khan begins to conquer an empire for the Mongols
1275	Marco Polo at the court of Kublai Khan
1405–33	Chinese fleets led by Cheng Ho make voyages of exploration in Pacific and Indian oceans
1498	Vasco da Gama sails from Portugal to India
1520s	Mogul empire in India
1600	Shogun Ieyasu becomes ruler of Japan
1760	French and British fight for power in India
1854	Japan forced to sign trade treaty with USA
1857	Indian Mutiny
1868	Meiji government begins to 'westernize' Japan
1900	Boxer Rebellion in China
1905	Japan defeats Russians in war
1912	Sun Yat-sen leads new Chinese republic
1930s	Rise of Japan as a military power
1939–45	World War II: first atomic bombs dropped on Japan
1947	India gains independence from British rule
1948	Creation of the state of Israel
1949	Mao Tse-tung's Communists win civil war in China
1954	French pull out of Indochina; beginnings of Vietnam War
1976	Vietnam War ends with victory for North Vietnam
1979	Shah of Iran overthrown; Iran becomes an Islamic republic
1980s	Civil war in Lebanon; war between Iran and Iraq (ends 1988); China becomes more open but clamps down on democratic students

EUROPE

BC

6000	Planting crops and animal husbandry reaches Europe from Asia
2000	Minoan bronze age civilization of Crete
1193	City of Troy destroyed by Greeks
509	Foundation of the Roman republic
331	Alexander the Great leads Greeks to victory over the Persian Empire

AD

43	Romans invade Britain
313	Christian religion tolerated throughout Roman Empire
330	Roman emperor Constantine founds Constantinople
476	Roman Empire collapses
732	Charles Martel leads Franks to victory over Moors
800	Charlemagne is crowned first Holy Roman Emperor
871	Alfred becomes king of Wessex in England
1066	William of Normandy conquers England
1096	First of six crusades against the Islamic rulers of the Holy Land (Palestine)
1215	English barons draw up Magna Carta
1300s	The Renaissance in arts and sciences begins
1348	The Black Death kills millions
1453	Constantinople is captured by the Turks
1517	Martin Luther's protest begins the Reformation
1522	First circumnavigation of the globe by Europeans (Magellan's fleet)
1588	English defeat the Spanish Armada
1642	Civil War in England
1700s	Revolutions in agriculture and industry; beginning of the Age of Machines
1789	French Revolution
1854–56	Crimean War
1870–71	Prussia defeats France in Franco-Prussian War
1914–18	World War I: Germany and its allies are defeated by Britain, France, USA, Russia and others. Over 10 million soldiers killed
1917	Communist revolution in Russia
1933	Hitler becomes ruler of Germany
1936–39	Civil war in Spain
1939–45	World War II: Allies defeat Germany and Italy in Europe
1957	Treaty of Rome establishes European Community (EC)
1980s	EC moves towards free market (1992); Gorbachev government brings new ideas in USSR; Eastern bloc countries move towards democracy
1991	Serbs and Croats fight in Yugoslavia; Soviet Union breaks up into independent states

AMERICAS AND AUSTRALASIA

BC

100,000?	Ancestors of Aborigines reach Australia
40,000	Ancestors of North American Indians migrate across 'land bridge' from Asia
20,000	Indians complete settlement of South America
8400	First domesticated dog (Idaho)
3372	Earliest date in Mayan calendar (Mexico)

AD

1100	Maoris sail to New Zealand from Pacific islands
1400	Inca empire in Peru
1492	Columbus 'discovers' America
1500	Cabral claims Brazil for Portugal
1518	Cortés begins conquest of Mexico, defeating Aztecs
1533	Pizarro conquers Inca empire for Spain
1584	Raleigh founds English colony in Virginia
1620	Voyage of the Pilgrim ship *Mayflower*
1626	Dutch found New Amsterdam (New York)
1642	Abel Tasman discovers Tasmania; French found Montreal in Canada
1763	Britain gains control of Canada, after defeating France
1770	Cook explores coast of Australia and New Zealand
1776	American Declaration of Independence
1783	End of American War of Independence
1788	First British settlement in Australia
1789	George Washington first US President
1824	South American republics break free from Spanish rule
1840	New Zealand becomes British colony
1861–65	American Civil War; Northern states defeat the South
1867	Canada becomes self-governing dominion
1901	Australia and New Zealand are independent
1917	USA enters World War I
1930s	Depression and unemployment in USA
1941	Japanese attack on Pearl Harbor brings USA into World War II
1959	Fidel Castro leads Communist revolution in Cuba
1963	President John F Kennedy of the USA is assassinated
1965	US troops fighting in Vietnam
1969	US lands astronauts on the Moon
1975	Last US forces leave Vietnam
1982	Britain sends forces to regain Falklands from Argentine occupation
1980s	USA is the strongest world power; civil war in Nicaragua (Central America); Australia and New Zealand make new trade partners in Asia

HONG KONG

CHINA

TAIWAN

HONG KONG

SOUTH CHINA SEA

PHILIPPINES

Government: Crown colony
Capital: Victoria
Area: Island 75 sq km
       New Territories etc. 971 sq km
Population: 5,801,000
Highest point: Tai Mo Shan 957 m
Climate: Tropical monsoon
Rainfall average: 2160 mm

Hong Kong

Hong Kong is a tiny British colony off the coast of China. Part of it is a small island, and the rest is a narrow strip of land called the New Territories, which is actually part of mainland China. Hong Kong has been governed by Britain since 1842. It is due to be handed over to Chinese rule in 1997.

Hong Kong has a fine harbour surrounded by mountains. The capital is Victoria, and another busy city is Kowloon. Hong Kong is a fascinating mixture of East and West. The people live by trade, fishing, and farming. Tall apartment buildings have been built to house them, but there is still little room for the millions of people.

Hormone

Hormones are chemical messengers found in all animals and plants. In many animals, hormones are produced in organs called GLANDS. Glands are found in several parts of the body. From these glands, the different hormones are carried in the blood to do certain jobs in other parts of the body.

The pituitary gland in the centre of the head produces several hormones. These 'master' hormones control the hormone secretion of several other glands. The thyroid gland in the neck, for example, is stimulated by the pituitary gland to make a hormone that controls how fast food is used up by the body. Too little of this hormone makes people overweight. The hormone adrenaline is controlled by nerve messages. When it flows, the heart beats faster, the blood pressure rises and the body prepares itself for strenuous physical exertion.

Many hormones can now be made in the laboratory and used to help people suffering from diseases caused by lack of certain hormones. Insulin is a hormone used in the treatment of diabetes, a disease in which too much sugar stays in the blood.

▼ *Hormones can affect how much – or how little – people grow. Jockey Willie Carson, shown here with his trainer, is exceptionally small.*

Horse

The horse was one of the first wild animals to be tamed. Today there are very few wild horses left. Many so-called 'wild' horses are actually descended from domestic horses which have run wild.

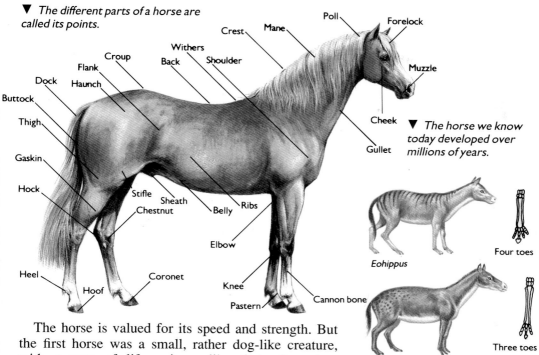

▼ The different parts of a horse are called its points.

Poll
Forelock
Crest
Mane
Withers
Croup
Back
Shoulder
Flank
Muzzle
Dock
Haunch
Cheek
Buttock
Thigh
Gullet
Gaskin
Hock
Stifle
Sheath
Chestnut
Ribs
Belly
Elbow
Heel
Coronet
Knee
Hoof
Cannon bone
Pastern

▼ The horse we know today developed over millions of years.

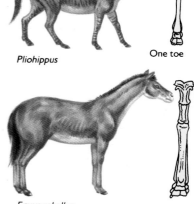

Eohippus
Four toes

Mesohippus
Three toes

Merychippus
Large middle toe

Pliohippus
One toe

Equus caballus

The horse is valued for its speed and strength. But the first horse was a small, rather dog-like creature, with a way of life quite unlike that of modern horses. Called *Eohippus*, or 'dawn horse', it lived millions of years ago. It had four toes on its front feet and three toes on its back feet, and it probably hid from its enemies in the undergrowth.

Later, horses came out to live on the wide grassy plains. There was no undergrowth to hide in, so they escaped from enemies by running away. Gradually, their legs grew longer, and they lost all their toes except one. Finally, after millions of years of EVOLUTION, the modern horse appeared. It, too, has only one toe, and actually runs on tiptoe. Its toe has become a tough nail or hoof.

Early man hunted wild horses for food. No one knows when horses were first tamed, but horses were being used for riding and for pulling chariots and carts in Egypt more than 5000 years ago. Until the 1800s the horse was the fastest form of transport and our strongest helpmate. Horses did all kinds of jobs, in towns and in the country, until the railway, the motor car and new, modern farm machinery replaced them. Though horses do not work for us as they once did, they are still very much a part of the world of horse races and shows, as well as valued pets which are great fun to ride.

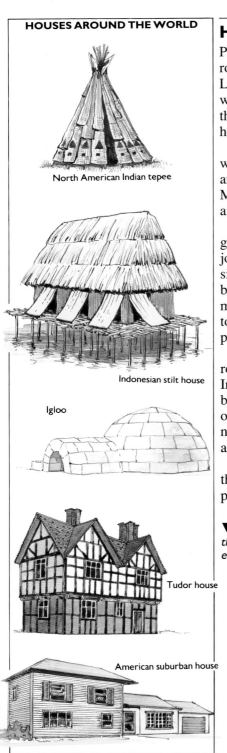

HOUSES AROUND THE WORLD

North American Indian tepee

Indonesian stilt house

Igloo

Tudor house

American suburban house

Houses

Prehistoric people lived in caves. The first houses were rough shelters, made of mud, branches and leaves. Later, people learned how to make bricks by drying wet clay in the sun. Brick, wood and stone were for thousands of years the materials from which almost all houses were built.

The modern house is built to keep out the cold and wet, and to keep in warmth. Double glazing of windows and insulation in the roof and walls help to do this. Many homes have central heating and, in hot climates, air conditioning.

In most countries a house is lived in by either a single family or a family group. A number of houses joined together form a terrrace. Two houses joined side-by-side are 'semi-detached'. A number of homes built on top of another form a block of flats or apartments. In many big cities, there are not enough houses to provide homes for everybody. In some countries, poor people have to live in slums and shanty towns.

People wanting to buy a house usually need to borrow most of the money, because houses are expensive. In Britain, house buyers can borrow money from a bank or from a building society. This is called taking out a mortgage. They have to repay the loan over a number of years. They will probably visit an estate agent to see what houses are for sale.

Not all houses are owned by the people who live in them. Many people live in rented flats or houses. They pay rent to the owner.

▼ *The Xanadu experimental house, in Florida, USA, could be the shape of things to come. It is built with concern for the environment and for maximum energy efficiency.*

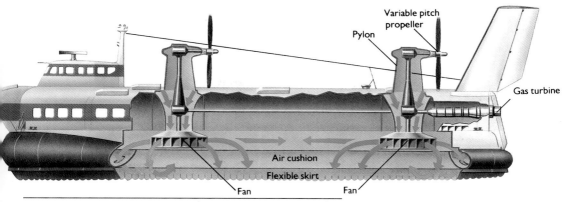

Variable pitch propeller
Pylon
Gas turbine
Air cushion
Flexible skirt
Fan
Fan

Hovercraft

Depending on how you look at one, a hovercraft is either a plane with no wings or a ship that rides out of the water.

Hovercraft ride on a cushion of air, blown downwards by fans, and held in by a skirt or side wall around the hovercraft. They work best over flat surfaces like water but can also cross beaches and flat land. The only danger is that rough ground may snag their bottoms.

Hovercraft are much faster than ships. Since they do not have to push against any water but simply skim smoothly through the air, they can easily manage speeds of 120 km/h. Their advantage over planes is the size of the load they can carry. A large craft can load dozens of cars and up to 400 passengers. And of course they do not need harbours or runways to land. They simply climb up the beach to settle on a simple concrete landing pad.

The hovercraft was invented in 1955 by the British engineer Christopher Cockerell. The first working model appeared four years later and had soon crossed the Channel from England to France. Today, fleets of hovercraft shuttle back and forth every day carrying hundreds of cars and passengers.

▲ *The cushion of air produced by powerful fans inside a hovercraft makes for a fast ride across water or land.*

▼ *If the history of the Earth to the present day were condensed into twelve hours, the earliest life in the sea would have begun just before nine o'clock. Life moved onto land at a quarter to eleven, and mammals appeared at twenty to twelve. Humans would have arrived just before the stroke of twelve.*

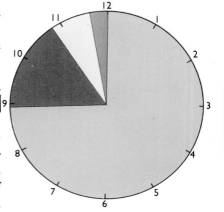

Human Beings

Human beings are mammals, but rather clever ones. They are very like their relatives, the apes. They have the same kind of bones, muscles and other parts inside their bodies. But the main difference between people and any other animal is the size of their brain. The human brain is enormous, compared

HUMAN BEINGS

to body size. People use their brain to think things out, and when they have found an answer to a problem, they can talk about it with other people. Language is a special human ability. This large brain is why the human being is so successful.

Scientists now agree that our ancestors were ape-like creatures who slowly, over millions of years, evolved (changed) into people. People something like ourselves have probably lived on Earth for about 500,000 years.

Today, all people belong to the same *species* (kind of creature). This creature is classified as *Homo sapiens* ('thinking man'). All people, in every country on Earth, are *Homo sapiens*.

Scientists divide human beings into three main *races*. The *Caucasoid* people are fair-skinned like the people of Europe and America or dark-skinned like the people of India, and others. The *Mongoloid* group takes in most of the yellow-skinned peoples of Asia, plus the American Indians. The *Negroid* group consists of the dark-skinned peoples of Africa and other regions.

▼ *Our ancestors of two million years ago were very different from us, but the world, too, was very different. A series of ice ages meant that huge glaciers covered much of the northern half of the Earth. One of the most important events in the development of people took place about one million years ago, when our ancestors started to make tools. By about 10,000 BC people were beginning to understand how to grow and harvest crops. The brown areas show where humans lived at different times.*

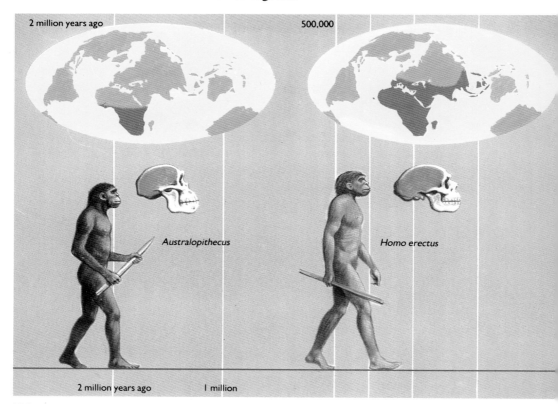

2 million years ago   500,000

Australopithecus   Homo erectus

2 million years ago   1 million

Human Body

Your body is a wonderful machine with many parts. Each part has a special job and all the parts work together to keep you alive and healthy. Like all machines, your body needs fuel – food. The oxygen you breathe in from the air helps turn the food you eat into energy. This energy allows you to play, work, think and grow.

Your body is made up of millions of tiny cells – many different kinds of cells. A group of cells that work together is called a *tissue*. For example, cells that allow you to lift things are called muscle tissue. Tissues that work together make up an *organ*. The heart is an organ that pumps blood. Other organs are the LIVER, the LUNGS, the STOMACH and the SKIN.

Organs that work together are called *systems*. You have a *digestive system* (mouth, stomach and intestines), a *circulatory system* (heart, arteries and veins), and a *nervous system* (brain and nerves). The study of the body is called *anatomy*.

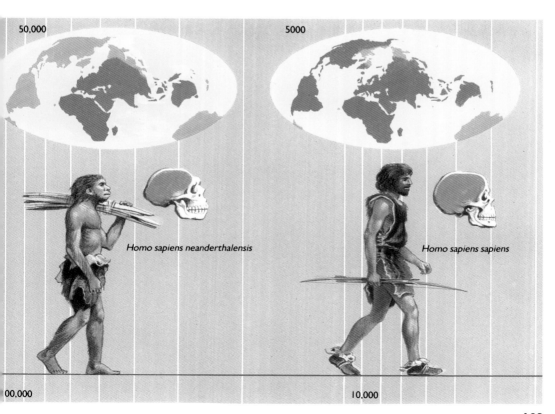

50,000

5000

Homo sapiens neanderthalensis

Homo sapiens sapiens

00,000

10,000

Humidity

All air has some water in it, although we cannot see it. Humidity is the amount of water in the air. If the air contains only a little water vapour, the humidity is low. When air holds a lot of moisture, we say the humidity is high. The warmer the air the more moisture it can hold. Humidity affects the way we feel. When the humidity is high we feel 'sweaty' and uncomfortable. This is because the sweat does not evaporate easily from our skin. But too low a humidity is not very good for us. Some people use *humidifiers* in their homes to put more moisture into the air.

Hummingbird

These birds are among the smallest in the world. They are found only in the New World, from Canada to the tip of South America. The tiniest of the 320 kinds lives in Cuba. It is less than 5 cm— hardly bigger than a large bumblebee.

The feathers of hummingbirds are coloured in brilliant metallic hues of blue, green, red and yellow. The colours flashing in the sun make hummingbirds look like glittering jewels on the wing.

▲ *The tiny hummingbird has a specially developed beak and tongue that let it feed from deep inside flowers.*

Hummingbirds can beat their wings up to 70 times a second. This is what causes their distinctive humming sound. It also lets them hover in mid-air and fly backwards and sideways like a helicopter. In this way, they dart from flower to flower and feed while flying. They take nectar and tiny insects from deep within the cups of flowers.

Hungary

This is a small, central European country that covers an area of some 93,000 sq km, not much bigger than Scotland. Hungary has a population of less than 11 million people.

Hungary has no coastline. The mighty Danube river flows across the country on its way to the Black Sea, dividing it almost in two. Ships can sail up-river as far as Budapest, the capital and biggest city.

Hungary is low-lying and fairly flat. To the east it becomes a vast grassy plain. Here herds of sheep, cattle and horses are grazed. The climate is hot and dry in summer, and bitterly cold in winter. Agriculture is important, but more Hungarians work in industry than on farms. There are also rich sources of coal, oil and bauxite for making aluminium.

After WORLD WAR I and the collapse of the Austro-Hungarian Empire, Hungary became an independent republic. After WORLD WAR II it was a communist country, but in 1989 the people achieved a more democratic government. In 1991 the last Soviet troops left Hungary.

Hurricane

A hurricane is a severe storm. To be called a hurricane, a storm must have wind speeds of at least 120 km/h. People who live around the Pacific Ocean call hurricanes *typhoons*. People who live on the Indian Ocean call them *cyclones*. Hurricane winds whirl around in a great circle and sometimes reach speeds of over 320 km/h. The largest hurricanes have measured 1600 km across. Hurricanes form over oceans near the Equator, where the air is very moist. At the centre of the hurricane is a narrow column of air that spins very slowly. This is the 'eye' of the hurricane. Around it swirl the hurricane winds, which are strongest nearest the eye.

HUNGARY

(map showing Hungary and surrounding countries: POLAND, GERMANY, CZECHOSLOVAKIA, UKRAINE, AUSTRIA, HUNGARY, ROMANIA, FORMER YUGOSLAVIA, ITALY, ADRIATIC SEA, BULGARIA)

Government: Multi-party system
Capital: Budapest
Area: 93,030 sq km
Population: 10,553,000
Language: Hungarian
Currency: Forint

▼ *Satellite pictures can help to predict the route a hurricane will take. Hurricane Allen is shown here over the Gulf of Mexico. You can clearly see the 'eye' in the centre of the storm.*

Hydroelectric Power

More than a quarter of the world's electricity is produced by using the energy of fast flowing water. This is called hydroelectric power. Most hydroelectric plants are found below dams, but some are powered by waterfalls.

Water is heavy. When it falls down through large pipes from a high dam it can be made to turn TURBINES with paddle-shaped blades. Shafts connected to the blades turn electric generators, as in ordinary coal- or oil-fired power stations.

▶ The huge turbine blades in a hydroelectric power station are turned by water as it flows down from a dam. They in turn rotate a shaft connected to generators which produce electricity in the same way as in ordinary power stations.

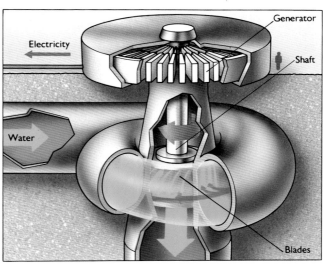

Hydrogen

Hydrogen is a gas. It is thought to be the most abundant ELEMENT in the whole universe. It is the single most important material from which stars, including our SUN, are made.

Hydrogen is the lightest of all elements. It is more than 14 times as light as air. It is colourless, has no smell and no taste. Hydrogen burns very easily. Great masses of hydrogen are always being burned in the Sun. It is this fierce burning that gives us light and heat from the Sun.

Coal, oil and natural gas all contain hydrogen. It is also a very important part of all plant and animal bodies. Hydrogen was once used in ballooning, but because it is highly inflammable there were many accidents. Now helium gas is used instead.

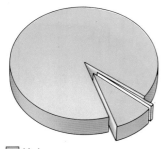

Hydrogen
Other gases
Helium

▲ This pie chart shows the proportions of the gases that make up our Sun. Hydrogen is the main component by a long way.

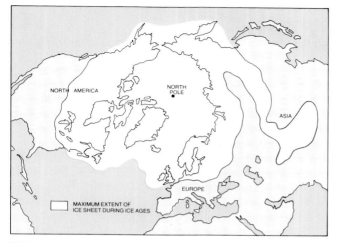

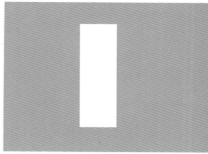

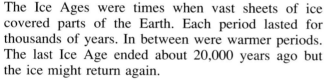

◄ *The glaciers that spread over large parts of the Earth during the Ice Ages carried huge rocks and boulders with them as they went. Geologists can trace the path of the glaciers by studying these rocks and working out where they came from.*

Ice Ages

The Ice Ages were times when vast sheets of ice covered parts of the Earth. Each period lasted for thousands of years. In between were warmer periods. The last Ice Age ended about 20,000 years ago but the ice might return again.

During the Ice Ages the weather was very cold. Endless snow fell and glaciers grew and spread. At times the glaciers covered much of North America and Asia, and Europe as far south as London. In some places the ice piled up more than a thousand metres high. This made the sea level lower than it is today. A land bridge was formed between Asia and North America. The first people in America came across this land bridge from Asia.

▼ *Huge icebergs float in the sea because when water freezes it expands, so ice is less dense than water.*

Iceberg

Icebergs are part of glaciers and ice shelves that have broken away and float in the sea. They are found in the waters of the ARCTIC and the ANTARCTIC.

Icebergs can be very big. Some weigh millions of tonnes. Most of an iceberg is hidden under the surface of the sea. Some icebergs may be 145 km long. They can be 120 metres high above water. An iceberg this high would be about another 960 metres deep under water.

Icebergs are dangerous to ships. Some icebergs float south from the Arctic into the Atlantic Ocean where they may obstruct ships's journeys.

ICELAND

Government: Constitutional republic
Capital: Reykjavik
Area: 103,000 sq km
Population: 255,000
Language: Icelandic
Currency: Krona

Iceland

Iceland is a small, mountainous island, about 100,000 sq km in size. It was first discovered by VIKINGS in AD 874. The island lies just south of the Arctic in the north Atlantic, between Greenland and Norway. Warm waters from the Gulf Stream keep most of the harbours free of ice all the year round.

Iceland has many VOLCANOES. About 25 of its volcanoes have erupted. There are many hot water springs too. Some are used to heat homes. The north of Iceland is covered by glaciers and a desert of stone and lava (cooled volcanic matter).

There are about 251,000 people in Iceland. Most live in the south and east where the land is lower. They live by farming and fishing. The capital city is Reykjavik.

Iceland became an independent country in 1944 after breaking its ties with Denmark.

Immunity

You have probably been vaccinated against the disease called polio. The substance the doctor or nurse put into your body contained polio germs, but these germs had been made harmless so you only caught a very mild case of polio. Your body did not know that the polio germs had been weakened, and it got to work fighting them. Your body produced *antibodies*—substances that attack certain disease-causing germs. The important thing is that these antibodies stay in your body to stop more of the same kind of germs from invading your body again. This kind of long-term protection against diseases is called immunity.

People also have *acquired* immunity to disease. This happens when they have a disease and produce

▼ *The presence of bacteria in the body stimulates the white blood cells which are always present to move in to attack them.*

1. A white blood cell is moving to attack a bacterium.

2. It surrounds the bacterium and takes it in.

3. The bacterium is killed by chemicals inside the cell.

4. The bacterium is expelled in the form of pus.

antibodies to fight it off. After that, the antibodies are waiting to ward off these germs should they appear again. If you have had measles, you are unlikely to get measles again.

However, some diseases are very difficult or impossible to vaccinate against. Your body stops making antibodies against the common cold almost as soon as you are over it. The VIRUS that causes AIDS damages the body's immune system so that it stops making antibodies against diseases.

Incas

The Incas were people who lived in SOUTH AMERICA. They ruled a great empire from the 1200s until the 1500s. The centre of their empire was in PERU. In the 1400s the empire grew. It stretched thousands of kilometres, from present-day Chile to Ecuador.

The Inca king and his nobles ruled over the people in the empire. They were very strict and told the farmers and craftsmen what to grow and make. The Incas built many roads through the empire.

In the 1500s, Spanish soldiers led by Francisco Pizarro reached America. They captured the Inca king Atahualpa and said they would free him in return for gold. Incas brought their treasure to free the king, but the Spanish still killed him. By 1569 the Spaniards had conquered the whole Inca empire.

The Incas' name comes from the title of their Emperor, who was called the Inca.

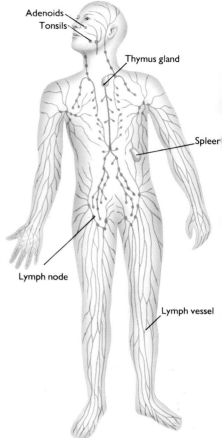

Adenoids
Tonsils
Thymus gland
Spleen
Lymph node
Lymph vessel

▲ The body protects itself against illness in various ways. The immune, or lymph, system fights diseases that attack the body.

◄ The Incas worshipped the Sun and other nature gods in elaborate ceremonies, at which their priests would offer sacrifices of animals.

▶ *The river Ganges is sacred to Hindus because, in legend, it flows from the head of the god Shiva.*

INDIA

Government: Federal republic
Capital: New Delhi
Area: 3,287,590 sq km
Population: 827,057,000
Languages: Hindi, English
Currency: Rupee

India

India has a population of over 800 million. It has more people than any other country except China. India is part of ASIA.

To the north of India are the HIMALAYAS. Many people live in the fertile northern plains, which are crossed by the great Ganges and Brahmaputra rivers. The south is high, flat land, with mountains called the Ghats along the coast.

India is very hot and dry in summer. Parts of the country are almost DESERT. But winds called *monsoons* bring heavy rain to the north-east every year.

Most Indians are farmers. They live in small villages and grow rice, wheat, tea, cotton and jute.

India is also a fast-growing industrial country. Cities such as Calcutta and Bombay are among the world's biggest. The capital is New Delhi.

Hindi and English are the two main languages, but there are hundreds of others. Most Indians practise HINDUISM, but many follow the religion of ISLAM. There are also many other religions in India, including Buddhism and Christianity.

Indonesia

Indonesia is a country in South-east ASIA. It is a chain of over 3000 islands around the EQUATOR. The islands stretch over a distance of 4800 km.

Indonesia has nearly 180 million people. More than half of them live in Java, one of the biggest islands. The capital city, Jakarta, is in Java. Most Indonesians are farmers. They grow many things, including rice, tea, rubber and tobacco. Indonesia also produces minerals, including petroleum.

INDONESIA

Government: Independent republic
Capital: Jakarta
Area: 2,027,087 sq km
Population: 179,300,000
Language: Bahasa Indonesian (Malay)
Currency: Rupiah

Industrial Revolution

The Industrial Revolution was a great change which took place in Europe in the 1700s and 1800s. People began to make things on machines in factories, instead of by hand at home. The new machines were run by STEAM ENGINES. They made things much faster than people could by hand. Mining and metal-

▼ *Arkwright's water frame was one of many machines invented during the industrial revolution. It altered work methods that had not changed for hundreds of years.*

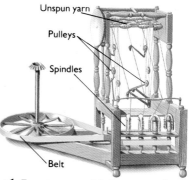

Unspun yarn

Pulleys

Spindles

Belt

◄ *Enormous social changes took place in the 18th century in Europe. Improved farming methods replaced traditional ways and many peasant farmers had to move to towns where the conditions were crowded and unhealthy.*

working became more important and the RAILWAYS began. Many people moved from the countryside and began to work in factories in the towns.

Some countries have experienced 'hyperinflation', when prices increased by more then 50 per cent *every month*. This means an inflation rate of more than 13,000 per cent a year. A bar of chocolate that cost 10p on January 1 would cost £13 by December 31!

Inflation

Inflation is a word used to mean rapidly rising prices. Every time prices go up, MONEY is worth less because people need more money to buy the same things. In turn, people ask for higher wages. If wages rise, then the cost of making things in factories goes up. This often makes prices rise again. Because prices and wages affect each other like this, inflation is hard to stop. There are many reasons why inflation starts. If inflation becomes very bad, money can become worthless.

Inoculation

Inoculation is a way of protecting people from diseases. It is also called *vaccination*.

Inoculation works by giving people a very weak dose of a disease. The body learns to fight the germs that cause the disease. In this way, the body becomes protected, or *immune,* from the disease.

IMMUNITY from a disease may last from a few months to many years, depending on the kind of disease and vaccine.

Insects

Insects live all over the world. They are by far the most numerous of all animal species. More than 850,000 different kinds of insects are known. Roughly eight out of ten of all the Earth's animals are insects!

Insects range in size from tiny fleas which can be seen only through a microscope to beetles as big as your hand. Many have interesting life stories, or cycles. Some insects, such as the desert locust of Africa, are destructive pests. But many others are helpful. Without bees and flying insects, flowering plants would not be pollinated and fruit trees would not bear fruit.

Among the most fascinating insects are the social insects, which live in highly organized communities or colonies. These include ants, bees and termites. Many insects make regular journeys. Some butterflies, beetles and dragonflies migrate at certain times every year.

▼ *These are just a few of the hundreds of thousands of different kinds of insects alive on Earth.*

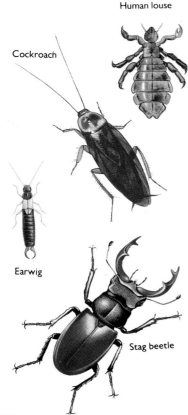

Human louse

Cockroach

Earwig

Stag beetle

Instinct

People have to learn to read and write, but bees do not learn how to sting. They are born knowing how to sting when there is danger. This kind of behaviour is called instinct. Parents pass on instincts to their young through GENETICS.

Animals do many things by instinct. Birds build nests this way. Simple animals, such as insects, do almost everything by instinct. They have set ways of finding food, attacking enemies or escaping. Animals that act entirely by instinct do not have enough INTELLIGENCE to learn new ways of doing things, and cannot easily change their behaviour.

Intelligence

When someone uses experience and knowledge to solve a new kind of problem, he or she shows intelligence. Intelligence depends on being able to learn. Creatures that act only by INSTINCT lack intelligence. People, apes and whales are the most intelligent creatures.

Internal Combustion Engine

In internal combustion engines, fuel burns inside the engines. The most common internal combustion engines are petrol engines and DIESEL ENGINES. In the petrol engine, fuel mixes with air inside a cylinder. A spark sets the mixture alight and it explodes. This happens over and over again. Hot gases from the explosions push a piston to and fro inside the cylinder. Most engines have several cylinders. The pistons work very quickly in turn. They move the crankshaft. This movement turns WHEELS or propellers.

Petrol and diesel engines are used in CARS and lorries, and in ships and some planes.

Iran

Iran is a country in ASIA. It lies between the Caspian Sea in the north and the Persian Gulf in the south. The country is nearly seven times larger than Great Britain but it has fewer people. Deserts, snowy mountains and green valleys cover most of the land. The country has hot, dry summers and cold winters.

▼ Instinctive behaviour is seen in humans and animals alike. Three examples are shown below. Bees sting as an instinctive reaction to danger; a new-born baby will grasp tightly enough with its hands to support its own weight; and a weaver bird makes an elaborate hanging nest out of grasses.

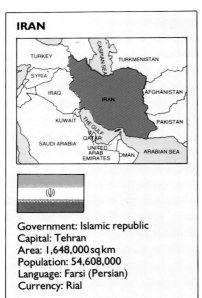

IRAN

Government: Islamic republic
Capital: Tehran
Area: 1,648,000 sq km
Population: 54,608,000
Language: Farsi (Persian)
Currency: Rial

Iranians speak Persian. (Persia is the old name for Iran.) Their religion is ISLAM. Tehran is the capital city.

Many Iranians are nomads who travel around with flocks of sheep or goats. Each time they camp, the women set up simple looms and weave beautiful rugs by hand. Iran's most important product is oil.

Iran has a long history. In about 550 BC the Persians had a leader called Cyrus. Cyrus and his army made an empire that stretched from Greece and Egypt to India. The Persian empire was then the largest in the world.

ALEXANDER THE GREAT conquered Persia about 330 BC. Later, the country was ruled by ARABS and MONGOLS. During this century Iran was ruled by emperors, or *shahs*. In 1979 the government of Iran changed and the shah left the country. Religious leaders now rule this Islamic Republic.

From 1980 to 1988 Iran fought a long and bitter war with Iraq.

Iraq

Iraq is an ARAB country in south-west ASIA. Much of Iraq is a dry, sandy and stony plain. It is cool in winter and very hot in summer. The Tigris and Euphrates rivers flow through the plain to the Persian Gulf. Their water helps the farmers to grow rice, cotton, wheat and dates. Iraq is also one of the biggest oil producers in the world. Pipelines carry the oil from the north of the country across the desert to ports in Syria and the Lebanon.

Many Iraqis are NOMADS. They live in the deserts with their sheep and goats. But nearly 4 million people work in the capital city of Baghdad.

Some of the first cities in the world were built near Iraq's big rivers. Ur was one of the earliest cities. It was built by a Bronze Age people called the Sumerians. Later, the Babylonians built their famous city, Babylon, in Iraq. Babylonia was one of the greatest civilizations of the ancient world. It rivalled EGYPT in its splendour. Babylonia lay between the valleys of the Tigris and Euphrates rivers.

Modern Iraq is a republic and was involved in a war with Iran from 1980 to 1988. In 1990 Iraq invaded Kuwait but was forced to leave after the Gulf War in 1991.

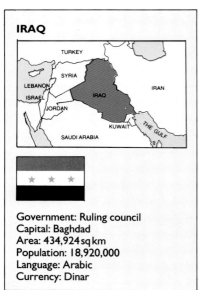

IRAQ

Government: Ruling council
Capital: Baghdad
Area: 434,924 sq km
Population: 18,920,000
Language: Arabic
Currency: Dinar

Ireland

Ireland is the second largest island of the BRITISH ISLES. It is shaped like a saucer. Mountains form the rim. The middle is a low plain. Through this flows the Shannon, the longest river in the British Isles. Irish weather is often mild and rainy. Meadows and moors cover much of the land. Northern Ireland is part of the United Kingdom. Southern Ireland is the Republic of Ireland, or Eire.

IRELAND

Government: Parliamentary republic
Capital: Dublin
Area: 70,283 sq km
Population: 3,557,000
Languages: English, Irish (Gaelic)
Currency: Irish pound (punt)

Iron and Steel

Iron is the cheapest and most useful of all metals. Much of our food, clothes, homes and cars are made with machines and tools made from iron.

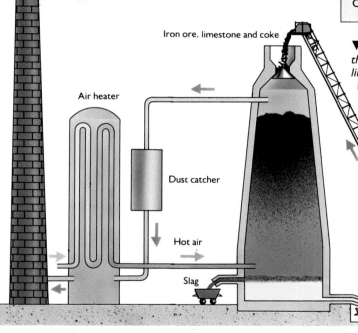

Iron ore, limestone and coke

Air heater

Dust catcher

Hot air

Slag

Iron

▼ To produce iron from iron ore, the ore is mixed with coke and limestone, then heated at a very high temperature. A poor quality iron, called pig iron, is made first and this can be made into steel or steel alloys, which are much stronger. Most steel (bottom) is made by the 'Linz-Donawitz' method. 1. The furnace is filled with scrap iron and molten iron. 2. Oxygen blown into the furnace produces enough heat to burn out impurities. 3. Molten steel is poured from the furnace into ingots.

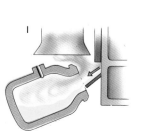

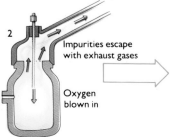

Impurities escape with exhaust gases

Oxygen blown in

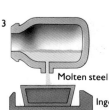

Molten steel

Ingot

Iron is mined, or *quarried*, as iron ore, or MINERALS. The ore is melted down, or *smelted*, in a blast furnace. The iron is then made into cast iron, wrought iron, or mixed with a small amount of CARBON to form steel.

Cast iron is hard but not as strong as steel. Molten cast iron is poured into moulds to make such things as engine blocks. Wrought iron is soft but tough. It is used for chains and gates. Steel is hard and strong. Steel ALLOYS containing metals such as tungsten and chromium are used to make many different things, from bridges to nails.

Shaduf

The shaduf was used for irrigation, as long ago as 5000 BC.

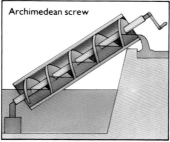

Archimedean screw

The Archimedean screw uses a rotating spiral to raise water.

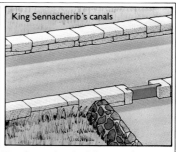

King Sennacherib's canals

King Sennacherib of Ancient Assyria built canals for irrigation.

▲ *Irrigation is as old as farming itself, and many ancient societies have developed their own methods for keeping their crops watered. Some of these are still used today.*

Irrigation

Farmers and gardeners who water plants are irrigating them. Irrigation makes it possible to grow crops and flowers in dry soils, even in a DESERT. Farmers in China, Egypt and Iraq have been irrigating large areas of land for thousands of years.

Many countries store water in lakes made by building DAMS across rivers. CANALS take water from the lakes to farms. One irrigation canal in Russia is 850 km long. Ditches or pipes carry water from each canal to the fields. In each field the water flows between the rows of plants. Sometimes it spurts up from holes in the pipes. It sprinkles the plants like a shower of rain.

Islam

Islam is a religion started in AD 622 by MUHAMMAD. It has more followers than any other religion except Christianity. Islam means 'submission'. Its followers are called Muslims. Muslim means 'submissive one'.

Muslims believe they must submit, or give in, to God's will. They believe in one God and in Muhammad as his prophet. Muslims pray five times a day and give gifts to the poor. For one month a year they go without food until sunset and they try to visit Mecca, Muhammad's birthplace, before they die. They also try to obey the rules for good living set out in the K*oran*, the holy book of Islam.

Islam began in Arabia. The Islamic calendar dates from 622 AD. In that year Muhammad went to Medina, where he was recognised as a prophet. Today Islam is the main religion in North Africa and most of south-west Asia.

Israel

Israel is a country in south-west ASIA, on the shores of the Mediterranean Sea. The state of Israel was only created in 1948 as a homeland for Jewish people from around the world. Since then, around two million Jewish people have migrated to Israel. Many go there to escape persecution in their own countries.

Farmers grow oranges, cotton and grain on fertile plains. More than half the land is dry mountain or desert. Summers are hot and winters are mild.

There are over four million Israelis. JERUSALEM is the capital city. Most Israelis are Jews. There are also many ARABS. The main language is Hebrew.

Italy

Italy is a country in southern EUROPE. It is shaped like a boot stuck out in the Mediterranean Sea to kick Sicily. Sicily and Sardinia are Italian islands.

Much of Italy is mountainous. The sharp, snowy peaks of the Alps cross northern Italy. The Apennines run like a backbone down the middle. Between the Alps and Apennines lies the plain of Lombardy. Italy is famous for its hot, sunny summers. Rain falls mostly in winter.

Crops grow on almost half the land. Italy produces more pears and olives than any other country. The farmers also grow a lot of grapes, lemons, wheat, rice and oranges. Big factories in northern Italy make cars, chemicals and machines.

The capital is Rome. Many tourists visit Rome to see the Vatican and ruins of the ROMAN EMPIRE.

ISRAEL

Government: Parliamentary
  democracy
Capital: Jerusalem
Area: 20,770 sq km
Population: 4,659,000
Languages: Hebrew, Arabic
Currency: Shekel

ITALY

Government: Republic
Capital: Rome
Area: 301,252 sq km
Population: 57,663,000
Language: Italian
Currency: Lira

Jaguar

No other American wild CAT is as heavy or perhaps as dangerous as the jaguar. From nose to tail a jaguar is longer than a man, and may be nearly twice his weight. The jaguar is yellow with black spots. The LEOPARD also has spots, but many of the jaguar's spots are in rings. Jaguars live in the hot, wet forests of Central and South America. They leap from trees onto wild pigs and deer. They also catch turtles, fish and alligators.

▶ *Jaguars look rather like the leopards of Asia and Africa but they are heavier.*

Jamaica

Jamaica is a tropical island in the Caribbean Sea. The name Jamaica means 'island of springs'. It is a beautiful island, with hundreds of streams flowing from springs on the sides of its green mountains.

There are more than two million people in Jamaica. Most of them are of African ancestry. Many work on farms that grow bananas, coconuts, coffee, oranges and sugar cane. Jamaica also mines bauxite. Kingston is Jamaica's capital city and an important Caribbean seaport.

Government: Constitutional
  monarchy
Capital: Kingston
Area: 10,991 sq km
Population: 2,420,000
Language: English
Currency: Jamaican dollar

James (kings)

James was the name of two kings of Great Britain. James I (1566–1625) was the son of MARY, QUEEN OF SCOTS and a cousin of ELIZABETH I. He became King James VI of Scotland when he was one year old. Queen Elizabeth died without any children in 1603. James VI (who was a descendant of King Henry VII of England) was next in line, and was crowned James I of England. In this way England and Scotland were joined under one ruler.

James II (1633–1701) was the grandson of James I. He tried to restore the ROMAN CATHOLIC CHURCH in England, but Parliament would not let him. In 1688 he was made to leave the country. He was replaced on the throne by his daughter Mary and her Dutch husband William of Orange. James's followers were called Jacobites. (Jacobus is Latin for James.) In the 1700s Jacobites twice began rebellions in Scotland. But they did not win the throne back for the Stuarts.

▲ *James I was king in 1605 when the Gunpowder Plot, in which Guy Fawkes and his friends planned to blow up parliament, was discovered.*

Japan

Japan is a long, narrow string of islands off the mainland coast of Asia. Altogether they make a country slightly larger than the British Isles.

Mountains cover most of Japan. The highest is a beautiful volcano called Fujiyama, or Mount Fuji. Parts of Japan have forests, waterfalls and lakes. Northern Japan has cool summers and cold winters.

Japan is a crowded country. It has more than 123 million people. To feed them, farmers grow huge amounts of rice and fruits. The Japanese eat a lot of fish and seaweed.

Japan does not have many minerals, so the Japanese buy most of their minerals such as iron ore from other countries. But no other country makes

▼ *There is very little space in Tokyo, so overhead railways are an ideal way of coping with commuter travel.*

JAPAN

Government: Parliamentary
  democracy
Capital: Tokyo
Area: 372,313 sq km
Population: 123,537,000
Language: Japanese
Currency: Yen

as many ships, television sets, radios, videos and cameras as Japan does. The Japanese also make a lot of cars.

Jazz

Jazz is a kind of music. The players use unexpected rhythms. They can play any notes they like, but they must fit the music made by the rest of the band. In this way, jazz musicians often *improvise*, or make up music as they go along. Jazz began in the United States in the 1800s.

Jenner, Edward

Edward Jenner (1749–1823) was a British doctor who discovered how inoculation works. He inoculated a boy with cowpox germs. Cowpox is a disease like smallpox, but it is less dangerous. Jenner then injected the boy with smallpox germs. Because the cowpox germs protected the boy, he did not develop smallpox. Today, millions of people are inoculated against many diseases.

Jerusalem

Jerusalem is the capital of ISRAEL. It is a holy city of the Jews, Christians and Muslims. David, Jesus and other famous people in the Bible lived or died here.

Jerusalem stands high up in hilly country. It has many old religious buildings. Huge walls surround the city's oldest part. In 1948 Jerusalem was divided between Israel and Jordan, but Israel took the whole city during a war in 1967.

Jesus

Jesus was a Jew. He started Christianity. The New Testament of the BIBLE says he was God's Son.

Jesus was born in Bethlehem. His mother was called Mary. When he grew up he travelled around, teaching and healing sick people. Some Jewish priests were jealous of Jesus. They told their Roman rulers that he was making trouble. The Romans killed Jesus on a cross, but the New Testament says that he came to life again and rose to heaven. Followers of Jesus spread his teachings worldwide.

▲ *The* Baptism of Christ *was painted by the Italian Renaissance artist Piero della Francesca in the 1400s. Many masterpieces of western art have had the life of Jesus as their inspiration.*

Jet Engine

A swimmer swims forwards by pushing water backwards. A jet engine works in a similar way. It drives an AIRCRAFT forwards by pushing gases backwards. Engines that work like this are called *reaction* engines. ROCKETS are also reaction engines. The main difference between jets and rockets is that jets take in oxygen from the air to burn their fuel, but rockets have a supply of oxygen in their fuel.

Long ago, in the first century AD, a Greek mathematician named Hero made the first jet engine. He suspended a hollow metal ball containing water. When he boiled the water, the steam escaped through a nozzle on either side of the ball. As the nozzles pointed in opposite directions, the ball began to spin.

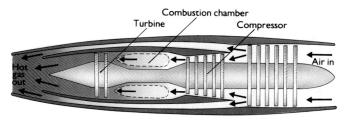

◄ *Jet engines provide a powerful thrust to drive both passenger and military planes.*

There are four main kinds of jet engine. These are turbojets, turboprops, turbofans and ramjets.

Jet engines have replaced propeller-driven piston engines in many kinds of plane. There are many reasons for this. Jet engines weigh less than piston engines. They also go wrong less often. Their moving parts spin instead of moving to and fro. This stops the plane from shaking about. Jet engines burn cheap paraffin (kerosene) instead of costly petrol. Jet engines can also carry planes faster and higher than piston engines can. Some jet fighters can travel at 3400 km/h.

▼ *Joan of Arc successfully took on the role of soldier to lead the French into battle against the English.*

Joan of Arc

Joan of Arc (1412–1431) was a French girl who believed that God told her to free France from its English invaders. At 17 she left the farm where she worked, and persuaded France's King Charles VII to let her lead his army. She won five battles. Then she was captured and burnt as a witch. But she had saved France. In 1920 the Pope made her a saint.

Judaism

Judaism is a religion that believes in one God and has as its holy book the Bible. The Hebrew Bible consists of the first five books of Moses (the Torah), historical accounts of the tribes of Israel, and books written by prophets and kings. (Christians include all this material in their Bible, calling it the Old Testament.) Judaism's followers are called Jews. They observe the Ten Commandments. They believe God gave the Law to Moses on top of Mount Sinai after Moses led their ancestors out of Egypt, where they had been slaves. The commemoration of this Exodus from Egypt is one of Judaism's most important festivals and is called Passover. Today Jews live all over the world, but regard Israel as their spiritual and historical home.

JUPITER FACTS

Average distance from Sun:
  778 million km
Nearest distance from Earth:
  630 million km
Average temperature: −150°C
Diameter across equator:
142,800 km
Atmosphere: Hydrogen, helium
Number of moons: 14 known
Length of day: 9 hours 50 minutes
Length of year: 11.9 Earth years

———Earth

———Jupiter

Jupiter

Jupiter is the largest of the PLANETS in our SOLAR SYSTEM. It is twice the size of all the other planets put together. You could fit 1300 planets the size of the Earth into the space filled by Jupiter. Jupiter's force of GRAVITY is great. Anyone on Jupiter would weigh twice as much as on the Earth. Astronomers believe that most of Jupiter is hot, liquid HYDROGEN. Jupiter is so hot that it would be a glowing star if it were ten times larger. It has 14 moons.

Jupiter spins so fast that a day and night last less than ten Earth-hours. But a year on Jupiter is 12 times longer than one of ours. This is because Jupiter is farther from the SUN than we are.

If an astronaut managed to 'land' on Jupiter, he or she would find that there are no seasons. The faint Sun, so distant as to be just a flickering star, would rise and set every nine and three-quarter hours. Jupiter's biggest moon, Ganymede, is bigger than the planet Mercury.

▶ The planet Jupiter appears to have light and dark belts around it in its atmosphere.

Kangaroo

Kangaroos are MARSUPIALS that live in New Guinea and Australia. Most of them live on grassy plains and most of them feed on plants. They move about in troops, springing along on their big, powerful hind legs and large feet. Their long tails help them to balance.

◀ Kangaroos are considered to be a pest in Australia, and to keep their numbers down, they are sometimes hunted.

There are more than 50 kinds of kangaroo. Red and grey kangaroos are the largest. A red kangaroo may be taller and heavier than a man. Grey kangaroos can bounce along at 40 km/h if chased. Wallabies are smaller kinds of kangaroo. The smallest of all are rat kangaroos. They are about the size of a rabbit. Tree kangaroos live in New Guinea.

Kenya

Kenya is a country in east AFRICA. It is just a bit larger than France. The south-west border touches Lake Victoria. The Indian Ocean is on the south-east. The EQUATOR goes across the middle of the country. Much of the land is covered by mountains and flat-topped hills. The rest looks like a huge open park. It is hot, dry country.

Kenya is a member of the COMMONWEALTH. Most of the people in Kenya are African. They belong to a number of different tribes. Some tribes, like the

KENYA

Government: Republic
Capital: Nairobi
Area: 582,646 sq km
Population: 24,032,000
Languages: Swahili, English
Currency: Shilling

203

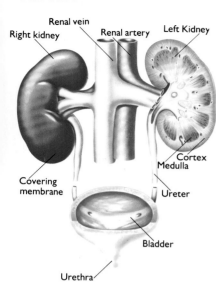

Renal vein
Right kidney
Renal artery
Left Kidney
Cortex
Medulla
Covering membrane
Ureter
Bladder
Urethra

▲ *The kidneys are part of a vital system for cleaning the blood of impurities and excess liquid. These are drained off through the ureters into the bladder, and leave the body as urine.*

▼ *Young koalas hold tightly to their mothers' backs as they climb through the trees that form their habitat.*

Masai, keep cattle. Kenyan farmers grow maize, tea and coffee. Kenya sells a lot of tea and coffee abroad. Many tourists visit Kenya to see the wild animals roaming the huge nature reserves.

Kidney

All VERTEBRATES (animals with a backbone) have two kidneys. Kidneys look like large reddish-brown beans. Human kidneys are about the size of a person's fist. They lie on each side of the backbone, at just about waist level.

Kidneys clean the BLOOD. They filter out waste matter and strain off any water that the body does not need. Blood pumped from the HEART flows into each kidney through an artery. Each kidney contains tubes that act as filters. Blood cells, tiny food particles, and other useful items stay in the blood to be used by the body. Filtered blood flows out of the kidney through a vein. All the waste matter and extra water mix together to make urine. This drips slowly into the bladder.

Kiwi

This strange bird from New Zealand gets its name from the shrill cries made by the male. The kiwi is a stocky brown bird as big as a chicken. It has tiny wings but cannot fly. Instead it runs on short, thick strong legs. Kiwi feathers look very much like hair.

Kiwis are shy birds that live in forests. By day they sleep in burrows. At night, they hunt for worms and grubs. Kiwis can hardly see. They smell out their food with the help of nostrils at the tip of their long, thin beaks. The females lay very large eggs but it is the male who sits on them and waits for them to hatch.

Koala

Koalas are MARSUPIALS that look like small, chubby bears. Koalas live in east and south-east Australia. They live much like sloths. Koalas climb slowly among the branches of trees and hardly ever touch the ground. Their only food is eucalyptus leaves. Forest fires and hunting nearly made them extinct, but many koalas now live safely on reserves.

Koran

The Koran is the sacred book of ISLAM. Its name means 'a recitation'. It has 114 chapters of Arabic verse, and teaches that there is one God whose prophets (messengers) included Abraham, JESUS and MUHAMMAD. The book teaches Muslims to be humble, generous and just. It is said that the Koran was revealed to Muhammad through the angel Gabriel. The way it is written has influenced Arab literature.

Korea

Korea is a peninsula in ASIA which juts out from CHINA into the Sea of Japan. The land has many mountains and small valleys. Forests cover most of the country. Korean farms produce much rice. Korean factories make steel and other products.

Korea was divided into two separate nations in 1945. They are now known as North Korea and South Korea.

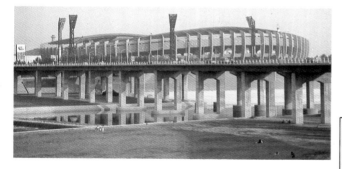

◄ *The Olympic Stadium in Seoul was the location of the 1988 games.*

War between North and South Korea broke out in 1950, with Soviet and Chinese forces supporting the North and United Nations (mostly American) forces helping the South. There is now peace.

Kremlin

This is the oldest part of MOSCOW. Some of its buildings date from the 1100s. The Kremlin was once the fortress home of Russia's *tsars*. Inside the high wall that surrounds it stand old palaces and cathedrals crowned by golden domes. For most of its history the Kremlin has been the seat of the Russian government.

NORTH KOREA

Government: Communist
Capital: Pyongyang
Area: 120,538 sq km
Population: 21,773,000
Language: Korean
Currency: Won

SOUTH KOREA

Government: Republic
Capital: Seoul
Area: 98,484 sq km
Population: 42,793,000
Language: Korean
Currency: Won

Lake

Lakes are large areas of water surrounded by land. The world's largest lake is the salty Caspian Sea. It lies between Europe and Asia, east of the Caucasus Mountains. The largest freshwater lake is Lake Superior, one of the GREAT LAKES.

Many lakes were formed in the ICE AGES. They began in valleys made by glaciers. When the glaciers melted they left behind mud and stones that formed DAMS. The melted water from the glaciers piled up behind the dams.

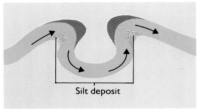

Silt deposit

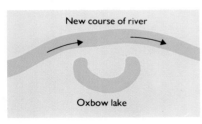

Silt deposit

New course of river

Oxbow lake

Language

Language is what we use to talk to, or communicate with, one another. Many animals have ways of communicating. These may include special body movements and sounds. But the speaking of words is something that so far only humans can do. Spoken language came first; later people invented a way of writing it down. This is known as written language. Language is always changing as some words are forgotten and others are added.

Today there are about 3000 languages in the world. They can be grouped into a number of language families. Some of the most widely spoken languages are English, French, German, Russian, Chinese, Hindi, Arabic and Spanish. There are about 160 *main* languages. A main language is one spoken by more than one million people.

▲ Rivers can gradually form bends by erosion of one bank and a build-up of material on the other. After a time the river cuts a straight channel through the neck of the bend. The loop of water left over is called an oxbow lake.

▶ This bewildering array of newspapers from countries all over the world gives an indication of how difficult international relations can be when people are divided by alphabet, language and culture.

Lapland

Lapland is a region in the ARCTIC. It lies in the far north of Sweden, Norway, Finland and Russia.

Some Lapps are nomads. They travel the land with herds of reindeer. They sleep in tents and eat reindeer meat. Other Lapps are fishermen or farmers. They live in small huts in villages. Lapps speak a language related to Finnish. They keep warm by wearing clothes made from wool and reindeer skins. Their clothes are brightly coloured.

Laser

A laser is a device that strengthens light and makes it shine in a very narrow beam. Many lasers have a ruby CRYSTAL or gas inside them. Bright light, radio waves or electricity are fed into the laser. This makes the ATOMS of the crystal or gas jump around very quickly. The atoms give off strong light.

The light of lasers can be used for many things. Doctors use small laser beams to burn away tiny areas of disease in the body. They also repair damaged eyes with laser beams. Dentists can use lasers to drill holes in teeth. Some lasers are so strong they can cut through DIAMONDS. Lasers are used in factories to cut metal and join tiny metal parts together.

Lasers can also be used to measure distance. The laser beam is aimed at objects far away. The distance is measured by counting the time it takes

Laser light is being used more and more to carry telephone conversations. A narrow cable containing 144 hairlike glass fibres can carry 40,000 telephone conversations at the same time.

▼ In this Los Angeles studio, experiments are being carried out into the use of lasers in games for the future.

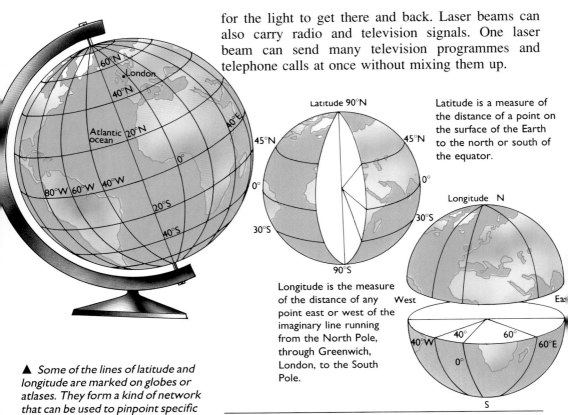

for the light to get there and back. Laser beams can also carry radio and television signals. One laser beam can send many television programmes and telephone calls at once without mixing them up.

Latitude is a measure of the distance of a point on the surface of the Earth to the north or south of the equator.

Longitude is the measure of the distance of any point east or west of the imaginary line running from the North Pole, through Greenwich, London, to the South Pole.

▲ *Some of the lines of latitude and longitude are marked on globes or atlases. They form a kind of network that can be used to pinpoint specific places.*

▼ *Lead was often used to make toys and, in particular, model soldiers, but for reasons of safety it is no longer used.*

Latitude and Longitude

Every place on Earth has a latitude and a longitude. Lines of latitude and longitude are drawn on MAPS. Lines, or *parallels*, of latitude show how far north or south of the *equator* a place is. They are measured in degrees (written as °). The equator is at 0° latitude. The North Pole has a latitude of 90° north, and the South Pole is 90° south.

Lines, or *meridians*, of longitude show how far east or west a place is. They are also measured in degrees. Greenwich, in London, is at 0° longitude. A place halfway around the world from Greenwich is at 180° longitude.

Lead

Lead is a soft, heavy, blue-grey metal. It does not rust. Lead is used for many things, but its greatest single use is in car batteries. Lead shields protect atomic energy workers from dangerous radiation. Lead is mixed with TIN to make pewter or *solder*.

Solder is used for joining pieces of metal. Many items are now made without lead because lead can be poisonous. It can also cause serious pollution and so today many people are adapting their car engines, so that they run on lead-free petrol.

Leaf

Leaves are the food factories of green PLANTS. To make food, leaves need light, carbon dioxide and water. Light comes from the Sun. Carbon dioxide comes from the air. Air enters a leaf through little holes called *stomata*. Water is drawn up from the ground by the plant's roots. It flows up the stem and into the leaf through tiny tubes called veins. Inside the leaf is a green colouring called chlorophyll. The chlorophyll uses light, water and carbon dioxide to make SUGAR. The way it does this is known as *photosynthesis*. The sugar then passes through tubes to the other parts of the plant.

In the autumn many trees lose their leaves. First they shut off the water supply to the leaves. This destroys the green colour and gives the leaves yellow, red and orange tints.

SEE IT YOURSELF

Make a leaf print by rubbing the back of a leaf lightly with shoe polish or paint. Lay the leaf, painted side down, on a clean sheet of paper and cover it with another sheet. Rub over the whole area of the leaf and you will have a clear picture of the veins. To make a leaf rubbing, lay a clean sheet of paper over a leaf and rub firmly all over with a crayon or soft pencil. The leaf pattern will gradually appear.

▶ Leaves come in many shapes, sizes and even colours. You can identify a tree by looking at one of its leaves, once you learn a bit about them.

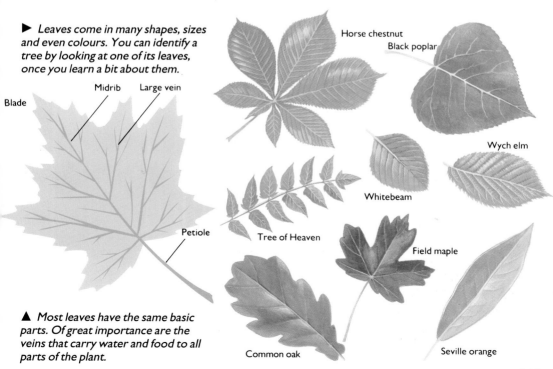

Blade

Midrib   Large vein

Petiole

Horse chestnut

Black poplar

Wych elm

Whitebeam

Tree of Heaven

Field maple

Common oak

Seville orange

▲ Most leaves have the same basic parts. Of great importance are the veins that carry water and food to all parts of the plant.

▲ *Lenin's revolutionary ideas united the group of communists called Bolsheviks, who overthrew the Russian government in 1917.*

Lenin, Vladimir

Vladimir Ilyich Lenin (1870–1924) helped to make Russia the first communist country in the world. Before his time, Russia was ruled by emperors, or *tsars*. Like Karl MARX, Lenin believed in COMMUNISM. He wanted every country run by the workers and no longer split into rich and poor groups. For many years Lenin lived outside Russia. He wrote books, and articles for communist newspapers. In 1917 he went back to Russia. He became the leader of a group of communists called Bolsheviks, who overthrew the government. Lenin then ruled Russia until he died.

Lens

Lenses are used to make things look bigger or smaller. They are usually made of glass or plastic. The lens inside your EYE is made of PROTEIN. Sometimes eye lenses do not work properly. Then people cannot see clearly. The lenses in spectacles make people's eyesight better. The lenses in MICROSCOPES, binoculars and TELESCOPES make faraway things or small things seem much larger.

Each lens has two smooth sides. Both sides may be curved, or one may be curved and the other flat. There are two main kinds of lens. Lenses where the edges are thicker than the middle are called *concave* lenses. Concave means 'hollowed out'. When LIGHT rays pass through a concave lens, they spread out. If

The 'burning glass' for producing fire from the Sun's rays has been known since ancient times. The magnifying property of a simple lens was recorded by Roger Bacon in the 13th century. Spectacle lenses were first used in the 14th century, and by the 16th century spectacles were commonly used. Benjamin Franklin invented the bifocal lens in 1760.

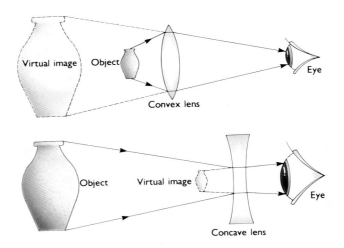

▶ *Light rays passing through a convex lens bend outwards, making the virtual image appear larger than it really is. The virtual image is what we see. A concave lens bends the rays inwards and the image looks smaller.*

you look at something through a concave lens, it looks smaller than it really is. Short-sighted people use spectacles that have concave lenses.

Lenses where the middle is thicker than the edges are called *convex* lenses. Convex means 'rounded'. When light rays pass through a convex lens, they come together. If you look at things through a convex lens, they seem larger. People with long sight have spectacles with convex lenses.

Leonardo da Vinci

Leonardo da Vinci (1452–1519) was an Italian artist and inventor. He lived during the RENAISSANCE. One of his most famous paintings is the *Mona Lisa*. It is a picture of a woman who is smiling mysteriously. Many people have wondered what she was smiling at. Leonardo made thousands of drawings of human bodies, water, plants and animals. He kept notes of his observations in secret back-to-front 'mirror' writing.

SHORT SIGHTEDNESS

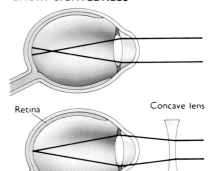

Retina   Concave lens

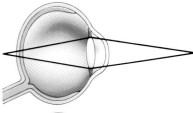

LONG SIGHTEDNESS

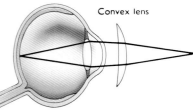

Convex lens

▲ In people with short sight, light from a distant object is focused by the lens of the eye before it reaches the back of the eye, or retina. This means the object looks blurred. In people with long sight, light from nearby objects is focused at a point beyond the retina, so they appear blurred. Corrective lenses in glasses make the images focus on the retina, so they look sharp and clear.

◄ Leonardo's famous painting, the Mona Lisa, hangs in the Louvre museum in Paris.

Leonardo worked as an engineer for Italian nobles and for the French king. He designed forts and canals. The canals had locks so that boats could travel up and down hills. Leonardo also drew ideas for things long before they were invented. His drawings include a helicopter, a flying machine and a machine gun.

Leonardo was interested in many other things, including music and architecture. He was also a good musician and singer.

Leopard

Leopards are large, wild cats just a bit smaller than LIONS. They live in Africa and southern Asia. Most leopards are spotted like jaguars, but some are nearly black. These are called panthers.

Leopards are very fierce, strong and agile hunters. They catch and eat antelopes, goats, dogs and sometimes people. Leopards are good climbers and they often hunt from trees, lying in wait on a branch. If they cannot eat all their catch at once, they may haul the carcass high up into a tree. Caracasses of animals weighing up to 68 kilograms have been found in trees. This is to stop lazier hunters such as lions or hyenas from stealing it. Leopards have two to four cubs at a time.

▼ *Although they are fierce hunters, female leopards are good mothers and take great care of their young until they can fend for themselves.*

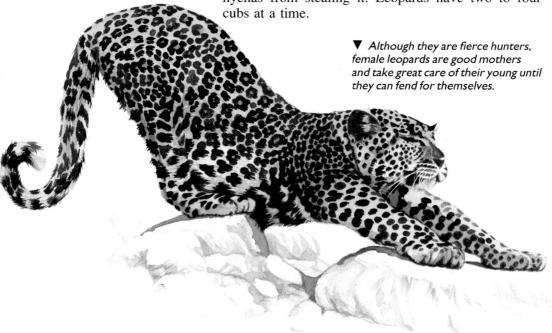

Libya

Libya is a large country in North AFRICA. It is more than three times the size of France, but very few people live there. This is because most of Libya lies in the SAHARA desert.

Most Libyans are ARABS who farm the land. Libya is also rich in oil. The country became part of the Turkish Ottoman Empire in the 1500s, and was a colony of Italy from 1912 to the end of World War II. It became an independent monarchy in 1952 as the United Kingdom of Libya. In 1969 army officers overthrew the king and took control, and Colonel Muammar al-Qaddafi became head of the government. Since that time Qaddafi has led a revolution in Libyan life and many nations have accused him of interfering in other countries' affairs.

LIBYA

Government: Islamic Arab Socialist
Capital: Tripoli
Area: 1,759,540 sq km
Population: 4,545,000
Language: Arabic
Currency: Libyan dinar

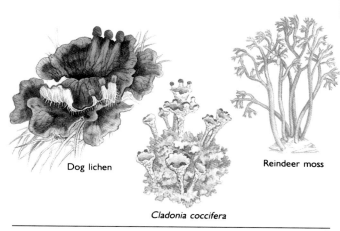

Dog lichen

Reindeer moss

Cladonia coccifera

 A lichen is actually made up of two plants – a fungus and an alga – growing together. Reindeer moss, though called a moss, is actually a lichen.

Lichen

A lichen is a simple PLANT. It has no roots, leaves or flowers. Some lichens grow as crusty patches on rocks, trees or walls. They grow very slowly. A patch no larger than your hand may be hundreds of years old. Other lichens grow as shrubby tufts. Lichens can live in places that are too bare, dry, cold or hot for any other plant.

Light

Light is a kind of ENERGY that we can see. Some objects—stars, lamps, certain chemicals—produce light. Most things do not produce light. We can see them only because they reflect light. For example,

▶ *A prism splits white light into a spectrum of colours. When the sun shines through rain, the raindrops act as a prism to make a rainbow.*

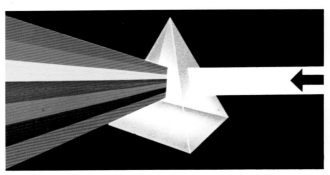

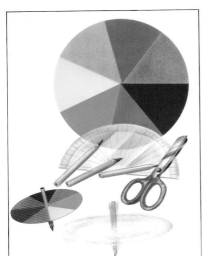

SEE IT YOURSELF

Here is a way to show that white light is made up of the seven colours of the rainbow. Cut a disc from card and divide it into seven equal sections. Colour each section as shown. Make a small hole in the middle of the disc and push a sharp pencil or stick through. Spin the disc quickly. What do you see?

▼ *When light rays travel through different substances, in this case air and water, they are bent so the image looks distorted.*

we can see the Moon and planets such as Venus and Jupiter in the sky only because they reflect light from the Sun.

Sunlight is the brightest light we normally see. Summer sunlight can be as bright as 10,000 candles burning close enough to touch. Bright sunlight seems white, but it is really made up of the colours of the RAINBOW. Isaac NEWTON showed this. He made a sunbeam shine through a specially shaped chunk of glass called a prism. Red, orange, yellow, green, blue, indigo and violet rays of light came out of the prism.

The prism had split the sunbeam into separate beams, each with its own *wavelength*. This is easy to understand if you think of light travelling in waves. The distance between the tops of the waves is the wavelength. We see each wavelength as a different colour. Long waves are red, short waves are violet, and wavelengths in between show up as all the other colours in the rainbow.

Light travels very fast, more than 300,000 km each second. Even so, it takes eight minutes for the light from the Sun to reach Earth, a distance of 150 million kilometres. A light year is the total distance a beam of light travels in one year— 9,470,000,000,000 kilometres. Scientists use light years to measure how far away STARS are. Some are millions of light years away.

Lincoln, Abraham

Abraham Lincoln (1809–1865) was president of the United States from 1861 to 1865. He had little schooling, but studied law on his own.

In 1854 a law was passed allowing people in new western territories to own slaves. In 1856 Lincoln joined the new, anti-slavery Republican Party and was elected president in 1860. Abraham Lincoln started a second term of office in 1865, just as he was trying to unite the nation at the end of the Civil War. But on April 14, 1865, on a visit to Ford's Theater in Washington, D.C., he was shot dead by John Wilkes Booth, an actor.

Lindbergh, Charles

Charles Augustus Lindbergh (1902–1974) was an American pilot who became the first man to fly the Atlantic Ocean alone. His single-engine aircraft, *Spirit of St. Louis,* left New York on May 20, 1927. He landed on May 21 in Paris, 33½ hours later, after flying about 5600 km non-stop. Lindbergh's flight made him an international hero. Later he helped to plan air tours to South America and over the Atlantic Ocean.

▲ Lincoln was the 16th president of the United States. He was shot just five days after the Civil War ended by John Wilkes Booth, an actor who supported the defeated South.

Lion

Lions are large, tawny-coloured wild CATS. An adult male weighs about 180 kg and measures about 2.7 metres from nose to tail. Females (lionesses) are slightly smaller and have no mane.

Lions usually live in groups called prides. A pride has one male, several females and all their cubs. Lions often hunt as a team. No other big cats seem to do this. They hunt mainly antelope and zebra. Lionesses do most of the hunting.

Many lions today lead protected lives on nature reserves where they are safe from humans.

▼ When lions are not hunting, they spend long periods resting to conserve their energy. Lions used to roam wild over southern Europe, India and Africa. Now they live only in South and East Africa and a tiny part of India.

215

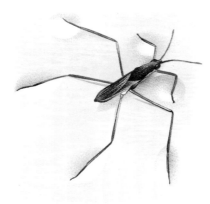

Liquid

A liquid can flow and change its shape. Liquids include water, milk, mercury and oil. When liquid is poured into a container, it takes the shape of the container but its volume remains the same. As a liquid gets hotter, the atoms or molecules in it move faster. They begin to leave the liquid. A GAS is formed. At the boiling point, the liquid boils and in time all of it turns into gas.

When a liquid gets colder, the atoms or molecules in it slow down. At the freezing point, they settle into rows and the liquid becomes a solid.

Lister, Joseph

Joseph Lister (1827–1912) was an English surgeon who found a way to stop his patients from dying of infection after operations. He used antiseptics to kill germs on surgeons' hands and instruments.

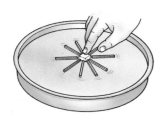

Liver

Your liver is a flat, triangular organ tucked under your right ribs. It is larger than your stomach. The liver is a kind of chemical factory and storage cupboard. It produces the digestive juice that burns up the fat you eat. It makes the PROTEINS used in blood. It gets rid of any poisonous substances in the blood or changes them so that they are harmless. Minerals and VITAMINS are stored in the liver until the body needs them.

Lizard

Lizards are REPTILES with dry, scaly skins and long tails. Most have four legs but some have none. These look like snakes. Some lizards are born live like MAMMALS, but most of them hatch from eggs.

There are about 3000 kinds of lizard. Most live in hot countries. Lizards that live in cooler places spend the winter in HIBERNATION. Lizards mainly eat insects.

Most lizards are only a few centimetres long, but the Komodo dragon of Indonesia is longer and heavier than a man. More typical lizards include the common lizard and the green lizard.

London

London is the capital of the United Kingdom. It has about seven million people. The river Thames runs through London.

People from all over the world visit London to see Buckingham Palace, the Houses of PARLIAMENT, Westminster Abbey and the Tower of London. There are many museums, theatres and parks in London, as well as offices and factories.

London began as a Roman settlement called *Londinium*. The plague came to London in the 1600s, followed by the Great Fire of 1666. The city was badly bombed in WORLD WAR II.

London is very slowly sinking into its foundations and the level of the river Thames is slowly rising. As a result, extra-high tides could flood a large part of London. To prevent this happening, a great barrier has been built across the Thames at Woolwich. If very high tides happen, the barrier can be raised and London will be safe.

Louis (French kings)

Eighteen French kings were called Louis.

The first was Louis I (778–840). Louis IX (1214–1270) led two CRUSADES. Louis XI (1423–1483) won power and land from his nobles. Louis XIII (1601–1643) made the French kings very powerful. Louis XIV (1638–1715) ruled for 72 years. He built a great palace at Versailles. All the French nobles had to live in his palace. Louis XVI (1754–1793) was beheaded after the FRENCH REVOLUTION.

Lung

Lungs are organs for BREATHING. People have lungs, and so do many animals. Lungs bring OXYGEN to the body from the AIR. They also remove waste carbon dioxide from the BLOOD.

Your lungs are two large, sponge-like masses in your chest. They fill with air and empty as you breathe in and out.

You breathe in air through the nose. The air flows down the windpipe, or *trachea*. Where the lungs begin, the trachea divides into two hollow branches called bronchial tubes, or *bronchi*. Each divides into smaller tubes called *bronchioles*. These end in cups called air sacs, or *alveoli*. This is where the lungs give oxygen to the blood and take away carbon dioxide.

Lungs need clean air. Smokers and people who live in smoky towns, or work in some kinds of dusty air, may get lung diseases.

▼ The soft, fragile lungs are well protected inside the rib cage, which expands and contracts to allow for the movements of breathing.

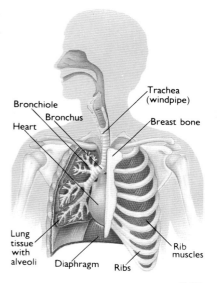

Bronchiole
Bronchus
Heart
Trachea (windpipe)
Breast bone
Lung tissue with alveoli
Diaphragm
Ribs
Rib muscles

Machine (Simple)

Some machines are very large and have many moving parts. Other machines are very simple. All the machines we see working around us are related to one or other of six simple machines. These machines were among people's oldest and most important inventions.

A machine is stronger than a person. It uses a greater *force*. When a force is used to move something, we can say that *work* is done. Machines make work easier. The *wedge*, for example, helps us to split things. A wedge hammered into a small crack in a tree trunk will split the trunk in two. Chisels, knives, nails and axes are all different forms of wedges.

The screw can pull things together or push them apart. With a screw jack, a man can quite easily lift a car weighing far more than himself. There are many kinds of *levers*. The simplest is a long pole, pivoted or balanced on a log and used to lift a heavy rock. The lever changes a small downward force into a bigger upward force.

The *inclined plane* makes it easier to raise heavy loads to higher levels. It is easier to pull a load up a slope than to lift it straight up. The PULLEY also makes lifting easier. A simple pulley is used in the winding mechanism that raises water from a well. A more complicated machine is the block and tackle, which has several sets of ropes and pulleys.

Probably the most important of all simple machines is the *wheel and axle*. This is used not only for moving loads, but also in all sorts of machines – such as clocks. An axle is a fixed shaft that lets wheels spin round instead of rolling under the vehicle.

▼ *Machines make it easier for us to do work. When we operate them, we do a little work over a long distance so that the machine can do a lot of work over a short distance. For example, in the screw jack shown below, you have to turn the lower bar many times to raise the upper bar only a little, but this bar can raise a very great weight.*

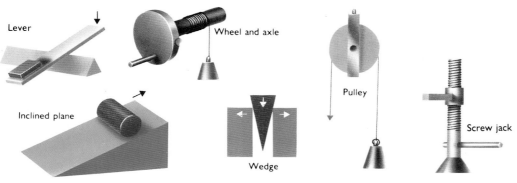

Lever

Wheel and axle

Pulley

Inclined plane

Screw jack

Wedge

Magnetism

A magnet attracts metals, particularly iron and steel. The Earth is a huge natural magnet. Invisible lines of magnetic force spread out round the planet, joining the North and South magnetic poles. We call this the Earth's *magnetic field*.

The needle in a COMPASS is a magnet. It always turns to face magnetic North. In ancient times people noticed that a kind of iron ore called a lodestone suspended from a string would always swing to point in the same direction. A lodestone is a natural magnet. Another name for it is magnetite.

An electromagnet is made by coiling wire round a metal core and passing electricity through the coil. Electromagnets can be made more powerful than ordinary magnets.

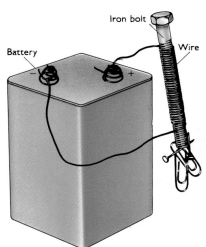

Iron bolt

Battery

Wire

▲ *In an electromagnet, a metal that is not normally magnetic, such as an iron bolt, can be made so by passing an electric current through a coil of wire wrapped around it. As soon as the current is broken, the magnetic field ceases to exist.*

Malaysia

Malaysia is a country in SOUTH-EAST ASIA. It is in two parts, West Malaysia on the Malay Peninsula, and East Malaysia, which is part of the island of Borneo. The capital, Kuala Lumpur, is in West Malaysia.

Malaysia has over 17,000,000 people, mostly Malays and Chinese. Its main exports are rubber, timber and tin.

Malaysia is a member of the Commonwealth. It is ruled by a sultan, who is head of state, and a prime minister, who is head of government.

Mammal

Mammals are not the largest group of animals on Earth. But they are the most intelligent and show a greater variety of forms than any other group of animals.

All mammals have warm blood and a bony skeleton. Many have hair or fur on their bodies to keep them warm. Female mammals give birth to live young, which they feed on milk from special glands in their bodies. Some mammals (such as mice) are born naked, blind and helpless. Others (such as deer) can run within hours of being born.

Mammals were the last great animal group to appear on Earth. They came long after fish, amphibians, reptiles and insects. When DINOSAURS

MALAYSIA

Government: Constitutional monarchy
Capital: Kuala Lumpur
Area: 329,749 sq km
Population: 17,861,000
Languages: Malay, Eng Chinese
Currency: Ringgit

219

EGG-LAYING MAMMALS

Echidna

Platypus

MARSUPIALS

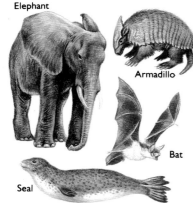

Koala   Tasmanian devil

PLACENTAL MAMMALS

Elephant

Armadillo

Bat

Seal

▲ *There are three families of mammals: egg-laying mammals, marsupials and placental mammals. The placental mammals are the most advanced group.*

ruled the Earth, millions of years ago, the only mammals were tiny creatures which looked like SHREWS. But after the dinosaurs died out, the mammals took over. During EVOLUTION, the mammals multiplied into many different forms which spread all over the world.

Scientists divide the mammals into three families. The most primitive mammals still lay eggs, like the reptiles and birds. There are only two left in this family, the echidna and the platypus. Then come the MARSUPIALS. These mammals give birth to tiny, half-developed young which have to be carried in their mother's pouch until they are big enough to look after themselves. The best known marsupial is the KANGAROO. Almost all the marsupials live in Australia.

The 'placental' mammals, the highest group of all, give birth to fully developed young. There are many different kinds, including flying mammals (BATS); gnawing animals or RODENTS; sea mammals (WHALES and DOLPHINS); and burrowing mammals (for example, moles). There are insect-eaters, plant-eaters and flesh-eaters. The flesh-eaters, or CARNIVORES, include the powerful CATS, WOLVES and BEARS. The most intelligent of all the mammals are the primates. This family includes MONKEYS, APES and HUMAN BEINGS.

Map and Chart

We need maps and charts to help us find our way about. There are different kinds of maps. Some show countries, towns, roads and railways. These

...day, aerial photographs are ...ake accurate maps. The ...is lost. ...n taken from a plane flying ...height. Each photo ...t slightly, so no detail

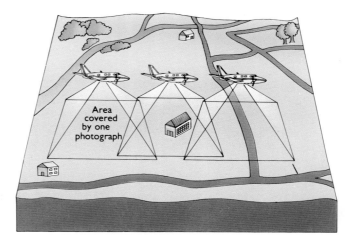

Area covered by one photograph

are *political* maps. *Physical* maps show natural features such as mountains, plains, rivers and lakes. The shape of features such as mountains is shown by colours or by contour lines.

Maps are drawn to different *scales*. The scale of some maps is so big that you might be able to find your house on one. The scale of other maps is very small so that we can even squeeze the whole world onto one page of an atlas. On a small-scale map, 2 cm on the map might represent 200 km, or 200,000 m, for example, on the ground.

Charts are maps of the sea. They tell sailors about lighthouses, rocks, channels and the depth of water in various places.

▲ *Marconi left Italy to continue his experiments in England because he did not get enough encouragement from the Italian government.*

Marco Polo *See Polo, Marco*

Marconi, Guglielmo

Guglielmo Marconi (1874–1937) was the man who, most people say, invented RADIO. His parents were rich Italians. When he was only 20 he managed to make an electric bell ring in one corner of a room, set off by radio waves sent out from the other corner. Soon he was sending radio signals over longer and longer distances. In 1901 he sent the first message across the Atlantic. In 1924 he sent signals across the world to Australia.

Marconi shared the Nobel Prize for physics in 1909 and was honoured throughout the world.

$A = 1/4$; $B = 3/8$; $C = 5/8$; $D = 4/5$;
$E = 3/5$; $F = 2/5$.

Mars (Planet)

The planet Mars is only about half the size of the Earth. It takes about two years to travel around the Sun. The surface of Mars has huge volcanoes and great gorges, far bigger than those on Earth. Most of Mars is covered with loose rocks, scattered over a dusty red surface. This is why Mars is called the 'Red Planet'. It has a North Pole and a South Pole.

Seen through a telescope, the red surface of Mars is criss-crossed by thin grey lines. Some early astronomers thought that these lines were canals which had been dug by intelligent beings. They said these canals had been dug to irrigate the soil, since Mars has very little water. But space probes to Mars

MARS FACTS

Average distance from Sun: 228 million km
Nearest distance from Earth: 78 million km
Temperature on sunlit side: 0 degrees C
Temperature on dark side: −170 degrees C
Diameter across equator: 6794 km
Atmosphere: Carbon dioxide
Number of moons: 2
Length of day: 24 hours 37 minutes
Length of year: 687 Earth days

Mars

Earth

▶ *The dusty, red surface of Mars shows no trace of life. Viking space probes to the planet appear finally to have put an end to any ideas that there could be alien beings living there.*

▼ *The kangaroo, like other marsupials, gives birth to its young before they are fully formed: (1) Before the birth, the female cleans her pouch and the fur around it. When the baby kangaroo is born, it crawls through the fur to the pouch (2). It attaches itself to one of the teats (3), and stays in the pouch for about 190 days until it is fully developed (4).*

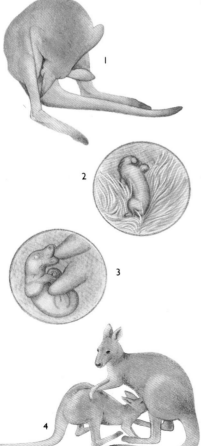

in 1965, 1969 and 1976 found no trace of the canals. The American Viking spacecraft landed on Mars and took samples of the planet's soil, but it was unable to find any kind of life on Mars.

The planet has two tiny moons – Phobos and Deimos. Phobos, the larger of the two, is only about 24 km across.

Because Mars has a smaller mass than the Earth, things on its surface weigh only about 40 per cent of what they would weigh on Earth. A day on Mars is about the same length as an Earth day.

Marsupial

Marsupials are MAMMALS with pouches – animals such as KANGAROOS, wallabies, bandicoots, KOALAS and OPOSSUMS. They all live in Australia, except the American opossum. A newly-born marsupial is very tiny. It crawls into its mother's pouch and stays there, feeding on her milk, until it can look after itself.

Marx, Karl

Karl Marx (1818–1883) was a political thinker and writer whose ideas brought about great social and political changes. Marx was born in Germany and his ideas were the starting point of COMMUNISM. He believed that people who own property, the capitalist class, keep those who work for them down so the owners can become richer. He also thought that the workers would one day rise against the capitalists and take control. Marx's ideas later inspired communist revolutions all over the world, notably the Russian Revolution.

Mary, Queen of Scots

Mary, Queen of Scots (1542–1587) was the last Roman Catholic ruler of SCOTLAND. The daughter of James V of Scotland, she was educated in France, and did not return to Scotland until she was 19. By that time she thought of herself as more French and Catholic than Scottish and Protestant.

Mary was the heir to the English throne after her Protestant cousin ELIZABETH I. In 1567 Mary was forced to give up the Scottish throne. Later she was imprisoned for 20 years in England. People said she was plotting against Queen Elizabeth. She was executed on the queen's orders in 1587.

Mathematics

We all use mathematics every day. We add up the coins in our pockets to find out how much money we have. We look at a clock and work out how much time we have left before going somewhere. In every business people are constantly using some kind of mathematics; often, nowadays, with the help of calculators and computers. The branch of mathematics that deals with numbers is called arithmetic. Algebra uses symbols such as x and y instead of numbers. Geometry deals with lines, angles and shapes such as triangles and squares.

> Some numbers are magic! Take the quite ordinary-looking number 142857, for example. Try multiplying it by 2. You get 285714. The same digits in the same order, but moved along. Now try multiplying our magic number by 3, by 4, by 5 and by 6. (A calculator will make it easier.) See what happens! And there's more. Try dividing it by 2 and by 5.

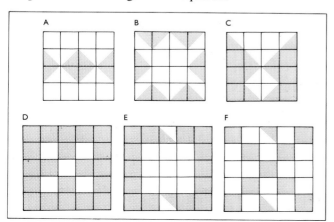

◀ *You can work out fractions by counting squares and half squares. What fraction of each grid has been coloured? The answers are on page 221.*

▼ *A Mayan carving in serpentine, a kind of rock, showing the god Tlaloc.*

▶ *Mayan temples are huge and imposing buildings, showing skill in architecture and engineering.*

Maya

The Maya Indians first lived in Central America in the AD 400s. They grew maize and sweet potatoes and kept pet dogs. Later they built cities of stone, with richly decorated palaces, temples, pyramids and observatories. Even today, many of these wonderful buildings are still standing, hidden in the jungle. The Maya were also skilled in astronomy and mathematics, and they had an advanced kind of writing.

The Maya people did not have any metals until very late in their history. They built with only stone tools, and had no knowledge of the wheel. Their lives were controlled by religion. They worshipped a sun god, rain gods, soil gods and a moon goddess who looked after women.

ADVANCES IN MEDICINE

1590	**Microscope** – Zacharias Janssen
1593	**Thermometer** – Galileo
1628	**Blood circulation** – William Harvey
1796	**Vaccination** – Edward Jenner
1846	**Anaesthetic** – William Morton
1865	**Antiseptic surgery** – Joseph Lister
1865	**Germs cause disease** – Louis Pasteur
1895	**X-rays** – William Roentgen
1898	**Radium** – Pierre and Marie Curie
1922	**Insulin for diabetes** – Frederick Banting and Charles Best
1928	**Penicillin** – Alexander Fleming
1954	**Polio vaccine** – Jonas Salk
1967	**Heart transplant** – Christiaan Barnard

Medicine

When we first think of the word 'medicine' perhaps we think about all the tablets, powders, pills and liquids people take when they are not feeling well. But medicine also means the science of healing. It has taken a long time for medicine to become truly scientific.

In the early days doctors relied mostly on magic cures, prayers and charms. But in the last few hundred years medicine has advanced faster than in all of human history. The development of anaesthetics in the last century was a vital step forward in progress in surgery. And in this century progress has

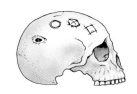

▲ Prehistoric men removed pieces from the skull to release evil spirits.

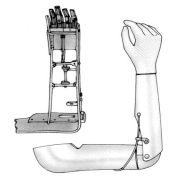

▲ An early 16th century iron hand (left) and a modern arm and hand (right).

▲ Joseph Lister's carbolic acid sprayer was used to sterilize operating theatres.

▼ This kidney machine helps patients with kidney failure.

▲ In Indian medicine, a steam pipe, called a Nadi-Svedi, was used from about 400BC to help wounds heal quickly.

► The iron lung was invented in 1876 to keep patients alive when their lungs failed to work.

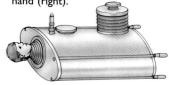

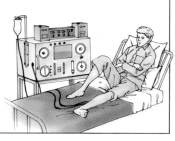

been fastest of all. Scientists have found out about VITAMINS; they have made all kinds of wonder drugs like penicillin; they have almost wiped out diseases such as tuberculosis and smallpox; they are finding out more and more about mental illness; and they can now give people spare parts for many parts of their bodies when these organs go wrong. But perhaps the most important area of a doctor's job is still *diagnosis*, finding out what is wrong with a patient by studying the symptoms.

▲ *Medicine has made huge advances from superstition and magic to the high-tech hospitals of today.*

Mendel, Gregor

Gregor Mendel (1822–1884) was an Austrian priest who became famous for his work on heredity. Heredity is the passing on of things such as eye colour, skin colour and mental ability from parents to their children.

Mendel grew up on a farm, where he became interested in plants. When he entered a monastery he began growing peas. He noticed that when he planted the seeds of tall pea plants, only tall pea plants grew. Then he tried crossing tall peas with short peas by taking pollen from one and putting it in the other. He found that again he had only tall plants. But when he crossed these new mixed tall

▲ *Mendel's important findings were not believed at first. It was some years before his laws were generally accepted.*

plants with each other, three-quarters of the new plants were tall and one quarter were short. Mendel had found out that things like the tallness or shortness are controlled by tiny *genes*, passed on from each parent. Mendel also showed that some genes are stronger than other genes.

MERCURY FACTS

Average distance from Sun: 58 million km

Nearest distance from Earth: 45 million km

Temperature on sunlit side: 350 degrees C

Temperature on dark side: −170 degrees C

Diameter across equator: 4878 km

Atmosphere: Almost none

Number of moons: 0

Length of day: 59 Earth days

Length of year: 88 Earth days

— Mercury

— Earth

Mercury (Planet)

The planet Mercury is one of the smallest planets in the SOLAR SYSTEM, and the closest to the Sun. A day on Mercury lasts 59 of our days. During the long daylight hours it is so hot that lead would melt. During the long night it grows unbelievably cold. Little was known about Mercury's surface until the space probe Mariner 10 passed within 800 km of the planet. It showed Mercury to have a thin atmosphere and big craters like those on the Moon.

Mercury travels very fast through space – at between 37 and 56 km per second. This great speed and its nearness to the Sun give it the shortest year of all the planets (a year is the time it takes a planet to go once round the Sun). Mercury's year lasts only 88 of our Earth days.

▶ *The Mariner 10 space probe passed Mercury three times in 1974 and 1975. It discovered that Mercury has a huge iron core, probably about three-quarters of the size of the planet.*

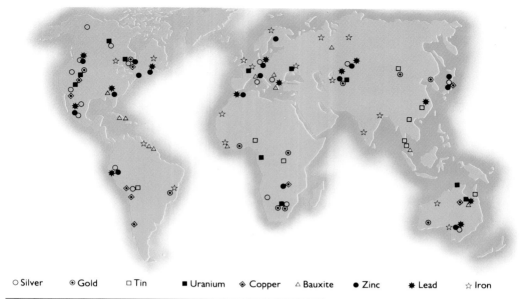

| ○ Silver | ◉ Gold | ▫ Tin | ■ Uranium | ◈ Copper | △ Bauxite | ● Zinc | ✳ Lead | ☆ Iron |

Metal

There are more than a hundred ELEMENTS on the Earth. About two-thirds of these are metals. The most important metals are IRON (for making steel), COPPER and aluminium.

People have used metals since early times. Copper, TIN and IRON were the first metals to be used. They were made into tools and weapons. GOLD and SILVER were also known very early on. They are often made into jewellery.

Most metals are shiny. They all let heat and electricity pass through them. Copper and silver are the best for this. Nearly all metals are solid unless they are heated.

Some metals are soft. They are easy to beat into shapes, and they can be pulled into thin wires. Other metals are *brittle*. This means they break easily. Some metals are very hard. It is difficult to work with them.

Metals can be mixed together to form ALLOYS. Alloys are different from their parent metals. Tin and copper are both soft. When mixed together, they form bronze. Bronze is a strong alloy. It is hard enough for swords and spears.

Metals are found in the ground. Some are found pure. They are not mixed with other things. Many metals are mixed up with other elements in MINERALS. The minerals must be treated to get the pure metal out.

▲ *This map shows known metal deposits throughout the world, but there must be many more deposits waiting to be discovered.*

▲ *Metals in the form of ore, such as this lump of iron, are quite unrecognizable except to an expert. An ore is a rock which contains minerals. When treated, these minerals release a pure metal.*

227

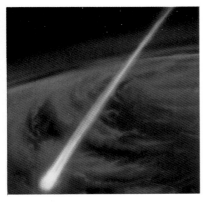

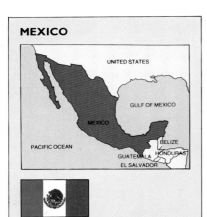 As a meteor enters the Earth's atmosphere, friction heats it and makes it glow.

Meteor

A meteor is a tiny piece of metal or stone. It travels through space at great speed. Millions of meteors fall on the Earth every day. Most of them burn up before they reach the ground. On clear nights you can sometimes see shooting stars. They are meteors burning up. Sometimes a large meteor reaches the ground. Then it is called a meteorite. Meteorites sometimes make large holes called craters.

Metric System

The metric system is used for measuring weight, length and volume. It is based on units of ten, or decimals. It was first used in France in the late 1700s. Now it is used in most parts of the world.

Mexico

Mexico is a country in NORTH AMERICA. It lies between the United States in the north and Central America in the south. To the east is the Gulf of Mexico, a big bay. On the west lies the Pacific Ocean.

Mexico has an area of 1,972,547 sq km. Much of the country is hilly, with fertile uplands. The highest mountains reach over 5700 metres. In the southeast, the low Yucatan Peninsula sticks out far into the Gulf of Mexico.

Mexico is a tropical country, but most of the land is high. This makes the climate cool and dry. The north has desert in places.

The first people in Mexico were Indians, such as the AZTECS.

MEXICO

Government: Federal republic
Capital: Mexico City
Area: 1,972,547 sq km
Population: 86,154,000
Language: Spanish
Currency: Peso

Michelangelo

Michelangelo Buonarroti (1475–1564) was a painter and sculptor. He lived in Italy at the time of the RENAISSANCE. Michelangelo is famous for the wonderful statues and paintings he made of people. He spent four and a half years painting pictures in the Sistine Chapel in the Vatican City. Many of his statues are large and very lifelike. His statue of David is 4 metres high. Michelangelo was the chief architect of St Peter's in Rome.

Microphone

A microphone picks up SOUND waves and turns them into electric signals. The signals can be made into a RECORDING or sent out as RADIO waves. They can also be fed through an amplifier and loud-speakers. These make the sound louder. The mouthpiece of a TELEPHONE has a microphone in it that turns your voice into electric signals.

Microscope

A microscope is an instrument used for looking at tiny objects. It *magnifies* things, or makes them look bigger. Things that are invisible to the naked eye are called *microscopic*. Many microscopic plants and animals, including BACTERIA, can be seen if you look at them through a microscope.

Microscopes work by using lenses. The simplest microscope is a magnifying glass. It has only one LENS. The lenses in many microscopes work by bending light rays. Small microscopes can magnify 100 times. Big microscopes used by scientists may magnify up to 1600 times. The electron microscope is much more powerful. It can magnify up to 2,000,000 times. Instead of bending light rays, it bends beams of electrons. Electrons are parts of ATOMS.

Anton van Leeuwenhoek, a Dutchman who lived in the 1600s, made one of the first microscopes. Using his microscope, he showed that fleas hatch from tiny eggs. Before this, people thought fleas came from sand or mud because they could not see anything as small as the eggs.

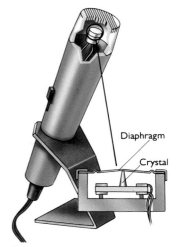

▲ In this microphone, sound waves hit the flexible diaphragm and make it vibrate. These vibrations are picked up by a crystal and turned into electric signals.

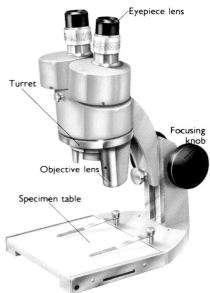

▲ In an optical microscope, the image can be seen by looking down through the eyepiece and tube, containing a series of magnifying lenses.

◄ This electron microscope image shows a dust mite, flakes of skin, soil particles, cat fur and fibres, all taken from a vacuum cleaner.

▶ *The heart of a microwave oven is a magnetron. A magnetron produces microwaves, which are usually reflected onto the food to be cooked. The waves shake up water molecules in the food. The molecules rub against each other and the friction produces heat, which cooks the food.*

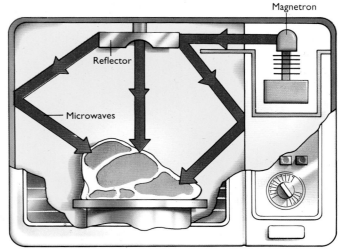

Magnetron

Reflector

Microwaves

Microwaves

Microwaves are a form of radiation. The waves have a wavelength of a few centimetres. They are used for communications, since their wavelength is a convenient size, easy to direct and control. Microwaves are usually produced from a metal cavity into which a whole number of wavelengths will fit exactly; this is very like the way in which SOUND is produced by an organ pipe. Very intense microwave beams can be produced using a maser. Microwaves can be used for cooking. In a microwave oven, the water molecules in the food absorb microwave ENERGY and so the food heats all through and cooks.

In the Middle Ages the value of spices was often greater than that of gold or jewels. Most spices were brought to Europe from India or the Moluccas – the Spice Islands. The route was from India to the Persian Gulf, then across the Arabian Sea by ship. The spices were then taken by caravan across the Middle East to the Mediterranean or the Black Sea, and from there to the countries of Europe. No wonder spices were very costly.

The Middle Ages

The Middle Ages in Europe began with the collapse of the Roman Empire in the AD 400s and lasted for about 1000 years. The 'Roman peace' ended, and much of Europe suffered wars and invasions. The learning of ancient times was almost forgotten, surviving only in the monasteries. Kings or nobles struggled for power, while the mass of people dwelt in poverty. The Black Death was spread by rats and killed 25 million people throughout Europe.

However, the Middle Ages also gave much to later generations. Great cathedrals were built. Universities were started. Painting and literature developed. With the 1400s came a rebirth of learning, the RENAISSANCE. The Middle Ages were over.

► In the feudal system, society was organized in a sort of pyramid, with the clergy and nobles at the top and a great many peasants at the bottom. In the middle were merchants and craftsmen.

THE KNIGHT

A knight was trained for war. He wore armour and rode a horse. Knights practised fighting at mock-battles called jousts. They were supposed to obey a code of knightly honour, known as chivalry.

THE SCIENTIST

Most medieval scientists practised alchemy, trying to turn lead into gold. A few, such as Roger Bacon (1214–1294), studied the stars and realized that the Earth was round.

THE PEASANT

Peasants worked on the land, and lived in huts which they often shared with their animals. They slept on straw mattresses on the floor. They ploughed the fields with ploughs pulled by oxen.

▼ Monarch butterflies migrate from Canada and the USA to Mexico in huge numbers each year.

Migration

Many animals make long journeys to breed or find food. Most make the journey every year. Some make the journey only twice in their life. These journeys are called migrations. Animals migrate by INSTINCT. They do not have to plan their journey.

Birds are the greatest migrants. Swallows leave Europe and North America every autumn. They fly south to spend winter in Africa or South America. These places are warm and the swallows find plenty of food there. The trip may be 10,000 km long. In spring, the swallows fly north again to breed.

MILK

▶ Each year, the short-tailed shearwater travels from Tasmania and Australia towards the Pacific. Following the wind, the bird flies all the way to Arctic regions via the Asian coast before returning along the North American coast to its breeding ground. It is a round trip of 32,000 km and takes the bird seven months.

The white beluga whale lives in the Arctic and migrates south in the summer and north again in the winter. Scientists are not sure why the whale follows this strange 'upside-down' path of migration.

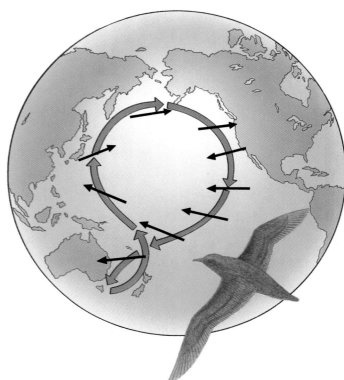

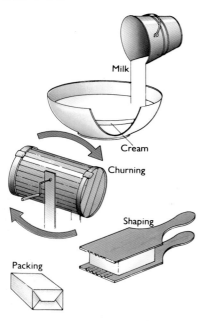

▲ Traditional methods of making butter involved skimming the cream off milk and 'churning' it by agitating it in a butter churn. This made the fat particles come together to form a thick yellow solid. It was patted into shape with wooden paddles, then wrapped and sold.

Whales and fish make long journeys through the sea to find food and breed. The eels of Europe's lakes and rivers swim thousands of kilometres across the Atlantic Ocean to breed. After breeding they die. The young eels take years to swim back to Europe. Monarch butterflies of North America fly south in great numbers for the winter.

Milk

Milk is a food that all baby MAMMALS live on. It comes from the breasts, or mammaries, of the baby's mother. The baby sucks the milk from its mother's teat or nipple.

At first, the milk is pale and watery. It protects the baby from diseases and infections. Later, the milk is much richer and creamier. It contains all the food the baby needs. Milk is full of FAT, SUGAR, STARCHES, PROTEIN, VITAMINS and MINERALS. After a while the baby starts to eat other kinds of food.

People use milk from many animals. These include cows, sheep, goats, camels, and even reindeer. The animals are kept in herds. Sometimes they live on farms, called *dairy* farms.

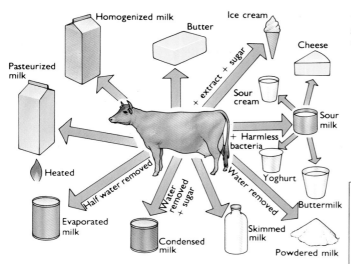

Milk is used to make many other foods. Cream, butter, yoghurt, cheese and some ice cream are all made from milk.

Milky Way

When you look at the sky on a clear, moonless night you can see a pale cloud of light. It stretches across the heavens. If you look at it through binoculars or a telescope, you can see that the cloud is really millions of stars. All these stars, and most of the other stars we see, are part of our GALAXY. It is called the Milky Way.

It is impossible to imagine the size of the Milky Way. It takes light from the Sun eight minutes to reach us (the Sun is 150,000,000 km away and light travels at a speed of 300,000 km per second). Light from the centre of the Milky Way takes about 30,000 *years* to reach the Earth. From where we are in the solar system it takes about 200 million years for the Earth to make just one trip around the Milky Way.

▼ *The view below shows how the Milky Way might appear from a few hundred light-years above the galaxy.*

Astronomers think that the Milky Way has about 100,000 million stars like our Sun. The Milky Way stretches over a distance of about 100,000 light-years. A light-year is the distance light travels in one year at a speed of 300,000 km a second. Our own SOLAR SYSTEM is 30,000 light-years from the centre of the Milky Way.

The Milky Way has a spiral shape. Its trailing arms turn slowly around the centre. They take 200 million years to make a full circle. From Earth, we see the Milky Way through the arms of the spiral. The cloud of stars in the picture is what we might see from a great distance above the galaxy.

The Milky Way is not a special galaxy. There are thousands of other galaxies with the same shape. There may be millions and millions of other galaxies in the UNIVERSE.

▼ A scale of hardness of minerals was devised by an Austrian, Friedrich Mohs, with the softest at the top and the hardest at the bottom. They are classed from 1 to 10. The hardness of other common things is shown alongside. Each mineral can scratch those above it on the scale, but not below.

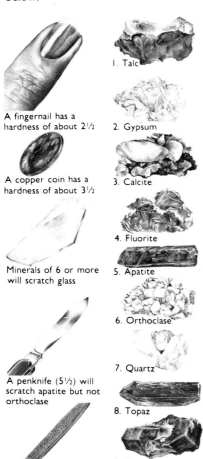

A fingernail has a hardness of about 2½

1. Talc

2. Gypsum

A copper coin has a hardness of about 3½

3. Calcite

4. Fluorite

Minerals of 6 or more will scratch glass

5. Apatite

6. Orthoclase

A penknife (5½) will scratch apatite but not orthoclase

7. Quartz

8. Topaz

9. Corundum

A special steel file will scratch quartz

10. Diamond

Mineral

The rocks of the Earth are made up of materials called minerals. There are many different kinds of mineral. Some, such as GOLD or platinum, are made up of only one ELEMENT. Others, such as QUARTZ and SALT, consist of two or more elements. Some minerals are metals, such as COPPER or SILVER. Other minerals are non-metallic, like sulphur.

Pure minerals are made up of ATOMS arranged in regular patterns, known as CRYSTALS. Minerals form crystals when they cool from hot GASES and LIQUIDS deep inside the Earth. Crystals can grow very large if they cool slowly. But large or small, crystals of the same mineral nearly always have the same shape.

Altogether there are over 2000 minerals. Yet most of the Earth's rocks are made up of only 30 minerals. The most common mineral of all is quartz. Most grains of sand are quartz. Pure quartz is made up of large, well-shaped crystals and has a milky colour.

Mining

Mining means digging MINERALS out of the Earth. It is one of the world's most important industries. When minerals lie in one place in large quantities they are known as ores. People mine minerals such as GOLD, SILVER and TIN. They also mine COAL.

Mines can be open pits or underground tunnels. When the ore is close to the surface the soil that lies on top of it is simply lifted away. Giant diggers then scoop up the rock that contains the minerals. Underground mines can be as deep as 3 km below the surface. Another form of mining is dredging. Here minerals are scooped up from the beds of rivers and lakes.

Mississippi River

The Mississippi River is the longest river in the UNITED STATES. It rises in Minnesota in the north and flows 3780 km southwards to the Gulf of Mexico. It has over 250 tributaries, small rivers that flow into it. The waters of the Mississippi carry a lot of mud. As a result its delta, where most of the mud is dumped, is growing out to sea at a rate of a kilometre every 10 years.

Mollusc

Molluscs are a large group of animals. There are about 70,000 different kinds. After insects they are the most numerous of all animals. They are found everywhere from deserts to the sea.

Most molluscs grow shells to protect themselves; some have shells inside parts of their bodies; some have no shells at all. But all molluscs have soft bodies and no bones.

▼ A great variety of molluscs are found in the sea, and some of them are good to eat.

THE DEVELOPMENT OF MONEY

The earliest form of trade was bartering, when goods would simply be exchanged.

Money has been made in all shapes and sizes, but it must be easy to use and store.

American Indians used beads and shells, often made into decorative patterns, as money.

Some shells are only a few millimetres wide. Others, such as that of the giant clam, are over a metre wide. As a mollusc grows, its shell grows with it. The shell is made of a hard limy material formed from the food the mollusc eats. Shells have many strange shapes and patterns.

The largest mollusc is the giant squid. This can grow to as much as 12 metres.

Money

We use money every day to pay for things we buy. We pay with either coins or paper notes. This sort of money is known as cash. There is also another kind of money. It includes cheques, credit cards and travellers' cheques.

Almost anything can be used as money. In the past people have used shells, beads, cocoa beans, salt, grain and even cattle. But coins are much easier to use than say, cattle. They are easy to store and to carry around.

Coins were first used in China. They were also used by ancient Greeks as early as 600 BC. They were valuable because they were made of either gold or silver. They were stamped with the mark of the ruler of the country for which they were made and also with how much each coin was worth.

Later, people began to use coins made of cheaper metals. The metal itself had no value, but the coins were still worth the amount stamped on them. They also started to use paper money. It no longer mattered that the money itself had no real value. It was backed by the government and banks. This is the kind of money we use today.

Coins have remained popular for centuries. They are easy to produce and last a long time.

Bank notes are a kind of promise, because they represent a sum of money.

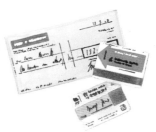

Credit cards and cheques are useful because they can be used instead of cash.

Mongolia

Mongolia is a republic in the heart of ASIA. It lies between Russia and China. The country has a population of about 2,000,000.

Mongolia is a high, flat country. It is mostly desert or rolling grassland, with mountain ranges in the west. The Gobi Desert covers a large part of the land.

The people of Mongolia are descended from the MONGOLS. Until recently a Communist state, Mongolia now has a multi-party system.

MONGOLIA

Government: Multi-party system
Capital: Ulan Bator
Area: 1,565,000 sq km
Population: 2,100,000
Language: Mongolian
Currency: Tugrik

Mongols

Mongols were NOMADS who lived on the great plains of central Asia. They herded huge flocks of sheep, goats, cattle and horses, which they grazed on the vast grasslands of the region. They lived in tent villages that they could quickly pack up and take with them when they moved on to find new pastures.

The Mongols were superb horsemen and highly trained warriors. In the 1200s they formed a mighty army under the great GENGHIS KHAN. Swift-riding hordes of Mongols swept through China, India, Persia and as far west as Hungary.

Under Genghis Khan, and later his grandson, Kublai Khan, the Mongols conquered half the known world. But they were unable to hold their empire together. In less than 100 years the Mongol empire had been taken over by the Chinese.

▼ Mongols were wanderers and expert horsemen. Their temporary shelters, known as yurts, were made of wood and hides.

Woolly monkey

Colobus monkey

Spider monkey

▲ *The colobus monkey lives in Africa. The spider and woolly monkeys live in the forests of South America.*

Monkey

Monkeys are MAMMALS that belong to the same group of animals as APES and HUMAN BEINGS. Most monkeys have long tails and thick fur all over their body. Monkeys are usually smaller than apes. Their hands and feet are used for grasping and are very similar to those of humans.

There are about 400 different kinds of monkey. Most live in the tropics, especially in forests, in Africa, Asia and South America. South American monkeys have long tails that they use like an extra arm or leg when swinging through the branches of trees.

On the ground monkeys usually move about on all four limbs. But when they are using their hands to hold something they can stand or sit up on two legs.

Monkeys live in family groups known as troops. They spend a lot of time chattering, playing, fighting and grooming each other. Each troop of monkeys has its own territory where it lives and feeds. It will fight fiercely to defend this area against other invading groups.

Moon

People have worshipped the Moon, made wishes on the Moon (because of superstition) and even walked on the Moon. The Moon is our nearest neighbour in space. It is the Earth's only natural SATELLITE, and was probably formed at the same time as our planet. But the rocks on the Moon's surface are older than those on the Earth's surface because the Moon has not changed in over 4000 million years. There has been no wind or water to wear the rocks away.

The diameter of the Moon is 400 times smaller than that of the Sun. However, the Moon is 400 times closer to the Earth. So to us, they look about the same size.

The Moon is a dry, lifeless world, without air. GRAVITY on the Moon is just one-sixth of gravity on Earth, yet the Moon's gravitational pull affects us every day. It is the Moon's pull that causes the rise and fall of the ocean tides. Astronauts landed to explore the Moon in 1969. One day in the future permanent bases may be built there.

MOON FACTS

- The Moon is 382,000 kilometres from the Earth.
- The Earth weighs 81 times as much as the Moon.
- The diameter (distance across) of the Moon is 3476 kilometres.
- The oldest Moon rock is 4600 million years old.
- The Moon has no seas. Its flat plains are called maria, because early astronomers mistook them for oceans and named them after the Latin *mare*, meaning 'sea'.
- The Moon's surface is pitted with craters. Almost all these holes were made by meteorites crashing into the Moon.
- The Latin word for the Moon is *luna*. From this we get our word 'lunar', meaning 'of the Moon'.
- The Moon once had active volcanoes, but almost all of its volcanoes are now dead.
- No one on Earth had seen the far side of the Moon until a spacecraft photographed it in 1959.

▲ *The maria, or plains, look dark in photographs. The Moon's craters and mountains cast long shadows.*

Mormon

Mormons belong to a religious group founded by Joseph Smith in 1830. The name comes from the *Book of Mormon*, which Mormons believe is a sacred history of ancient American peoples. The Mormons began in New York, but were persecuted for their beliefs and driven out. They finally settled in Salt Lake Valley, Utah.

Morocco

Morocco is a country right at the top of north-west AFRICA. It is nearly twice the size of Great Britain and has two coastlines. On the west is the Atlantic Ocean and to the north is the Mediterranean Sea.

Moroccans are well-known for the fine leather goods, pottery and rugs they produce. Such art often shows the influence of Spanish and French styles, for both these nations formerly controlled Morocco.

Most of Morocco's 25 million people are farmers. They grow wheat, maize, fruit, olives and nuts. Some keep sheep, goats and cattle. Most of the people are Muslims. Casablanca is the largest city and main seaport. The country is ruled by a king.

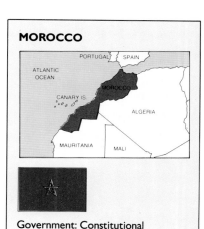

MOROCCO

Government: Constitutional monarchy
Capital: Rabat
Area: 446,550 sq km
Population: 25,061,000
Language: Arabic
Currency: Dirham

INTERNATIONAL MORSE CODE

A ·—		P ·——·	
B —···		Q ——·—	
C —·—·		R ·—·	
D —··		S ···	
E ·		T —	
F ··—·		U ··—	
G ——·		V ···—	
H ····		W ·——	
I ··		X —··—	
J ·———		Y —·——	
K —·—		Z ——··	
L ·—··		Full stop (.) ·—·—·—	
M ——		Comma (,) ——··——	
N —·		Query (?) ··——··	
O ———		Error ········	

Morse Code

Morse code is a simple way of sending messages. It is an alphabet of dots and dashes. Each letter has its own dot and dash pattern. The code was invented by Samuel Morse, an American artist, to send messages along a telegraph wire. The telegraph operator presses a key at one end to send a signal along the wire to a sounder at the other end. A short signal is a dot and a long signal is a dash. The first official telegraph message was sent in 1844.

Mosaic

A mosaic is a picture made from small pieces of coloured stone or glass set into cement. The pieces are arranged to make a design or a portrait or to show a scene.

Mosaic making is a very ancient art. The Sumerians made mosaics nearly 5000 years ago. Mosaics are a very practical way of decorating floors and walls, as they can be washed without being spoiled. In ancient Rome, every villa and palace had its dazzling mosaics showing scenes from everyday life. Religious mosaics were common in Greece and Italy.

▼ *St Basil's Cathedral is in one of the most historic parts of Moscow, near Red Square and the Kremlin.*

Moscow

Moscow is the capital of Russia. It is also the biggest city in the country. More than eight million people live there. Moscow lies on a plain across the river Moskva. It is the largest industrial and business centre in the country. Everything is made in Moscow, from cars to clothes. It is also the political and cultural centre of the country.

Moscow was first made the capital of Muscovy in 1547, during the reign of Ivan the Terrible, the first *tsar* (emperor) of Russia. It grew up around the KREMLIN, an ancient fort from which the Muscovy princes used to defend their country. Moscow remained the capital of the tsars until 1712 when Peter the Great moved the capital to St Petersburg. The city remained very important, even after it was nearly all burnt down during NAPOLEON's occupation of 1812. After the Revolution of 1917, Moscow became the seat of the Soviet government. In 1992 it became the capital of Russia again.

Mosquito

Mosquitoes are a small kind of FLY. They have slender, tube-shaped bodies, three pairs of long legs and two narrow wings. There are about 1400 different kinds. They live all over the world from the tropics to the Arctic, but must be able to get to water to lay their eggs.

Only female mosquitoes bite and suck blood. They have special piercing mouths. Males live on the juices of plants. When the female bites, she injects a substance into her victim to make the blood flow more easily. This makes mosquito bites itch.

Some kinds of mosquito spread serious diseases. Malaria and yellow fever are two diseases passed on by mosquitoes.

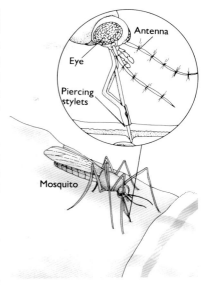

Moss

This is a very common kind of PLANT that grows in low, closely packed clusters. There are more than 12,000 different kinds. They are very hardy plants and flourish everywhere, except in deserts, even as far north as the Arctic. Most mosses grow in damp places. They spread in carpets on the ground in shady forests, or over rocks and the trunks of trees.

Mosses are very simple kinds of plants, like LICHENS. They were among the first plants to make their home on land. They have slender creeping stems that are covered with tiny leaves. Instead of proper roots that reach down into the soil, mosses simply have a mass of tiny hairs that soak up moisture and food. Mosses do not have flowers. They reproduce by spores, just like ferns. One kind, called sphagnum moss, grows in bogs and is the plant that makes peat.

▲ The female mosquito uses its stylets to pierce tiny blood vessels in its victims.

▼ When mosses are ready to reproduce they produce capsules containing tiny spores. They soak up moisture and nutrients through tiny root-hairs called rhizoids.

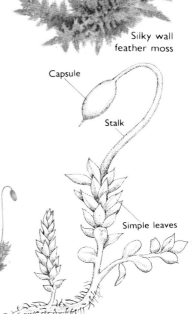

Silky wall feather moss

Capsule

Stalk

Simple leaves

Rhizoids

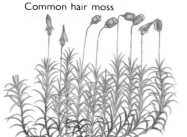

Common hair moss

Bryum capillare

241

WORLD'S HIGHEST MOUNTAINS		
Peak	Range	Metres
Everest	Himalayas	8848
Godwin Austen	Karakoram	8610
Kanchen junga	Himalayas	8598
Lhotse	Himalayas	8510
Makalu	Himalayas	8470
Dhaulagiri I	Himalayas	8172
Manaslu	Himalayas	8156
Cho Oyu	Himalayas	8153
Nanga Parbat	Himalayas	8126
Annapurna I	Himalayas	8078
Gasherbrum I	Karakoram	8068
Broad Peak	Karakoram	8047
Gasherbrum II	Karakoram	8033
Gosainthan	Himalayas	8013
Gasherbrum III	Karakoram	7952
Annapurna II	Himalayas	7937
Gasherbrum IV	Karakoram	7925
Kangbachen	Himalayas	7902
Gyachung Kang	Himalayas	7897
Himal Chuli	Himalayas	7893
Disteghil Sar	Karakoram	7885
Kunyang Kish	Karakoram	7852
Dakum (Peak 29)	Himalayas	7852
Nuptse	Himalayas	7841

▼ Different plants grow at different altitudes in mountain areas. This is because the air gets thinner and colder the higher you go.

Mountain

A large part of the Earth's surface is covered by mountains. The greatest mountain ranges are the Alps of Europe, the Rockies and the ANDES of America and the HIMALAYAS of Asia. The Himalayas are the greatest of them all. They have many of the world's highest peaks, including the biggest, Mount EVEREST.

There are mountains under the sea, too. And sometimes the peaks of under-sea mountains stick up above the sea's surface as islands. One mountain called Mauna Loa which rises from the floor of the Pacific Ocean is very much higher than Everest.

Mountains are formed by movements in the Earth's crust. Some mountains are formed when two great land masses move toward each other and squeeze up the land in between. The Alps were made in this way. Other mountains are VOLCANOES, great heaps of ash and lava that poured out when the volcano erupted.

But even the greatest mountains do not last for ever. The hardest rock gets worn away in time by rain, wind, sun and frost. RIVERS cut valleys, glaciers grind their way down, wearing away the mountains after untold centuries into gentle hills.

When the height of a mountain is given, it means the height above sea level. This can be a lot more than the height from the base.

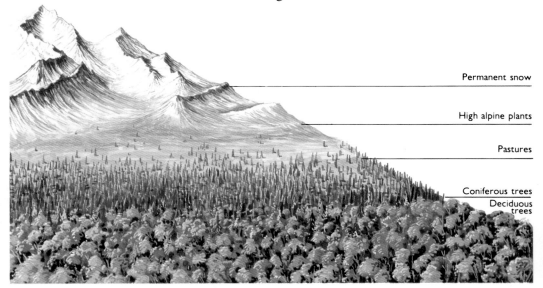

Permanent snow

High alpine plants

Pastures

Coniferous trees

Deciduous trees

Mozart, Wolfgang Amadeus

Wolfgang Amadeus Mozart (1756–1791) was an Austrian and one of the greatest composers of music that the world has known. He began writing music at the age of five. Two years later he was playing at concerts all over Europe. Mozart wrote over 600 pieces of music, including many beautiful operas and symphonies. But he earned little money from his hard work. He died at the age of 35.

Muhammad

Muhammad (AD 570–632) was the founder and leader of the religion known as ISLAM. He was born in Mecca in what is now Saudi Arabia. At the age of 40 he believed that God had asked him to preach to the ARABS. He taught that there was only one God, called Allah.

In 622 he was forced out of Mecca, and this is the year from which the Muslim calendar dates. After his death his teachings spread rapidly across the world.

▲ *From a very early age, Mozart was taken on concert tours by his father Leopold, also a musician.*

Muscle

Muscles are the things that make the parts of our bodies move. When you pick up this book or kick a ball you are using muscles. There are two different kinds of muscles. Some work when your brain tells them to. When you pick up a chair, your brain sends signals to muscles in your arms, in your body and in your legs. All these muscles work together at the right time, and you pick up the chair. Other kinds of muscles work even when you are asleep. Your stomach muscles go on churning the food you have eaten. Your heart muscles go on pumping blood. The human body has more than 500 muscles.

Mushroom and Toadstool

Mushrooms grow in woods, fields and on people's lawns – almost anywhere, in fact, where it is warm enough and damp enough. Some mushrooms are very good to eat. Others are so poisonous that people die from eating them. Many people call the poisonous ones toadstools. Mushrooms are in the

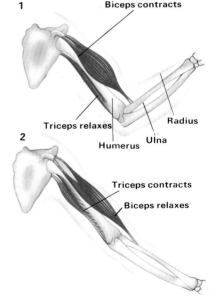

▲ *Muscles often work in pairs, with one contracting as the other relaxes. They are said to be antagonistic, or working against each other. This is how the arm muscles work.*

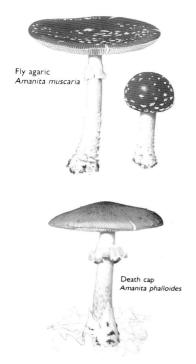

Fly agaric
Amanita muscaria

Death cap
Amanita phalloides

▲ *Poisonous toadstools like these sometimes look dangerous, but even some harmless-looking ones can kill.*

▼ *In music some notes have two names. C sharp, for instance, is the same note as D flat. A ♯ by a note means that it is raised by a semi-tone, a ♭ by a note means it is lowered a semi-tone.*

fungus group of plants. They have no green colouring matter (CHLOROPHYLL); instead they feed on decayed matter in the soil or on other plants.

Music

People have been making some kind of music all through history. The very earliest people probably made singing noises and beat time with pieces of wood. We know that the ancient Egyptians enjoyed their music. Paintings in the tombs of the PHARAOHS show musicians playing pipes, harps and other stringed instruments. The ancient Greeks also liked stringed instruments such as the lyre. But we have no idea what this early music sounded like, because there was no way of writing it down.

By the MIDDLE AGES, composers were writing music for groups of instruments. But it was not until the 1600s that the ORCHESTRA as we know it was born. The first orchestras were brought together by Italian composers to accompany their OPERAS. It was at this time that violins, violas and cellos were first used.

As instruments improved, new ones were added to the orchestra. BACH and HANDEL, who were both born in 1685, used orchestras with mostly stringed instruments like the violin. But they also had flutes, oboes, trumpets and horns. Joseph Haydn was the first composer to use the orchestra as a whole. He invented the *symphony*. In this, all the instruments blended together so that none was more important than the others.

A new kind of music began with the great German composer BEETHOVEN. He began writing

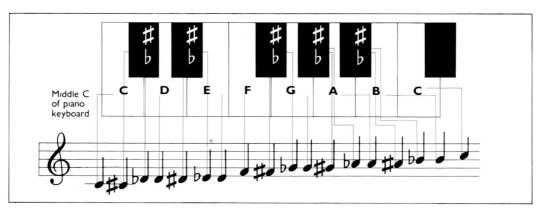

Middle C
of piano
keyboard

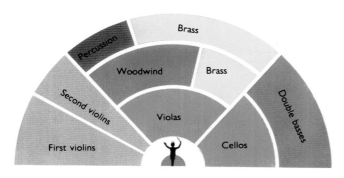

◀ The layout of a modern symphony orchestra has been developed over many years.

music in which some of the notes clashed. This sounded rather shocking to people who listened to his music in his day. Later musicians tried all kinds of mixtures of instruments. In the 1900s new kinds of music were made by composers such as Igor Stravinsky and Arnold Schoenberg. Others since then have used tape recorders and electronic systems to produce new sounds which are often rather strange to our ears.

But much music still has three things: *melody, harmony* and *rhythm*. The melody is the tune. Harmony is the agreeable sound made when certain notes are played together. Often these notes form a *chord*, an arrangement of notes within a particular musical key. Rhythm is the regular 'beat' of the music. The simplest kind of music is just beating out a rhythm on a drum.

SEE IT YOURSELF
You can make a simple guitar from a cardboard box and some elastic bands. Cut a hole in the lid of the box and tack lengths of elastic of varying thickness tightly across it. Fit a wedge of wood beneath the elastic bands as shown. The bands will give out different notes when they are plucked.

Musical Instrument

There are four kinds of musical instrument. In wind instruments, air is made to vibrate inside a tube. This vibrating air makes a musical note.

All *woodwind* instruments such as clarinets, bassoons, flutes, piccolos and recorders have holes that are covered by the fingers or by pads worked by the fingers. These holes change the length of the vibrating column of air inside the instrument. The shorter the column the higher the note. In *brass* wind instruments, the vibration of the player's lips makes the air in the instrument vibrate. By changing the pressure of the lips, the player can make different notes. Most brass instruments also have valves and pistons to change the length of the vibrating column of air, and so make different notes. The tuba and trombone are brass instruments.

What is probably the oldest kind of musical instrument has been found by archaeologists in Stone Age sites. It is a bull-roarer, consisting of a small oval-shaped piece of bone with a hole in one end in which a cord is tied. It is whirled around by the player and produces a buzzing sound – the faster it is whirled, the higher the buzz.

▼ *Percussion instruments are played by striking them. The note made by the timpani can be changed by tightening or loosening the skin.*

Vibrating skin

Mallet

Skin

Bowl

Stringed instruments work in one of two ways. The strings of the instrument are either made to vibrate by a bow, as in the violin, viola, cello and double bass; or the strings are plucked, as in the guitar, harp or banjo.

In *percussion* instruments, a tight piece of skin or a piece of wood or metal is struck to make a note. There are lots of percussion instruments – drums, cymbals, gongs, tambourines, triangles and chimes.

Electronic instruments such as the electric organ and the synthesizer make music using sounds produced by electronic circuits.

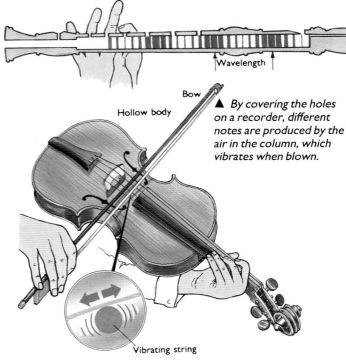

Wavelength

Hollow body

Bow

▲ *By covering the holes on a recorder, different notes are produced by the air in the column, which vibrates when blown.*

► *Friction between the strings and the bow of a violin causes the vibrations that make sound. The pitch can be changed by shortening or lengthening the string.*

Vibrating string

▲ *Mussolini was known in his native Italy as* Il Duce, *which means 'the leader'.*

Mussolini, Benito

Mussolini (1883–1945) was a dictator and leader of Italy's Fascists. In 1922 he bluffed the king of Italy into making him prime minister. Soon he made himself dictator. He wanted to make Italy great; he built many new buildings and created new jobs. But he also wanted military glory and led Italy into World War II on the side of HITLER. His armies were defeated by the Allies and Mussolini was finally captured and shot by his own people.

Napoleon Bonaparte

In 1789 the people of France rebelled against the unjust rule of their king and his nobles. The FRENCH REVOLUTION was supported by a young man born on the island of Corsica 20 years before. His name was Napoleon Bonaparte (1769–1821).

Napoleon went to the leading military school in Paris, and by 1792 he was a captain of artillery. Three years later he saved France by crushing a royalist rebellion in Paris. Soon Napoleon was head of the French army and won great victories in Italy, Belgium and Austria. In 1804 he crowned himself emperor of France in the presence of the Pope. Then he crowned his wife, Josephine.

But Napoleon could not defeat Britain at sea. He tried to stop all countries from trading with Britain, but Russia would not cooperate. So Napoleon led a great army into Russia in the winter of 1812. This campaign ended in disaster. His troops were defeated by the bitter weather. Then he met his final defeat at the battle of Waterloo in 1815. There he was beaten by the British under Wellington and the Prussians under Blücher. He was made prisoner by the British on the lonely Atlantic island of St Helena, where he died in 1821.

Napoleon was a small man. His soldiers adored him and called him 'the little corporal'. Napoleon drew up a new French code of law. Many of his laws are still in force today. He introduced important reforms into almost every area of French government.

▲ With political skills equal to his skills as a general, Napoleon reorganized the government of France.

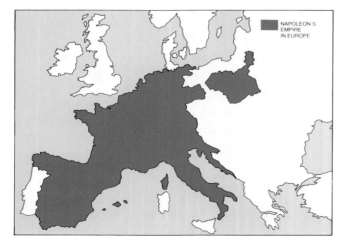

NAPOLEON'S EMPIRE IN EUROPE

◀ Napoleon set out to conquer the whole of Europe. Shown here is the extent of his empire at the height of his power.

NATO (North Atlantic Treaty Organization)

NATO is a defensive alliance set up after World War II. In 1949, 12 countries signed a treaty in which they agreed that an attack on one member should be considered an attack on them all. The 12 were Belgium, Canada, Denmark, France, Iceland, Italy, Luxembourg, the Netherlands, Norway, Portugal, the United Kingdom and the United States. Greece and Turkey joined in 1951, West Germany in 1954, and Spain in 1982. The original NATO headquarters were in Paris.

The purpose of the alliance is to unify and strengthen the military defences of the nations of Western Europe. Each member nation contributes soldiers and supplies to NATO forces. But the members of NATO also cooperate on political and economic issues.

In the 1960s some NATO members felt that the United States had too much power in the alliance. France withdrew her NATO forces in 1966. France is still a NATO member, but the headquarters have been moved from Paris to Brussels. With the collapse of many of the Communist governments of Eastern Europe in 1990, NATO is looking closely at its role for the future. In 1991 NATO forces were restructured as the Cold War came to an end.

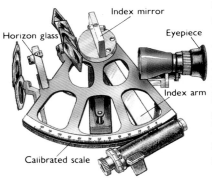

Index mirror

Horizon glass

Eyepiece

Index arm

Calibrated scale

▲ *A sextant can be used to work out a ship's position by measuring the angle between a star or the Sun and the horizon (see below).*

Navigation

Navigation means finding the way, usually in a ship or an aircraft. For hundreds of years, navigators at sea used the changing positions of the Sun and stars to work out their LATITUDE. Knowing the difference

▶ *Once the angle has been measured, the star's position at that particular time can be looked up in a very accurate table. This allows the position of the ship to be calculated. By taking a series of sextant readings the ship can be kept on the right course.*

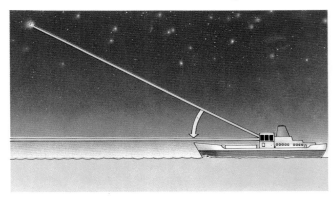

between the time on the ship and the time set at 0° longitude at Greenwich helped them to work out their position more precisely.

Today, many navigational instruments are electronic and are very accurate. Radio beacons and SATELLITES send out signals from which a ship can find its position. Then the navigator uses a COMPASS to keep the ship on the right course. COMPUTERS help ships, aircraft and spacecraft navigate exactly.

Nelson, Horatio

Horatio Nelson (1758–1805) was a famous British admiral at the time when Britain was at war with the French, led by NAPOLEON BONAPARTE.

Nelson was born in Norfolk, the son of a country clergyman. He joined the navy when he was 12 and was captain of a frigate by the time he was 20. He was made a rear-admiral in 1797. By then he had lost an eye in battle. Soon he lost an arm too.

▲ *Nelson once ignored an order to stop an attack by pretending he couldn't see the signal – he held his telescope to his blind eye.*

In 1798 he led his ships to victory against the French at Alexandria in Egypt. While he was in the Mediterranean he met and fell in love with Lady Hamilton, the wife of the British ambassador to Naples. Nelson loved Lady Hamilton all his life. Many people thought this was shocking as they were both married to other people.

Nelson's most famous battle was his last. It was fought against a French fleet led by Admiral Villeneuve. For nearly 10 months in 1805, Nelson's ships chased Villeneuve's across the Atlantic and back. Then, on October 21, they met off the Cape of Trafalgar in southern Spain. Nelson defeated the French in the battle that followed but was killed on board his ship, the *Victory*.

Before the battle Nelson sent a famous message to all the ships in his fleet: 'England expects that every man will do his duty.'

NEPTUNE FACTS

Average distance from Sun: 4500 million km
Nearest distance from Earth: 4350 million km
Average temperature (clouds): −240 degrees C
Diameter across equator: 49,000 km?
Atmosphere: Hydrogen, helium?
Number of moons: 6 known
Length of day: 18–20 hours?
Length of year: 165 Earth years

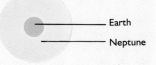

Earth

Neptune

Neptune (Planet)

The PLANET Neptune is named after the Roman god of water and the sea. It is a large planet far out in the SOLAR SYSTEM. It is about 4493 million km from the SUN. Only PLUTO is farther away. It takes Neptune 165 years to circle the Sun. (The Earth takes 365 days.)

▲ *If we could observe Neptune from its large moon, Triton, it would probably look like this. The light from the Sun would be no brighter than that of a star.*

Being so far from the Sun, Neptune is a very cold place. Scientists think its atmosphere is rather like JUPITER's, which is mostly made up of the gas HYDROGEN. Neptune has six moons, and scientists have recently discovered a system of thin rings around the planet.

Early astronomers were unable to see Neptune, but they knew it had to be there. They could tell there was something affecting the orbit of the nearby planet URANUS. In 1845 two astronomers, Adams in England and Leverrier in France, used mathematics to work out where Neptune should be. Astronomers used this information the next year, and spotted Neptune.

▼ *If the size of the various parts of your body corresponded to the number of nerve cells in them, you would look rather like this.*

Nerve

Nerves are tiny fibres made up of CELLS. They reach all through the body. When a part of the body touches something, the nerves send a message through the spinal column to the BRAIN. If we feel

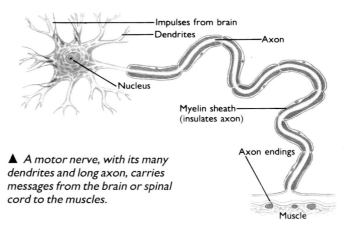

▲ *A motor nerve, with its many dendrites and long axon, carries messages from the brain or spinal cord to the muscles.*

pain, a message is sent back to make us move away from whatever is hurting. Nerves also carry the senses of sight, hearing and taste. The sense organs have special nerve endings that respond to heat, light, cold and other stimuli around us.

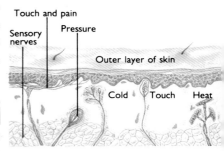

▲ Various receptors in the skin deal with different sensations. They transmit these sensations to the brain with the help of nerve cells.

Nest

A nest is a home built by an animal, where it has its young and looks after them. BIRDS build nests when they are ready to lay EGGS. Sometimes the female builds the nest, sometimes the male will give her some help. Some nests are very complicated, and may be lined with wool, hair or feathers. Others are simple or rather untidy.

A few MAMMALS such as mice and SQUIRRELS make nests for their young, but these are not as complicated as birds' nests.

Some INSECTS make the most complicated nests of all. These are not at all like birds' nests. They are often built for a whole group, or colony, of insects. There will be one queen, who lays eggs, and hundreds or even thousands of workers to look after them. Most BEES and wasps make this sort of nest. Some wasps build their nests out of paper. Termites make huge mud nests.

▲ Coots live on open stretches of water, but build their nests on piles of stones or sticks raised above the water.

Netherlands

The Netherlands, or Holland, as it is also known, is a low-lying country in western EUROPE. The sea often floods the flat land near the coast, so sea walls have been built for protection against storms. Living so near the sea, the people of the Netherlands (who call themselves the Dutch) have a long and successful history of seafaring, trade and exploring. A lot of the land is reclaimed from the sea.

The Netherlands is a land of canals, windmills, farms and bulb fields which burst into colour in spring. It was once part of a group of countries called the Low Countries, but it became self-governing in 1759. Important cities are Amsterdam, the capital, and Rotterdam, which is the busiest port in Europe. The Netherlands is a prosperous country and one of the first members of the EUROPEAN COMMUNITY. It has a queen, but is governed by a democratic parliament.

NETHERLANDS

Government: Constitutional monarchy
Capital: Amsterdam
Area: 40,844 sq km
Population: 14,700,000
Language: Dutch
Currency: Guilder

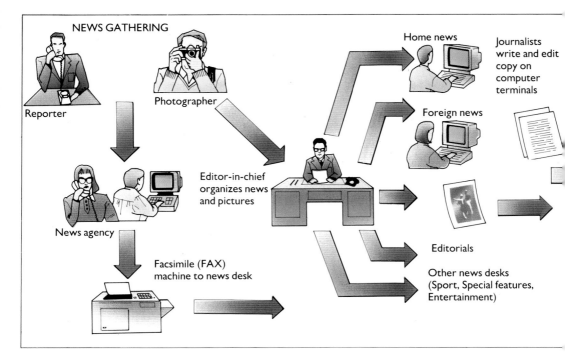

NEWS GATHERING

Reporter

Photographer

News agency

Editor-in-chief organizes news and pictures

Facsimile (FAX) machine to news desk

Home news

Journalists write and edit copy on computer terminals

Foreign news

Editorials

Other news desks (Sport, Special features, Entertainment)

▲ *There are many stages and many workers involved in producing a newspaper.*

▼ *Newton determined the laws of motion that are still used in physics today.*

Newspaper

Newspapers are just what their name says they are – papers that print news. They first appeared in the 1400s, just after PRINTING began. Printers produced pamphlets telling people what was happening in the country and what they thought about it.

Modern newspapers first appeared in the 1700s. Today, there are newspapers in almost every country in the world, in many different languages. Some are printed every day, some every week.

One of the oldest newspapers is *The Times* which is printed in London. It began in 1785 when it was called the *Universal Daily Register*. It changed its name to *The Times* in 1788. Other famous newspapers are the *New York Times* and the *Washington Post* in the United States, *Pravda* in Russia, and *Le Monde* in France.

Newton, Isaac

Sir Isaac Newton (1642–1727) was an English mathematician and scientist who made some of the world's greatest scientific discoveries. He left Cambridge University in 1665 when plague shut the

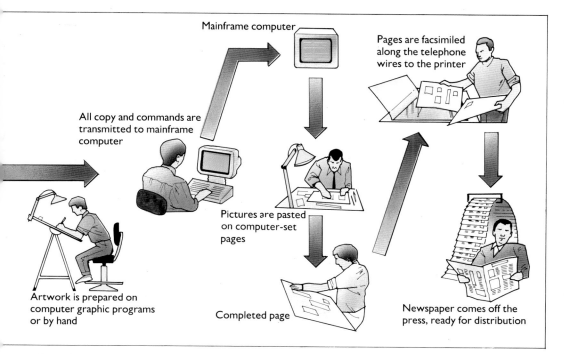

Mainframe computer

All copy and commands are transmitted to mainframe computer

Pages are facsimiled along the telephone wires to the printer

Artwork is prepared on computer graphic programs or by hand

Pictures are pasted on computer-set pages

Completed page

Newspaper comes off the press, ready for distribution

university. In the 18 months before the university reopened, Newton did much of his most important work.

Newton's experiments showed that white LIGHT is a mixture of all the colours of the rainbow (the spectrum). By studying the spectrum of light from a star or other glowing object, scientists can now find out what that object is made of. Newton's studies of light also led him to build the first reflecting TELESCOPE.

NEWTON also discovered GRAVITY. He realized that the same kind of force that makes apples fall from trees also gives objects weight and keeps PLANETS going round the SUN.

New York

New York City is the largest city in the UNITED STATES. More than 11 million people live in New York and its suburbs.

The city stands mainly on three islands that lie at the mouth of the Hudson River. The island of Manhattan holds the heart of New York, and many of its most famous sights. Some of the world's tallest skyscrapers tower above its streets. Fifth Avenue is

New York probably has the most mixed population of any city in the world. Its black community is the largest in the United States. The world's largest Jewish population lives in the New York area. The city has a Little Italy and a Chinatown.

NEW ZEALAND

Government: Parliamentary
Capital: Wellington
Area: 268,676 sq km
Population: 3,346,000
Languages: English, Maori
Currency: Dollar

▲ The kiwi lives in the forests of New Zealand. Since it cannot fly, it does not need the strong, stiff feathers most birds have. Its feathers look more like shaggy fur.

When the first European settlers arrived in New Zealand, the only animals there were dogs and rats. All the country's cattle, sheep, pigs, deer, rabbits and goats were brought in by Europeans.

a famous shopping street, and Broadway is known for its theatres. Perhaps New York's best-known sight is the Statue of Liberty, one of the largest statues on Earth. It stands on an island in New York Harbor.

Ships from every continent dock at New York's port, which is the largest anywhere. New York is one of the world's great business centres. Its factories produce more goods than those of any other city in the United States.

New Zealand

New Zealand is a remote island nation in the Pacific Ocean, south-east of Australia.

New Zealand is actually two main islands. North Island is famous for its hot springs and volcanoes. South Island has a range of mountains called the Southern Alps, and many lakes and waterfalls.

The country also has plains and valleys. Here, the mild climate helps farmers to grow grains, vegetables and apples. They also raise millions of sheep and cattle. New Zealand is the world's third largest producer of sheep and wool.

There are over three million New Zealanders. Two in three people live in a city or town. Auckland is the largest city, but the capital is Wellington. Both are in North Island.

New Zealand is a member of the COMMON-WEALTH. Many of its people are descended from British settlers. Others are Maoris, descended from Pacific islanders, who lived in New Zealand before the British came. They fought many battles with the first European settlers.

Niagara Falls

The Niagara Falls are waterfalls on the Niagara River in North America. Water from most of the GREAT LAKES flows through this river. Each minute about 450,000 tonnes of water plunge about 50 metres from a cliff into a gorge.

The falls stand on the border between Canada and the United States. The water pours down on each side of an island. Most of it plunges down the Horseshoe Falls in Canada. The rest plunges down the American Falls in the United States.

◀ *The sheer size of Niagara Falls has challenged people's courage and ingenuity for many years – Charles Blondin walked across the top of the falls on a tightrope on June 30, 1859.*

As the water plunges over the edge of Niagara Falls, it slowly erodes (wears away) the rock. In this way, the position of the falls is gradually changed. The falls are about 11 km farther north than they were when the water first flowed over them thousands of years ago. In several thousand more years, Niagara Falls as we know them will have disappeared.

Nigeria

This nation in West AFRICA is named after the Niger River that flows through it to the Atlantic Ocean. Nigeria has about 110 million people, more than any other nation in Africa. The capital is Lagos.

Nigeria is hot. Dry grass and scrubby trees are scattered across the country. Swamps and forests line the coasts.

There are a great number of different tribes and many of them speak different languages.

Half the people follow the religion of ISLAM. Most of the people grow maize, yams or other food crops. Nigeria is one of the world's main cocoa growers, and one of Africa's top two oil producers. It has been an independent nation since 1960.

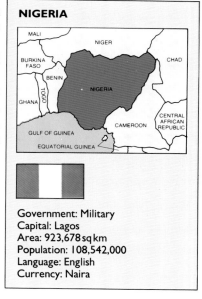

NIGERIA

Government: Military
Capital: Lagos
Area: 923,678 sq km
Population: 108,542,000
Language: English
Currency: Naira

◀ *There are various types of national dress in Nigeria. From left to right: the* bubu *and skirt made from Guinea brocade, the* babariga *worn by northerners, and the wrapper and blouse worn mostly by Ibo and Benin women.*

▼ *A ship unloads at the quay in an Ancient Egyptian city. The civilization that grew up in Ancient Egypt depended on the Nile for transport, so most large cities were built beside this great river.*

▼ *When Alfred Nobel died in 1896, he left $9,000,000 to set up the prizes that now bear his name. The interest that this money earns each year forms the awards.*

Nile

The Nile River in Africa is generally thought to be the longest river on Earth. (Some people think that the AMAZON is longer.) The Nile has been measured at 6690 km. It rises in Burundi in central Africa and flows north through Egypt into the Mediterranean Sea. It is very important to farmers, who rely on it for irrigation.

Nobel Prize

These money prizes are given each year to people who have helped mankind in different ways. Three prizes are for inventions or discoveries in physics, chemistry, and physiology and medicine. The fourth is for literature. The fifth prize is for work to make or keep peace between peoples and the sixth is for economics. Money for the prizes was left by the Swedish chemist Alfred Nobel, who invented the explosive dynamite.

Nomad

People without a settled home are nomads. Many nomads live in lands too dry to farm. Such people keep herds of animals and travel to find fresh pasture for them. They live in portable homes, such as tents. Many nomads still live in or near the great deserts of Africa and Asia.

North America

The continent of North America stretches north from tropical Panama to the cold Arctic Ocean, and east from the Pacific Ocean to the Atlantic Ocean. Only Asia is larger.

North America has the world's largest island (Greenland), and the largest freshwater lake (Lake Superior). It contains the second largest country (CANADA), the second longest mountain range (the Rocky Mountains), and the third longest river (the MISSISSIPPI RIVER). North America's natural wonders include NIAGARA FALLS and the Grand Canyon (the largest gorge on land).

The cold north has long, dark, frozen winters. No trees grow here. Farther south stand huge evergreen forests. Grasslands covered most of the plains in the middle of the continent until farmers ploughed them up. Cactuses thrive in the deserts of the southwest. Tropical trees grow quickly in the hot, wet forests of the south.

Peoples from all over the world have made their homes in North America. First, from Asia, came the ancestors of the AMERICAN INDIANS and ES-KIMOS. Later came Europeans, who brought black slaves from Africa. Most North Americans speak English, French or Spanish, and are Protestant or Roman Catholic Christians. They live in more than 30 nations. The UNITED STATES and Canada are large, powerful and rich. But many of the nations of Central America and the WEST INDIES are small and poor.

Only one person in every 12 people in the world lives in North America. Yet North Americans make half the world's manufactured goods. This is because North America produces huge amounts of food and raw materials to feed the workers and supply factory machines.

▲ *Three-quarters of North America is occupied by just two countries – Canada and the United States.*

NORTH AMERICA

Area: 24,240,000 sq km – 15.7 per cent of world's land area
Population: 432,000,000 – 8 per cent of world population
Coastline: 148,330 km
Highest mountain: Mount McKinley, Alaska, 6194 m
Lowest point: Death Valley, California, 86 m below sea level
Principal rivers: Mackenzie, Mississippi, Missouri, St Lawrence, Rio Grande, Yukon, Arkansas, Colorado
Principal lakes: Superior, Huron, Michigan, Great Bear, Great Slave, Erie, Winnipeg, Ontario
Largest city: Mexico City, 20,000,000
Busiest port: New Orleans

NORTH AMERICA

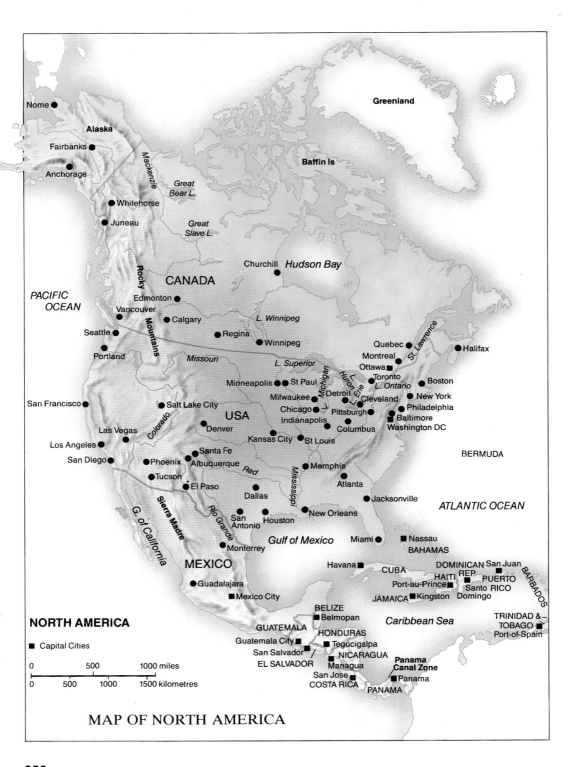

Nome
Alaska
Fairbanks
Anchorage
Mackenzie
Whitehorse
Great Bear L.
Juneau
Great Slave L.
Churchill
Hudson Bay
Greenland
Baffin Is
PACIFIC OCEAN
CANADA
Edmonton
Vancouver
Calgary
Regina
Winnipeg
L. Winnipeg
Rocky Mountains
Seattle
Portland
Missouri
L. Superior
Quebec
Montreal
Ottawa
St. Lawrence
Halifax
Minneapolis
St Paul
L. Michigan
L. Huron
Toronto
L. Ontario
Boston
San Francisco
Salt Lake City
USA
Milwaukee
Chicago
Detroit
L. Erie
Cleveland
New York
Philadelphia
Indianapolis
Pittsburgh
Baltimore
Denver
Columbus
Washington DC
Las Vegas
Colorado
Kansas City
St Louis
BERMUDA
Los Angeles
Santa Fe
San Diego
Phoenix
Albuquerque
Red
Memphis
Tucson
Mississippi
Atlanta
El Paso
Dallas
Jacksonville
ATLANTIC OCEAN
Sierra Madre
Rio Grande
San Antonio
Houston
New Orleans
G. of California
Monterrey
Gulf of Mexico
Miami
Nassau
BAHAMAS
MEXICO
Havana
CUBA
DOMINICAN REP
San Juan
PUERTO RICO
HAITI
Port-au-Prince
Santo Domingo
BARBADOS
Guadalajara
JAMAICA
Kingston
Mexico City
BELIZE
Belmopan
Caribbean Sea
TRINIDAD & TOBAGO
Port-of-Spain

NORTH AMERICA

- Capital Cities

| 0 | 500 | 1000 miles |
| 0 | 500 | 1000 | 1500 kilometres |

GUATEMALA
Guatemala City
San Salvador
EL SALVADOR
HONDURAS
Tegucigalpa
NICARAGUA
Managua
San Jose
COSTA RICA
Panama Canal Zone
Panama
PANAMA

MAP OF NORTH AMERICA

North Sea

This part of the Atlantic Ocean separates Great Britain from Scandinavia and other northern parts of mainland Europe. The North Sea is quite shallow. If you lowered St Paul's Cathedral in London into the middle of the North Sea, the top would show above the waves. Winter storms often make this sea very dangerous for ships.

The North Sea is an important waterway. Some of the world's largest and busiest ports stand on its shores. Its waters are rich in fish, and the seabed holds oil and natural gas.

NORWAY

Government: Hereditary
   constitutional monarchy
Capital: Oslo
Area: 324,219 sq km
Population: 4,242,000
Language: Norwegian
Currency: Krone

Norway

Norway is EUROPE's sixth largest country. This long, northern kingdom is wide in the south but narrow in the centre and the north. Mountains with forests, bare rocks and snow cover much of Norway. Steep inlets called FIORDS pierce its rocky coast.

Summers in Norway are cool and the winters long. It is very cold in the ARCTIC north, but the rainy west coast is kept fairly mild by the Gulf Stream.

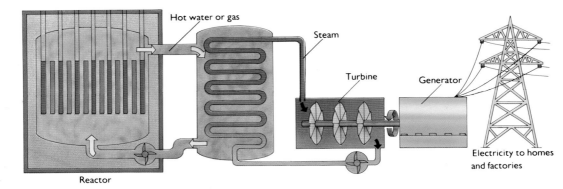

▲ *In a nuclear power station the energy, in the form of heat, from the controlled nuclear reaction is used to make steam. The steam drives turbines which generate electricity in the same way as in any other type of power station.*

Nuclear Energy

The tiny nucleus at the centre of the atom contains the most powerful force ever discovered. This force gives us nuclear energy – sometimes called atomic energy. The most complicated ELEMENT that occurs in nature is URANIUM. The nuclear fuel used in nuclear power stations is a rare form of uranium called uranium-235.

When the nucleus of a uranium-235 atom is struck by a neutron (see ATOM), it breaks apart and more neutrons shoot out. These new neutrons strike other uranium nuclei, causing them to split and give out still more neutrons. In this way, more and more nuclei split and many atoms give up their energy at once. If the action is not controlled, a tremendous explosion takes place – the atomic explosion that powers nuclear weapons.

Nuclear energy can be controlled to provide us with power. In a nuclear power station, control rods are lowered into the reactor to keep the reaction in check. But the uranium still gets very hot and so a coolant – a liquid or a gas – moves through the reactor. When the hot coolant leaves the reactor it goes to a boiler to make steam. It is this steam that powers generators to make electricity for our homes and factories.

▲ *The 'mushroom cloud' formed by the huge release of destructive energy from a nuclear explosion.*

▶ *Bombarding an atom of uranium-235 with a neutron can start a chain reaction. As the nucleus of the atom splits, more neutrons are given out to split more atoms, and great amounts of energy are released.*

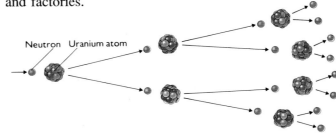

260

Number

In STONE AGE times people showed a number like 20 or 30 by making 20 or 30 separate marks. In certain caves you can still see the marks that they made.

In time people invented special signs or groups of signs to show different numbers. Such signs are called *numerals*. For centuries many people used Roman numerals. But these are rather clumsy. For instance, the Roman numerals for 38 are XXXVIII. Our simpler system uses Arabic numerals that were first used in India. The most important numeral in our system is the 0. If we write 207 we mean *two* hundreds, *no* tens and *seven* ones. Without the 0 we would not be able to write 207.

1	2	3	4	5	6	7	8	9	10		
▼	▼▼	▼▼▼	▼▼▼▼	▼▼▼▼▼	▼▼▼▼▼▼	▼▼▼▼▼▼▼	▼▼▼▼▼▼▼▼	▼▼▼▼▼▼▼▼▼	◄		Babylonian
A	B	Γ	Δ	E	Z	H	Θ	I	K		Greek
I	II	III	IV	V	VI	VII	VIII	IX	X		Roman
一	二	三	四	五	六	七	八	九	十		Chinese
•	••	•••	••••	—	·—	··—	···—	····—	═	◯	Mayan
?	?	?	?	?	?	?	?	?	?	०	Indian

(Top-right legend: Arabic)

There are many very large numbers. The population of the world is very large. The number of blades of grass, and of leaves on the trees must be enormously large. The famous Greek scientist Archimedes estimated the number of grains of sand it would take to fill the universe. He did not know the number exactly, but he said it was *finite*. He also knew that some numbers are *infinite*. If we go on counting 1, 2, 3, 4, 5, . . . and so on, we will never come to the end. This set of numbers is infinite.

◄ The earliest known written numbers were those used by the Babylonians about 5000 years ago. All the great civilizations have had their own way of writing and using numbers.

Nursing

People who are very ill, old or handicapped need nursing in their homes or in a hospital. Nursing can mean feeding, washing and giving treatment ordered by a doctor. It is hard work and requires special skills. Men and women train for several years before becoming nurses. Modern nursing owes much to Florence Nightingale.

The word 'nursing' comes from the Latin word *nutricia*, meaning 'nourishing'. Records from ancient Egypt and Greece mention various nursing practices, including the giving of herbal remedies. The Roman armies employed male nurses to care for the wounded.

Nutrition

Nutrition is the process by which we take in and use food. We need food to keep our bodies running smoothly and to provide the energy for work and play. Malnutrition is a weakening of the body caused by eating too little food, or eating food that lacks enough of the nutrients that keep your body strong and healthy. Nutrients can be divided into six groups: proteins, carbohydrates, fats, vitamins, minerals and water. No one nutrient is more important than another. Each has its own work to do. A well-balanced diet contains all of them.

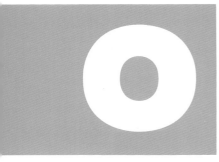

Oak

Oaks are trees with nuts called acorns. Some oaks measure over 11 metres around the trunk. They grow slowly and may live for 900 years. There are about 275 kinds of oak. Most have leaves with deeply notched (wavy) edges. But evergreen oaks have tough, shiny, smooth-edged leaves.

Oak wood is hard and slow to rot. People used to build sailing ships from it. Tannin from oak bark is used in making leather. CORK comes from cork oak bark.

Stalked acorns

Pendunculate oak

▶ Most types of oak tree are deciduous; that is, they lose their leaves in autumn each year and grow new ones in spring. The fruit of an oak tree is called an acorn (above). Although squirrels eat them, humans cannot.

Ocean

Oceans cover nearly three-quarters of the surface of the Earth. If you put all the world's water in 100 giant tanks, 97 of them would be full of water from the oceans. The oceans are always losing water as water vapour, drawn up into the air by the Sun's heat. But most returns as RAIN. Rain water running off the land takes salts and other MINERALS to the oceans. For instance, enough sea water to fill a square tank one kilometre long and one kilometre high would hold four million tonnes of magnesium. The oceans supply most of the magnesium we use.

There are four oceans. The largest and deepest is the PACIFIC OCEAN. The second largest is the Atlantic Ocean. This is only half as large as the Pacific Ocean. The Indian Ocean is smaller but deeper than the Atlantic Ocean. The Arctic Ocean is the smallest and shallowest ocean of all.

The oceans are never still. Winds crinkle their surface into waves. The Gulf Stream and other

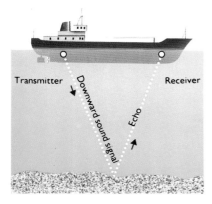

Transmitter   Receiver

Downward sound signal

Echo

▲ To work out the depth of the water they are sailing in, ships use sonar devices. They send sound waves to the bottom of the sea and measure the time it takes for the echo to return.

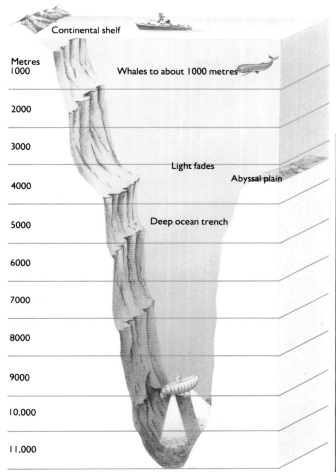

Continental shelf

Metres
1000   Whales to about 1000 metres

2000

3000

Light fades

Abyssal plain

4000

5000   Deep ocean trench

6000

7000

8000

9000

10,000

11,000

◀ Most life in the sea exists in the top levels where sunlight can penetrate. The exploration of the deepest levels, more than 10,000m down, was first carried out using special underwater vehicles called bathyscaphes.

OCEAN FACTS

Arctic Ocean
Surface area 12,173,000 sq km
Average depth 990 m
Greatest depth 4600 m

Indian Ocean
Surface area 73,426,500 sq km
Average depth 3890 m
Greatest depth 7450 m

Atlantic Ocean
Surface area 82,000,000 sq km
Average depth 1800 m
Greatest depth 9144 m

Pacific Ocean
Surface area 166,000,000 sq km
Average depth 4280 m
Greatest depth 11,022 m

WAVE, CURRENT AND TIDE FACTS

Highest storm wave: 34 m

Fastest waves: 500–800 km/h set off by earthquakes.

Largest ocean current: Antarctic Circumpolar Current. It carries 2200 times more water than the world's largest river pours into the sea.

Fastest ocean current: Nakwakto Rapids, off Western Canada: 30 km/h

Greatest range of tides on Earth: Bay of Fundy, Canada. A spring high tide here can be more than 16 m above a spring low tide.

---

currents (some warm, others cold) flow like rivers through the oceans. Every day the ocean surface falls and rises with the TIDES. In winter, polar sea water freezes over. ICEBERGS from polar seas may drift hundreds of kilometres through the oceans.

Oceans are home to countless living things. The minerals in sea water help to nourish tiny plants drifting at the surface. The plants are food for tiny animals. These animals and plants are called plankton. Fish and some whales eat the plankton. In turn, small fish are eaten by larger hunters.

Octopus

There are about 50 kinds of octopus. They are soft-bodied MOLLUSCS that live in the sea. Octopus means 'eight feet', but the eight tentacles of an

---

The octopus is the most intelligent of the animals without backbones. It can be trained to find its way through a maze and to solve simple problems, such as removing the stopper from a sealed jar containing food.

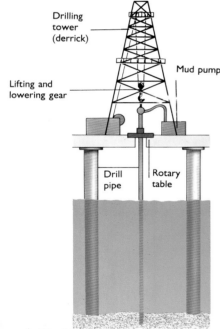

▲ *In many countries, particularly those bordering the Mediterranean Sea, octopuses are eaten regularly.*

Drilling tower (derrick)

Lifting and lowering gear

Mud pump

Drill pipe

Rotary table

▲ *The biggest part of an oil drilling platform is the derrick – the tall metal tower that houses the drilling equipment. The drill bit, at the end of the drill pipe, cuts through rock with sharp metal teeth. By examining the fragments of rock cut by the drill, scientists can tell when they are getting near an oil deposit.*

octopus are usually called arms. The largest octopus has arms about 9 metres across, but most octopuses are no larger than a person's fist. Suckers on the tentacles grip crabs, shellfish or other prey. An octopus's tentacles pull its victim towards its mouth.

Each octopus hides in an underwater cave or crevice. It creeps about the seabed searching for food. Its two large eyes keep a watch for enemies. If danger threatens, the octopus may confuse its enemy by squirting an inky liquid. The ink hangs in the water like a cloud. An octopus can also dart forwards by squirting water backwards from a tube in its body.

Oil

Oils are FATS and other greasy substances that do not dissolve in water. But when we say 'oil' we usually mean mineral oil. Mineral oil was formed millions of years ago from dead plants and animals. The oil was trapped under rocks. Engineers drill holes down through the surface rocks to reach the mineral oil beneath. It gushes up or can be pumped up to the surface.

Oil refineries separate the oil to make petrol, paraffin and lubricating oil. Mineral oil is also used in making artificial fertilizer, many kinds of medicine, paint, plastics and detergent. We may need to find new ways to make these things because the world's supplies of oil are running out. Scientists are working on new ways of extracting oil from shale, a kind of rock, and from tar sands.

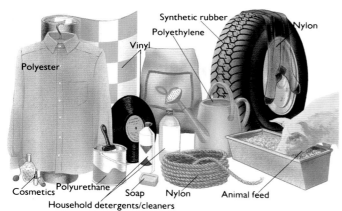

Synthetic rubber
Polyethylene
Nylon
Vinyl
Polyester
Cosmetics
Polyurethane
Soap
Nylon
Animal feed
Household detergents/cleaners

◄ *When petroleum oil is refined it is separated into many different chemicals. As well as producing petrol and paraffin, oil by-products can be used to make plastics, perfumes, soaps, paint and even animal feed.*

The world's largest known oil deposits lie in the Middle East, in the countries of Saudi Arabia, Iran, Iraq and Kuwait.

Olympic Games

This athletics competition is the world's oldest. The first known Olympic Games took place at Olympia in Greece in 776 BC. The Greek Games ended in AD 394. The modern Olympic Games began in 1896. They are held once every four years, each time in a different country. Athletes from different nations compete in races, jumping, gymnastics, football, yachting, and many more contests. The winners gain medals, but no prize money.

Opera

An opera is a play with music. The 'actors' are singers who sing all or many of their words. An ORCHESTRA accompanies them.

The first opera was performed in Italy, nearly 400 years ago. Famous composers of serious opera include MOZART, Verdi, Puccini and Wagner.

Light, short operas are called operettas. Operettas of the 1800s gave rise to the tuneful musical comedies of the 1900s.

Opinion Poll

Political parties and manufacturers want to know what people think of their party's policy or the goods they make. They employ a research firm to conduct an opinion poll – to ask questions and

▲ *Papageno, the comic bird-catcher, from the 1816 Berlin production of Mozart's opera* The Magic Flute.

265

SEE IT YOURSELF
You can take your own opinion poll. Decide on the question you want to ask, then pick your sample group. It can be everyone in your class, or, better still, everyone in your form. You do not have to record people's names, just their answers or whether they are undecided, and whether they are a boy or girl.

QUESTION: Do you prefer vanilla or chocolate ice cream?

TOTAL SAMPLE		ALL BOYS		ALL GIRLS	
Vanilla	40	Vanilla	18	Vanilla	22
Chocolate	50	Chocolate	28	Chocolate	22
Undecided	10	Undecided	4	Undecided	6
Total polled	100	Total polled	50	Total polled	50

FINDINGS: According to this poll, 50 per cent of the sample pupils prefer chocolate ice cream and 40 per cent prefer vanilla. However, 56 per cent of boys prefer chocolate and only 36 per cent vanilla. The girls are equally divided between the two. What do you think would happen if the whole school were polled and divided into two age groups – those below 12 and those above?

analyse the answers. It would be impossible to ask questions of everyone, everywhere, so a carefully selected group of people, called a *sample*, is chosen to represent a larger group. The sample may be only 1 per cent of the larger group, but it must contain the same sort of people. For example, if 20 per cent of the larger group are under 18 years of age, 20 per cent of the sample group must also be under 18.

Opossum

Opossums are MARSUPIALS found in North and South America. Some look like rats, others look like mice. The Virginia opossum is as big as a cat. This is North America's only marsupial. It climbs trees and can cling on with its tail. A female has up to 18 babies, each no larger than a honeybee at birth. If danger threatens, the Virginia opossum pretends to be dead. If someone pretends to be hurt, we say he or she is 'playing possum'.

▲ *Like all marsupials, the American opossum gives birth to its babies when they are still in a very immature state. After about three months, they are able to ride around on their mother's back.*

Orang-utan

This big, red-haired APE comes from the islands of Borneo and Sumatra in south-east Asia. Its name comes from Malay words meaning 'man of the woods'. A male is as heavy as a man, but not so tall. Orang-utans use their long arms to swing through the branches of trees as they hunt for fruit and leaves to eat. Each night they make a nest high up in the trees. A leafy roof helps to keep out rain.

Orchestra

An orchestra is a large group of musicians who play together. The word *orchestra* once meant 'dancing place'. In ancient Greek theatres, dancers and musicians performed on a space between the audience and the stage. When Italy invented OPERA, Italian theatres arranged their musicians in the same way. Soon, people used the word orchestra to describe the group of musicians, and not the place where they performed.

The modern orchestra owes much to the composer Haydn. He arranged its MUSICAL INSTRUMENTS into four main groups: strings, woodwind, brass and percussion. Most orchestras have a conductor.

▼ *The ostrich is one of the record-breaking birds for the number of eggs it lays – up to 15 at one time.*

Ostrich

This is the largest living BIRD. An ostrich may weigh twice as much as a man and stand more than 2 metres high. Ostriches cannot fly. If an enemy attacks, an ostrich runs away. It can kick hard enough to rip a lion open. Frightened ostriches never hide their heads in sand, as people used to think.

Ostriches live in Africa. They roam in herds, led by a male. The females lay large, white eggs in a nest dug in the sand.

Otter

Otters are large relatives of the weasel. They have long, slender bodies and short legs. An otter is a bit heavier than a dachshund dog. It hunts in water for fish and frogs. Thick fur keeps its body dry. It can swim swiftly by waggling its tail and body like an eel, and using its webbed hind feet as paddles.

Otters are wanderers. By night they hunt up and down a river, or roam overland to find new fishing grounds. They love to play by sliding down a bank of snow or mud.

▼ The number of otters in the wild is going down steadily, and they are now quite a rare sight. This could be due to pollution, but no one is sure.

Owl

These birds of prey hunt mainly by night. They have soft feathers that make no sound as they fly. Their large, staring eyes help them to see in the dimmest light. Owls also have keen ears. Some owls can catch mice in pitch darkness by listening to the sounds they make. An owl can turn its head right round to look backwards.

When an owl eats a mouse or bird, it swallows it complete with bones and fur or feathers. Later, the owl spits out the remains in a pellet. You can sometimes find owl pellets on the ground.

▲ The long-eared owl's tufted 'ears' are not ears at all, just feathers. But they help in the recognition of this bird, which is found in most of Europe, northern Asia and North America.

Ox

Oxen are a group of big, heavy animals that include domestic (farm) cattle, bison, wild and tame buffalo, and the yak. Oxen have split hooves and a pair of curved horns. They eat grass. The heaviest domestic cattle can weigh two tonnes.

For thousands of years, the ox has been a beast of burden, pulling carts or ploughs. People probably began domesticating cattle 9000 years ago in Greece.

Oxygen

Oxygen is a GAS. It is one of the most abundant ELEMENTS on Earth. It makes up one part in every five parts of AIR. Oxygen is found in water and many different rocks. Most of the weight of water, and half that of rocks, comes from the oxygen in them.

FIRE needs oxygen to burn. Almost all living things need oxygen for BREATHING and to give them the energy just to stay alive. Animals need extra oxygen to move about. PLANTS give out oxygen into the air during the process of making their food. This process is known as *photosynthesis* and is a valuable service to animal life.

Oyster

Oysters are MOLLUSCS with a soft body protected by a broad, hinged shell. This is rough on the outside. The inside of a pearl oyster's shell is smooth, shiny mother-of-pearl. Pearl oysters make pearls.

Several kinds of oyster are eaten as a food. People farm oysters in shallow coastal water. Oysters cling to empty shells, rocks or wooden posts on the seabed. When they have grown large enough they are harvested.

Ozone Layer

The ozone layer is a layer of gases that surrounds the Earth and shields it from harmful radiation from the Sun. The layer is found in the region between 10 and 50 km above the Earth's surface. Ozone is a form of the gas oxygen, and although the ozone layer contains only a very small quantity of ozone, it shields us from most of the Sun's dangerous ultra-violet rays. Without the protection of the ozone layer, animals and plants probably could not live on Earth.

Recently, scientists have been worried about a thinning of the ozone layer, especially over polar regions. They believe this may have been caused by the use of substances called *chlorofluorocarbons*, or CFCs, in aerosol dispensers, refrigerators and to make the bubbles in foam plastic. Most countries are now trying to stop the manufacture and use of these substances.

SEE IT YOURSELF

Nothing can burn without oxygen. To find out roughly how much oxygen there is in the air, stand a candle in a bowl of water. Light the candle and cover it with a glass jar. Rest the jar on plasticine so that water can get under the rim. Mark the level of water in the jar. As the candle burns, oxygen is used up and water rises to take its place. Soon the candle goes out – all the oxygen has gone. You will find that the water has risen about one-fifth of the way up the jar. A fifth of the air is oxygen.

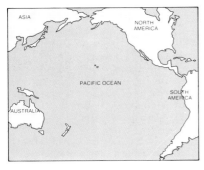

Pacific Ocean

This is the largest and deepest of all the OCEANS. Its waters cover more than one-third of the world. All the CONTINENTS would fit inside the Pacific Ocean with room to spare. Its deepest part is deep enough to drown the world's highest mountain.

The Pacific Ocean lies west of the Americas, and east of Australia and Asia. It stretches from the frozen Arctic to the frozen Antarctic. There are thousands of tiny islands in the Pacific. Most were formed when VOLCANOES grew up from the seabed. Sometimes earthquakes shake the seabed and send out huge tidal waves.

Painting

Painting is a form of ART in which people use coloured paint to make pictures on canvas, plaster, wood or paper. Today most people paint for their own pleasure. But this was not always so.

STONE AGE hunters probably used painting as magic. They drew wounded wild beasts on their cave walls. They probably thought that such pictures would help them to kill real animals on their next hunt.

In the MIDDLE AGES most artists worked for the Church. Their paintings showed scenes from Bible stories. Such paintings helped people who could not read to understand the Bible.

By the 1400s Europe's rich princes and merchants were paying artists to paint pictures to decorate their

SEE IT YOURSELF

There are lots of fun ways to paint. Try this one: Put a spoonful of watery paint on a piece of white paper. Place one end of a drinking straw near the paint and blow gently through the other to spread out the paint. Using a clean spoon for each colour, put some other colours onto the paper and blow them around too.

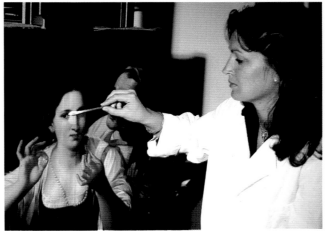

▶ *The cleaning and restoration of dirty or damaged old paintings is a delicate and highly skilled craft.*

homes. The pictures might be family portraits, still-life scenes of flowers and fruit, or landscapes showing their cities and country estates.

In the 1800s many artists began trying out new ideas. For example, some tried to give a feeling of the light and shade in a landscape. Others used bright, flat colours to bring out the patterns in still-lifes and landscapes. In the 1900s Pablo PICASSO and other artists began to experiment with abstract paintings. These concentrate on the basic shapes, colours and patterns of the things painted. Today, many artists are still experimenting.

Pakistan

Pakistan lies between India and Iran. There are more than 110 million Pakistanis. Most of them follow the religion of ISLAM.

Much of Pakistan is hot and dry, but crops such as wheat and cotton grow with the help of water from

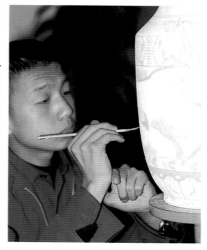

▲ Once this boy has finished painting the design on the vase, it will be glazed and fired in a kiln to complete the finish.

◀ Street traders, selling all kinds of food, are a common sight in the city of Karachi in Pakistan.

the Indus River. Until 1947 Pakistan was part of British-ruled INDIA. It then broke away to become an independent Muslim republic. In 1971 East Pakistan broke away and became Bangladesh. In 1988 Benazir Bhutto was elected prime minister but she was defeated in the 1990 elections.

Palestine

Palestine is a land on the eastern shore of the Mediterranean Sea. Most of the stories in the BIBLE took place there. Palestine gets its name from the Philistines who once lived in part of it.

PAKISTAN

Government: Parliamentary democracy
Capital: Islamabad
Area: 803,943 sq km
Population: 112,050,000
Languages: Urdu and English
Currency: Rupee

Historic Palestine covers an area of only 27,000 sq km, little more than a third the size of Scotland. People lived in Palestine at least 200,000 years ago, during the Old Stone Age.

By 1800 BC the Hebrews had made Palestine their home. Later they ruled it as two nations, called Israel and Judah. Both of these nations were then taken over by foreign rulers.

Today, most of what used to be called Palestine lies in the nation of ISRAEL. The rest is part of Jordan, Lebanon and Syria. There have been frequent clashes between Palestinians and Israelis.

Panama

Panama is a country about the size of Scotland. It occupies the narrow neck of land that joins Central and South America. Panama has a damp, tropical climate. Rice, bananas and pineapples are grown.

The Panama CANAL cuts the country in half. Much of Panama's wealth comes from the canal and it has made Panama City an international finance centre.

The world's shipping uses the Panama Canal as a short cut between the Atlantic and Pacific oceans.

▶ *Many huge cargo ships pass through the Panama Canal every day.*

Government: Constitutional democracy
Capital: Panama City
Area: 75,650 sq km
Population: 2,418,000
Languages: Spanish and English
Currency: Balboa

Sets of locks on the canal raise and lower ships as they cross the hilly countryside. In 1903, Panama granted the occupation and control of the canal to the United States. A new treaty in 1978 provided for the gradual takeover by Panama of the canal. The takeover will be completed in 1999.

Panda

There are two kinds of panda. Both live in the forests of east Asia. The giant panda looks like a black and white bear. It lives in bamboo forests in

China. The red panda is not much larger than a cat. It has a bushy tail and reddish fur. Both kinds eat plants. Their nearest relatives are the raccoons of North and South America.

Paper

Paper gets its name from papyrus, a plant that grows in swamps in Egypt. The ancient Egyptians made a kind of paper from papyrus. But the Chinese invented paper as we know it. About 1900 years ago they learned to separate the fibres from mulberry bark. They soaked these, then dried them, making a flat, dry sheet that they could write on. Paper is still made of plant fibres. Some of the best paper is made from COTTON. Newspaper is made from wood.

▼ *The steps in making paper from softwood pulp.*

The bark is removed from the logs at the paper mill

The logs are cut into small chips

The chips are 'cooked' with chemicals and the pulp produced is washed, bleached and beaten into finer fibres. It is mixed with resins and dyes depending on the type of paper required.

It is dried in steam-heated cylinders and polished in calender rollers

The pulp is passed through a series of rollers

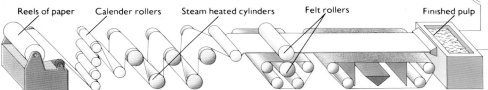

Reels of paper   Calender rollers   Steam heated cylinders   Felt rollers   Finished pulp

Today, people are more concerned about taking care of the environment. Interest in recycling, or reusing, paper is growing. Old paper can be taken to mills to be made into new paper or cardboard. However, dyed or specially finished paper cannot be recycled.

▼ *Traffic skirts the Arc de Triomphe in Paris. Built by Napoleon I, it is one of the city's most famous landmarks.*

Paris

Paris is the capital of FRANCE, and France's largest city. More than 2,000,000 people live there. The River Seine divides the city into the Left Bank and the Right Bank.

If you gaze down on Paris from the Eiffel Tower you will see many parks and gardens, fine squares and tree-lined avenues. Other famous landmarks are the cathedral of Notre Dame, the basilica of the Sacré Coeur, the Arc de Triomphe and the Louvre Palace, now a famous museum.

Paris is famous for its fashions, jewellery and perfume. Another important industry is car manufacturing.

▲ *Pasteur developed vaccines against cholera, rabies, anthrax and other diseases.*

Parliament

A parliament is a meeting of people held to make a nation's laws. One of the first parliaments was Iceland's *Althing*, which was founded more than a thousand years ago.

In Great Britain, the Houses of Parliament stand by the River Thames in London. Members of Parliament elected by the people sit in the House of Commons. Peers (nobles) and churchmen (who are not elected) sit in the House of Lords. The British Parliament was started in 1265. It grew gradually out of a meeting of nobles who advised the king. In the 1300s it was divided into the two Houses, and by the 1700s Parliament had become more powerful than the king.

Pasteur, Louis

Louis Pasteur (1822–1895) was a great French scientist. He proved that BACTERIA and other germs cause diseases. Pasteur injected weakened germs into animals and people to stop them catching the diseases those germs usually caused. He invented *pasteurization*, a way of heating milk and cooling it quickly to stop it going bad. Pasteur also found out how tiny yeast cells turn sugar into alcohol.

Penguin

Penguins are swimming birds. They cannot fly, because their wings are shaped as flippers. Penguins use their wings to 'row' themselves through the sea. They swim and dive well. A penguin in the water can leap up nearly 2 metres to land on a rock or ice.

▼ *Four of the 18 different types of penguin.*

Emperor penguin

Chinstrap penguin   Gentoo   Macaroni penguin

All penguins come from the southern part of the world. Emperor penguins live in the ANTARCTIC. In winter each female lays one egg on the ice. Her mate rolls the egg onto his feet and warms it for two months until it hatches. As the fathers, male Emperor Penguins put up with hard conditions. While they are warming the eggs with their feet, they cannot feed for 64 days.

◄ *Lake Titicaca is the highest navigated lake in the world. Situated between Peru and Bolivia, it is 3810m above sea level.*

Peru

Peru is the third largest nation in SOUTH AMERICA. You could fit France, Great Britain, Spain, West Germany and Yugoslavia inside Peru with room to spare.

Peru touches five other countries. Western Peru is washed by the Pacific Ocean. The sharp, snowy peaks of the high Andes Mountains cross Peru from north to south like a giant backbone. Between the mountains and the ocean lies a thin strip of desert. East of the mountains hot, steamy forests stretch around the AMAZON RIVER.

Peruvians grow sugarcane and coffee. The sheep and llamas in the mountains produce wool. Peru mines copper, iron and silver. Its ocean fishing grounds usually hold plenty of fish.

People have been building towns in Peru for several thousand years. The most famous people were the INCAS who ran a mountain empire. In the 1530s the Spaniards seized Peru. Since the 1820s Peru has been an independent nation.

PERU

Government: Constitutional republic
Capital: Lima
Area: 1,285,216 sq km
Population: 22,332,000
Language: Spanish
Currency: Inti

▲ *The funeral procession of a pharaoh. Four yoked oxen pull the sledge of the funeral boat, in which rests the coffin containing the mummy, the embalmed and wrapped body of the pharaoh.*

Pharaoh

We use the word *pharaoh* to mean 'king' when we talk of the kings of ancient EGYPT. (The ancient Egyptians gave their kings other titles as well.) 'Pharaoh' comes from *peraa*, which means 'great house'. This was the royal palace where the pharaoh lived.

Egyptians believed that each pharaoh was the same god in the shape of a different man. He lived in certain ways said to have been fixed by the gods. The pharaoh was said to look after all the needs of his people. He was supposed to rule everything and everyone in Egypt. He owned all the land. All of Egypt's nobles, priests and soldiers were supposed to obey him. But in fact the priests and nobles largely ran the country.

Philosophy

The word *philosophy* comes from Greek words meaning 'love of wisdom'. Philosophers are thinkers who ask deep questions like these: How much can we really know about anything? If we argue that something is what we say it is, how can we be sure that our ideas are really right? When we say that God exists, what do we mean by 'God' and what do we mean by 'exists'? What is goodness? What is just? What is beauty?

The first great philosophers were Greeks, including Socrates, Plato and Aristotle.

Philosophers will often ponder over the oddest questions. It is said that two famous 13th century philosophers, St Thomas Aquinas and Albert the Great, used to argue for hours about how many angels could sit on the point of a pin.

Photography

The word *photography* comes from Greek words that mean 'drawing with light'. When you take a photograph, rays of LIGHT produce a picture on the film in your CAMERA.

What happens is this. First you look through a viewfinder at the subject you want to photograph. Then you press a button or lever that opens a shutter to let light from the subject enter the camera. The light passes a LENS that produces an image of your subject on a film in the camera. But the image shows up only when the film is developed (treated with chemicals). A developed film is called a *negative*. This shows black objects white, and white objects black. From negatives you can print *positives*, the final photos, either as paper prints or slides.

Physics

Physics is one of the sciences. Physicists are interested in *matter* – in solids, liquids and gases, and in the tiny atoms of which all matter is made up. They are interested in the different forms of *energy* – electric energy, light energy, sound energy, mechanical energy, chemical energy and nuclear energy. Some of the major fields of study in physics include mechanics (forces and motion; solids, liquids and gases); optics (light); acoustics (sound); electricity and magnetism; atomic, molecular and

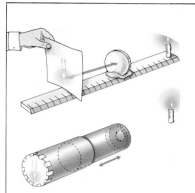

SEE IT YOURSELF

You can make a toy camera. Take the lens out of a magnifying glass. Fix the lens upright with plasticine on a ruler. Put a lighted candle in front of the lens. Hold a piece of white paper on the ruler behind the lens and move it backwards and forwards until you see a sharp image of the candle. Read off the distance between the lens and the paper. This is the focal length of that lens. Now take two cardboard tubes, one of which fits inside the other. Cover one end with tissue paper fixed with sticky tape. Cover the other end with card and make a hole about a centimetre across. Fix the lens here with plasticine or sticky tape. Focus the camera by sliding the tubes in or out until you get a clear image on the tissue paper. The image will be upside down.

◄ *A hair-raising experience: the steel ball is a Van de Graaff generator that makes static electricity. When the girl puts her hand on it her hair springs to attention! The generator is on display at the Science Centre, Toronto, Canada.*

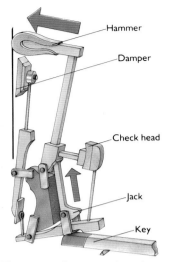

▲ *The action of a piano is based on a lever movement by the key which is transmitted to a felt-covered hammer that strikes the piano string. A damper prevents the note from sounding after the key is released.*

nuclear physics; and cryogenics (the study of extremely low temperatures and their effects, including superconductivity).

Physicists try to find things out by doing careful experiments. They record the results of their experiments so that other people can try the same experiments if they want to. Physics is a very big subject and no one physicist today understands all the different parts of the subject. For example, nuclear physicists who study the tiny atom and its parts may know little about outer space and the movements of planets, stars and galaxies as studied by astrophysicists. But one subject they must all understand is mathematics.

Two of the greatest physicists who ever lived were Sir Isaac NEWTON and Albert EINSTEIN.

Piano

Piano is short for the Italian word *pianoforte*, meaning *soft* and *loud*. The piano was invented by Bartolomeo Cristofori in 1709. The name refers to its great range compared with the harpsichord that came before it. The piano has 88 keys. When a key is struck, a system of levers makes a felt-tipped hammer strike a stretched wire. At the same time a *damper*, which normally prevents the wire from vibrating, drops back from the wire and stays back until the key is released.

Picasso, Pablo

Pablo Picasso (1881–1973) was the most famous artist of this century. He was born in Spain but lived mostly in France.

People said Picasso could draw before he learned to talk. He disliked paintings that looked like photographs, and admired the curving shapes of African sculpture. Picasso began painting people as simple shapes such as cubes. He also produced sculpture and pottery.

Pig

▲ *Pablo Picasso was a very influential artist whose work changed the course of modern art.*

These farmyard animals have a long, heavy body; short legs ending in hoofed toes; a long snout; and a short, curly tail. Males are called boars. Females are called sows. The heaviest boars weigh over a tonne.

Pigs provide us with bacon, ham, pork and lard. Different parts of a pig's body are used to make brushes, glue, leather and soap.

Planet

The word planet comes from a Greek word meaning 'wanderer'. Long ago, skywatchers gave this name to 'stars' that appeared to move. We now know that planets are not STARS, but are heavenly bodies that travel around stars.

▲ The wild boar is a tough, fierce animal, unlike most of its domestic relatives.

◀ Scientists think the Earth was born about four and a half thousand million years ago. The spare material around the Sun formed a ring, or 'doughnut', of gas and dust, whirling around the Sun at high speed. The planets may have formed out of the 'doughnut' rather like this.

1. To begin with, the doughnut was a spinning ring of gas and dust.

2. The solid particles began to strike each other and stick together, forming larger bodies. At first, these were mostly carbon and ice.

3. These particles rapidly grew to planetary size. As they grew larger they began to 'pull' against each other, which meant that if they passed too close to each other, they were pulled into a different orbit. Some of the very small carbon-ice bodies were pulled so violently by the larger ones that they were thrown right out towards the stars. Others found themselves pulled into very long orbits that carried them far beyond the planets and back again very near to the Sun. These are the comets.

4. Eventually there were just a few large bodies going around the Sun in orbits that did not meet each other, and so there were no more collisions or near misses – the nine major planets were formed. See p. 280.

5. With the passage of thousands of millions of years the planets continued to pull against each other, until their orbits have become almost level.

The EARTH and other planets of our SOLAR SYSTEM travel around the star we call the SUN. Each planet travels in its own orbit. But they all move in the same direction, and, except for Mercury and Pluto, they lie in the same plane (at about the same level).

Astronomers think the planets came from a band of gas and dust that once whirled around the Sun. They think that GRAVITY pulled parts of this band together as masses that became planets.

The nine planets in the solar system are MERCURY, VENUS, EARTH, MARS, JUPITER, SATURN, URANUS, NEPTUNE and PLUTO. Mercury is closest to the Sun, Pluto usually farthest away.

THE PARTS OF A PLANT

Flower: concerned with reproduction. Most flowers have male and female parts.
Leaf: concerned with food-making.
Stem: supports the leaves and flowers. Tubes in the stem carry, and also store, food and water.
Roots: anchor the plant in the soil. They also take in water and minerals through delicate hairs.

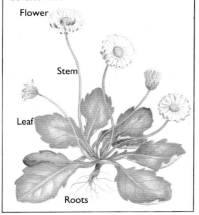

Flower

Stem

Leaf

Roots

Plants

Plants differ from animals in several ways. For example, green plants can make food with the help of chlorophyll. Only plants are able to use sunlight to build up living matter. They use the carbon dioxide gas (breathed out as waste by animals) and 'breathe out' life-giving oxygen. Without plants there would be no animal life on Earth. Plants provide animals with food. People not only eat plants (and animals such as cattle that feed on plants) but also make use of plant products in all kinds of ways.

There are more than 360,000 different kinds of plant. Some trees may grow a hundred metres tall and live for hundreds of years. Other plants are so tiny they can be seen only through a microscope. Plants are found in the oceans, in deserts, on windswept mountains and cold tundra plains. When people first learned how to cultivate plants, civilisation began. Today, many wild plants are endangered because their habitats are under threat. It is important to protect wild plants, and to save them for future generations.

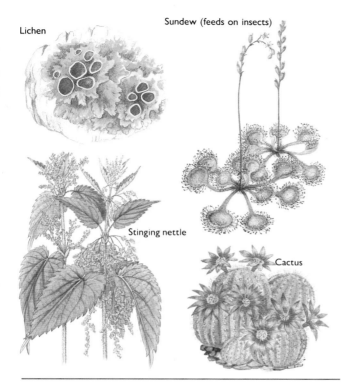

Lichen

Sundew (feeds on insects)

Stinging nettle

Cactus

Oak tree (deciduous – sheds its leaves)

◄ *Plants come in all shapes and sizes ranging from the very small algae in lichen to the huge oak tree.*

Plastic

Plastics are man-made substances and can be moulded into many different shapes. They are used to make anything from furniture and car seats to shoes and bags or cups and plates.

Most plastics are largely made from chemicals obtained from petroleum oil. Coal, limestone, salt and water are also used. Plastics can be hard, soft or runny. They can be made to look like glass, metal, wood or other substances.

Hard plastics are used in radio and camera cases. But fine threads of the hard plastic nylon make soft stockings.

Plastic bags and squeeze bottles are made of soft plastics like polyethylene. The first plastic was celluloid, discovered in the 1800s.

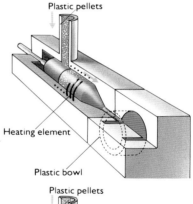

Plastic pellets

Heating element

Plastic bowl

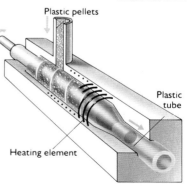

Plastic pellets

Plastic tube

Heating element

Pluto

The PLANET Pluto is named after the Greek god who ruled the dreary world of the dead. Pluto must be bitterly cold, because it is farther away from the Sun than any of the other planets. It is almost 40 times farther from the Sun than the EARTH is.

▲ *Hot plastic can be squeezed, or extruded (above) into a long, thin tube shape by forcing it through a specially shaped hole. A bowl (top) is made by 'injection moulding'. Hot plastic is forced into a mould which is cooled to harden the plastic.*

281

▶ *Pluto has one moon, Charon, which is about half as large as the planet it orbits. Many astronomers consider them a twin planet rather than a planet with a moon.*

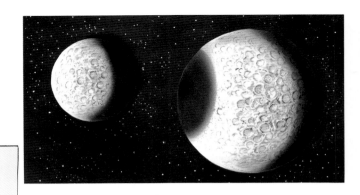

PLUTO FACTS

Average distance from Sun: 5900
  million km
Nearest distance from Earth: 5800
  million km
Average temperature: −220°C
Diameter across the equator:
  3000 km
Atmosphere: None?
Number of moons: 1 known
Length of day: 6 days 9 hours
Length of year: 248 Earth years

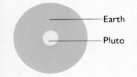

Earth
Pluto

Pluto spins and moves around the Sun much more slowly than the Earth. A day on Pluto may equal nearly a week on Earth. One year on Pluto lasts almost 248 of our years.

Pluto is much smaller than the Earth, and weighs one-sixth as much.

Poetry

Poetry is the oldest form of literature. Before people developed a system of writing, they found that the best way to remember a story was to sing it or put it in a rhyming pattern. In this way, poetry was born. Poets choose words carefully, for their sound as well as their meaning. Poetry is something like music because it creates beautiful sounds with words.

Much poetry is written in *rhyme*. This means that the words at the ends of lines sound alike. A simple rhyme is:

I wish I were an octopus, with arms on every corner;

I'd scare my granny half to death; I wouldn't even warn her!

Can you see that 'corner' and 'warn her' rhyme?

Rhyme is not necessary in poetry, however. Many poets use rhyme in some poems and not in others.

Poems are usually written in verses. The lines have a *rhythm* built up by strong and weak sounds. Can you see where the strong sounds occur in the lines above? You will find that there are 7 strong sounds in each line.

There are three main types of poetry. They are *narrative, lyric* and *dramatic*. Narrative poetry tells a story. Lyric poetry tells of the poet's own feelings.

▼ *T.S. Eliot (1888–1965), whose poem 'The Wasteland' (1922) broke with 19th century poetic traditions and made him famous.*

Dramatic poetry has characters who tell a story, just as a play does. SHAKESPEARE wrote nearly all his plays in verse.

SOME POISONOUS SUBSTANCES

Many things around us – in our kitchens, our garages, or our garden sheds – can be poisonous if they are not used properly. These are just a few of them:

• Some **household substances** may be poisonous if swallowed. These include bleach, toilet cleaners, most detergents, furniture polish, petrol, lighter fuel, paraffin and household ammonia.

• Garden and farm **insecticides** and **weedkillers** can kill.

• **Carbon monoxide**, a gas given off by car exhausts, is poisonous, especially in badly ventilated areas. Car antifreeze is also a poison.

• Taken in excess, many **drugs and medicines** can be poisonous, including aspirin and sleeping pills.

• **Poisonous plants** include holly (berries), lily of the valley, hydrangea (leaves and buds) and deadly nightshade.

" THE JABBERWOCK, WITH EYES OF FLAME, CAME WHIFFLING THROUGH THE TULGEY WOOD "

▲ *An illustration for the poem 'Jabberwocky' by Lewis Carroll. This poem, from the book* Through the Looking-Glass, *is a superb example of a nonsense rhyme.*

Poison

Poisons are chemical substances that kill or damage living things. Some poisons get into the body through the skin. Some are swallowed. Poisonous gases are harmful if someone breathes them in with air.

Different poisons work in different ways. Strong ACIDS or alkalis 'burn'. NERVE poisons can stop the heart. Some other poisons can make the body bleed inside.

DRUGS called antidotes can cure people who are suffering from certain poisons.

Poland

Poland lies in eastern Europe, south of the Baltic Sea, and is the seventh largest country in EUROPE. Most of Poland is low farmland, although forests sprawl across the Carpathian Mountains in the south. Poland's largest river is the Vistula. It rises in the mountains and flows into the Baltic Sea. Rivers often freeze in Poland's cold, snowy winters.

There are more than 38 million Poles. Most of them speak Polish, and most are Roman Catholics. Only three countries mine more coal than Poland.

POLAND

Government: Socialist
Capital: Warsaw
Area: 312,677 sq km
Population: 38,180,000
Language: Polish
Currency: Zloty

In 1989 Poland had the first free elections in 40 years. The independent trade union Solidarity swept into power and Poland became the first non-communist country in the Eastern bloc.

Police

Police work for a government to keep law and order in their country. Their main task is to see that everyone obeys their country's laws. Part of this job is protecting people's lives and property. Police also help to control crowds. They help people hurt in accidents, and take charge of lost children.

Police officers try to prevent crime, and track down and capture criminals. This can be dangerous and sometimes officers are killed.

Pollution

Pollution means the spoiling of air, soil, water or countryside by wastes. Before the INDUSTRIAL REVOLUTION most of the wastes produced by living things have been used by other living things. But today, people produce more wastes than nature can cope with.

Cars and factories pour smoke and fumes into the air. Chemical fertilizer and pesticides can kill off wild plants and animals. Poor sewage disposal and spilt oil make seas and rivers filthy.

▲ *This plastic rubbish polluting a rocky shore in Wales must be cleared up by hand – it will not decompose naturally.*

▶ *Lichens that normally grow on trees in the countryside are sensitive to polluted air. As you get closer to towns, only certain types of lichen can survive. Where there are heavy concentrations of sulphur dioxide gas in the air only a thin film of algae will grow on trees and stones.*

CLEAN   POLLUTED

Polo, Marco

Marco Polo (1254–1324) was an Italian traveller. He is famous for the long journey he made to faraway China at a time when the people of Europe knew little about the East. His father and his uncle were merchants from Venice and they decided to take the young Marco with them when they set out

for the East in 1271. They crossed Persia and the vast Gobi Desert. In 1275 they reached Peking (Beijing) and were welcomed by Kublai Khan, a great MONGOL conqueror. The Polos stayed for many years during which Marco travelled all over China in the service of the Khan. They left China in 1292 and arrived home in Venice in 1295. Later, Marco's stories of his travels were written down. The *Travels of Marco Polo* is one of the most exciting books ever written.

▲ *Marco Polo and his companions were kindly received by Kublai Khan, who was interested in other countries and their customs.*

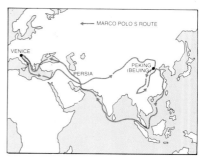

▲ *Even by modern standards, Marco Polo's journey was a long one, but in the 1200s it was a tremendous achievement.*

Pompeii

Two thousand years ago, Pompeii was a small Roman city in southern Italy. A sudden disaster killed many of its citizens and drove out the rest. But the same disaster preserved the streets and buildings. Today, visitors to Pompeii can learn a great deal about what life was like inside a Roman city.

Mount Vesuvius had been dormant for 800 years. Even those who realized it was a volcano believed it to be extinct. But in AD 79 Vesuvius erupted, and showered Pompeii with volcanic ash and cinders. Poisonous gases swirled through the streets. Out of a population of around 20,000 people, about one citizen in every ten was poisoned by fumes or burned to death by hot ash. The rest escaped. Ash and cinders soon covered up the buildings. In time people forgot that Pompeii had ever been there.

The Roman writer Pliny the Younger described what happened when Vesuvius destroyed Pompeii. Pliny saw the ground shake, the sea sucked back and then hurled forward and great tongues of flame spurt from the black cloud that boiled up from the volcano.

▲ *Archaeologists have uncovered almost half of the city of Pompeii (right). Bodies of Pompeiians trapped while fleeing (left) have been recreated by making plaster casts of their imprints in the volcanic ash.*

For centuries Pompeii's thick coat of ash protected it from the weather. At last, in the 1700s, people began to dig it out. The digging still goes on today. Archaeologists discovered buildings, streets, tools and statues. They even found hollows left in the ash by the decayed bodies of people and dogs killed by the eruption. The archaeologists poured plaster into these hollows. They let the plaster harden, then they cleared away the ash. They found that the plaster had formed life-size models of the dead bodies.

PORTUGAL

Government: Parliamentary democracy
Capital: Lisbon
Area: 92,082 sq km
Population: 10,525,000
Language: Portuguese
Currency: Escudo

Pope

'Pope' is a title of the head of the ROMAN CATHOLIC CHURCH. (The word 'pope' comes from *papa*, which means 'father'.) The Pope is also the Bishop of Rome. He lives in the Vatican City inside the city of Rome.

Roman Catholics believe that Jesus made St Peter the first Pope. Since then there have been hundreds of Popes. Each time one dies, church leaders choose another. The Pope makes church laws, chooses bishops and can declare people saints.

Portugal

This is a long, narrow, country in south-west EUROPE. It is sandwiched between the Atlantic Ocean and Spain, a country four times the size of Portugal. It forms part of the Iberian Peninsula (a peninsula is an area of land nearly surrounded by water).

Much of Portugal is mountainous. Rivers flow from the mountains through valleys and across plains to the sea. Portugal's mild winters and warm summers help its people to grow olives, oranges and rice. Its grapes produce port, a wine named after the Portuguese city of Oporto. Portugal's woods yield more CORK than those of any other nation. Its fishermen catch sardines and other sea fish. Portugal also has mines and factories.

There are about 10 million Portuguese. They speak Portuguese, a language much like Spanish. Their capital is Lisbon.

▲ Partridges are small game birds, about 30 cm long, with brown and chestnut markings. They are often raised for their meat. In the wild they live on farmland and moorland.

Poultry

All birds kept for meat or eggs are known as poultry. To most people, poultry means chickens, DUCKS, geese and turkeys. But guinea fowl, OSTRICHES, partridges, peacocks, pheasants and pigeons can be kept as poultry too.

Chickens outnumber other kinds of poultry. There are probably more chickens than people, and they lay enough eggs to give everyone on Earth several hundred eggs each year. Chickens also produce meat more cheaply than sheep or cattle. This is because it costs less in food to produce a kilogram of chicken meat than it costs to make a kilogram of beef, lamb or mutton.

Prehistoric Animals

Prehistoric animals are those that lived before history began, about 5000 years ago. Animal life on Earth began in the oceans, more than 570 million years ago. Simple crab-like animals and shellfish swarmed in the sea, but there was no life on dry land until much later – about 350 million years ago. Then air-breathing fish crawled out onto the land, and from them evolved AMPHIBIANS and later REPTILES. For many millions of years DINOSAURS, some of them huge, roamed the Earth. They died out about 65 million years ago, and their places were taken by MAMMALS. No one knows exactly why the dinosaurs became extinct. Today, only their fossilized bones remain to provide a clue for us of their size, and how they lived.

▼ The largest dinosaurs, such as Brontosaurus, weighed over 150 tonnes. These vast creatures were harmless planteaters.

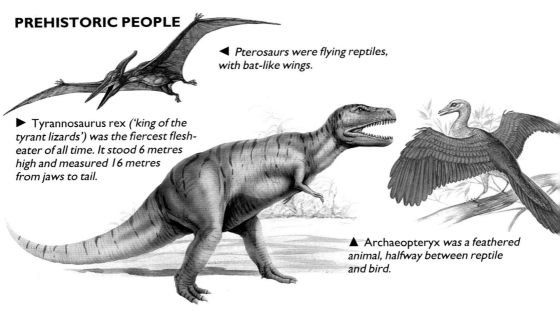

◀ *Pterosaurs were flying reptiles, with bat-like wings.*

▶ Tyrannosaurus rex *('king of the tyrant lizards') was the fiercest flesh-eater of all time. It stood 6 metres high and measured 16 metres from jaws to tail.*

▲ Archaeopteryx *was a feathered animal, halfway between reptile and bird.*

▼ *We know little about the first mammals. They were small creatures that probably ate insects and worms.*

▼ Homo habilis *was probably the first human being to make and use tools.*

The earliest mammals, tiny shrew-like animals, lived in the shadows of the great dinosaurs. After the dinosaurs died out, mammals developed and spread rapidly. The exact pattern of this rapid evolution is difficult to make out from the fossil record because things were happening so quickly. From these early mammals (some of which were very curious looking) developed the mammals of today. Some were much larger than their modern relatives. Animals that could not adapt to changing conditions (like the Ice Ages) died out. Others were hunted by human beings, the most powerful of all animals, whose primitive ancestors first appeared on Earth some 35 million years ago.

Prehistoric People

Prehistoric people lived long ago before there were any written records of history. We know about them from the remains of their tools, weapons and bodies. Prehistory is divided into the STONE AGE, the Bronze Age and the Iron Age. The ages are named after the materials that people used to make their tools and weapons.

The Stone Age lasted for a long time. It began around 2½ to 3 million years ago when human-like creatures began to appear on the Earth. They were different from the ape-like animals that lived at the same time. They had larger brains, used stone tools and could walk upright.

◀ *About 20,000 years ago modern humans lived in caves or crude huts of wood or hides. They used tools of stone and bone for hunting and preparing food and for making clothing and shelters.*

Around 1½ million years ago, a more human-like creature appeared. Scientists call this kind of early man *Homo erectus*. This means 'upright man'. *Homo erectus* is probably the ancestor of more advanced types of man, called *Homo sapiens*. This means 'intelligent man'. One kind of *Homo sapiens* was Neanderthal man, who appeared about 100,000 years ago. Modern man, called *Homo sapiens sapiens*, first appeared in Europe and Asia around 35,000 years ago.

Towards the end of the Stone Age, prehistoric people began to use metals. The first metal they used was copper. They made copper tools about 10,000 years ago. About 5,000 years ago, people invented bronze. Bronze is a hard ALLOY of copper and tin. This was the start of the Bronze Age, when the earliest civilizations began. It ended about 3300 years ago when people learned how to make iron tools, which were more hard-wearing than bronze.

It is difficult for us to imagine how few people there were in Stone Age times. It has been estimated that only a few thousand people lived in all of Africa and another few thousand in Asia. People moved around in small groups. During his or her whole lifetime, a Stone Age person might see only 25 to 50 other people.

▼ *The evolution of human beings, from the ape-like Ramapithecus to modern man.*

Ramapithecus	*Australopithecus*	*Homo habilis*	*Homo erectus*	*Neanderthal man*	*Modern human*
15 million years ago. Africa, Asia	1 – 4 million years ago. Africa	1.5 – 2 million years ago. Africa	0.2 – 1.5 million years ago. Africa, Asia Europe	35,000–100,000 years ago. Europe	Since 35,000 years ago. Worldwide

▲ *Thomas Jefferson wrote the text of the American Declaration of Independence and became third president of the United States.*

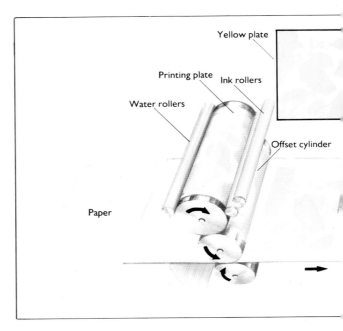

Yellow plate

Printing plate Ink rollers

Water rollers

Offset cylinder

Paper

▼ *Margaret Thatcher became the first woman to be elected Prime Minister of Great Britain in May 1979.*

President of the United States

The president of the UNITED STATES is the world's most powerful elected person. He is head of state, like the queen or king of Britain. He is also head of the government, like a PRIME MINISTER. The president is also the commander-in-chief of the army, navy and air force. The American people elect a president for a four-year term. A president may serve two terms. From 1789 to 1988 the USA had 40 presidents. The first was George WASHINGTON. Other famous presidents of the past include Thomas Jefferson and Abraham LINCOLN.

Prime Minister

A prime minister is a head of government. Britain and many other countries have a prime minister. The prime minister is usually the leader of the political party (or group of parties) with the greatest number of seats in PARLIAMENT. He or she chooses a group of people to help run the government. These people are called *ministers*. The group is called a *cabinet*. The cabinet decides government policy.

In some countries, like Australia, there is a distinction between the prime minister of the whole country, and the *premier* who is head of an individual state.

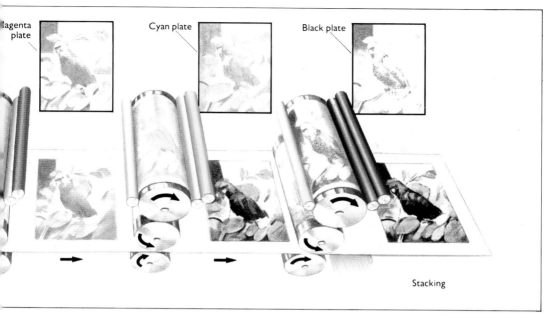

Magenta plate | Cyan plate | Black plate | Stacking

Printing

Printing is a way of copying words and pictures by mechanical means. It is used to produce books, newspapers, magazines and other items such as food can labels and printed carrier bags.

In *relief* printing, ink is put onto raised images, such as letters. The letters are then pressed against paper. The most common relief method is called *letterpress* printing. In *intaglio* or *gravure* printing, the image is not raised but cut away, or etched.

In other kinds of printing, the ink is put onto a flat surface. *Offset lithography* uses printing plates that are made photographically. The plates are treated with chemicals so that the greasy ink sticks only to the images to be printed.

The earliest printing, using wooden blocks, was done in China, probably as early as the AD 500s. Johannes GUTENBERG of Germany founded modern printing in the 1400s. He used movable type letters that could be used again and again.

▲ *When a colour picture is printed, it is actually made up of tiny dots of the three primary colours – blue (cyan), yellow and red (magenta) – and black. Four different printing plates are prepared for the picture, one for each colour. In offset lithography, the flexible plates are rolled around cylinders and moistened by water rollers. The ink rollers spread colour over the image areas on the plate. This colour is transferred to the offset cylinder and from there to the paper passing beneath it. The paper moves from one colour to the next: the black is printed last.*

Protein

Proteins are substances in food which are vital to life. They contain CARBON, HYDROGEN, OXYGEN and nitrogen. They build up body tissue, especially

▲ *Meat, fish, eggs, cheese and nuts are all rich sources of protein.*

muscle, and repair broken-down CELLS. They also give heat and energy, help us to grow, and help to protect us from disease. Our bodies do not store extra protein, so we must eat a regular supply.

Foods that come from animals provide most of our proteins. But some plant foods, such as groundnuts, peas and beans, are also rich in protein.

Protestant

Protestants are Christians who do not belong to the Roman Catholic or the Eastern Orthodox churches. Protestants believe that the things written in the BIBLE are more important than any rules made by church leaders. There are some passages in the Bible that can be explained in different ways. Protestants believe that people should make up their own minds about what these mean.

Protestantism began with the REFORMATION, when Martin Luther led a movement to change the ROMAN CATHOLIC CHURCH. Luther was a German priest, who was angry about the corruption in the Church at that time. He did not like the way priests forgave people's sins in return for money. In 1529, the Roman Catholic Church in Germany tried to stop people from following Luther's ideas. Luther's followers protested against this and were then called Protestants. Early Protestant groups included the Lutherans, Calvinists (Presbyterians) and Anglicans. Later groups included the Baptists, Congregationalists, Methodists and QUAKERS.

▲ *John Bunyan, who wrote* The Pilgrim's Progress, *joined a Nonconformist (a kind of Protestant) church in 1653. He was arrested in 1660 for preaching without a licence and spent almost 12 years in prison.*

▶ *In France, the fight between Protestants and Catholics was very bitter. In 1572, on the eve of August 24th, St Bartholomew's Day, thousands of Protestants known as Huguenots were murdered by Catholics. This terrible event became known as the St Bartholomew's Day Massacre.*

Psychology

Psychology is the study of the behaviour of animals and people. Psychologists are interested in how the mind and senses work. They are able to measure some things, such as INTELLIGENCE, by using special tests.

There are several branches of psychology. For example, child psychology is the study of how children behave and what they can do at different ages. *Psychiatry* is a similar science. But psychiatrists are doctors who cure mental illness and abnormal kinds of behaviour such as drug addiction and depression.

Pulley

A pulley is a simple MACHINE. It consists of a wheel on a fixed axle. A rope or belt passed over the wheel is tied to a load. When the rope is pulled, the load is raised.

A *movable pulley* runs along a rope. One end of the rope is fixed to a support. The load hangs from the pulley itself. When the other end of the rope is pulled, the pulley moves the load along the rope. Pulleys are used in machines such as cranes. The weight of the load that can be lifted depends on the number of wheels and the way they are connected. If the pulley has one rope, with a 6-wheel pulley you can lift a load six times greater than you could with only one wheel.

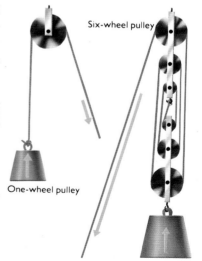

Six-wheel pulley

One-wheel pulley

▲ *Pulleys make it easier to lift heavy loads. A six-wheel pulley (right) can lift a much heavier load than a one- wheel pulley (left). This is because the amount of force applied to the weight increases six times.*

293

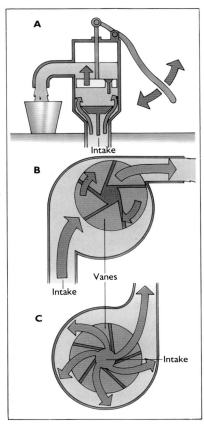

Pump

Most pumps are used to move liquids, but some move gases or powders such as flour. There are several kinds of pumps. For example, a bicycle pump is a simple *reciprocating pump*. It has a piston which moves up and down inside a cylinder. A similar pump is the *lift pump*. This can raise water about 9 metres from the bottom of a well. It has an upright barrel with a close-fitting piston worked by a handle. *Force pumps* are used to raise water from greater depths.

Pyramid

Pyramids are huge, four-sided buildings. They have a square base. The sides are triangles that meet in a point at the top.

The Egyptians built pyramids as royal tombs. The first was built in about 2650 BC at Sakkara. It is 62 metres high. The three most famous pyramids are near Giza. The Great Pyramid, built in the 2600s BC by the PHARAOH Khufu, is 137 metres high. Khafre, who ruled soon after Khufu, built the second pyramid. It is 136 metres high. The third, built by Khafre's successor Menakaure, is 73 metres high. About 80 pyramids still stand in Egypt.

Central and South American Indians also built pyramids as temples during the first six centuries AD. One huge pyramid is at Cholula, south-east of Mexico City. It is about 54 metres high.

▲ In a reciprocating pump (A), a piston forces liquid through an intake opening and out through a spout. A valve in the piston allows more liquid through as the piston is forced down. Rotary pumps (B) allow a steady flow of liquid, sucking the liquid in through the intake opening by means of a wheel instead of a piston. In a centrifugal pump (C) the liquid enters in the centre and is whipped round and out by the spinning blades.

▼ The huge pyramids built thousands of years ago in Egypt are great feats of engineering but it took countless numbers of slaves to move the great blocks of stone.

Quaker

The Quakers are also known as the Society of Friends. They are a PROTESTANT group that began in England during the 1650s.

They were called Quakers because some of them shook with emotion at their meetings. Early Quakers were often badly treated because of their belief that religion and government should not be mixed. Quakers have simple religious meetings and have elders not priests.

Quantum

We think of light and other forms of energy such as radio waves and X-rays as travelling in waves. Light can also be thought of as a stream of tiny quanta (the plural of quantum) or *photons*. The energy of each photon depends on the wavelength and therefore the colour of the light. A photon of white light has more energy than a photon of red light. Scientists combine the two ways of thinking about light. They think of light streaming out in packets of waves, each packet being a quantum or photon. They also think that tiny particles of matter such as electrons behave like waves as well as behaving like solid particles.

> When you look at the light from a light bulb, it seems to be quite steady. Actually, light is not as steady as it seems. It is given off in a vast number of tiny packages of energy, like the bullets from a machine gun. Each package is a quantum.

Quarrying

Quarries are huge pits where rocks are cut or blasted out of the ground. As long ago as prehistoric times, people had quarries where they dug up flint to make into tools and weapons.

Today rock is quarried in enormous amounts. Explosives blast loose thousands of tonnes. This is scooped up by bulldozers and diggers, and taken to crushers. The rock is ground into stones for use in roads, railways, concrete and cement. Not all rock is removed in this way. Stone that is used in building and paving is cut out of the ground rather than blasted. Electric cutters, wire saws and drills are used to cut the rock.

The beautiful rock called marble, which is used by some sculptors, is quarried by hand. It is then highly polished, which brings out its colours and sparkle.

QUARTZ

▶ *This thin disc of quartz will vibrate at a very regular frequency when exposed to an electric field. Such crystals are used as timers in watches and clocks because they are so accurate.*

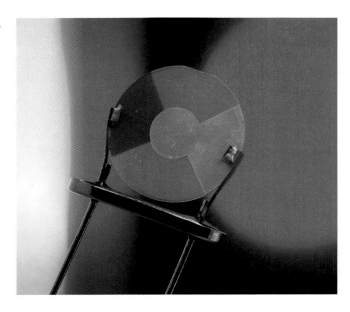

▼ *Quasars are still a mystery to astronomers. They can only be detected by the most powerful radio telescopes. If we could get close enough to one, it might appear as a brilliant core of light surrounded by a spinning disc of shining material.*

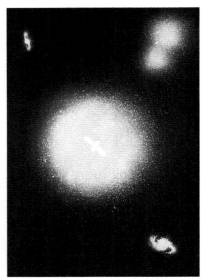

Quartz

Quartz is one of the most common MINERALS in the world. It is found everywhere. Sand is mostly made of quartz, and many ROCKS, for example granite, have quartz in them.

Quartz forms six-sided CRYSTALS. It is very hard, harder even than steel. In its pure form it has no colour and is as clear as glass. But most is smoky white or tinted with various colours. Many semi-precious gems, such as agate, amethyst, opal and onyx, are quartz.

Quartz is an important mineral. It is used in many things, including abrasives (such as sandpaper), lenses and electronics.

Quasar

Quasars are very distant, very powerful objects farther out in space than the most remote GALAXIES. They may be galaxies with some extra-powerful energy source at their centre. Quasars send out strong RADIO waves and X-RAYS. From Earth they look like very faint stars because they are so far away. All quasars are millions of light-years away, and so we see them now as they were that length of time ago. Quasars were not discovered by astronomers until the 1960s.

Rabbit

Rabbits originally came from Europe. Today they are found all over the world. They are small MAMMALS with a short tail and long pointed ears. Rabbits live in burrows in the ground. Each burrow is the home of a single family. A group of burrows is known as a warren.

Raccoon

In North America, raccoons are common creatures of the wild. They have long grey fur, a short pointed nose and a bushy tail ringed with black. They may grow to as much as 90 cm long.

Raccoons live in forests. They make their homes in tree holes and are good climbers. At night, they leave their hollows to hunt for food. They will eat almost anything: fruit and plants, eggs, insects, fish, birds and small mammals. But their main food comes from rivers, so their tree holes are usually found close by.

Wild rabbit

▶ *Raccoons are often thought of as pests in the United States, and are sometimes hunted. The frontiersman Davy Crockett's famous hat was made of raccoon fur, with the striped tail left hanging down at the back.*

Dwarf lop-eared rabbit

Himalayan rabbit

Radar

Radar is a device for tracking objects by RADIO beams. Because these beams work in the dark, in fog, and over distances well out of eyesight, radar is an enormously useful invention. It can detect objects thousands of kilometres away.

Radar works by sending out a narrow, high- powered beam about 500 times a second. It travels at a steady 300 metres every millionth of a second. When the beam strikes an object a faint echo

▲ *All types of pet rabbit have been bred from wild rabbits. They now come in different sizes, colours and even shapes. The tiny dwarf lop-eared rabbit has ears that droop. The Himalayan rabbit is not really from the Himalayas. It just means a certain type of coat marking with darker face, ears, legs and tail.*

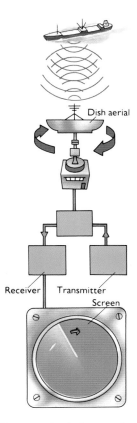

bounces back. The echo is picked up and turned into a light 'blip' on a screen. A radar operator can tell by studying the blip how far away the object is, in what direction it is moving, and at what speed. Radar is used by air traffic controllers at airports, by the military to track missiles and planes, and by weather stations to find and follow the paths of storms. SATELLITES fitted with radar can map the ground.

Radio

The common household object we call a radio is only the receiving end of a great system of radio communications. Most of the system is never even seen.

A radio programme begins in a studio. There, voices and music are turned into electronic signals. These are made stronger (amplified), and then sent out from tall masts as radio waves. These are picked up by the radio in your home and changed back into sounds you can hear. Radio waves travel at the speed of light. This is so fast that a signal can circle the world 7½ times in one second.

▲ The name 'radar' comes from the phrase '**ra**dio **d**etecting **a**nd **r**anging'. The aerial that sends out the special radio signal usually acts as a receiver too, detecting the signal as it bounces back. To do this it has to change from one sort of operation to the other. This 'change-over' is controlled from inside the radar installation. When the signals are displayed on the screen, objects detected by the radar show up as bright spots. Experienced operators can tell the direction and distance of objects from the 'blips' on the screen, even though the 'blips' look nothing like the objects in real life.

▶ How a radio broadcast is carried to your radio. Inside the radio, the voice signals are separated from their carrier waves and turned back into sounds by the loudspeaker.

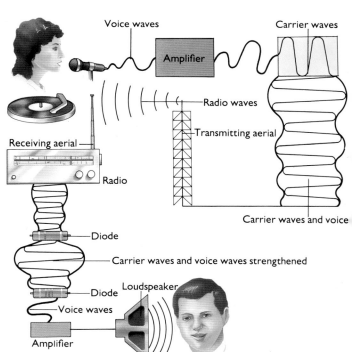

The first person to generate radio waves was Heinrich Hertz in 1887. But it was Guglielmo MARCONI who sent the first messages in 1894. His first signals travelled only a few metres. Seven years later he sent signals across the Atlantic. Today, radio waves are used to transmit television and radio programmes and computer information.

Radioactivity

The atoms of some substances are always shooting off tiny particles and rays that we cannot see or feel. This is called radioactivity. These strange rays were discovered in 1896. It was soon found that nothing could be done to stop the rays shooting out. It was also found that in time these radioactive substances changed into other substances, and that they did this at a steady rate. If a piece of radioactive uranium was left for millions of years it would 'decay' and turn into a piece of lead. Scientists measure the rate of decay in radioactive carbon in animal and plant remains to find out how many thousands of years ago the animals and plants lived. Radioactive materials can be dangerous. A nuclear explosion causes dangerous levels of radioactivity.

Carrier wave

Sound signal

Amplitude modulation (AM)

Frequency modulation (FM)

▲ The station selector on your radio may have the initials AM and FM on it. These initials tell you how the carrier wave was joined with the signals at the transmitter. AM stands for 'amplitude modulation'. This means that the amplitude (height) of the carrier wave was altered to match the signals. FM – 'frequency modulation' – means that the frequency – the number of carrier waves passing each second – was changed to match the signal at the transmitter.

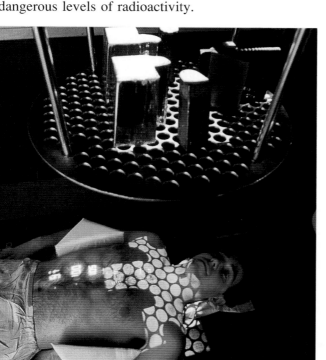

◀ The power of radioactivity can be used to treat some types of illness, such as cancer. Radiotherapy can be used to destroy the cancer cells without harming the healthy cells. The illuminated discs over this patient's chest show the areas which are to receive radiation. The pattern can be altered by changing the position of the lead blocks (at the top of the picture) which shield the lungs from too much radiation.

▲ *The huge VLA (Very Large Array) radio telescope at Socorro, New Mexico, is made up of 27 dish aerials. Each of them is 25 metres in diameter, and they can be moved along a Y-shaped track to exactly the position the astronomers choose.*

▼ *This image received by the Socorro radio telescope is of a galaxy 20 million light-years away from Earth. The colours are produced by computer, and show how much energy is coming from each part. Red is the highest energy level, and purple is the lowest.*

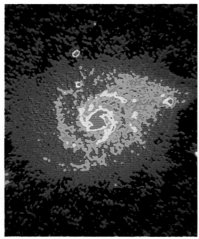

Radio Astronomy

A heavenly body, such as a STAR, does not only give off LIGHT waves. It sends out many kinds of radio waves too. Radio astronomers explore the UNIVERSE by 'listening' to the radio signals that reach Earth from outer space. These signals are not made by other forms of life. They come from natural events, such as exploding stars or heated clouds of gases. By studying these signals, radio astronomers can find out many things about different parts of the universe.

Radio telescopes have giant aerials – often dish-shaped. They pick up faint signals that have come from places much deeper in space than anything that can be seen by ordinary TELESCOPES. The first large radio telescopes were built after World War II. Today, the biggest in the world is at Arecibo in Puerto Rico. Its huge receiving dish has been built across a mountain valley. It is 305 metres wide.

Railways

Railways have been in use since the 1500s. At first, rails were made of wood and wagons were pulled by horses. However, what we call the railway age began when a Cornish engineer named Richard Trevithick drove a steam rail engine along a steel-plate track in South Wales. The year was 1804. The man who did more than any other to make the railways an important

▼ *A huge Union Pacific 'Big Boy' locomotive of the 1940s. It weighed 534 tonnes.*

▶ *A modern electric locomotive. It picks up electricity from overhead wires through the hinged pantograph on the roof.*

▲ *Mallard set the world speed record for a steam locomotive in 1938 – 202 km (126 miles) an hour.*

▲ *Japan's streamlined electric 'bullet trains' run at an average speed of more than 160 km (100 miles) an hour.*

form of transport was another Englishman, George Stephenson. He built and equipped the first railways to carry passengers on trains pulled by steam locomotives.

Today, the age of steam is over, though you can still enjoy the thrill of riding on one of the many steam trains kept running by enthusiasts. Modern diesel and electric locomotives use less fuel and need less looking after. Railways are particularly useful for carrying heavy freight and for taking commuters to and from their jobs in city centres while underground railways carry passengers quickly across cities.

Rain and Snow

When rain pours down, it is only the sky returning the same water to Earth that originally evaporated from the land and sea.

Rain forms when water vapour in the air starts to cool. As the vapour cools it turns first of all into tiny droplets, which form wispy CLOUDS. The droplets

High mountains usually force rain out of any moist wind that strikes them. They force the air up to cooler heights, and as the moist air cools it makes rain. Most rain falls on the slopes that face the wind. The other side of the mountain receives little rain. Waialeale peak in Hawaii has the highest rainfall in the world – an average of 1200 cm a year. Yet only a few miles away, on the other side of the peak, the average rainfall is less than 50 cm.

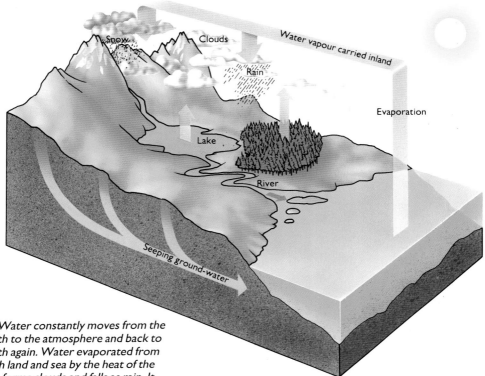

▲ *Water constantly moves from the Earth to the atmosphere and back to Earth again. Water evaporated from both land and sea by the heat of the Sun forms clouds and falls as rain. It flows into lakes and rivers and eventually into the sea, where it is turned into water vapour again, and so on. We call this movement of water the water cycle.*

and the clouds thicken and turn a dull grey. At last the drops become so heavy that they start to fall. If it is cold enough to freeze them, the drops hit the ground as either hail or snow.

The amount of rain that falls is widely different from place to place. In the Atacama Desert in Chile, less than 25 mm of rain falls in 20 years. But in eastern India, monsoon rains drop 1080 cm every year.

Rainbow

The gorgeous colours of a rainbow are formed by sunlight shining on drops of rain. The best time for rainbows is right after a shower, when the clouds break up and sunlight streams through.

Rainbows can be seen only when the Sun is behind you and low over the horizon. When the Sun's rays strike the raindrops, each drop acts as a prism and splits the LIGHT into a SPECTRUM of colours ranging from red to violet. The lower the Sun, the higher the rainbow and the fuller its curved arch.

An old fairy story says that there is a crock of gold at the end of a rainbow. Nobody has ever found the treasure because a rainbow really has no end. It is a full circle. The bottom half of the circle lies below the horizon and out of sight.

Recording

Making a record is a complicated process. First a microphone turns the voices and music into electronic signals. These are made stronger, or amplified, in order to make a sapphire 'chisel' vibrate as it cuts a very fine groove into a smooth disc. This is the master disc.

A metal copy in reverse is made from the master disc so that the grooves stand out as ridges on the copy. Next, metal stampers are made. They are used to press thousands of records.

A TAPE RECORDER works by changing sound waves into magnetism. The sound is recorded as a magnetic pattern along the recording tape. When the tape is played, the magnetic pattern is turned back into sound.

You can record a television programme on a VIDEO cassette using a video recorder. The video cassette contains tape like a sound cassette. It records the electric signal coming from the television aerial. Sound recording was pioneered by Thomas EDISON.

> As many as 48 separate sound recordings can be made on one tape in parallel paths called 'tracks'. Any single track is a 'mono' recording. Two tracks are needed for stereophonic sound.

Reformation

The Reformation is the name given to the period of great religious upheaval that began in Europe in the 1500s.

At that time, a revolt occurred in the ROMAN CATHOLIC CHURCH. In protest at what they saw as

▼ The Reformation reached England when King Henry VIII broke all ties with the Pope. He decided that all the monasteries should be closed, and their great wealth should go to the Crown. This act is often called the dissolution of the monasteries.

> The Reformation saw the start of many long years of religious wars and persecution that have continued to this day. The Thirty Years' War was the result of rivalry between Catholics and Protestants. It began in Germany, but spread to involve most of the European countries. Most European countries now allow freedom of religion, but the two sides still think the other's beliefs are mistaken.

bad practices and errors in the Church, groups of people broke away to set up their own churches. These people became known as PROTESTANTS.

What many Protestants wanted was a simpler, more basic form of Christianity, and one that allowed them greater freedom to worship as they chose. As the Protestant movement grew, many kings and rulers saw the new movement as a chance to widen their power at the expense of the Church. They were happy to support the Protestant cause because in many ways the religious protest also helped them to gain more influence. The Reformation led to wars between Protestant and Catholic rulers.

▼ Part of Einstein's theory of relativity was that gravity could make light bend. Thus from the Earth, it would be easy to make a mistake about the real position of a distant star, because the light coming from it could have been bent by the Sun's gravitational pull. Another part of the theory says that time slows down for an object travelling at almost the speed of light. The example shows a rocket with a clock on board which takes off from Earth at 3 o'clock. As it nears the speed of light, its clock will be showing 5 o'clock. But time has slowed down on the rocket, and the clocks back on Earth will be showing 6 o'clock.

Relativity

If you are travelling in a car at 60 km/h and you are overtaken by another car travelling at 80 km/h, the second car pulls away from you at 20 km/h. Its true speed relative to the ground is 80 km/h, but its speed *relative* to you is 20 km/h. This is the basic idea of relativity: assuming that you are not moving and working out the speed of something that is moving relative to you.

At the end of the last century scientists discovered that the speed of light is always the same, no matter how fast the source of the light is moving. In 1905, Albert EINSTEIN put forward his *special* theory of relativity to explain this strange fact. His theory

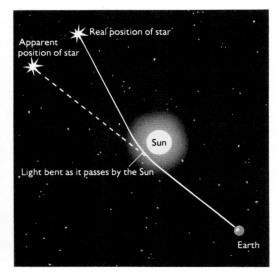

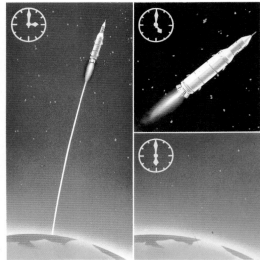

concerns, among other things, the effect of motion on time, length and mass. For instance, the theory predicts that in a spaceship hurtling across the universe at nearly the speed of light, time would pass more slowly, the spaceship's length would become smaller and its mass would become greater than on a similar spaceship stationary on Earth.

Later, in 1915, Einstein produced his *general* theory of relativity. This theory has helped scientists understand more about space, gravity and the nature of the universe.

Renaissance

The Renaissance is the name given to a period of about 200 years in the history of Europe. The word means 'rebirth' in French, and the Renaissance was the time when people again became interested in every aspect of art, science, architecture and literature.

Since the times of the ancient Greeks and Romans there had been little interest in new ideas.

▼ *Goldsmiths working in Florence, Italy, during the Renaissance. Trading brought great wealth to the city.*

▼ A statue of Perseus holding the head of Medusa, by the Italian Renaissance sculptor Cellini.

Then, during the 1300s, Italian scholars began to take a fresh interest in the past. They also looked for new scientific explanations of the mysteries of the world and the universe. During the Renaissance a great number of painters, sculptors and architects were at work in Italy. The works of art of LEONARDO DA VINCI and MICHELANGELO are among the most famous products of this time. From Italy, the ideas of the Renaissance quickly spread to the rest of Europe.

At the same time as all these artistic and scientific ideas, there was a great growth in trade. Later, there were voyages to explore Africa and India, and in 1492 America was discovered by COLUMBUS.

▶ Florence cathedral is a supreme example of Renaissance architecture. The dome was designed by the artist Brunelleschi in 1420, but it was not completed until 15 years after his death, in 1461.

▼ An amoeba is one of the simplest forms of life – a single-celled animal. It can reproduce on its own. First the nucleus, in the middle of the cell, divides in two. Then the cell splits apart to become two identical amoebas.

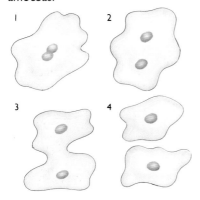

Reproduction

Reproduction is the process by which plants and animals make new plants and animals like themselves. Some plants and animals can reproduce on their own. Some just split in two. Many plants reproduce *asexually* by producing buds that drop off and start a new life of their own. Other plants produce spores that may be carried away by wind or water until they land in a suitable place to grow into new plants.

In *sexual* reproduction, a male cell, called a *sperm*, joins with, or fertilizes, a female cell, called an *ovum* or egg, to form a new fertilized cell. This cell divides over and over again until a whole new organism has been formed.

Most female FISH lay their eggs in the water. Then the male swims over the eggs and releases his

◄ *Part of the egg rope of a perch. Once a female fish has laid her eggs, and the male has fertilized them, the tiny fish embryos develop, one inside each egg. Once they have used up the food store in the egg it is time for them to hatch.*

sperm on them. After fertilization, the embryo (developing) fish grows while using the store of food in the egg.

In most higher animals, fertilization takes place inside the female's body. After fertilization the female BIRD or REPTILE lays her eggs. The embryo then develops inside the egg until it is ready to hatch out. In MAMMALS, fertilization also takes place inside the female, but the embryo develops inside its mother until it is ready to be born. The embryo receives food from its mother's bloodstream. After it is born, the mother feeds it with her milk.

The number of offspring a mother gives birth to at one time depends on the number of eggs fertilized. In human mothers, only one egg is usually fertilized. If more than one is fertilized there may be twins, triplets or even more babies. Identical twins come from the same egg which divides after fertilization.

SEE IT YOURSELF

Some seeds grow in an amazingly short time. Buy a packet of cress seeds. Put some potting compost or damp blotting paper in a shallow dish, and sow the seeds on top of it. It is fun to make the first letter of your name. After only a few days the seeds will start to grow, and in 12 to 15 days the cress will be ready to eat.

Take a leaf from an African violet or begonia and make cuts through some of the veins. Put the leaf on moist soil, and first roots and then a new plant will grow.

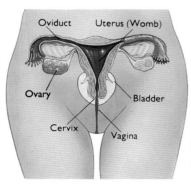

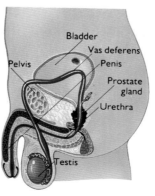

◄ *The reproductive parts of the body are very different in men and women. The woman produces eggs in her ovaries. These travel down the oviducts and, if fertilized by sperm provided by a man during sexual intercourse, may develop into a baby in the woman's uterus, or womb. Men produce millions of sperm in their testicles. The sperm and the egg each contain half of what is needed to make another human being.*

Galapagos giant tortoise

Red-eared terrapin

▲ *The Galapagos giant tortoise can have a shell over 1.5 metres long, and often weighs more than 200 kilograms. Red-eared terrapins are found in fresh water in North America.*

Reptile

Reptiles are the most advanced of all cold-blooded animals. They live on land and in the sea.

Reptiles live in all parts of the world except for the North and South Poles. Most, however, live in warm regions. This is because they are cold-blooded and must get their warmth from their surroundings.

When it is cold they become very sleepy and cannot move fast enough to catch food or escape from enemies. Most reptiles that live in cold places spend the winter in HIBERNATION.

Reptiles played a very important part in the EVOLUTION of the Earth. About 360 million years ago, the first reptiles appeared. They soon became the strongest form of life on Earth. They ruled the planet for close to 100 million years. One group of reptiles, the DINOSAURS, were the most spectacular creatures ever to walk the land. The biggest weighed more than 100 tonnes.

Today there are four main groups of reptiles: ALLIGATORS and CROCODILES, LIZARDS and SNAKES, TORTOISES and TURTLES, and the rare tuatara. The biggest reptiles are the alligators and crocodiles. The estuarine crocodile of South-east Asia grows to 6 metres in length, and is the biggest of them all.

There are over 5000 kinds of lizards and snakes. They live everywhere, from deserts to jungles and faraway ocean islands. Some have poisonous bites with which they kill their prey. Turtles and tortoises

▶ *These primitive reptiles lived over 250 million years ago. They are called sail-backs because on their backs they had bony spines covered in skin. They used these to help control their body heat. If they turned sideways to the Sun, the sails could absorb heat. If they turned their backs to the Sun, the sails gave out heat and the creatures cooled down.*

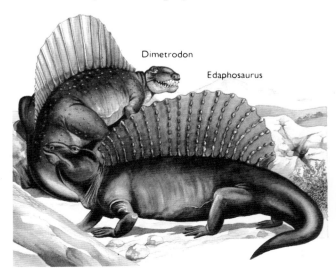

Dimetrodon

Edaphosaurus

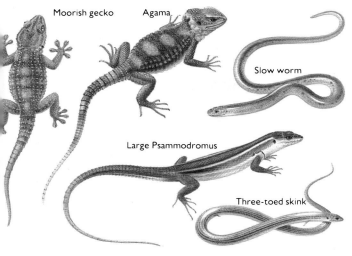

Moorish gecko   Agama

Slow worm

Large Psammodromus

Three-toed skink

◄ There are many different types of lizard, ranging in size from a few centimetres to three metres. Lizards are far more ancient reptiles than snakes. Lizard fossils have been found dating from 200 million years ago, but snakes appeared only about 100 million years ago. The slow worm is in fact a lizard, though its legs have disappeared.

are well protected by their hard shells. The biggest are the lumbering giant tortoises of the Pacific and Indian Ocean islands.

Rhinoceros

Sometimes described as a 'tank on legs', the rhinoceros is one of the largest and strongest of all land animals. A full grown male weighs up to 3.5 tonnes.

This massive beast has a tough leathery skin and sprouts one or two horns (actually made of hair) on its snout. These may grow as long as 127 cm.

The rhinoceros lives in Africa and in south-eastern Asia. There it feeds on leafy twigs, shrubs and grasses.

▼ Although their poor eyesight may make them an easier target for hunters, rhinos have a good sense of hearing and smell.

Although an adult rhino has no natural enemies, it is so widely hunted for its horns that it has become an endangered species. When ground into a powder, rhino horn is believed to be a powerful medicine. Some people claim it can be used to detect poisoned wine. None of these beliefs are true.

River

Rivers are one of the most important geographical features in the world. They range in size from little more than swollen streams to mighty waterways that flow for thousands of kilometres.

The greatest rivers in the world are the AMAZON, the MISSISSIPPI and the NILE. They all drain huge areas of land. The basin of the Amazon, for example, stretches over an area larger than all of western Europe.

Some rivers serve as transport links that allow ocean-going ships to sail far inland. In tropical jungles they are often the only way to travel. Rivers with DAMS supply us with electric power. Water from rivers is also used to irrigate farmland in desert lands and other dry parts of the world.

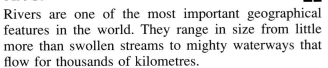

LONGEST RIVERS	
	km
Nile Africa	6690
Amazon South America	6437
Chang Jiang (Yangtze) China	6342
Mississippi-Missouri USA	6212
Irtysh Russia	5570
Huang He (Yellow) China	4672
Zaire (Congo) Africa	4667
Amur Asia	4509
Lena Russia	4269
Mackenzie Canada	4241
Mekong Asia	4184
Niger Africa	4168

The longest river in the British Isles is the Shannon in Ireland at 386 km. The Severn is the longest river in Great Britain – 354 km in length. The Thames is 346 km long.

▶ *Over hundreds of years, rivers carve valleys out of the land as they flow towards the sea. From tiny mountain streams made from melted snow, they grow and swell, picking up mineral and other deposits as they flow through the landscape. These deposits sink to the bottom when the rivers slow down as they near the sea, forming great deltas.*

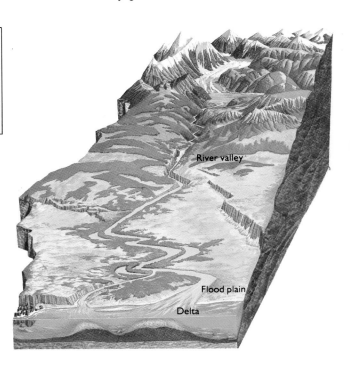

River valley

Flood plain

Delta

◄ *Complex road systems have to be planned to cope with ever growing numbers of cars and other vehicles. In St. Louis, Missouri, USA, this huge interchange had to be built where two major highways cross the Mississippi River.*

▼ *Roman roads (below) were some of the first paved roads to be built in the world. They were built by the Roman army and had gutters built in for drainage. Modern roads (bottom) are made up of smooth layers of tar, or asphalt, over concrete or macadam.*

Road

The Romans were the first great road builders. Some of their long, straight roads still survive. The Romans made roads of gravel and stones. The surface paving stones were arched so rain ran off into ditches.

Modern road building began during the INDUSTRIAL REVOLUTION. In the early 1800s a Scottish engineer, John McAdam, became the pioneer of modern road-making. But the stony surfaces of his roads were not good for vehicles with rubber tyres. Later, *macadamized* roads were built. They are covered with tar or asphalt to make them smooth. Many roads, especially motorways, are now made of concrete.

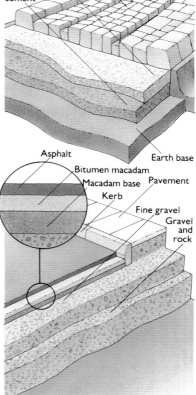

Stone slabs
Stone filling
Stones and cement

Asphalt
Bitumen macadam
Macadam base
Kerb
Earth base
Pavement
Fine gravel
Gravel and rock

Robot

In films and books set in the future, robots often look like metal people and they can walk, talk and even think.

Real robots are very different. They are machines with arms that can move in several directions. Robots are *programmable* machines. This means they can be instructed to carry out different tasks. The instructions, or programs, are stored in the robot's computer brain.

Most robots work in industry and do jobs such as paint spraying, welding, and heavy lifting.

Rock

Rocks consist of grains of MINERALS. *Igneous rocks* form when magma (molten rock) hardens. Some harden on the surface to form rocks like basalt and obsidian. Some harden underground to form rocks like granite. *Sedimentary rocks* are composed of sediments, like sand. For example, conglomerates are rocks made up of pebbles and sand. Many limestones are made of sediments formed mainly from the remains of dead plants and animals. *Metamorphic rocks* are igneous or sedimentary rocks that have been changed by great heat and pressure. For example, limestones may be *metamorphosed* (changed) into marble.

Almost all of the minerals that make up rocks are made up of compounds of only about eight elements: oxygen, silicon, aluminium, iron, calcium, sodium, potassium and magnesium.

Collecting rocks can be fun, and it will teach you much about the Earth. It is easy to find rocks, even in a city. You can start by getting hold of a book that will tell you how to find and identify interesting rocks. Good hunting grounds for rocks are quarries, building sites and the base of ocean cliffs.

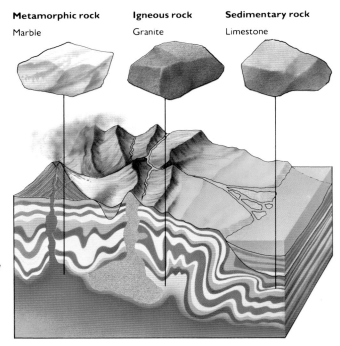

Metamorphic rock
Marble

Igneous rock
Granite

Sedimentary rock
Limestone

▶ *Granite is a rock that has hardened underground and limestone is made from layers of sediment made up of dead sea creatures. Heat and pressure on limestone inside the Earth forms marble, a metamorphic rock.*

Rocket

A firework rocket and the rockets that took astronauts to the MOON work in much the same way. Both burn fuel to produce hot gases. The gases shoot out backwards. This creates a *reaction* force that thrusts the rocket forwards. Rockets do not need air for their engines, unlike jets. So they are ideal for moving in space (where there is no air).

The Chinese used rockets as weapons as early as the 1200s. Rockets used to launch SATELLITES and spacecraft were developed after World War II. They are *multistage* rockets, which means several rockets joined together. Each stage fires in turn.

Fuel for early rockets, such as Germany's V2 in World War II, was kerosene and oxygen. Today's rockets use liquid fuels. Not only do liquid fuels give more energy, weight for weight, but they allow more control. The most powerful rocket in use today is the *Energia* rocket used in the Soviet shuttle.

▼ *Most engines run on fuel that burns in oxygen from the air, but out in space there is no air. If the rocket fuel is going to burn the rocket has to carry its own oxygen, in frozen liquid form. The rocket fuel is usually liquid hydrogen.*

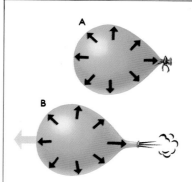

SEE IT YOURSELF

When air is let out of a balloon, it acts like a simple rocket. Fill a balloon with air. The balloon will stretch as you force a large amount of air into its small space. Once you close the mouth of the balloon (A), the air pushes equally in all directions. Now open the mouth (B). The balloon collapses as the air under pressure escapes. As this happens, the air pressure on the side opposite the mouth becomes greater than the pressure around the mouth, and the balloon flies in the direction of greater pressure. All rockets work on this principle.

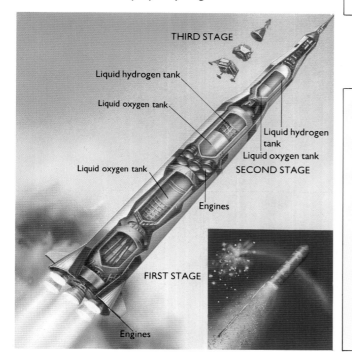

THIRD STAGE

Liquid hydrogen tank

Liquid oxygen tank

Liquid hydrogen tank

Liquid oxygen tank

SECOND STAGE

Liquid oxygen tank

Engines

FIRST STAGE

Engines

Today's space rockets use liquid fuels – usually a liquid called hydrazine or liquid hydrogen. In a liquid-fuel rocket, the fuel needs oxygen before it will burn. The fuel and the oxidizer are stored in separate tanks. When they are both pumped into a combustion chamber they burn explosively and produce the gases that rush out of a nozzle and give lift. Liquid hydrogen and liquid oxygen have to be refrigerated to stay liquid, so space rockets need complicated systems of refrigeration pipes.

Flying squirrel

Alpine marmot

Siberian chipmunk

Rodent

Rodents are a group of gnawing animals. They have large, sharp front teeth that grow all the time. The animals wear down these teeth by gnawing their food. They also use their teeth to dig burrows in the ground for their homes and nests. BEAVERS even cut down good-sized trees with their gnawing teeth.

The 2000 or so rodents also include mice, RATS, porcupines and SQUIRRELS. The South American capybara is the largest rodent. It looks like a giant guinea pig. It grows to a length of 1.25 metres and weighs over 45 kg. The smallest rodent is the European harvest mouse. It grows only about 7 centimetres long.

Roman Catholic Church

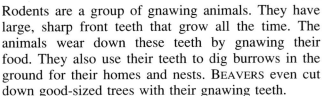

The Roman Catholic Church is the oldest and largest of all Christian churches. It has about 996 million members. The POPE is the head of the Church. He lives in Vatican City in Italy.

Roman Catholics follow the teachings of JESUS Christ. The Church also helps its followers by giving them rules for good living. The main church service is called the Mass. Some Roman Catholics become nuns, monks and brothers. They devote their lives to their faith in orders (societies) such as the Franciscans or Benedictines.

▲ *Three of the many species of rodent. The flying squirrel does not actually fly, but glides with the help of extra flaps of skin between its fore and hind legs. The marmot and chipmunk are both ground dwellers.*

▶ *In the Roman Catholic Church, great importance is given to celebrations and ceremonies.*

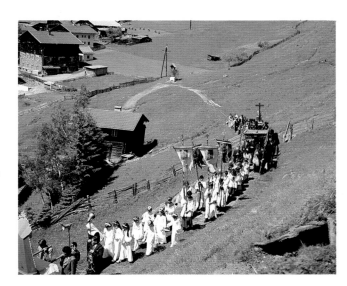

The Roman Empire

The story of the Roman Empire began about 2700 years ago, in small villages on hills above the river Tiber in Italy. The people of these villages founded the mighty Roman Empire.

According to legend, Rome was founded by twin brothers called Romulus and Remus, who were reared by a wolf. About 590BC the Romans set up a republic, and created a strong army. They began to conquer their neighbours.

The capital of this state was Rome, a city built on seven hills. Here was the Forum, or meeting place, and the Senate, or parliament. There were temples, markets, triumphal arches and villas (large houses). The language of Rome was Latin.

In 45BC the soldier Julius Caesar made himself dictator of Rome. In 27BC his nephew Octavian (Augustus) became the first Roman emperor. The Romans ruled most of Europe and the lands around the Mediterranean. They brought peace and firm government. Roman ideas spread everywhere. The Romans were skilful engineers and many remains of their roads, walls, forts and other buildings can still be seen. The crane was a Roman invention.

In AD 364 the empire was divided: the western half was governed from Rome, the eastern half from Constantinople (Byzantium). For a thousand years, Eastern Roman, or Byzantine, emperors ruled from Constantinople.

Rome was now in decline. Its army struggled to fight off attacks from barbarian tribes. Around 476 Rome itself fell, and the empire in the west collapsed. The eastern empire lasted (in name) until 1453, when Constantinople was captured by the Turks.

HISTORY OF ROME	
753 BC	Founding of Rome (according to legend).
590 BC	Foreign kings driven from Rome; the republic set up.
264 BC	Punic Wars, against Carthage.
146 BC	Greece now controlled by Rome.
73 BC	Slaves revolt, led by Spartacus.
31 BC	Octavian defeats Mark Antony and Cleopatra.
AD 150	Peak of Roman power.
AD 330	Constantinople founded.
AD 364	Division of the empire.
AD 378	Roman legions defeated at Adrianople by Goths.
AD 410	Alaric's Visigoths capture Rome.
AD 451	Attila the Hun attacks Rome.
AD 476	Fall of western empire.

▲ A Roman senator. He is wearing a loose, flowing robe called a toga.

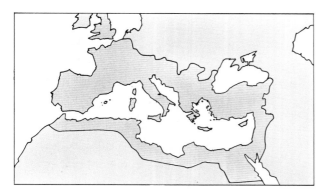

◄ This map shows the Roman Empire when it was at its greatest, in AD 117. At this time it was ruled by the emperor Trajan.

315

ROMANIA

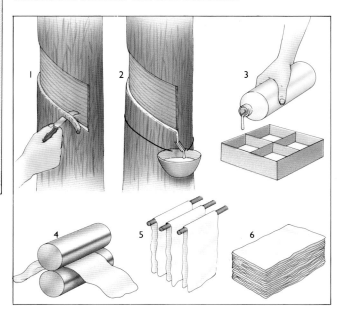

(Map showing Romania with neighbouring countries: POLAND, CZECHOSLOVAKIA, UKRAINE, MOLDOVA, HUNGARY, ROMANIA, FORMER YUGOSLAVIA, BLACK SEA, BULGARIA)

Government: Multi-party system
Capital: Bucharest
Area: 237,500 sq km
Population: 23,200,000
Languages: Romanian, Hungarian, German
Currency: Leu

▶ *Steps in rubber production: (1) The rubber tree is tapped for latex. (2) Each tapping produces about a quarter of a litre of latex. (3) Formic acid is added to the latex to make the rubber particles stick together (coagulate). (4) The rubber is rolled into sheets, which are hung up to dry (5). The crude rubber sheets (6) are dyed and treated, and shaped by machines into various products.*

Romania

Romania is a small country in southeastern EUROPE. It has beautiful mountains and many forests. Most people are farmers, but there are also mines, and oil is produced too. In 1989, the people overthrew the corrupt communist government. They demanded democratic reforms and free elections.

Rubber

Rubber is an important material with many uses in industry and in the home. Most natural rubber comes from the rubber tree. When the bark of the tree is cut, a white juice called *latex* oozes out. The juice is collected and made into rubber. Today most natural rubber comes from Malaysia and Indonesia.

Russia

Russia is by far the largest of the countries that formed from the former SOVIET UNION. It contains more people than the other states put together and has most of the great cities, including MOSCOW and St Petersburg. Russia is rich in mineral resources and is industrially powerful, with significant steel and textile industries. Farming, including such crops as cereals, fodder and cattle, is also important.

Sahara Desert

The Sahara is the world's largest hot DESERT. It covers about 9.1 million square km in North Africa. It extends from the Atlantic Ocean in the west to the Red Sea in the east. In the north, it stretches to the Mediterranean coast in Libya and in Egypt. Recently, the lands south of the Sahara have had very little rain. Because of this, the desert is slowly spreading southwards.

About a third of the Sahara is covered by sand. Other parts are covered by gravel and stones, or by bare rock. The Sahara is the hottest place on earth. The world's highest air temperature in the shade, 57.7°C, was recorded there.

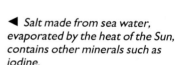

AFRICA

SAHARA DESERT

◄ Salt made from sea water, evaporated by the heat of the Sun, contains other minerals such as iodine.

Salt

The chemical name for the salt we eat is sodium chloride. We need some salt to stay healthy, but not too much. Salt is also used to preserve foods and it is important in many industries. Much of our salt comes from sea water, but some is mined from deposits in the ground.

Satellite

A body that moves in orbit around another body is called a satellite. The EARTH and the other planets are satellites of the SUN. The MOON is the Earth's satellite, but the Earth has many more satellites. These are the artificial satellites launched by rockets into fixed orbits. Weather satellites have cameras that send back pictures of cloud and storm formations. Communications satellites relay television

The most useful satellites are the communications and weather satellites, most of which are launched into *geostationary* orbit. This means that they are placed in a fixed orbit 36,000 km high where they orbit the Earth in exactly 24 hours. Because of this they appear to remain stationary in the sky, always over the same spot on Earth.

SATURN

► *The first satellite in space was the Soviet* Sputnik 1, *launched in 1957.*

▼ *A cutaway view of an Intelsat news satellite. Its small rocket motor is used to position the satellite exactly after launching from Earth. Electrical power is provided by solar panels.*

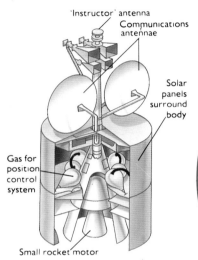

'Instructor' antenna

Communications antennae

Solar panels surround body

Gas for position control system

Small rocket motor

► *There are many Intelsat communications satellites positioned over different parts of the world. The satellites relay signals between each other as well as to hundreds of ground stations.*

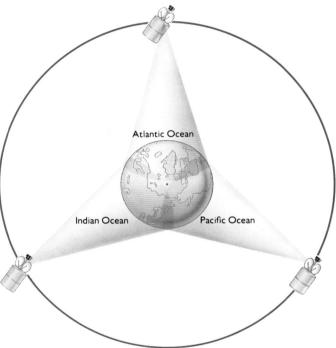

Atlantic Ocean

Indian Ocean

Pacific Ocean

and telephone signals around the world. They have radio and other equipment powered by batteries charged by the Sun's rays. The satellites receive a signal from the transmitting station on Earth, amplify it, and beam it down to another Earth station, which may be thousands of kilometres away.

The first artificial satellite was *Sputnik 1*, launched by the USSR in 1957.

Saturn

Saturn is the second largest PLANET in the SOLAR SYSTEM after JUPITER. It is about 120,000 km across. Saturn is famous for the rings that circle it. These rings are made of billions of icy particles. The rings are more than 272,000 km across, but they are very thin. The particles in the rings may be the remains of a moon that broke up.

To the naked eye, Saturn looks like a bright star. The planet is actually mostly made up of light gases, and it is less dense than water, but scientists think that it may have a solid core. Saturn has 24 satellites. The largest is Titan. It measures about 5,200 km across – larger than MERCURY. Titan is the only known moon to have an atmosphere – a layer of gases surrounding it.

SATURN FACTS

Average distance from Sun: 1430 million km
Nearest distance from Earth: 1280 million km
Average temperature (clouds): –190 degrees
Diameter across equator: 120,000 km
Diameter of ring system: 272,000 km
Atmosphere: Hydrogen, helium
Number of moons: 24 known
Length of day: 10 hours 14 minutes
Length of years: 29.5 Earth years

Earth
Saturn

◀ *Saturn's rings are made up of pieces of ice, rock and dust. They form a band that, measured across, is more than 20 times the diameter of the Earth.*

Science

The main divisions of science are ASTRONOMY, BIOLOGY, CHEMISTRY, GEOLOGY, MATHEMATICS, MEDICINE, and PHYSICS, which deals with types of ENERGY.

Modern scientists use the *scientific method*. First they *observe*, or look at, something carefully to find out everything they can about it. Then they make a *theory* which explains what the thing is made of, or how it works. Then they test the theory with *experiments*. If the experiments agree with the theory, it becomes a *law* of science. Sometimes a law changes when scientists discover new facts.

SCIENCE FICTION

► *Scientific research is often aimed at making life easier and safer for people. This walking robot is for use in the nuclear industry. It can be controlled remotely.*

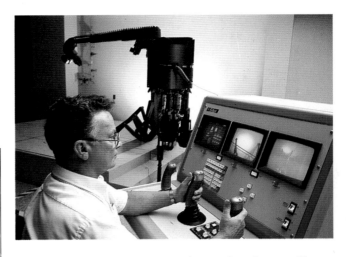

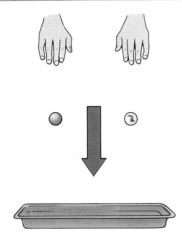

SEE IT YOURSELF

The famous scientist Galileo found out that objects always gather speed as they fall to the ground. Try dropping two objects onto a tray at the same time. Use objects which have the same shape but different weights. Do they land together? Galileo proposed that objects of the same size and shape fall at the same speed no matter what they weigh.

Scientific studies began in early times. Great advances were made during the first civilizations, especially in ancient Greece and China. Science nearly died out in Europe in the MIDDLE AGES, but during the RENAISSANCE scientists began making discoveries that changed the way people thought and lived. This process speeded up during the INDUSTRIAL REVOLUTION, and scientific research has been increasing ever since.

Science Fiction

Imaginative stories which are set in the future or on other planets are called science fiction. The writers often use new scientific discoveries in their stories. They imagine how these discoveries might change

► *This is one artist's idea of how an alien spacecraft heading towards Earth might look. Many science fiction stories are set in outer space.*

the world in the future. Many of the stories are about space travel and time travel, and meetings between creatures from different planets. Some writers describe life in the future to show how many things they think are wrong in the world today.

Jules Verne (1828–1905) and H.G. Wells (1866–1946) were two of the first great science fiction writers. Recent writers include Isaac Asimov, Ray Bradbury and Arthur C. Clarke.

Science fiction is not new. In the AD 100s, the Greek writer Lucian of Samosata described journeys to the Moon and the strange creatures to be met there. Johannes Kepler, the famous astronomer who lived in the 16th century, wrote a book entitled *Somnium* in which he also described a trip to the Moon and the serpent-like creatures met by the hero.

Scorpion

Scorpions are animals related to spiders, with poisonous stings in their tails. Most live in warm, dry places and grow to 15 cm long. They have four pairs of legs, and a pair of large claws. Scorpions use their sting to stun or kill their prey. The poison can also make people ill, but it very seldom kills them.

Scotland

Scotland is part of the United Kingdom of Great Britain and Northern Ireland. Most Scots live in a narrow belt in the south where most industry is. In this belt are Glasgow, Scotland's largest city, and Edinburgh, the capital. The Highlands of Scotland have very few people and many beautiful mountains and lochs. The highest mountain in Britain is Ben Nevis, 1343 metres high. There are many islands off the Scottish coast. These include the Hebrides, Orkneys and Shetlands.

Scotland joined with England and Wales in 1707, but the Scots have kept many of their own traditions. Some Scots want their own government.

Sculpture

Sculpture is a way of making attractive models, statues and objects as works of ART. They may be carved from stone or wood, or they may be made by *casting*. In making a cast, the sculptor first makes a model in clay or wax. He or she uses this model to make a mould. Hot molten metal, such as bronze, is then poured into the mould. When the metal has cooled and hardened, it is taken out of the mould. The metal 'cast' is a perfect copy of the original model.

▲ *When scorpions are frightened, they curl their tails up over their heads and may sometimes sting.*

SCOTLAND

Area: 78,772 sq km
Population: 5,094,000
Agriculture: About 75% of land in use
Chief products: Barley, cattle, oats, sheep, wheat
Fishing: Crabs, herring, lobsters and white fish.
Chief industries: Iron and steel, motor vehicles, textiles, industrial machinery, chemicals, whisky and shipbuilding.

Female figure dating from about 5750 BC, found in Anatolia.

Bronze head of an ancient Akkadian king, who ruled in Mesopotamia.

A Phoenician ivory carving dating from about the 800s BC.

An ivory carving of a Byzantine empress from the AD 700s.

Neapolitan Fisherboy, a marble sculpture by Carpeaux (1800s).

A famous modern sculpture by Brancusi, called *The Kiss* (1908).

▲ *Sculpture is a very ancient art, as some of the earliest examples show.*

▼ *Sea anemones attach themselves to rocks by a suckerlike disc. The upper end of the column expands into the mouth opening.*

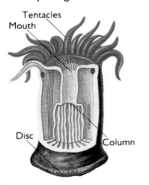

Early Greek statues were models for RENAISSANCE sculptors such as MICHELANGELO, who was possibly the finest sculptor ever.

Modern sculptors have moved away from lifelike figures. Great artists such as Henry Moore have made *abstract* figures and groups.

Sea Anemone

Sea anemones are soft-bodied, tube-like animals. They are closely related to CORALS. Many live on or near the seashore. They look like flowers because they have one or more rings of petal-like tentacles around their mouths. The tentacles have stinging CELLS, and trap small fish for food and other tiny animals that float by. The sea anemone then pulls the food into its stomach through its mouth, and digests it.

Seal and Sea Lion

Seals and sea lions are large sea mammals. Many of them live in icy waters. They spend most of their time in the sea, but sometimes come ashore to lie in the sun. They also have their young, called pups, on land. Seals have streamlined bodies and legs shaped like flippers for swimming. They also have a thick layer of fat, or blubber, under their skin to protect them from the cold. Seals and sea lions eat fish and other sea creatures.

Sea lions have small ears outside their heads and have fur all over their bodies. The males often have a shaggy mane. The Californian sea lion is the smallest. It is often seen in circuses and zoos.

▼ Seals and sea lions are wonderful swimmers, but on land they move slowly. They spend most of their time at sea, but they come ashore to breed.

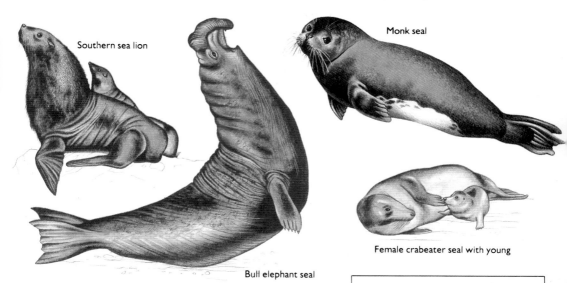

Southern sea lion

Monk seal

Bull elephant seal

Female crabeater seal with young

Season

The year is divided into four seasons. They are spring, summer, autumn and winter. Each season has its own kind of weather.

In spring, for example, the days become warmer; plants begin to grow again after the winter cold and most animals have their young. In autumn, the days are cooler; leaves fall from the trees and many birds fly to warmer places for the winter.

Seasons happen because the EARTH is tilted on its *axis* (a line through the centre of the planet between the North and South Poles). As the Earth travels

One of the factors affecting seasonal temperatures is how far a place is from the ocean. Somewhere on the coast or on a small island has seasons that are much less marked than places that are far inland. This is because water is slow to heat up and cool down. The sea therefore helps to keep a fairly even temperature at places near it. In the centre of vast continents, it can be very hot in summer and very cold in winter.

SEAWEED

SEAWEED

▶ *The Earth's axis always tilts in the same direction. In June, the northern half, or hemisphere, of the planet is in summer because it is leaning towards the Sun. It receives more direct rays and therefore more heat, and the days are longer. At the same time the southern hemisphere is in midwinter. Six months later in December, the Earth has gone halfway around the Sun, and the seasons are reversed. In March and September both hemispheres have an equal share of day and night.*

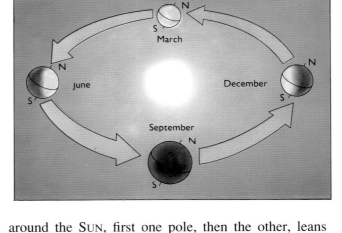

▼ *Seaweeds all belong to the class of simple plants we call algae. They live in shallow water where they give out oxygen and feed and shelter many creatures.*

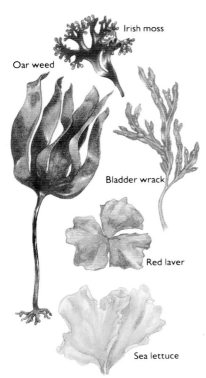

Oar weed

Irish moss

Bladder wrack

Red laver

Sea lettuce

around the SUN, first one pole, then the other, leans towards the Sun. When the North Pole tips towards the Sun it is summer in the northern half of the world and winter in the southern half. Six months later, it is the South Pole's turn to lean sunward, making it summer in southern lands and winter in northern ones. Spring and autumn, the halfway seasons between summer and winter, happen when the Earth is between its summer and winter positions.

At the poles, there are only two seasons: summer and winter. During the polar winter the sun never rises and days are dark. In the summers the sun shines all the time and there are no real nights.

Farthest from the poles, at the EQUATOR, the Earth's tilt has no effect. There are no clear differences between the seasons.

Seaweed

Seaweeds are a group of plants that live in the sea. They grow on rocks or on the seabed. Like most plants, seaweeds need sunlight to make food. Because the Sun's rays do not reach very far down into the sea, there are no seaweeds in deep water.

In some countries people eat different types of seaweeds as vegetables.

Seed

Seeds are the most important part of a PLANT; they are the beginnings of new plants. A seed is formed when pollen reaches the female part of a FLOWER.

◄ *Seeds are scattered in many different ways. Some, such as the pea, are in pods that burst open when ripe. Others, such as the dandelion, are carried by the wind. Acorns and blackberries are stored or eaten by animals, while the burdock has tiny hooks that cling to animals' fur.*

The new seed grows inside a FRUIT, which protects it. In a grape, for example, the fleshy part is the fruit and the pips are the seeds.

Seeds have to be scattered to find new ground to grow on. Some fruits have wings and are carried by the wind. Others are prickly and stick to the fur of passing animals. Many seeds contain the baby plant and a little supply of food. When the seed begins to grow, the baby plant takes in this food until it has roots and leaves and can make its own food.

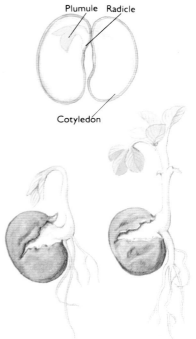

Semiconductor

Some materials allow ELECTRICITY to pass through them easily – they are good *conductors*. Most of these materials are metals. Other materials do not allow electricity to pass–they are *insulators*. Semiconductors are materials such as silicon, germanium and gallium arsenide, which are neither conductors

▲ *A bean seed (top, split open), has large fleshy cotyledons (seed leaves) and a radicle and plumule. The radicle grows downwards into the soil, then the plumule appears, growing upwards (above left). To protect the young shoot, it remains bent over until it reaches the surface (above right).*

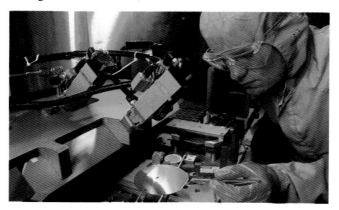

◄ *Wafer-thin slices of the semiconductor silicon are prepared for cutting into microchips.*

nor insulators. When small amounts of other elements are added to semiconductors, important electronic devices can be made. These devices – such as the 'chip' – can be made to pass low or high amounts of electric current, to block it completely, or to allow it to pass in one direction only. Transistors are made from semiconductors.

Seven Wonders of the World

The Seven Wonders of the World were seven outstanding man-made objects that were built in ancient times and were so called because people marvelled at them. Only one of these wonders, the PYRAMIDS, exists today. The others have all been destroyed. They were:

It has been estimated that to build the Great Pyramid today would require at least 400 men using modern equipment to work for more than five years at a cost of about £600 million!

▶ The Seven Wonders of the Ancient World – only the Egyptian pyramids remain.

SEVEN WONDERS OF THE WORLD
1 The Pyramids of Egypt. 2 The Lighthouse of Pharos at alexandria. 3 The Colossus of Rhodes. 4 The Statue of Zeus at Olympia. 5 The Hanging Gardens of Babylon. 6 The Temps of Artemis. 7 The Mausoleum at Halicarnassus.

The Hanging Gardens of Babylon, which were probably built high up on the walls of temples. They were probably a gift from King Nebuchadnezzar II to one of his wives.

The Temple of Artemis at Ephesus (now in Turkey). This temple was one of the largest in the ancient world. Some of its marble columns are in the British Museum in London.

The Statue of Zeus at Olympia, Greece, which showed the king of the gods on his throne. It was made of gold and ivory.

The tomb at Halicarnassus (now in Turkey), which was a massive tomb built for Mausolus, a ruler in Persia. It became so famous that all large tombs are now called *mausoleums*.

The Colossus of Rhodes in Greece, which was a huge, bronze statue of the sun god, Helios. It stood towering high over the harbour entrance.

The Pharos of Alexandria in Egypt, which was the first modern lighthouse. It was built in 270 BC on the island of Pharos outside Alexandria harbour. It had a wood fire burning on top.

▲ *William Shakespeare is probably the most famous name in English literature, but very few facts are known about his life.*

Shakespeare, William

William Shakespeare (1564–1616) is thought by most people to be England's greatest writer. He is most famous for his plays—about 40 altogether—which include *A Midsummer Night's Dream, Hamlet, Macbeth,* and *Romeo and Juliet.*

Very little is known about Shakespeare's life. He was born in Stratford-upon-Avon and was the son of a glovemaker. When he was 18, he married Anne Hathaway, a farmer's daughter, and had three children. Then, at the age of 20, he left Stratford and went to London where he became an actor and playwright. At the end of his life he returned to Stratford. Shakespeare's plays are acted and studied all over the world. Many of the words and phrases we use today were first used by Shakespeare.

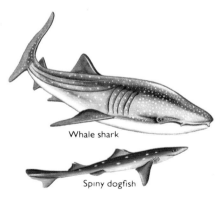

Whale shark

Spiny dogfish

Shark

The shark family includes the world's largest and fiercest fish. Many sharks have a wedge-shaped head, a long body and a triangular back fin that often sticks out of the water. Their skeletons are

▲ *The smallest and the largest members of the shark family. The dogfish is about 60 centimetres long, while the whale shark is more than 15 metres long.*

made of rubbery gristle, not bone. Most sharks live in warm seas. They vary greatly in size. The dogfish, one of the smallest sharks, is only 60 cm long. The largest fish in the oceans, the whale shark, measures over 15 metres—as long as two buses.

The whale shark and the basking shark are harmless to people and other animals because they live on plankton. But many sharks are cruel killers with rows of razor-sharp teeth. Several will attack humans. The greediest monster, the great white shark, swallows its prey whole. The remains of big animals, such as horses, seals and other sharks, have been found in its stomach.

Other dangerous sharks are the blue shark, the tiger shark and the leopard shark, which has leopard-like spots. The smell of blood in water can cause sharks to attack anything nearby, even other sharks.

▼ These sharks are all hunters. They have sharp teeth that grow in rows. As one set wears out, the row behind takes over (inset).

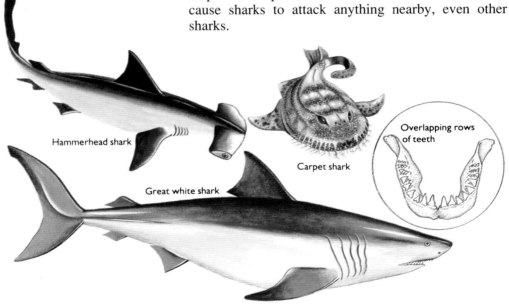

Hammerhead shark

Carpet shark

Overlapping rows of teeth

Great white shark

Sheep

Sheep have been kept as domestic animals for thousands of years. At first, sheep were kept for their milk and skins. Milk could be made into cheese and the skins were used for clothing. Then people discovered that the animals' thick coats could be *sheared* (shaved off) and the wool woven into cloth. Today sheep are kept mostly for wool and for meat (*mutton* or *lamb*).

Merino

Ile-de-France

Dorset horn

Suffolk

◄ *Modern sheep have been specially bred to give the best combination of wool and meat.*

Shells and Shellfish

Many animals live inside shells. This is because they have soft bodies that need protection. Shells are usually hard and are all sizes and colours. The shells of some sea snails are no bigger than a grain of sand, but the giant clam of the Pacific Ocean has a shell 120 cm across.

Some land animals such as SNAILS have shells, but most creatures with shells belong in the sea. Shelled sea animals include MOLLUSCS and CRUSTACEANS. Some of these, such as OYSTERS, scallops, and lobsters, can be eaten. These are often called shellfish although they are not really fish at all. Shellfish have been an important food for thousands of years. In

▲ *The mouflon is a truly wild sheep that lives in mountainous areas in mainland Europe and in open country on Mediterranean islands.*

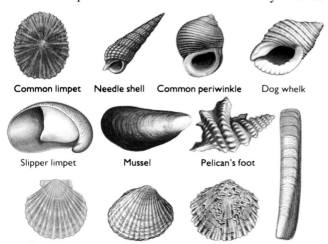

Common limpet   Needle shell   Common periwinkle   Dog whelk

Slipper limpet   Mussel   Pelican's foot

Queen scallop   Cockle   Oyster   Razor shell

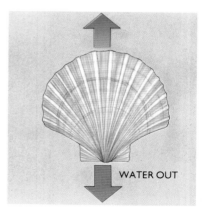

WATER OUT

▲ *Scallops swim by opening their shells then shutting them quickly. The jet of water they force out pushes them along.*

◄ *Many different types of mollusc shell can be found on the seashore.*

▲ The tellin buries itself in the sand then sucks tiny pieces of food from the water through a tube it extends above the surface.

some place, kitchen refuse of prehistoric people has been found that consists entirely of enormous mounds of shells, as high as a two-storey house.

Ship

Today most ships are cargo vessels. They are usually built to carry a certain type of cargo. *Tankers* carry liquids such as oil or wine. Some oil tankers are so long that the crew can ride bicycles around the deck. *Bulk carriers* take dry cargoes like coal and wheat that can be loaded loose. *Container ships* carry all kinds of goods packed in large boxes called containers. *Refrigerator ships* are for carrying fresh food such as fruit and meat. Planes have replaced most passenger ships, but there are still ferries that take people

▲ This super-tanker is 380 metres long – over a third of a kilometre. It is 62 metres wide, with a cruising speed of 16 knots (29.6km/h). Yet it has a crew of only 35 to 50.

▶ Roll-on roll-off ferries can take cars, lorries and their passengers.

◀ Aircraft carriers must have enough room on deck for planes and helicopters to take off and land.

and vehicles across smaller stretches of water. There are also luxury cruise liners. Various kinds of warship are used by the navy.

Silicon Chip

Silicon chips are tiny pieces of the ELEMENT silicon. (Silicon is a SEMICONDUCTOR.) They can be made to carry very small electrical circuits, called micro-circuits. These are used in transistor radios, digital watches, calculators and computers. Because the chips are so small, the electronic devices in which they are used can be small too.

▲ This silicon chip, the tiny square in the centre of the panel, is smaller than any of the cherries around it. Yet its circuits are capable of running a small computer.

Silk

Silk is a natural fibre made from the cocoon of one kind of moth. Silkworms, which are really cater-pillars, are kept in special containers and fed on

▼ Once the silkworms have eaten enough mulberry leaves they start to spin their cocoons. They produce a liquid through a hole in their lower lip which hardens in the air, and makes the fine silk thread. The cocoons are put into hot water to loosen the threads for winding. The threads from several cocoons are wound together to make a stronger thread.

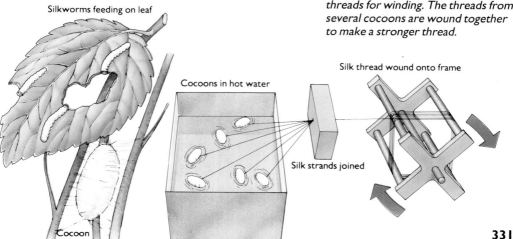

Silkworms feeding on leaf

Cocoons in hot water

Silk thread wound onto frame

Silk strands joined

Cocoon

331

mulberry leaves for about four weeks. At the end of this time they spin their cocoons and start to turn into moths. Then they are killed and each cocoon is unwound as a long thread between 600 and 900 metres long.

Silk was first used in Asia centuries ago, especially in China and Japan. Silk WEAVING in Europe began in the 1400s. Silk makes a very fine, soft material. It was used for stockings before nylon was invented. Silk can be made into other fabrics such as satin and chiffon, and can be dyed in beautiful colours.

> The chemical symbol for silver is Ag, from the Latin *argentum*, meaning 'white and shining'. It melts at 960.8°C and boils at 2210°C. A tiny gram of the metal can be drawn into a wire nearly 2 km long. The main silver-producing countries are the United States and Mexico.

Silver

Silver is a precious metal. It has been used by people all over the world for thousands of years. Although many countries have silver deposits, the mining process is very expensive.

Silver bends very easily, and can be beaten into many shapes and patterns. Like gold, it can be hammered out into thin sheets. It is used to make useful and decorative things such as spoons and forks, bowls, and jewellery. Sometimes it is used as a coating on cheaper metals such as copper or nickel, to make them look like silver. It can also be mixed with another metal (usually copper), and then it is called *sterling* silver.

Silver carries electricity well and is used for this in industry. Some chemicals made from silver react to light and are used in photography. Another chemical, silver nitrate, is painted on the back of glass to make mirrors.

▶ This set of silverware consists of a mug, napkin ring, knife, spoon and fork, all made in 1903.

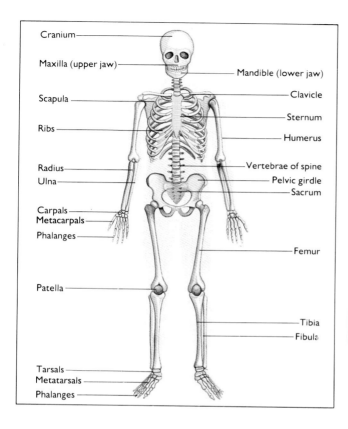

Cranium
Maxilla (upper jaw)
Mandible (lower jaw)
Scapula
Clavicle
Sternum
Ribs
Humerus
Radius
Vertebrae of spine
Ulna
Pelvic girdle
Sacrum
Carpals
Metacarpals
Phalanges
Femur
Patella
Tibia
Fibula
Tarsals
Metatarsals
Phalanges

◄ The skeleton provides a framework for your body, holding it together and supporting its weight. Bones also protect important organs.

Babies are born with about 350 bones. But as a child grows, some of these bones join together and an adult ends up with about 206. The number varies because some people have more bones in their hands and feet than others. The largest bone in your body is the *femur*, or thigh bone. The smallest is the *stapes*, or stirrup bone, in your middle ear. It is only about 2.6 to 3.4 mm long.

Skeleton

Our skeleton is made up of BONES. If we did not have a skeleton, our bodies would be shapeless blobs. The skeleton protects our vital organs, such as the heart, liver and lungs. It is also an anchor for our MUSCLES.

In humans and other animals with backbones (VERTEBRATES), the skeleton is inside the body, covered by the flesh and skin. In other animals, such

▲ Lobsters have an exoskeleton, that is, their skeleton is in the form of hard plates on the outside of their body.

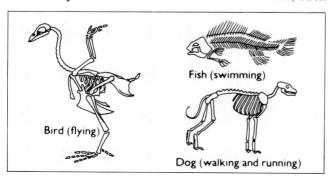

Fish (swimming)

Bird (flying)

Dog (walking and running)

◄ Examples of animals with internal skeletons. The shape of their skeleton is perfectly adapted to the way they move.

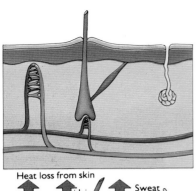

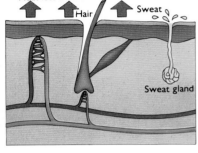

▲ *The skin goes through changes to make you warmer or cooler. When you are cold, erector muscles make the tiny hairs on the skin stand upright to trap a layer of warm air (top). When you are hot, the hairs lie flat to let the air circulate, and sweat evaporates from the skin to cool you (above).*

as INSECTS and SPIDERS, the skeleton is like a hard crust on the outside of the body. It is called an *exoskeleton*. Some animals, such as the jellyfish and octopus, do not have a skeleton. Their bodies are supported by the water they live in.

There are more than 200 bones in the human skeleton. These include the bones of the spine, skull (which protects the brain), ribs, pelvis, breastbone and limbs. Joints are places where bones meet. Some joints (like those in the skull) do not move. Others, like those in the shoulders and hips, help us to move about. Muscles across the joints tighten, or *contract*, to move the bones.

A human skeleton develops before the baby is born, and grows along with the body.

Skin

Skin is the covering on the outside of our bodies. It protects our bodies and is sensitive to heat, cold and pain. Human skin can be quite thick and hard on places that get a lot of wear, such as the soles of the feet. It can also be very thin on other places, such as the eyelids.

Human skin is made up of two layers. The outer layer, the *epidermis*, has a chemical called melanin which gives skin its colour. The inner layer, the *dermis*, contains nerves, blood vessels, sweat glands and the roots of hairs. The skin of an adult human covers about 1.7 square metres.

▶ *The skin is a waterproof, elastic covering for the body. It helps to keep germs and dirt out, and can even repair itself. Sebaceous glands give off oil that keeps the skin from becoming too dry.*

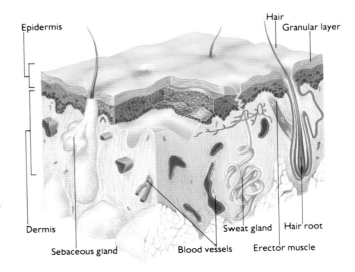

Epidermis
Hair
Granular layer
Dermis
Sebaceous gland
Blood vessels
Sweat gland
Hair root
Erector muscle

◀ *The conditions suffered by the people who were kidnapped and made slaves were appalling. Many died on the ships carrying them from Africa to the Americas.*

Slavery

Slavery means owning people to work for you, just as you would own a car. Slaves can be bought and sold. In ancient civilizations, prisoners captured in war were often made into slaves, and poor people sometimes sold their children as slaves.

From the 1500s, the Spanish took people from Africa as slaves for their colonies in America. By the 1770s, British ships were carrying slaves to America. Hundreds were packed tightly into ships. Conditions were terrible, and many slaves died on the way. Britain abolished the slave trade in 1808. Slavery was ended in the USA in 1865, after the Civil War. But racial discrimination continued even after civil rights laws were passed to guarantee equal rights for black people.

▲ *The abolition of the slave trade was largely due to William Wilberforce (1759–1833). He was a Church of England priest who became a politician and campaigned for more than 20 years to have slavery banned.*

Sleep

Sleep is a time when we are unconscious and resting. People and some animals need sleep to stay healthy. Without it, people become short-tempered and after a long time they may start having *halluci-*

Most people need less sleep as they grow older. Someone who slept 8 hours a day when he or she was 30 years old may need only 7 hours of sleep at the age of 60. Young babies sleep most of the time; 4-year-olds average from 10 to 14 hours sleep a day; 10-year-olds from 9 to 12 hours.

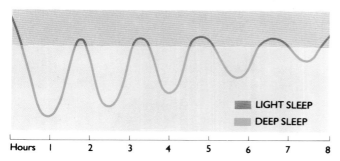

LIGHT SLEEP

DEEP SLEEP

Hours 1 2 3 4 5 6 7 8

◀ *The electrical waves given off by the brain during sleep can be measured to show the periods of light and deep sleep. Dreams happen during periods of light sleep. As morning comes near, the periods of light sleep last longer.*

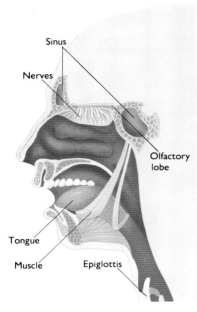

Sinus

Nerves

Olfactory
lobe

Tongue

Muscle   Epiglottis

▲ *Our sense of smell is closely linked to our sense of taste. When we have a cold and lose our sense of smell, it makes our food taste less interesting.*

nations—seeing things that are not actually there.

There are four different stages of sleep. At each stage the electrical waves given off by the BRAIN change. When we are deeply asleep, these waves are slow and large. When we are only lightly asleep the waves are faster.

Different people need different amounts of sleep. Babies need a lot. Adults need between six and nine hours a night.

Smell

Smell is an important sense, like sight and hearing. Humans and other MAMMALS smell through the nose. We sniff the air, and the scents given off by the things around us are picked up by special cells in the nose. These cells send messages to the BRAIN.

Our sense of smell is useful when we are eating. It helps us to TASTE things. It can also let us know when food is bad. Most other animals have a much better sense of smell than humans. Dogs can use their sense of smell to track down and follow prey. Moths do not have noses, but they can still smell things. Some male moths can smell a female moth many kilometres away.

Snail

Snails are MOLLUSCS with a coiled shell on their back. There are more than 80,000 kinds in the world. Some live on land, some in fresh water and some in the sea. Snails move slowly, leaving a glistening, slimy trail on land. They feed on plants.

Most snails are less than 3 cm long. But one of the largest, the giant land snail, is about 20 cm long.

▼ *The coral snake's bright colours are not just decoration. They are a warning to other creatures that the snake is poisonous.*

Snake

Snakes are REPTILES. They are long and thin and have no arms or legs. They move along by wriggling their bodies.

Snakes have a dry, smooth skin. Most live in warm places. Those that live in colder climates spend the winter in HIBERNATION.

A few snakes have poison glands. They inject this poison into animals that they bite. The rattlesnake and the cobra are both poisonous snakes.

Most snakes hatch from eggs. A female snake can lay up to ten eggs at a time. Others give birth to live young. The largest snakes are pythons and anacondas.

▲ *Pythons can grow to as long as 10 metres. They can unhinge their jaws to swallow quite large prey.*

Snow *See* Rain and Snow

Soap

Soap is used for cleaning things. It is made by mixing FAT or vegetable oil with a chemical such as caustic soda. It loosens dirt in clothes and carries it away. Today chemical cleaners called DETERGENTS are often used instead. Detergents clean better than soap in hard water, but they do not by themselves make suds. Suds are not necessary for cleaning, but substances that make suds are added to detergents.

▼ *Solar panels can be used to collect energy from the Sun. The energy can be made into electricity or just used to help heat a house.*

Solar Energy

Solar energy is energy from the Sun. It reaches the Earth as light and heat. Without these things there could be no life on Earth.

Only about 15 per cent of the Sun's energy that reaches the Earth is absorbed by the Earth's surface. Much of it bounces off the Earth and back into space. Solar energy can be collected by special panels and mirrors and used to make electricity.

Solar panels on the roofs of houses trap the sun's rays. They warm water flowing through the panels. In this way solar power helps to produce hot water for washing and heating.

► *Seen in comparison with the Sun and the four 'giant' planets, the Earth looks very small. The nine planets in our solar system are:*
1 *Mercury*
2 *Venus*
3 *Earth*
4 *Mars*
5 *Jupiter*
6 *Saturn*
7 *Uranus*
8 *Neptune*
9 *Pluto*

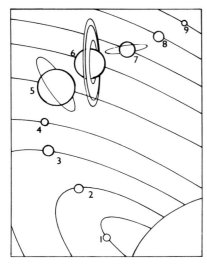

▼ *Sound waves travel outwards from the source of the sound like ripples on a pond. They make vibrations in the air and, when they reach your ear they make your ear drum vibrate too, so you can hear the sound.*

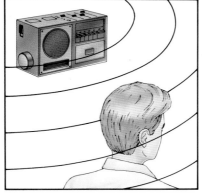

Solar System

The solar system is made up of the SUN and the planets travelling around it. MERCURY is the planet nearest the Sun. Next comes VENUS, EARTH, MARS, JUPITER, SATURN, URANUS, NEPTUNE and PLUTO.

Until the 1500s, most people thought that the Earth was the centre of the universe, and that the Sun and planets travelled around it. In 1543 a Polish astronomer, Nicolaus COPERNICUS, discovered that, in fact, the Earth moved around the Sun.

Sound

Sound is made by vibrating objects that send sound waves through the air. When these vibrations reach our EARS, we hear them as sounds.

Sound travels through air at about 334 metres a second. This is slow enough for us to see a far-off explosion, for example, before we hear it. The sound takes time to reach us.

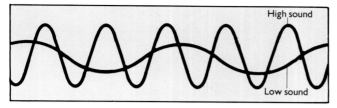

High sound

Low sound

◀ *The frequency of sound waves makes sounds high or low. High sounds make waves that are close together. The waves of low sounds are farther apart.*

The speed of the vibrations makes a difference to the kind of sound we hear. If the vibrations are very fast, they are said to be 'high frequency' and the sound we hear is high-pitched. If they are slow, the sound is said to be 'low frequency' and the sound we hear is low-pitched.

South Africa

South Africa is a country in southern AFRICA. Most of the country is tableland, a high region of flat-topped hills. Around the coast is a narrow plain. The climate is warm and dry.

South Africa is a rich country. Factories make a wide range of goods. Mines produce gold, diamonds, uranium, copper, iron and other minerals. Farms grow big crops of maize, wheat and fruit. Millions of sheep graze on the grasslands in the centre of the country.

Just over 35 million people live in South Africa. Almost three-quarters of them are black Africans. There are fewer than 5 million whites. The whites, who are descended mainly from Dutch and British settlers, control the country's government and money. Since the 1940s, South Africa has had a policy of apartheid or 'apartness'. This means that whites and non-whites live separately. In the late 1980s the white minority government took steps to end apartheid and extend democratic rights to all South Africans.

South America

South America is the world's fourth largest continent. Lying between the Atlantic and Pacific oceans, it stretches from the EQUATOR in the north to the ANTARCTIC in the south, from the ANDES Mountains in the west to the AMAZON delta in the east.

The Andes are the longest mountain range in the world. They run along the Pacific coast for 8000 km.

SOUTH AFRICA

Government: Republic
Capitals: Cape Town (legislative),
  Pretoria (administrative),
  Bloemfontein (judicial)
Area: 1,221,037 sq km
Population: 35,282,000
Languages: Afrikaans, English
Currency: Rand

▼ *South America is a huge continent. It stretches from the Antarctic right up to north of the equator.*

339

SOUTH AMERICA

SOUTH AMERICA
Area: 17,829,560 sq km
Population: 302,000,000
Highest mountain: Mount Aconcagua
  in Argentina, 6960 m
Lowest point: Valdes Peninsula,
  Argentina, 40 m below sea level
Principal rivers: Amazon (6437 km),
  Madeira, Magdalena, Orinoco,
  Plate-Paraguay-Parana system,
  Purus, Sao Francisco,
  Uruguay
Principal lakes: Maracaibo, Mirim,
  Poopo, Titicaca
Largest city: Buenos Aires, 10,500,000
Highest waterfall: Angel Falls, 979 m,
  highest in the world

▼ *Many of the creatures of the South American rain forest live high above the forest floor. These and the forests themselves are under threat as thousands of hectares of rain forest are felled for valuable hardwoods or to create farmland.*

They are also the starting point of one of the world's greatest rivers, the Amazon. This huge waterway travels nearly 6450 km across South America and empties 118 million litres of water into the ocean every second. The huge area drained by the Amazon includes thick tropical rain forest.

Two other great rivers are the Orinoco in the north and the Plate in the south. The land south of the Amazon jungle has swamps, lakes, grasslands and, near the continent's tip, the Patagonian desert.

There are 13 countries in South America. The largest, BRAZIL, takes up half the continent. Most South Americans speak Spanish. But in Brazil they speak Portuguese, in Guyana they speak English, in French Guiana, French, and in Surinam, Dutch. These different languages are the leftovers of history. South America was explored by the Spanish and Portuguese in the 1500s. Then Spain, Portugal and other European countries set up colonies. In the 1800s, most of these colonies won their independence.

The first people of South America were Indians. Most of them, including the INCAS, were killed by foreign conquerors. Later the Europeans brought in African slaves. Today most South Americans come from European and African ancestors. There are still some Indians in the Andes and Amazonia.

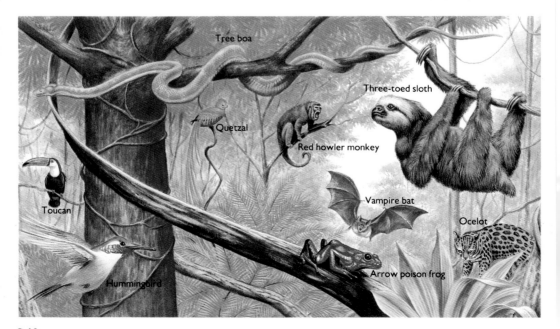

Barranquilla
Caracas
Maracaibo
Orinoco
Georgetown
Medellin
VENEZUELA
Paramaribo
Llanos
Cayenne
Bogotá
GUYANA
SURINAM
**FRENCH
GUIANA**
Cali
COLOMBIA
ATLANTIC OCEAN

Quito
GALAPAGOS IS.
ECUADOR
Manáus
Belém
Guayaquil
Amazon

PERU
Selvas
Fortaleza
Chiclayo
Trujillo
Recife

BRAZIL

Callão
Lima
Cuzco
Salvador

BOLIVIA
La Paz
Cochabamba
Brasilia
Oruro
ANDES
Sucre
Brazilian Highlands

ATACAMA DESERT
MOUNTAINS
PARAGUAY
PACIFIC OCEAN
Gran Chaco
Paraná
Rio de Janeiro
Asunción
São Paulo

Córdoba
Pôrto Alegre
Mt Aconcagua
Valparaiso
Rosario
URUGUAY
Santiago
Buenos Aires
Montevideo
ARGENTINA
La Plata

CHILE
PAMPAS
Bahia Blanca
Colorado
ATLANTIC OCEAN

■ Capital Cities

| 0 | 500 | 1000 miles |
| 0 | 500 | 1000 | 1500 kilometres |

Chubut

Patagonia

FALKLAND IS.

**Tierra
del Fuego**
Cape Horn

South America has rich natural resources. The rocks of the Andes are full of minerals. There is silver in PERU, tin in BOLIVIA and copper in CHILE. There are also huge amounts of oil in VENEZUELA in the north. The open grasslands of ARGENTINA, URUGUAY, and PARAGUAY provide food for millions of sheep and cattle. Brazil's farmers produce a third of the coffee in the world. so far all this wealth has not been used properly. Most South Americans are poor. Bad government and poor management of the land have held back South America's progress.

▲ An Indian of the Amazon region ferries his son in a dugout canoe. The lives of many of the Indians of the South American rain forests are changing as the forests diminish.

South-east Asia

South-east Asia is a large spread-out area that lies to the south of CHINA and to the east of INDIA. It is not one country, but many. Joined to the Asian mainland are BURMA (Myanmar), THAILAND, MALAYSIA, SINGAPORE, CAMBODIA, VIETNAM and Laos. Farther south there is a chain of islands forming the countries of INDONESIA, Brunei, Papua New Guinea and the Philippines.

South-east Asia is mainly mountainous. It has a tropical climate, with heavy rainfall in the wet season. Most of the people are farmers. They grow rice, maize, rubber, sugarcane and tea.

▶ At the Floating Market in Bangkok, Thailand, traders sell their wares from small boats.

From the 900s to the 1400s, much of South-east Asia was ruled by people called Khmers, who built up a powerful empire. The Khmer built hundreds of beautiful stone temples, canals, reservoirs and roads. The temple of Angkor Wat in Kampuchea is their greatest architectural achievement. The enormous temple is 1550 metres long by 1400 metres wide, with an entrance hall of more than a hundred square columns.

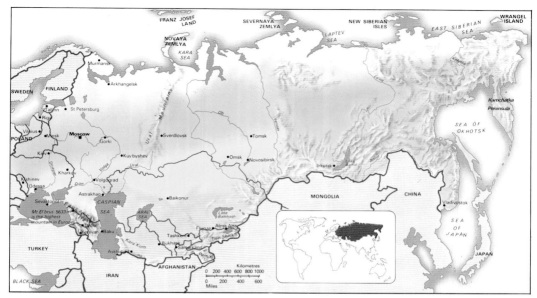

▲ *The international boundaries of the former Soviet Union.*

Soviet Union

The vast area that was the Soviet Union in 1990 is now a complex of independent states, each trying to come to terms with its freedom from Kremlin control. Latvia, Lithuania and Estonia, the three BALTIC STATES declared their independence from the USSR at the end of 1991. This was followed by the setting up of the Commonwealth of Independent States, with the founding membership of RUSSIA, the Ukraine and Byelorussia. The Commonwealth has been dominated economically and militarily by the power of Russia under the leadership of Boris Yeltsin, who displaced Mikhail Gorbachev to organize the breakup of the Soviet Union. The Communist Party was disbanded, but the entire former Soviet economy was in danger of collapse, with acute food shortages.

Before 1917, Russia was a poor country ruled by *tsars*, or emperors. In 1917, there was a revolution. A COMMUNIST government took over, led by Vladimir LENIN. Between 1918 and 1920 Russia was nearly destroyed by a civil war between the communists and their enemies. The communists won, and began to turn Russia into a great industrial nation.

During World War II Germany invaded the Soviet Union, but after fierce fighting the Soviet Army drove the Germans back. The Soviets occupied Hungary, Romania, Czechoslovakia, Poland

FORMER SOVIET UNION

Government: Communist
Area: 22,402,000 sq km
Population: 229,000,000
Capital and largest city: Moscow, 8,500,000
Highest point: Communism Peak, 7495 m
Chief crops: grain, cotton, sugar beets, potatoes
Chief industries: Steel, machinery, machine tools, vehicles
Languages: Russian and others
Currency: Rouble

Slavs   Siberia

Ukraine

▲ *No other region has such variety in its peoples as the former USSR, with more than 100 different nationality groups in the population. Different regions have their own languages, dress and customs.*

▶ *The republics of the former Soviet Union and their boundaries.*

and part of Germany itself. After the war, communist governments closely tied to the Soviet Union were set up in these countries.

The United States and the USSR grew to distrust each other and what was called the Cold War developed. Under its last leader, Mikhail Gorbachev, the USSR entered a period of change and unrest. US and Soviet leaders signed agreements to reduce the numbers of nuclear and conventional weapons. The countries of the West have been helping the former Soviet states with aid.

Space Exploration

The Space Age began in 1957, when the Russians launched the first artificial SATELLITE. In 1961 came the first manned flight, and only eight years later astronauts were exploring the surface of the MOON.

People had long dreamed of escaping the EARTH's GRAVITY and flying in space. It was the multi-stage ROCKET, developed in Germany during World War II, that made space flight possible. The Russians and Americans dominated the early years of space exploration. But Europe has its own space rocket, and other countries such as China and India have also launched satellites.

The Americans call their space travellers 'astronauts', while the Russians call theirs 'cosmonauts'. The Americans were the first to build a reusable Space

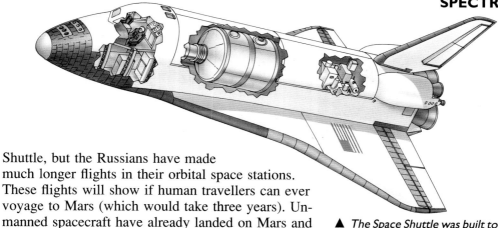

Shuttle, but the Russians have made much longer flights in their orbital space stations. These flights will show if human travellers can ever voyage to Mars (which would take three years). Unmanned spacecraft have already landed on Mars and sent TV pictures back from other planets.

▲ The Space Shuttle was built to launch satellites cheaply and carry scientists into orbit. It is about the same size as a medium-range airliner such as the DC-9. The Shuttle glides down to land like an aeroplane, and can be used over and over again.

Spain

Spain lies in south-west EUROPE, beyond the Pyrenees. Most of the country is covered by high plains and mountains, with a low plain around the coast. The highlands have hot summers, cold winters and little rain. The coast is milder and wetter, especially in the north.

Half the people work on farms, growing potatoes, wheat, grapes, olives and fruits. Wine, olive oil and oranges are exported. Many Spaniards who live on the coast are fishermen. They catch sardines and anchovies. Others work in the tourist trade. Each year, millions of tourists visit Spain to enjoy its sunny beaches. The two main industrial areas are around Bilbao and Barcelona.

Spectrum

Where do the colours in a rainbow come from? The answer was found in 1666 when Sir Isaac NEWTON put a triangle-shaped block of glass called a *prism* in front of a beam of sunlight. The prism bent the light and separated it into the different colours of the rainbow. Newton showed that sunlight is made up of different colours – a spectrum of colours. Sunlight is white only because all the colours of the rainbow are mixed together in it.

The spectrum of light is only one small part of the whole *electromagnetic spectrum*. The electromagnetic spectrum is arranged according to the *wavelength* (distance between waves) and *frequency* (number of

SPAIN

Government: Constitutional monarchy
Capital: Madrid
Area: 504,782 sq km
Population: 38,959,000
Language: Spanish
Currency: Peseta

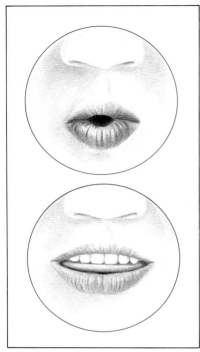

▲ Your tongue, teeth and lips work together to make sounds. The lips here (top) are pushed forwards to make the sound 'oo'. In the lower picture, the sound 'th' is formed by the tongue, teeth and lips combined.

▼ The name tarantula has been given to many different types of spider – usually larger ones. The tarantula of southern Europe was once thought to have a sting deadly to humans, but it causes serious harm only to the small insects it eats.

waves per second) of the waves. Radio waves have the lowest frequency and the longest wavelength. Gamma rays have the highest frequency and shortest wavelength. In between these come ultraviolet rays, X-rays and other rays.

Speech

Once, the only sounds people could make were grunts, yells and other simple sounds. Then, over tens of thousands of years, they learned to form words. Languages slowly developed.

Speech sounds are made by air from our lungs passing around two membranes called vocal cords. We change the pitch of the sound by altering the tension of the vocal cords, just as we can alter the pitch of a guitar by tightening or slackening the strings. By changing the shape of the passages in our throat, mouth and nose, and by using our tongue, we can alter the sounds produced. We can make the words of speech.

Women usually have higher-pitched voices than men because their vocal cords are shorter.

Spider

Spiders are small animals. Although they look like insects, they are not. Insects have six legs; spiders have eight. Insects have feelers and wings; spiders do not. Insect bodies have three parts; spiders' bodies have two.

All spiders spin silk threads. Many of them use the threads to make a sticky web for catching insects. Not all spiders trap their food in webs. Some are hunters and chase their prey; others lie in wait, then pounce. When a spider catches something, it stuns or kills it with a poisonous bite. All spiders have poison, but in most cases it does not hurt people. There are only about 30 species that are really dangerous to us.

There are about 30,000 kinds of spider. They are all sizes. The comb-footed spider is no bigger than a pinhead, but some bird-eating spiders can be 25 cm across. They have different life stories. Some live for only a year, others for 20 years. Some mate in winter, others in spring. Tiny spiders lay a few eggs, perhaps just one, but the largest lay up to 2,000.

Squirrel

Most people think of squirrels as a kind of RODENT that is good at climbing trees. Tree squirrels are exactly that. They have sharp claws for climbing and a long, bushy tail that helps them to steer and keep their balance. Tree squirrels can leap 3 metres to reach one tree from another.

Flying squirrels jump 10 times farther than that. These little creatures have flaps of skin between their front and back legs. The flaps form a parachute when a flying squirrel jumps and spreads its limbs. Tree squirrels and flying squirrels feed on leaves, twigs or seeds.

Ground squirrels live in burrows under the ground. They include the chipmunks, prairie dogs and woodchucks.

The most common squirrel in Britain is the grey squirrel. There are more than 300 different kinds of squirrel.

▲ *The red squirrel is the only native tree squirrel in Europe. It lives mostly in coniferous woodland, where it eats seeds and shoots.*

Sri Lanka

Sri Lanka is an island country off the southern tip of INDIA. Sri Lanka used to be called Ceylon. The island is near the equator, and so the climate is tropical. Most of the tropical trees and shrubs have been cleared away to make room for crops, but there are still bamboo and palm trees. Animals such as elephants, leopards, monkeys, snakes and colourful birds live in the wilder areas. Sri Lanka's crops include tea, rubber and coconuts.

Stalactites and Stalagmites

Stalactites and stalagmites are like icicles made of stone. They are formed in limestone caverns or in other places where water is able to drip. Stalactites are those which hang down from the roof of the cave, while the ones that grow upwards from the floor are the stalagmites.

Water which flows through limestone country dissolves some of the lime from the limestone and carries it in a sort of water mixture, called a solution. If this water then drips into a cavern, some of the lime comes out as some of the water evaporates. Carbon dioxide is released to the atmosphere. Lime builds up as a stony

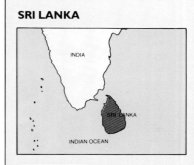

SRI LANKA

INDIA

SRI LANKA

INDIAN OCEAN

Government: Republic
Capital: Colombo
Area: 65,610 sq km
Population: 16,993,000
Languages: Sinhala, Tamil
Currency: Rupee

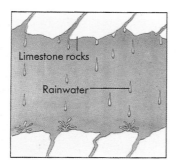
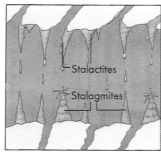
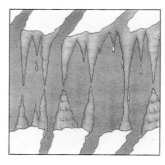

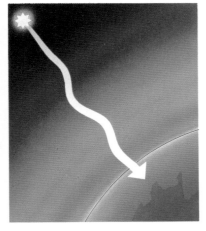

▲ *Stalactites and stalagmites are made of calcium carbonate. Rainwater draining through limestone rock dissolves calcium carbonate, which comes out of solution as the water evaporates after dripping through caves and caverns.*

deposit. Slowly, the stalactite builds up and hangs from the roof of the cave. Where the water falls, more lime comes out of solution as the drops hit the floor. A growing pinnacle is formed. The world's longest stalactite is in a cave in County Clare, Ireland.

Stalin, Joseph

Joseph Stalin (1879–1953) ruled the USSR from 1929 to 1953. After LENIN died, Stalin made the Soviet Union one of the two most powerful nations in the world. He killed or imprisoned millions who disliked him or disagreed with his kind of COMMUNISM. The name Stalin is Russian for 'man of steel'.

Stamp

A stamp can be a special mark, or a piece of printed paper with a sticky back. A passport and many other kinds of documents must bear the correct government stamp. Postage stamps are stuck on letters and parcels to be carried by the post office. Each nation has its own postage stamps. Millions of people collect postage stamps. Some kinds are scarce and valuable. A very rare stamp can cost more than a house.

▼ *Stars appear to us to twinkle because their light bends as it travels through the Earth's atmosphere.*

Star

The stars we can see from earth are just a few of the many billions scattered through space. Stars look small because they are so far away. But most are huge, fiery balls of gas like our SUN.

Stars begin as clouds of gas. GRAVITY pulls the gas particles in towards the middle of each cloud. There the particles collide and grow hot, and other particles press in.

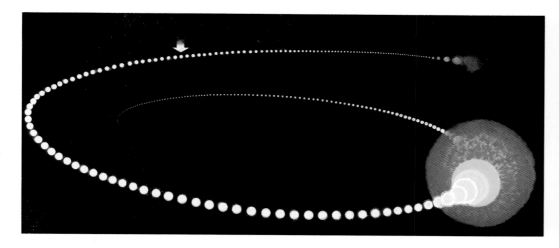

HYDROGEN atoms change into helium atoms by a process called nuclear fusion. That process gives off NUCLEAR ENERGY. This is what makes stars glow.

Stars swell as they use their hydrogen. Astronomers call such stars *red giants*. Red giants later shrink into tiny white-hot stars called *white dwarfs*. In time, these fade into the darkness of space.

▲ *An artist's impression of the life of a star, first formed by a cloud of gas that condenses and solidifies. Over thousands of millions of years, the star grows larger. Suddenly, it expands into a red giant, then begins to shrink and fade. The arrow shows where our Sun is in this process.*

Starch

Starch is a substance found in plants. Cereals such as wheat, rice and maize are particularly rich in starch. Starch is a *carbohydrate*, which means that it is made up of carbon, oxygen and hydrogen, the same ingredients found in sugar. It is important to have starch in our diet because it gives energy.

Starch makes up about four-fifths of rice and three-quarters of wheat, rye and maize. About 80 per cent of all commercial starch is made from maize and is called corn starch.

Statistics

Statistics is the science of collecting and classifying numerical facts. It can simply summarize these facts, or it can lead to conclusions about larger numbers of which the facts supplied are just a sample. The theory of statistics is part of MATHEMATICS.

Steam Engine

Boiling water turns into steam. Steam will fill 1700 times more space than the water that it came from. So if you squash steam into a small container it presses hard against the sides. If one side is free to move, the steam pressure will push it outwards.

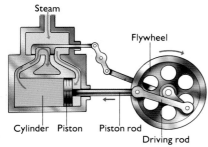

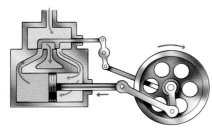

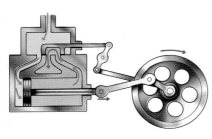

▲ *Inside a steam engine, steam is produced by heating water to boiling point. The pressure of the expanding steam is used to push a piston to and fro in a hollow tube called a cylinder. The piston fits tightly inside the cylinder so the steam cannot seep around the sides of the piston head. The piston is attached to the piston rod. As the piston rod goes in and out, it drives another rod called the driving rod. The driving rod turns a wheel called the flywheel, which turns steadily even when the piston is at the end of its stroke and is not pushing. In a steam locomotive, the driving rod is attached to a driving wheel.*

In the 1700s British inventors began to use this fact to build engines powered by steam. Early steam engines worked with a simple to-and-fro motion. In Thomas Newcomen's engine, a furnace heated water in a boiler. The water gave off steam that pushed a piston up inside a cylinder. When the steam cooled and turned back to water, air pressed the piston down again. Newcomen's engine was used to pump water from flooded mines.

James Watt built a more powerful engine where steam pushed the piston first one way and then the other. Rods from the piston spun a wheel. By the early 1800s, such engines were moving heavy loads faster than men or horses could. Yet, unlike men and horses, steam engines never tired.

Steam engines powered factory machines that made the INDUSTRIAL REVOLUTION possible. They also powered locomotives and steamships. For the first time, people travelled faster than horses.

The INTERNAL COMBUSTION ENGINE has largely taken the place of steam engines. But many ships' propellers and power station GENERATORS are worked by steam which spins wheels called TURBINES.

Stomach

Your stomach is a muscular bag, open at both ends and shaped like a fat letter J. It plays an important part in the DIGESTION of food.

When you eat a meal, food travels down your throat to your stomach. The stomach can store a large meal. Juices produced in the stomach kill germs in food. They also moisten and start digesting the food. Stomach muscles churn the mixture, then force it into the small intestine.

Stone Age

The Stone Age was the great span of time before people learned how to make metal tools. Stone Age people used stone, wood, and bone instead of metal. The Stone Age probably began more than three million years ago. It ended in Iraq and Egypt when the Bronze Age began there 5000 years ago.

The Stone Age had three parts: Old, Middle and New. The Old Stone Age lasted until 10,000 years ago in the Middle East. When it began, hunters could scarcely chip a stone well enough to sharpen it. When the Old Stone Age ended, people had learned to chip flint into delicate spearheads, knives and scrapers.

In the Middle Stone Age, hunters used tiny flakes of flint in arrows and harpoons.

The New Stone Age began in the Middle East about 9000 years ago. New Stone Age people made smooth axe heads of ground stone. Farming replaced hunting in the New Stone Age.

> The words 'Stone Age' do not mean a fixed period of time that began and ended on certain dates. When the people of Britain were still in the Stone Age, the ancient Egyptians were living in cities and using metals. On the other hand, there are some people today in remote regions who are living as the people of Britain did in their Stone Age.

Submarine

Submarines are boats that can travel under water. To dive, the crew of a submarine make it heavier than the amount of water needed to fill the space taken up by the submarine. To rise, the crew make the submarine lighter than that amount of water. When water and submarine both weigh the same, the boat stays at the same level under the surface.

In 1620 someone rowed a wood and leather submarine down the river Thames. But the first submarine that worked well was not built until the 1770s. Both these early submarines were worked by hand. They were slow and under-powered.

In the 1870s an English clergyman invented a submarine powered by a steam engine. But each time it dived the crew had to pull down its chimney and put out the fire that heated water to produce steam.

By 1900 the American inventor John P. Holland had produced a much better underwater boat. Petrol engines drove it on the surface. But petrol needs air to burn. Under water the boat ran on battery-driven motors that did not need air.

In 1955 came the first nuclear-powered submarine. Such boats can travel around the world without having to come to the surface.

▲ One of the earliest submarines, the Turtle *was powered by a hand propeller and had room for just one person. In 1776 it was used for the first submarine attack on a warship.*

▼ *This cutaway view of a nuclear submarine shows how much of its interior is taken up with the nuclear reactor and turbines that drive it. The crew's quarters and operating area occupy relatively little space.*

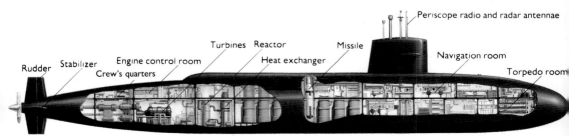

Rudder · Stabilizer · Engine control room · Crew's quarters · Turbines · Reactor · Heat exchanger · Missile · Periscope radio and radar antennae · Navigation room · Torpedo room

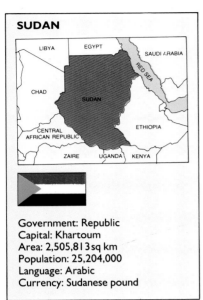

SUDAN

LIBYA EGYPT SAUDI ARABIA

RED SEA

CHAD

SUDAN

CENTRAL
AFRICAN REPUBLIC ETHIOPIA

ZAIRE UGANDA KENYA

Government: Republic
Capital: Khartoum
Area: 2,505,813 sq km
Population: 25,204,000
Language: Arabic
Currency: Sudanese pound

Sudan

This is the largest nation in AFRICA. It is nearly four times the size of France.

Sudan is a hot country in north-east Africa. Desert sprawls across the north. There are flat grasslands in the middle. The south has forests and a huge swamp.

Sudanese people include Arabs and blacks. Most live near the NILE, which flows north across the country. The Sudanese raise cattle and grow crops.

Suez Canal

The Suez Canal crosses Egypt between Port Said on the Mediterranean Sea and Suez on the Red Sea. It is the world's longest canal that can be used by big ships. It measures 160 km from end to end and 60 metres across its bed. Ships use it as a shortcut on voyages between Europe and Asia. This saves them from sailing 9650 km around southern Africa.

The canal was begun in 1859 by a French company run by the engineer Ferdinand de Lesseps. More than 8000 men and hundreds of camels worked on it for 10 years. France and England operated the canal until Egypt took it over in 1956.

Sunken ships blocked the canal for eight years after Egypt's war with Israel in 1967. But dredging has now made it much wider and deeper than it was a century ago.

▼ *The Suez Canal crosses the narrow isthmus between the Mediterranean and the long, thin Gulf of Suez, at the northern end of the Red Sea.*

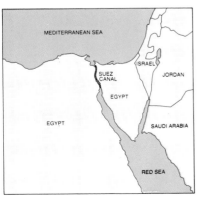

MEDITERRANEAN SEA

ISRAEL

SUEZ
CANAL JORDAN

EGYPT

EGYPT

SAUDI ARABIA

RED SEA

Sugar

Sugar is a sweet-tasting food. We eat it as an ingredient in ice cream, sweets and soft drinks. We use sugar crystals to sweeten cereals, coffee and tea.

Sugar gives our body energy more quickly than any other food. But eating too many sugary things can cause your teeth to decay.

All sugar contains carbon, hydrogen and oxygen. Different groupings of these ATOMS produce different kinds of sugars. The kind we eat most of is known as *sucrose*.

Every green PLANT produces sugar. But most of the sugar that we eat comes from two plants. One is sugarcane, a type of giant grass. The other is sugar beet, a plant with a thick root rich in sugar.

Sun

The Sun is just one of many millions of STARS in the MILKY WAY. But it is also the centre of the SOLAR SYSTEM. The PLANETS and their moons all whirl around it. The heat and light given out by the Sun make it possible for planets and animals to live on EARTH.

The Sun seems small because it is so far away from our planet. A spacecraft that took an hour to zoom around the Earth would need five months to reach the Sun. In fact, the Sun is so big that you could fit a million Earths inside it with room to spare. A bucketful of the Sun's substance would weigh far less than a bucketful of rock from the Earth. But the whole Sun would weigh over 750 times more than all the planets put together.

The Sun is a great glowing ball of gases. In the middle of the Sun a process called nuclear fusion turns HYDROGEN gas into helium gas. The change releases huge amounts of NUCLEAR ENERGY. The Sun beams out its energy in all directions as *electromagnetic waves*. Some of these waves give us HEAT and LIGHT. But there are also radio waves, ultraviolet rays, X-rays and others.

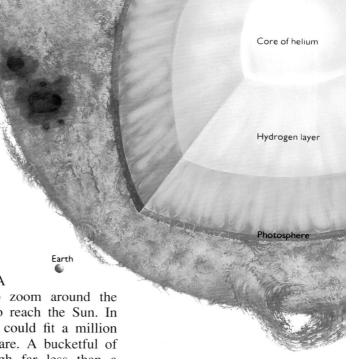

Core of helium

Hydrogen layer

Photosphere

Earth

▲ You can see just how tiny the Earth is compared to the Sun when they are drawn to the same scale. The Sun is bigger than a million Earths.

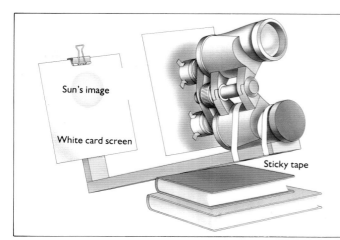

Sun's image

White card screen

Sticky tape

SEE IT YOURSELF
This is a safe way to study the Sun. Clip a sheet of white card onto an L-shaped wooden frame. Place a pair of binoculars onto the frame so that the eyepieces are about 30 cm away from the card. Move the binoculars around until images of the Sun appear on the card. Focus the binoculars to get a sharp image. Now stick another sheet of card over the eyepieces, cutting a round hole for one of them in the card. Tape the binoculars onto the wooden frame. Cover one of the lenses. You should get a single, sharp, steady image of the Sun on the card.

If scientists succeed in making substances superconductive at ordinary air temperatures, it will be possible to produce electromagnets that generate large magnetic fields without losing any energy. These could be used for high-speed trains supported above the track by powerful magnets. But perhaps the most important use for superconductive materials will be in super-efficient power generation plants.

Superconductivity

Some materials allow electricity to flow through them more easily than other materials. Good conductors such as copper and silver have little resistance to an electric current – but they do have some. Electricity struggling to pass through them makes them warm. However, in 1911 it was discovered that the metal mercury loses all its electrical resistance when it is cooled to about minus 270°C – very, very cold indeed. It became a superconductor – but it was very expensive and difficult to produce such a low temperature.

Then, in 1987, scientists began to experiment with new materials. They found that certain ceramic (clay-based) mixtures could be made to superconduct at higher temperatures – as high as about minus 170°C – still very cold, but easier to achieve. Now the race is on to find materials that are superconductors at room temperature. If this is achieved, the whole electronics industry will be changed.

▼ A plane flying slower than the speed of sound (left) creates disturbances in the air pressure, which travel at the speed of sound and so move along ahead of the plane. A plane moving at the speed of sound (centre) is moving as fast as the disturbances it causes. These pile up in front of the plane and form a shock wave. A plane travelling faster than the speed of sound (right) breaks through the sound 'barrier', but creates a shock wave which, when it reaches the ground, is heard as a sonic boom.

Supersonic Flight

'Supersonic' flight means flying faster than sound travels through the air. This speed is about 1225 km/h at sea level. Higher up, sound travels at a slower speed.

When a plane flies slower than the speed of sound, the air ahead has time to divide smoothly and flow around the plane. But with supersonic flight the air ahead has no time to prepare for the coming of the plane. Instead, the air is disturbed so much it forms a shock wave that makes a loud bang and may badly buffet the plane.

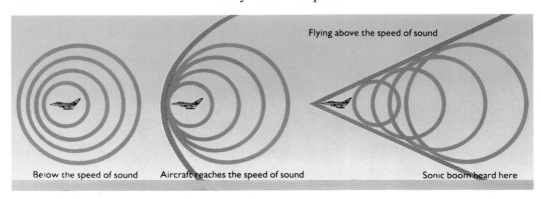

Flying above the speed of sound

Below the speed of sound   Aircraft reaches the speed of sound   Sonic boom heard here

Surveying

Surveying means using measuring instruments and working out certain sums to find out the exact positions of places on the Earth's surface. This kind of information makes it possible for people to make maps and charts and to build bridges, roads and buildings.

> The ancient Egyptians used surveying methods as early as 1400 BC to position boundary marks that were covered each year by the Nile's flood waters. They must also have used surveying to build the pyramids as accurately as they did. The Babylonians, about 3500 BC, made maps to an accurate scale.

Swan

These big, graceful waterbirds are among the heaviest birds able to fly. To take off, they need a long, clear stretch of water.

Swans swim with webbed feet, lowering their necks to feed on underwater plants. They build bulky nests by pools or rivers. Their young are known as cygnets.

Some kinds of swan fly south in spring and autumn. They fly in V-shaped flocks.

Sweden

Sweden is the fourth largest nation in EUROPE. The country lies in the north between Norway and the Baltic Sea. Mountains cover most of the west, and forests take up more than half of the land. Their conifer trees yield much of the world's softwood. Most of Sweden's electricity comes from rivers flowing down the mountains. Farmers produce milk, meat, grains and sugar beets on farmlands near the coast. The north is too cold for farming, but it has rich iron mines.

Most of the eight million Swedes live in the south. The capital, Stockholm, is there.

SWEDEN

Government: Constitutional monarchy
Capital: Stockholm
Area: 449,964 sq km
Population: 8,559,000
Language: Swedish
Currency: Swedish krona

Swimming

Swimming is the skill or sport of staying afloat and moving through water. Swimming is healthy exercise, and being able to swim may save your life if you fall into water by accident. Many animals know how to swim from birth. But people have to learn, usually with help from a trained instructor.

Learners often start in a pool or at the edge of the sea. First they should float or glide. Then they can try kicking. Arm movements come last. Beginners

SWITZERLAND

Government: Federal state
Capital: Bern
Area: 41,288 sq km
Population: 6,712,000
Languages: German, French, Italian
Currency: Swiss franc

must learn to fit in breathing with arm movements. Swimmers usually use one or more of five main strokes. These are called the breaststroke, butterfly stroke, backstroke, sidestroke, and crawl.

Switzerland

This small, mountainous country lies in the south-central part of EUROPE. The sharp, snowy peaks of the Alps and their steep-sided valleys fill most of southern Switzerland. In summer, tourists pick wild flowers and watch dairy cattle grazing on the mountain meadows. Winter visitors to the many resorts ski down the snowy alpine slopes.

Most of the country's crops are grown where the mountains meet the lower land of the Swiss Plateau. Here, too, stand most of Switzerland's cities, including Bern, the capital. Swiss factories make chemicals, machinery, watches and chocolates.

Sydney

Sydney is the largest city in AUSTRALIA, and the capital of New South Wales. More than three million people live in Sydney. It stands on a fine natural harbour (Port Jackson) crossed by a famous steel-arch bridge. Sydney makes chemicals, machinery and ships and is an important port. It was founded in 1788 as a settlement for convicts sent out from England.

SYRIA

Government: Socialist
Capital: Damascus
Area: 185,180 sq km
Population: 12,116,000
Language: Arabic
Currency: Syrian pound

Syria

This Arab country lies just east of the Mediterranean Sea. Much of Syria is covered by dry plains that are hot in summer and chilly in winter. There are nearly ten million people. Nomads drive flocks of sheep and goats over the dry lands. Farmers grow grains, grapes and apricots in areas where rivers or rain provide water.

Most Syrian towns grew up on the roads used long ago to bring goods from the East. In 1516, Syria was conquered by the Turks, and was ruled by Turkey for 400 years. After World War I, the French ruled the country on behalf of the League of Nations. Syria gained its independence in 1943 and has close ties with Libya.

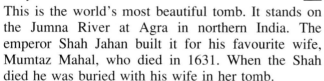

◀ *The Taj Mahal, in Agra, India, is a marvel of Islamic architecture.*

Taj Mahal

This is the world's most beautiful tomb. It stands on the Jumna River at Agra in northern India. The emperor Shah Jahan built it for his favourite wife, Mumtaz Mahal, who died in 1631. When the Shah died he was buried with his wife in her tomb.

At the centre of the Taj Mahal is a dome and there is a prayer tower at each corner. The walls are decorated with passages from the Koran.

> The building of the Taj Mahal and its ornamentation took 20,000 men from 1632 to 1650. The inside of the tomb is adorned with semi-precious stones and lit through carved-marble screens set near the tops of the walls.

Tape Recorder

A tape recorder turns sound waves into a magnetic pattern on tape. When played, the pattern changes back into sound.

A microphone inside or connected to the recorder changes sound into an electrical signal. This is amplified (made stronger) and fed to the recording head. The head produces a magnetic field which magnetizes the tape as it passes the head.

When playing the tape back, the magnetic field produces an electrical signal which goes to an amplifier and loudspeaker.

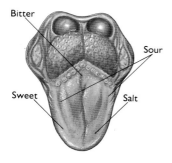

▲ *Each patch of taste buds on the tongue picks up one kind of taste.*

Taste

We can taste food because we have taste buds on our TONGUES. Your tongue is covered in tiny bumps. The taste buds are buried in the sides of these bumps. There are clusters of buds on the back, tip and sides of the tongue. NERVES running from the buds to the brain tell you whether the food you are eating is sweet, sour, bitter or salty.

Flavour is a mixture of the taste and the SMELL of food. If you have a bad cold and your nose is blocked, food hardly tastes of anything. The most comfortable way to take bad-tasting medicine is to hold your nose while you swallow.

Tax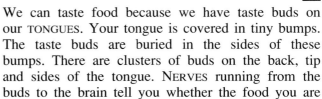

The government of a country must have money to carry on its work. It gets most of this money by taxing people. *Direct* taxes are those people pay directly to the government on their income – income tax. How much income tax a person pays depends on several things. The higher a person's income, the more he or she pays in tax. A married person pays less than a single person with the same income.

Indirect taxes are those charged on some goods bought in the shops or elsewhere. Every time a motorist buys petrol, a part of the cost is tax which goes to the government.

▼ *The taxes that people pay are used to keep essential services running so that they are available to everyone. Some of the things paid for by taxes are shown in this picture, but there are many more, too.*

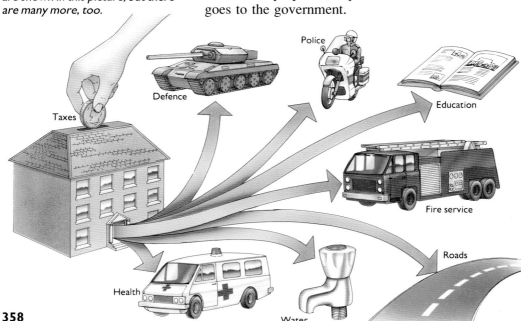

Taxes
Defence
Police
Education
Fire service
Health
Water
Roads

Teeth

Teeth are made to cut, tear or crush food so that it can be swallowed. Cutting teeth are called incisors; tearing teeth are called canines; and crushing teeth are called molars. Meat-eating animals have large canines for tearing flesh. Plant-eaters have sharp incisors and large molars for snapping off and grinding stringy stalks. Humans have all three kinds of teeth because we eat all kinds of food.

There are two parts to a tooth. The root, which has one, two, or three prongs, is fixed in the jawbone. The crown is the part you can see. Tooth decay happens when bacteria mix with sugar. This dissolves tooth enamel, making holes that let infection get inside the tooth.

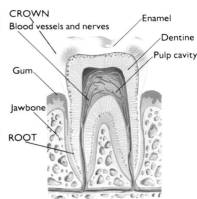

CROWN
Blood vessels and nerves
Enamel
Dentine
Pulp cavity
Gum
Jawbone
ROOT

▲ *There are three layers in a tooth. At the centre is a space full of nerves and blood vessels; around that is a bony wall of dentine. On top is a layer of hard, shiny enamel.*

Telephone

Telephones let you speak to someone far away. When you pick up a telephone receiver, a weak electric current is switched on. When you speak into the mouthpiece, you speak into a microphone.

Waves of SOUND from your voice hit a metal disc inside the microphone and make it vibrate. These vibrations travel along the telephone wires as electrical waves. When they reach the other end, they hit another metal disc in the earpiece. This changes the vibrations back into sound waves, which the person you are calling hears as your voice.

The first electric telephone, made by Alexander BELL in 1876, produced only a very weak sound over long distances. Today, telephone networks use a worldwide system of cables and communications SATELLITES.

▶ *Speaking into a telephone mouthpiece makes a diaphragm vibrate and compresses carbon granules, to make an electric current vary. The current flows along wires to another telephone and enters the earpiece, where an electromagnet makes a diaphragm vibrate to produce the sound of your voice.*

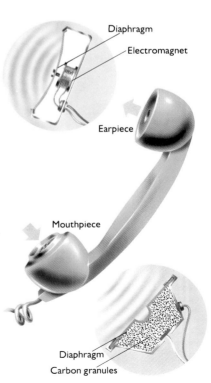

Diaphragm
Electromagnet
Earpiece
Mouthpiece
Diaphragm
Carbon granules

Telescope

Telescopes make things that are far away look nearer. They work by gathering the LIGHT from an object and bending it to make a tiny picture called an image which is made larger so we can see it.

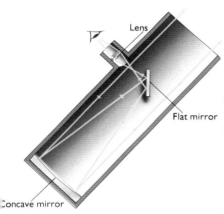

There are two kinds of telescope. The *lens* or refractor telescope uses two lenses fixed in a tube to keep out unwanted light. A large lens at one end of the tube collects the light. It is called the object lens. A smaller lens called the eyepiece makes the image larger.

The image you see through this kind of telescope is upside down. If you want to turn the image the right way around, a third lens is needed. Binoculars are two lens telescopes fixed together.

The other kind of telescope is called a reflecting telescope. Instead of a lens it has a curved mirror to collect light. The mirror is shaped so that the light rays bouncing off it are directed at a second mirror which reflects the ray towards the eyepiece. Since 1900, most of the big astronomical telescopes built have been reflectors.

The idea of the lens telescope was discovered by accident in 1608 by Hans Lippershey, a Dutch eyeglass maker. While holding up two lenses he noticed that the church weathervane looked much closer through them.

▲ *A refracting telescope uses two lenses to focus rays of light from distant stars and planets.*

▲ *Reflecting telescopes use a large concave mirror to reflect light onto a smaller mirror that directs it through a lens to the eye.*

John Logie Baird's first television set was made of old cans, bicycle parts, lenses, sealing wax and string.

Television

Television is a way of sending sounds and pictures through the air. Scientists have been interested in the idea of television since the 1880s. Although John Logie Baird was the first to show how television worked, his success was based on work by many other scientists from all over the world. Baird showed his set in 1926.

At first, all television was black and white. Few people owned television sets because they were very expensive. Now nearly every home has one.

Television works by changing LIGHT waves into electric signals. This happens inside the TV camera. A picture of what is happening in front of the camera forms on a special screen behind the LENS. Behind the screen is an electron gun. This *scans* the screen. It moves from left to right to cover each part of the picture. Each part is turned into an electric signal which is made stronger, then sent to the transmitter. All the signals are broadcast by the transmitter as RADIO waves. They are picked up by home TV aerials and changed back into electric signals. These pass into the TV set.

Inside the set is a large glass tube called the CATHODE RAY TUBE. The screen that you look at is the front of this tube. The screen is covered with tiny chemical dots. In a colour set, these are arranged in groups of three: one red, one blue, one green. At the back of the tube are three electron guns. These fire beams of electrons to scan the screen just as the camera gun does. As each electron hits the screen, it lights up a dot. These tiny flashes of colour build up the picture on your screen. You do not see lines of coloured flashing lights, because the electron gun moves too fast for the eye to follow. What you see is a picture of what is happening in the television studio.

Live television programmes show you what is happening as it happens. Most programmes are recorded on film or *videotape* and sent out later.

▼ The main part of a television set is the cathode ray tube. The big end is the screen. The narrow end contains three electron guns that fire electrons through the shadow mask onto the phosphor dots on the screen. All the colours you see on a colour television screen are made up from three colours – red, blue and green – and each of the colours is supplied by one of the guns. To receive the signals that provide the programmes, you need an aerial. The aerial may be attached to the set, as here, or installed high up on the roof of a building, so it can receive the radio waves broadcast by the transmitter as clearly as possible.

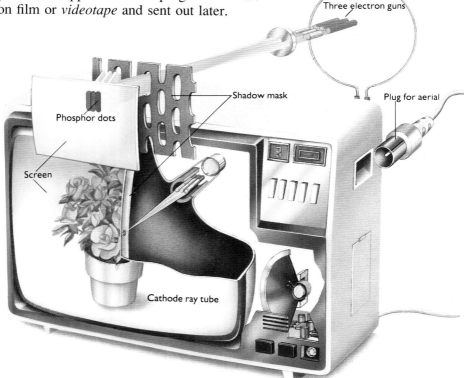

Three electron guns

Shadow mask

Plug for aerial

Phosphor dots

Screen

Cathode ray tube

Temperature

Temperature is the measurement of heat. It is measured on a scale marked on a THERMOMETER. The Fahrenheit scale is most often used in the United States but the Celsius scale is common elsewhere.

TEMPERATURE CONVERSION TABLE		
	Celsius (Centigrade)	Fahrenheit
Freezing Point	0	32
	10	50
	20	68
	30	86
	40	104
	50	122
	60	140
	70	158
	80	176
	90	194
Boiling Point	100	212
	110	230
	120	248
	130	266
	140	284
	150	302
	200	392
	250	482
	300	572

To convert Fahrenheit to Celsius, subtract 32, multiply by 5, and divide by 9. To convert Celsius to Fahrenheit, multiply by 9, divide by 5, and add 32.

Some animals, including mammals such as humans, are warm-blooded. Their temperature stays much the same. Humans can stand quite a wide range of body temperatures. A healthy person's normal body temperature is 37°C. When he or she is ill, their temperature might go up to 41°C or more, and they could still survive.

Other animals, such as snakes, lizards and frogs, are cold-blooded. Their body temperature goes up and down with the temperature of their surroundings. Many cold-blooded animals can survive until their body temperature drops almost to freezing point.

Tennis

Tennis is a game for two or four people played on a specially marked court, which is divided in half by a net 3 feet (91 cm) high. If two people play it is called a singles match. If four people play it is called a doubles match.

A tennis match is divided into sets. Usually women play three sets and men play five. Each set has at least six games. To win a game, one player must score at least four points. Modern tennis is a simple version of an old French game called real tennis or royal tennis.

Textile

A textile is any cloth made by WEAVING. Before the INDUSTRIAL REVOLUTION, all cloth was made by hand from natural fibres of wool, silk, cotton or linen. Since then, scientists have developed many kinds of man-made fibre. Rayon is made from wood. Nylon comes from oil.

▼ *Different patterns of cloth are made by different kinds of weaving. These include (left to right): looped weft threads; weft threads woven in and out of warp threads; plaited weave; a third thread added to a plain (criss-cross) weave.*

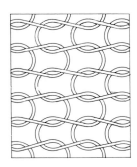
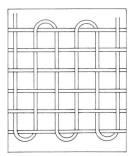
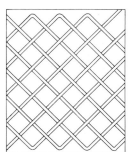
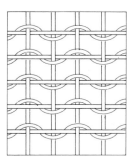

Thailand

Thailand is a country in SOUTH-EAST ASIA. It is surrounded by BURMA (Myanmar), Laos and CAMBODIA. The south coast opens onto the Gulf of Thailand, which is part of the South China Sea.

Most of the people live in the central part of the country. Many rivers flow through this area, making it very fertile. Most people are farmers. Rice is the main crop. They also grow cotton, tobacco, corn, coconuts and bananas. In the north there are large forests of teak, which is a major export. The peninsula in the south-west is very rich in minerals, especially tin.

Thailand was called Siam before 1939. Thai means 'free', so Thailand means the land of the free. There is a king, but the country is ruled by an elected government.

THAILAND

Government: Constitutional monarchy
Capital: Bangkok
Area: 514,000 sq km
Population: 55,020,000
Language: Thai
Currency: Baht

Theatre

A theatre is a place where plays are performed by actors and watched by an audience. The theatre may be just a patch of ground or a large, expensive building.

The earliest theatres we know about were in Greece. They were simply flattened patches of ground on a hillside. The audience sat in rows on the hill above so that they could all see the 'stage'. When the Greeks built theatres, they cut a half-moon shape in the hillside and lined it with rows of stone seats that looked down on a round, flat stage.

The Romans copied the Greek pattern, but they built most of their theatres on flat ground. The rows of seats were held up by a wall. The Romans built a theatre in nearly every large town in the Roman Empire.

In Britain, there were no theatre buildings before the 1500s. Troupes of actors travelled around using their carts as stages. Later, they performed in rich people's houses and in the courtyards of inns. The first theatres to be built were made of wood and looked very much like inns. The stage jutted out into a large yard. Galleries of seats ran all round the sides. There were even seats on the stage, but only for rich people. These theatres had no roofs. When it rained, the *groundlings*, people who stood in the

▼ *The theatre at Delphi in Greece was built in the 300s BC. It was so skilfully built that even people sitting right at the back could hear every word the actors spoke.*

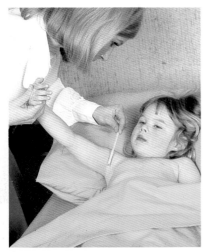

▲ A medical thermometer placed under this feverish girl's arm will indicate how high above normal (37° C) her body temperature is. It is safer to take a very young child's temperature in this way than to risk putting a glass thermometer into his or her mouth.

yard around the edge of the stage, got wet. SHAKE-SPEARE's plays were performed in theatres like this.

Later on, theatres had proper roofs. The stage was moved back and the audience sat in rows in front of it. Today, a large modern theatre is an elaborate building. Theatres have the latest lighting and sound-equipment to provide atmosphere and effect.

Thermometer

A thermometer is an instrument that measures TEMPERATURE. It is usually a glass tube marked with a scale. Inside is another, thinner glass tube, which ends in a bulb containing mercury or alcohol. When the temperature goes up, the mercury or the alcohol gets warm and expands (grows bigger). It rises up the tube. When it stops, you can read the temperature on the marked scale. When it gets cold, the mercury contracts (grows smaller) and sinks down the tube. If alcohol is used in a thermometer it is usually coloured red. Most thermometers measure temperatures between the boiling and freezing points of water. This is between 0° and 100° on the Celsius scale. Most countries use the Celsius scale, but some, such as the United States, also use Fahrenheit, in which the freezing and boiling points of water are 32° and 212°.

Medical thermometers, which are small enough to go in your mouth, measure your blood heat. Household thermometers tell you how warm or cold the air is inside or outside your house.

► Maximum and minimum thermometers are used to indicate the highest and lowest temperatures recorded. In a maximum thermometer, mercury flows through a narrow neck in the tube. As the thermometer cools, a small amount of mercury stays above the neck, showing the highest temperature to which the thermometer has been exposed. A minimum thermometer is usually an alcohol thermometer which stays at the lowest point reached. Oven thermometers (below right) make use of the difference in expansion of different metals. As the temperature rises, the bimetallic strip bends as one metal expands, moving a pointer on a dial.

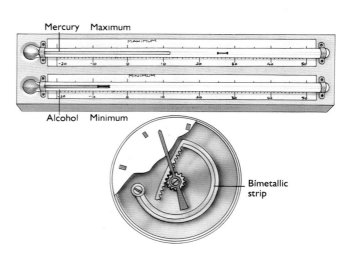

Mercury   Maximum

Alcohol   Minimum

Bimetallic strip

Third World

The Third World is a polite way of describing the poorer nations in our world. The first two 'worlds' are the rich and powerful nations of the East, including the communist countries led by the former SOVIET UNION; and the western countries, of which the most powerful is the UNITED STATES.

The Third World countries are in ASIA, AFRICA and SOUTH AMERICA. Many of them supply the rest of the world with cheap food, minerals, timber and fibres, as well as cheap labour. This pattern of wealth in one part of the world and poverty in another is very difficult to change. The rest of the countries in the world do not want to give up the wealth and power they have been used to for so long. This means that many countries in the Third World go on getting poorer while the rich countries go on getting richer.

▲ The terrible conditions that many people suffer in these slums in Rio de Janeiro, Brazil, are typical of those in many Third World countries.

INFANT MORTALITY IN VARIOUS NATIONS			
Third World	Per 1000	Other	Per 1000
China	50	Australia	9
Bangladesh	140	Canada	8
Bolivia	123	Denmark	7
Brazil	70	Finland	6
Burma	96	France	8
Cameroon	113	Greece	13
Chile	22	Italy	12
Congo	110	New Zealand	10
Gabon	162	Poland	18
Gambia	217	Portugal	18
Ghana	98	Sweden	3
India	101	United Kingdom	10
Liberia	127	United States	10

◄ The number of infant deaths per thousand people in a country is one indication of that country's wealth and standard of living. In poorer countries, lower standards of health and education usually result in a greater number of infant deaths.

Thunder and Lightning

Thunderstorms are caused by ELECTRICITY in the air. Different electrical charges build up inside big rain clouds. When the charges are strong enough, a spark leaps from one charged part of the cloud to another. Sometimes the spark jumps from the cloud to the ground. We see the spark as lightning. Lightning heats up the air. The air expands (gets bigger) so quickly that it explodes, making the crashing noise we call thunder.

Since sound travels much slower than LIGHT, you always hear thunder after you see lightning. It takes the noise of thunder about three seconds to travel

Thunderstorms are most frequent in the tropics. In some areas they may occur on as many as 200 days a year. In the British Isles they may happen on more than 15 days a year, but along western coasts thunder is seldom heard on more than 5 days a year.

one kilometre. To find out how many kilometres away the storm is, count the seconds between seeing the lightning and hearing the thunder, and divide the number by three.

Tibet

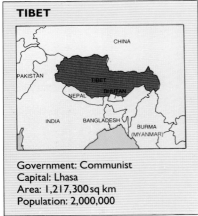

TIBET

CHINA

PAKISTAN

TIBET

NEPAL BHUTAN

INDIA BANGLADESH

BURMA (MYANMAR)

Government: Communist
Capital: Lhasa
Area: 1,217,300 sq km
Population: 2,000,000

Tibet is a country in central ASIA. It is the highest country in the world. The flat part of Tibet, which is in the middle, is as high as the peaks of the Alps. Enormous mountain ranges surround this high plain. In the south lie the HIMALAYAS, the home of Mount EVEREST.

Tibet used to be ruled by Buddhist monks called *lamas*. In 1959, the country was taken over by China.

Tide

Tides are regular movements of the OCEANS. They are mainly caused by the MOON. The Moon is like a giant magnet. It tugs the oceans towards it as it loops around the Earth. The Earth is spinning at the same time, so most places get two high tides and two low tides about every 24 hours.

High tide happens when the water flows as far inland as it can. Low tide happens when it flows out as far as it can.

Tiger

Tigers are the biggest members of the cat family. They live in the forests of Asia and Indonesia, and hunt deer or large cattle. Tigers usually lie still during the day, and hunt alone by night. They are very strong. One tiger can pull a dead buffalo that is so heavy a group of people would find it difficult to move.

Until the 1800s, thousands of tigers roamed through the forests of Asia. Then men began to shoot them, and as a result they are now very rare.

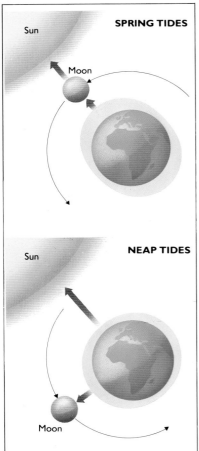

SPRING TIDES

Sun

Moon

NEAP TIDES

Sun

Moon

▲ *When the Sun and the Moon 'pull' in the same direction, there is a spring tide; when they pull at right angles, a neap tide.*

Time

Nobody has ever really explained what time is. But people have invented many ways of measuring it. First, they divided up the years and months by

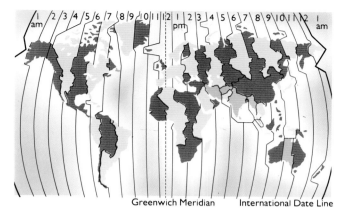

◄ *Because of the rotation of the Earth, sunrise in, for example, the eastern United States occurs three hours earlier than in the western part. For this reason, the world has been divided into 24 time zones. At the International Date Line the date changes.*

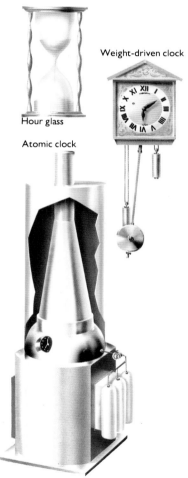

Weight-driven clock

Hour glass

Atomic clock

natural things that happened regularly, such as the SEASONS and the size and shape of the Moon. The position of the SUN in the sky told them the time of day.

The very first clock was probably invented by the Egyptians. It was a sundial. As the Sun moved across the sky, an upright rod in the middle of the dial cast a shadow onto a scale of hours drawn around it.

But this was no good at night time. Other ways of telling the time, without the Sun's help, were invented. One was the hour glass. This was two glass bulbs joined together. Sand in one bulb took exactly one hour to trickle through a hole into the other bulb.

Mechanical CLOCKS were not made until the 1200s. These were driven by weights. Clocks which worked by springs were made in the 1500s. In the early 1600s, the pendulum was being used to make clocks more accurate. Modern clocks are very accurate. They work by ELECTRONICS. Scientists need ever more accurate timekeeping. They use atomic clocks that are accurate to 10 millionths of a second.

We think of time as being something that is always the same in all situations, but this is not necessarily so. Albert Einstein showed that the rate at which time passes varies according to the speed at which we are travelling. On a supersonic jet, clocks and watches move just very slightly slower than they do on the ground. The difference would only be noticeable, however, in a spacecraft travelling at close to the speed of light – that is, at approximately 299,800 km (186,000 miles) a second.

▲ *Hour glasses were one of the earliest ways of measuring time. Pendulum clocks came into use in the 1600s. More precise methods of timekeeping have been developed over the years. An atomic caesium clock is so accurate that it should lose only one second in 1000 years.*

Packaging

Tin plate

Pewter

▲ Tin is useful for packaging because it does not rust. It can also be used for plating other metals to give a bright shiny surface. Mixed with antimony and copper it makes pewter, a soft alloy once used for most tableware.

▼ Tobacco leaves are picked, then dried and packaged to be sent abroad for processing to make cigarettes, cigars, loose tobacco or snuff, a powder that can be sniffed. Cheap tobacco is dried in the sun. More expensive types are dried by hot air or over fires in sheds.

Tin

Tin is one of the oldest metals known to us. People were mining tin before IRON was discovered. Tin was mixed with COPPER to make bronze.

Tin was mined in Cornwall long before the birth of Christ. An ancient people called the Phoenicians sailed from the Mediterranean to trade cloth and precious stones for it.

Tin cans are made from sheets of steel that have been coated with tin. Tin does not rust.

Tin is not a common metal. The main tin mines are in Bolivia, south-eastern Asia, and western Africa.

Tobacco

Tobacco is made from the dried leaves of the plant *Nicotiana*, which belongs to the same family as potatoes. It was first found in America, but is now grown all over the world. The Spanish traveller Francisco Hernandez brought it to Europe in 1599.

Tobacco leaves can be rolled together to make cigars, or shredded up to be smoked in pipes or cigarettes. Smoking is very bad for your health. It is particularly harmful to the lungs and heart.

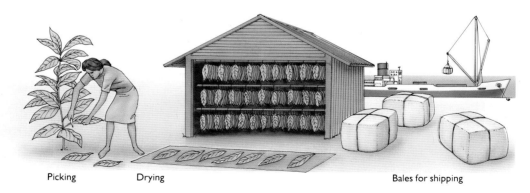

Picking   Drying   Bales for shipping

Tokyo

Tokyo is the capital of JAPAN. It is one of the biggest cities in the world. Tokyo is on the south-east coast of Honshu, the main island of Japan.

Almost every kind of work goes on in this enormous city. There are factories which make paper, electronic and electrical goods, cars and motorbikes. There are also huge shipyards and oil refineries on the coast. So many people work in Tokyo that most of them have to live on the outside edge of the city. Some people have to spend four hours a day going to and from their work. Tokyo has some of the worst traffic jams in the world.

Much of the city was destroyed by an EARTHQUAKE in 1923. What was left was badly bombed in WORLD WAR II. Since then the city has been almost entirely rebuilt, but a number of beautiful old buildings remain. The Imperial Palace is an old *shogun* castle, and there are many ancient temples and shrines.

> Tokyo has had an unusual population history. In 1787 it had a population of 1,400,000, making it the world's largest city at that time. Then Tokyo's population became smaller and smaller until by 1868 it was only half that size. When the city was almost completely destroyed by an earthquake in 1923, the population had again risen to 2,200,000.

Tongue

The tongue is a muscular, flexible flap fixed inside the mouth. Only VERTEBRATES have tongues. Our own tongues help us to TASTE and eat food, and to talk. The letters T and D for instance, cannot be said without using the tongue in a special way.

In toads, the tongue is fixed to the front of the mouth. Snakes have forked or split tongues which can 'smell' the air. Cats' tongues are covered in tiny hooks of flesh. Cats can use their tongues like combs to clean their fur.

Tonsils

Tonsils are two small lumps at the back of the throat. There is one on each side. They help to protect the body from germs coming in through the mouth.

Children have very large tonsils. These gradually shrink as they grow older. Sometimes, tonsils can become infected. They swell up and are very painful. This illness is called tonsillitis. The tonsils may have to be taken out by doctors in a hospital. Having our tonsils taken out does not seem to harm our bodies in any way.

Tornado

Tornadoes are violent, whirling windstorms. Most of them happen in America, but they can occur anywhere in the world.

Hurricanes are strong winds that build up over the sea. Tornadoes build up over land. They happen

▼ The cat's tongue is long and flexible. The little hooks that make it rough are called papillae. They help the cat lap up liquids and keep its fur clean.

Cup-shaped papillae —carry taste buds

Hook-shaped papillae—carry no taste buds

The most violent tornadoes happen in the centre of the United States. They travel at about 50 kilometres an hour with a roaring sound that can be heard 40 kilometres away. Many farmhouses have special cellars where people can shelter from tornadoes.

when large masses of cloud meet. The clouds begin to whirl around each other. Gradually, these whirling clouds join together to make a gigantic, twisting funnel. When this touches the ground, it sucks up anything in its path – trees, houses or people.

Tortoise

Giant tortoises live in the Galapagos Islands and islands in the Indian Ocean. They can weigh up to 225 kg and be 1.8 metres long. Some large tortoises live for over 150 years.

Tortoises are slow-moving REPTILES. They can walk only about 5 metres in a minute. When frightened, they pull their heads and legs inside their domed shells. The 40 or so kinds of tortoise live on land, mostly in warm parts of the world. They are similar to TURTLES and terrapins, but these reptiles live in water.

▲ *The Hermann's tortoise is a European type. The shell has three layers: a thin layer of living skin is sandwiched between horny plates on the outside and bony plates on the inside.*

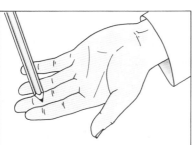

SEE IT YOURSELF
Some parts of your body are more responsive to light touch than others. Try this experiment with a friend. Blindfold yourself and ask your friend to press either one or two pencil points lightly on your fingertip. You will probably be able to tell how many pencil points your friend is using each time. Try doing this on your back, shoulders and on other parts of your body. Can you tell how many pencil points are being used each time? Which areas are receptive to light touch?

Touch

There are different nerve cells in your skin called receptors that respond to five main kinds of sensation. These are light touch, heavy touch (pressure), pain, heat and cold. Receptors pass sensations along NERVES to the brain.

Pain receptors are the most numerous; cold receptors the least numerous. Some parts of the body, such as the tongue and fingertips, have more receptors than others.

We also have receptors inside the body. Usually we do not realize that these are working, except when they produce sensations such as hunger or tiredness. These receptors help to protect the body from accidental damage.

Trade Union

Trade unions are groups formed by workers. Their main aim is to get better wages for their members. They also ask for shorter hours and better working conditions, and some form of job security. Some unions look after their members and their families in times of trouble. If a trade union has a serious disagreement with an employer, it may ask its members to stop working. This is called a *strike*.

Modern trade unions were formed in the early days of the INDUSTRIAL REVOLUTION. They were first made legal in Britain in the 1870s. Since then, unions have gradually increased their power. Today, trade unions play an important part in the affairs of many countries.

Transistor

Transistors are small ELECTRONIC devices. They are usually made to amplify (strengthen) electric currents in electronic equipment such as radios, televisions, computers and satellites. They can also switch electric currents on and off. Transistors have largely replaced other devices, called valves, which were once used for the same purpose.

▲ John L. Lewis was a powerful American trade union leader and was president of the United Mine Workers of America for 40 years.

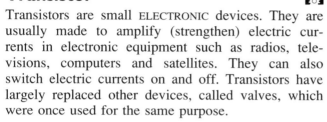
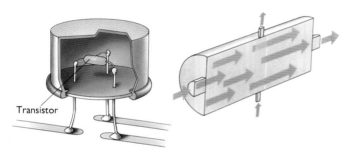

Transistor

◀ A transistor in a circuit (left), and shown in section (right). The transistor shown here is made of a sandwich of three differently treated pieces of silicon. This type of transistor amplifies a signal and has the same effect as the more old-fashioned triode valve. The flow of electrons is shown by the blue arrows.

Today complicated circuits containing thousands of transistors can be put into SILICON CHIPS that are only a centimetre square. The first practical transistors were developed in the 1940s by the American scientists Walter Brattain, John Bardeen and William Shockley. The invention of transistors completely revolutionized electronics and millions of these devices are now made every year.

The first research into transistors was done, not with silicon, but with the hard greyish-white metal germanium. William Shockley, the American scientist, used germanium to make the first transistor in 1948.

Trees

Trees are the largest of all PLANTS. They are woody with a thick stem, or trunk. Trees are beautiful to look at and also very useful. Some give us fruit and nuts. Many trees, especially the conifers, are grown for timber. Wood is not only a valuable building material. It is also used to make PAPER and in some countries it is burned for fuel. Trees are vital to the environnment, for they enrich the atmosphere.

TROJAN

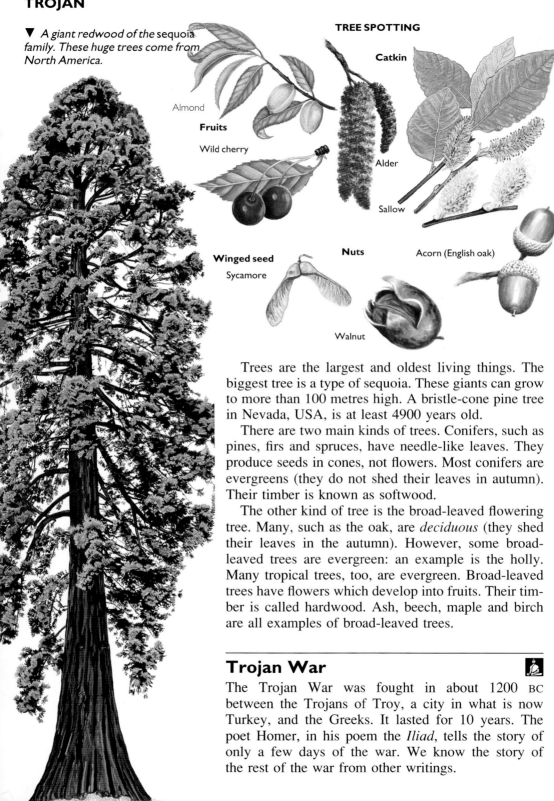

▼ *A giant redwood of the sequoia family. These huge trees come from North America.*

TREE SPOTTING

Catkin

Almond

Fruits

Wild cherry

Alder

Sallow

Winged seed

Sycamore

Nuts

Walnut

Acorn (English oak)

Trees are the largest and oldest living things. The biggest tree is a type of sequoia. These giants can grow to more than 100 metres high. A bristle-cone pine tree in Nevada, USA, is at least 4900 years old.

There are two main kinds of trees. Conifers, such as pines, firs and spruces, have needle-like leaves. They produce seeds in cones, not flowers. Most conifers are evergreens (they do not shed their leaves in autumn). Their timber is known as softwood.

The other kind of tree is the broad-leaved flowering tree. Many, such as the oak, are *deciduous* (they shed their leaves in the autumn). However, some broad-leaved trees are evergreen: an example is the holly. Many tropical trees, too, are evergreen. Broad-leaved trees have flowers which develop into fruits. Their timber is called hardwood. Ash, beech, maple and birch are all examples of broad-leaved trees.

Trojan War

The Trojan War was fought in about 1200 BC between the Trojans of Troy, a city in what is now Turkey, and the Greeks. It lasted for 10 years. The poet Homer, in his poem the *Iliad*, tells the story of only a few days of the war. We know the story of the rest of the war from other writings.

Paris was a prince of Troy. He fell in love with Helen, the wife of King Menelaus of Sparta in Greece. Paris took Helen to Troy, and Menelaus with other Greek kings and soldiers went to get her back. They besieged Troy for years. In the end they won by tricking the Trojans with a huge wooden horse filled with Greek soldiers, which they left standing outside the city. The Trojans, thinking that the horse was a gift, took it inside the city walls. The hidden soldiers then opened the gates and Troy was destroyed. No one knows if the story is true.

Tropical Fish

Tropical fish are among the prettiest fish in the world. They live in the warm seas of tropical regions, often along the edges of CORAL reefs.

Many small, brightly coloured freshwater tropical fish are popular aquarium pets. Marine fish can also be kept, but they are more expensive and difficult to look after. They have to have salt water containing just the right amount of salt to live in.

Tropical fish live in warm water. Most tanks have a heater to keep the water at around 24°C. A cover on the tank holds the heat in and stops the water from evaporating (drying up). Electric light bulbs in the cover light the tank and also heat the water. Most aquariums have air pumps that add OXYGEN to the water and filter it to keep it clear. Water plants also provide oxygen. Special food for tropical fish can be bought at pet shops.

The most common tropical freshwater fish is the guppy. Other common tropical fish are angelfish, barbs and neon tetras.

▼ The porcupine fish inflates itself like a balloon and erects sharp spines if it senses danger nearby.

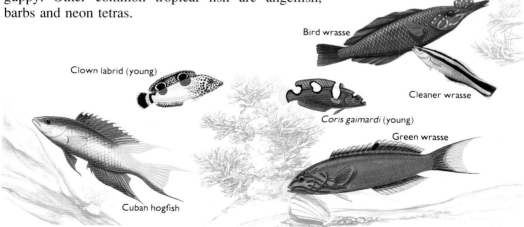

▼ These tropical fish are all members of the wrasse family. They can be kept in aquariums, provided the conditions are just right.

Bird wrasse

Clown labrid (young)

Cleaner wrasse

Coris gaimardi (young)

Green wrasse

Cuban hogfish

TUNISIA

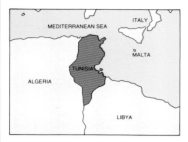

TUNISIA

MEDITERRANEAN SEA — ITALY — MALTA — TUNISIA — ALGERIA — LIBYA

Government: Republic
Capital: Tunis
Area: 163,610 sq km
Population: 8,180,000
Languages: Arabic, French
Currency: Tunisian dinar

Tunisia

Tunisia is a sunny country in North AFRICA. Its beaches attract many tourists from Europe. The north is rugged. It has the most rain. The south is part of the dry SAHARA. Farming is the main industry in this small nation, but oil and phosphates are important exports.

There are about 8,000,000 people, most of whom are Muslims. Near the capital, also called Tunis, are the ruins of Carthage. Carthage was a great Mediterranean Sea power until it was destroyed by the ROMAN EMPIRE in 146 BC.

Tunnel

Tunnelling is important in mining, transport and water supply. The Romans built tunnels to carry water. And today, a tunnel that brings water to New York City is the world's longest. It is 169 km long.

Different methods are used to build tunnels. In hard rock, the tunnel is blasted out with explosives. Cutting machines, like those used to drill oil wells, are used in softer rock. In the softest rocks, *tunnel shields* are used. These are giant steel tubes, the same size as the intended tunnel. The front edge of the shield is sharp and is pushed into the earth. The earth is dug out, and the tunnel behind the shield is lined to stop it from caving in.

Some tunnels under rivers are built by lowering sections of tunnel into the river. Divers join them together. When the tunnel is complete, the water is pumped out. Underground railway tunnels can be built in deep trenches. When they are finished the tunnel is covered over. The biggest tunnelling operation taking place today is digging the Channel Tunnel between England and France.

LONGEST TUNNELS

	Km	Opened
Railway		
Seikan (Japan)	53.9	1985
Oshimizu (Japan)	22.2	1982
Simplon (Switz./Italy)	19.8	1906
Road		
Arlberg (Austria)	14.0	1978
Mont Blanc (France/Italy)	11.6	1965
Underwater		
Seikan (Japan)	23.3	1985
Shin Kanmon (Japan)	18.7	1974

A Channel tunnel between France and England was first suggested to Napoleon in 1802 by the French engineer, Albert Mathieu. He decided that the tunnel should come to the surface on an island half-way across the Channel. This was so that men and horses could have a breath of fresh air.

Turbine

A turbine is a machine, in which a wheel, drum or screw is turned around by fast flowing water, or by steam or gas. Water wheels and windmills are simple turbines.

Water turbines are used at HYDROELECTRIC POWER STATIONS. These stations are next to DAMS or water-falls. The force of falling water carried through a

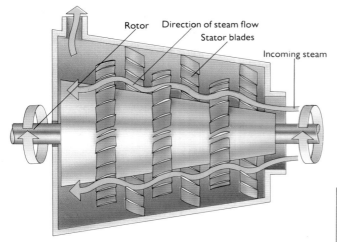

Rotor   Direction of steam flow
Stator blades
Incoming steam

◀ *In a steam turbine, high pressure steam is directed through fixed, or stator, blades to strike a series of blades on a central shaft. The steam expands as it passes through each set of blades, driving the shaft round. The fixed blades direct the steam onto the turbine blades at the correct angle.*

> **Small turbines driven by compressed air are used for dentists' drills. These turbines drive the drill at more than 250,000 revolutions per minute, so the drilling of a tooth is quickly done. There is also less vibration than with an electric drill.**

pipe from a dam turns the turbine. The turbine does not produce electricity. But as the turbine spins it drives a GENERATOR, which produces the electricity. Some turbines are wheels or drums, with blades or cup-shaped buckets round their edges. Others are shaped like screws or propellers.

Steam turbines are operated by jets of steam. They have many uses. They are used to produce electricity, to propel ships and to operate PUMPS. Gas turbines are turned by fast-moving jets of gas. The gases are produced by burning fuels such as oil. Gas turbines are used to turn the propellers of aircraft.

Turkey

Turkey is a country that is partly in EUROPE and partly in ASIA. The small European part covers three per cent of the land. It lies west of the waterway which links the Black Sea to the Mediterranean Sea. This part includes the largest city, Istanbul, which was once called Constantinople. The Asian part, which is sometimes called Anatolia or Asia Minor, includes the capital, Ankara.

Most of Turkey's people follow the religion of ISLAM. Much of the land is mountainous and large areas are covered by dry plateaus (tablelands). But the coastal plains are fertile and farming is the main industry. Turkey also produces chromium.

Turkey was once part of the Byzantine empire, which was the eastern part of the ROMAN EMPIRE.

TURKEY

Government: Republic
Capital: Ankara
Area: 780,576 sq km
Population: 55,687,000
Language: Turkish
Currency: Turkish lira

The Ottoman Empire of the Turks produced brave and well-led soldiers, but they had many cruel practices. It was, for example, the custom to kill all the sultan's brothers so that none of them should be able to take the throne. After 1610, the brothers were no longer killed. Instead they were shut up for all their lives in a building surrounded by a walled garden.

But after Constantinople fell in 1453, the Muslim Ottoman conquerors built up a huge empire. At its height, it stretched from southern Russia to Morocco, and from the Danube River to the Persian Gulf. But it slowly declined after 1600 and collapsed in World War I. After that war, Turkey's president, Kemal Atatürk (1881–1938) modernized the nation. Atatürk means 'Father of the Nation'.

Turtle and Terrapin

Some people give the name 'turtle' to all shelled REPTILES, including TORTOISES. But generally, the name is just used for those that live in water. The shells of turtles are similar to those of tortoises. These are both made of bony 'plates' which are covered by large horny scales. Small turtles that live in fresh water are called terrapins.

Marine, or sea, turtles spend most of their lives in warm seas. They swim great distances to find food, and many of them have webbed toes, or flipper-like legs to help them swim well. They eat water plants, such as seaweed, and some small sea animals. Turtles often swim under water, but they come up to the surface to gulp air into their lungs.

Turtles go ashore to lay their eggs. They usually bury their eggs in sand, or hide them among weeds. The baby turtles hatch out on their own. When they have hatched, they dig themselves out of their nest and head for the sea.

There are several kinds of marine turtle. The largest kind is called the leatherback turtle. It can weigh over 725 kg and be up to 1.8 metres long. The green turtle is used for turtle soup and its eggs are eaten in Asian countries. The hawksbill turtle almost became extinct.

▼ Snapping turtles are not very good swimmers. They usually walk over the bottom of the rivers and lakes where they live. They are found in central and eastern parts of the United States and in some parts of Central America.

Uganda

Uganda is a small republic in the middle of East AFRICA. It was ruled by Britain until 1962, when it became independent. General Idi Amin seized power in 1971. Many people were murdered under his dictatorship. But in 1979, Ugandan and Tanzanian soldiers took over Uganda and Amin fled.

Part of Africa's largest lake, Lake Victoria, lies in Uganda. Most of the people are farmers. The main crops are coffee, tea and cotton.

Ultraviolet Light

If LIGHT from the Sun shines through a prism it splits up into a rainbow of colours, called a SPECTRUM. Red is at one end of the spectrum and violet at the other. Ultraviolet light lies just beyond the violet end of the spectrum. We cannot see it, but it will blacken photographic film and make some chemicals glow. Most ultraviolet light from the Sun is lost in the atmosphere. But enough rays reach Earth to give us suntans. If more ultraviolet rays reached us, they would be very harmful.

UGANDA

Government: Military
Capital: Kampala
Area: 236,036 sq km
Population: 18,795,000
Languages: Luganda, Swahili, English
Currency: Ugandan shilling

◄ Ultraviolet (UV) light is useful to scientists. In this photograph, taken through a high powered microscope, antibodies used in cell research have been stained with a green dye which fluoresces (shines) when exposed to ultraviolet light to make them visible.

United Nations

Most of the world's countries belong to the United Nations. This is an association that works to keep peace and help people everywhere.

Each member country sends delegates to regular meetings of the United Nations' General Assembly in New York City. The General Assembly suggests how countries should behave. It cannot make them

▲ *The flag of the United Nations. It shows a map of the world surrounded by an olive wreath. The olive branch is a symbol of peace.*

take its advice. But the United Nations' Security Council can ask member countries for troops to help stop nations from fighting.

The United Nations works largely through 14 agencies. The Food and Agriculture Organization helps countries to grow more food. The World Health Organization fights disease. The International Monetary Fund lends countries money.

The United Nations has managed to prevent some wars and has helped millions of people.

SOME UNITED NATIONS AGENCIES	
FAO Food and Agriculture Organization	**UNCTAD** United Nations Conference on Trade and Development
IBRD International Bank for Reconstruction and Development (World Bank)	**UNESCO** United Nations Educational, Scientific and Cultural Organization
ICAO International Civil Aviation Organization	**UNICEF** United Nations Children's Emergency Fund
ICJ International Court of Justice	**UNIDO** United Nations Industrial Development Organization
IFC International Finance Corporation	
ILO International Labour Organization	**UNRWA** United Nations Relief and Works Agency
IMF International Monetary Fund	**WHO** World Health Organization

United States of America

UNITED STATES OF AMERICA

Government: Federal republic
Capital: Washington, D.C. (635,185)
Area: 9,363,123 sq km
Population: 249,975,000
Largest city (population): New York, 7,071,639
Highest point: Mount McKinley, Alaska, 6194 m
Agriculture: Nearly 50% of land in use
Chief crops: Soya beans, cotton, fruits, maize
Chief industries: Coal, oil, steel, textiles, tobacco
Language: English
Currency: US dollar

The United States of America is the world's fourth largest nation. Russia, Canada and China are bigger in area, and more people live in China, India and Russia. There are 50 states in the United States. Forty-eight are in the same part of NORTH AMERICA. The other two are Alaska in the north, and the Pacific islands of Hawaii.

The mainland United States stretches from the Pacific to the Atlantic. Long mountain ranges run down the Pacific coast. Inland are flat-topped mountains and basins. In this region is Death Valley, the lowest place in the Americas. Here, too, is the Grand Canyon, a huge gorge cut by the Colorado River. Farther east lie the tall peaks of the Rocky Mountains that run from Canada to Mexico. Beyond these stretch the Great Plains where the mighty MISSISSIPPI RIVER flows. Another mountain range, the Appalachians, runs down the eastern side of the United States.

The United States is a young country. In 1976 it was just 200 years old. The original 13 colonies declared their independence from Britain in 1776. George WASHINGTON was elected first president in 1789. By the mid 1800s the United States had grown to much the same size as it is today. Explorers had added new land to the original colonies, and the country stretched as far west as the Pacific. From 1861 to 1865 a civil war was fought between the South, which believed in SLAVERY, and the North, which wanted every man to be free. The northern states won and slavery was abolished. Between 1870 and 1900 thousands of Europeans came and settled in the United States. They were seeking land and a new life. By 1900 the country's population had doubled.

The 250 million citizens of the United States include Eskimos, Indians, and people whose ancestors came from Europe or Africa. Seventy in every 100 Americans live in cities. Washington, D.C. is the capital but NEW YORK is the largest city. Los Angeles and Chicago each have over three million inhabitants.

▲ *The bald eagle is a symbol of the United States.*

The United States is one of the world's richest countries. Its farms produce huge wheat crops, and more oranges, meat, eggs and cheese than any other country. American miners mine more coal, copper, lead and uranium.

Until recently the United States produced enough coal, oil and gas of its own to run its farms, factories and homes. But now it has to buy oil from abroad.

Universe

▲ *A husky waits patiently outside a trapper's hut in Alaska.*

The universe is made up of all the STARS, PLANETS, MOONS and other bodies scattered through the emptiness of space. The EARTH is just a tiny part of the SOLAR SYSTEM, in a great group of stars known as the MILKY WAY. Beyond our GALAXY lie possibly 10,000 million other galaxies. Some are so far away that the light from them takes thousands of millions of years to reach us.

Scientists think that all matter in the universe was once squashed together as a fireball that exploded, shooting matter out in all directions. As the matter spread it cooled, and clouds of gas and dust came together to form the stars, planets, moons and so on. This idea is called the BIG BANG THEORY.

▲ *The island of Maui is the second largest island in Hawaii.*

379

University

Some people who leave school at 18 go on to university. At school people are taught a little about several subjects. But at university a student often learns about just one or two subjects. He or she goes to talks called *lectures*, and smaller study groups known as *tutorials* or *seminars*. The student has to write essays and maybe carry out experiments in a laboratory. University students use libraries to find out much of what they need to know from books.

After three years or so students take their final examinations. If they pass they are given a degree, usually a Bachelor of Arts or a Bachelor of Science. If they continue their studies they can earn higher degrees.

Arab peoples had universities more than 1000 years ago. Europe's first university was founded in the 1000s at Bologna in Italy. Soon after, universities were founded at Paris in France, Salamanca in Spain and Oxford in England. Today most countries have universities.

Uranium

This metal is one of the heaviest of all known ELEMENTS. It was named after the planet Uranus. Uranium gives off RADIOACTIVITY. As it loses atomic particles it decays, and ends up, after millions of years, as LEAD. People working with uranium often need protective clothing to shield their bodies from radiation damage.

Uranium is the fuel used to make NUCLEAR ENERGY in atomic bombs and nuclear power stations. It is mined in many countries. Most of the western world's uranium comes from the United States and Canada.

Uranus

The PLANET Uranus is 19 times farther away from the Sun than the Earth is. We cannot see Uranus just with our eyes. It was the first planet discovered with the help of a TELESCOPE. It looks like a greenish-yellow disc.

Uranus is unlike our Earth in many ways. For one thing, it is much larger. You could fit 52 planets the

Uranium was discovered in 1789 by the German chemist Martin Heinrich Klaproth. He named it after the planet Uranus.

One tonne of uranium can produce as much energy as 30,000 tonnes of coal.

URANUS FACTS

Average distance from Sun: 2800 million km
Nearest distance from Earth: 2650 million km
Average temperature (clouds): −220 degrees C
Diameter across equator: 52,000 km
Atmosphere: Hydrogen, helium
Number of moons: 15 known
Length of day: 16 hours
Length of year: 84 Earth years

Earth

Uranus

◀ *The American space probe, Voyager 2, passed Uranus in June 1986. The pictures it sent back showed that the planet has rings, and is tilted on its axis. This tilt is shown by the red lines.*

When William Herschel discovered Uranus in 1781 he named it Georgium Sidus (Star of George) in honour of King George III. This name was never popular in other countries, and the present name, that of one of the Greek gods, was chosen by the German astronomer J. E. Bode.

size of the Earth inside Uranus. The distance through the middle of Uranus is nearly four times the distance through the middle of the Earth.

Unlike our planet, Uranus is mainly made up of gases. Its whole surface is far colder than the coldest place on Earth.

Uranus spins at a speed that makes one of its days about the length of 16 Earth hours. But Uranus takes so long to ORBIT the Sun that one of its years lasts 84 of ours.

In 1986, *Voyager 2* flew close to Uranus and took pictures that told scientists a great deal about the planet. It has at least 15 moons, one of which – Miranda – has mountains 26 km high.

Uruguay

Uruguay is one of the smallest countries in SOUTH AMERICA. It lies in the south-east, between the Atlantic Ocean and its two big neighbours, Argentina and Brazil. Uruguay was formerly a province of Brazil. It became independent in 1825.

Low, grassy hills and lowlands cover most of Uruguay. Many rivers flow into the big Uruguay River or into the river mouth called the River Plate. Uruguay has mild winters and warm summers.

Most of Uruguay's inhabitants are descended from Spanish or Italian settlers. More than one in three of them live in the capital, Montevideo.

URUGUAY

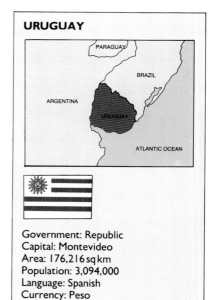

Government: Republic
Capital: Montevideo
Area: 176,216 sq km
Population: 3,094,000
Language: Spanish
Currency: Peso

Many people are vegetarians – they do not eat the flesh of animals, including red meat, poultry and fish. The vegetarian diet consists mostly of vegetables, cereals, nuts, seeds and fruits. Soya beans are a popular source of protein. People who eat a well-balanced vegetarian diet generally have lower blood pressure and less excess fat than those who eat meat. Vegetarians must take care, however, to consume enough proteins and vitamins.

Vacuum

A vacuum is a space with nothing in it. It gets its name from *vacuus*, the Latin word for 'empty'. In fact there are no complete vacuums. When you try to empty a container by pumping out the air, a small amount of air always stays behind. This partly empty space is called a partial vacuum. New air always rushes in to fill the space. This is how your LUNGS work. When you breathe out, you make a partial vacuum in your lungs. Air rushes to fill the space, making you breathe in.

You can see partial vacuums at work in many ways. The space does not always fill up with air. When you suck air from a straw dipped in lemonade, it is the lemonade that rushes to fill the vacuum and so reaches your mouth. It is a partial vacuum that helps to keep aircraft in the air. As an aeroplane flies along, its wings are so shaped that they make a partial vacuum just above them. Air underneath the wings pushes them up to fill the space.

Vegetable

Vegetables are plants with parts that we can eat. They taste less sweet than the plant foods we call FRUIT. Vegetables such as lettuce and spinach are eaten for their leaves. Other vegetables are eaten for their roots or stems. Carrots and parsnips are roots. Celery and asparagus are stems. Peas, beans, and sweet corn are seeds. Tomatoes and squash are fruits.

Peas and beans supply body-building PROTEINS. Leafy and root vegetables provide VITAMINS, minerals and fibres to help keep our DIGESTION working properly. Potatoes contain *starches*, which the body can burn up to make energy.

▲ De-oxygenated blood flows back to the heart through the veins. Blood flowing in the right direction (left) forces valves in the vein open. Blood flowing the wrong way (right) forces the valves shut. The valves make sure that blood always flows towards the heart.

Vein

Veins are narrow tubes that carry used BLOOD from all parts of your body back to the HEART. Blood flowing through the arteries is pushed along by the pumping of the heart. Blood in the veins has nothing to push it along. So many veins have flaps, or *valves*, inside them which close the tube if the blood begins to flow backwards.

Venezuela

Venezuela is a large country on the north coast of SOUTH AMERICA. Most of southern Venezuela is covered by flat-topped mountains. Here stand the Angel Falls, the highest waterfall in the world. A grassy plain stretches across the middle of the country on either side of the Orinoco river.

Venezuela grows coffee, cotton and cocoa. But its minerals, especially oil, make it the richest country in the continent.

Venus (planet)

The PLANET Venus is named after the Roman goddess of beauty and love. Venus is the brightest planet in the SOLAR SYSTEM. We see it as the morning star or the evening star, depending on where it is on its journey around the Sun. If you look at Venus through binoculars, you may see it looking like a small Moon, showing just the part that is lit by the Sun.

Venus takes only 225 days to go around the Sun. So more than three years pass on Venus for every two on Earth. But Venus itself spins so slowly that one day on Venus lasts for 117 days on Earth. It is the only planet to spin in the opposite way to the direction of its orbit.

Venus is about the same size as Earth, but weighs a little less. It is also much hotter, because it is much closer to the Sun. The surface of Venus is hidden under a dazzling white cloak of cloud. This may be made up of tiny drops of sulphuric acid.

▼ From the Earth, we have an almost edge-on view of the orbit of Venus. As it travels around the Sun, we see different amounts of its sunlit surface. These are known as its 'phases'.

VENEZUELA

Government: Federal republic
Capital: Caracas
Area: 912,050 sq km
Population: 19,735,000
Languages: Spanish, Indian
Currency: Bolívar

VENUS FACTS

Average distance from Sun: 108 million km
Nearest distance from Earth: 40 million km
Average temperature: 455 degrees C
Diameter across equator: 12,103 km
Atmosphere: Mainly carbon dioxide
Number of moons: 0
Length of day: 117 Earth days
Length of year: 225 Earth days

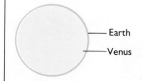

— Earth
—Venus

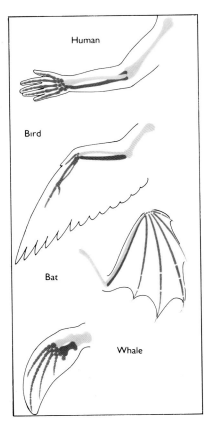

▲ *The forelimbs of these vertebrates show that the animals may have evolved from the same ancestor.*

Vertebrate

Vertebrates are animals with a backbone or spine. The backbone is made up of short bones called *vertebrae*. This name comes from a Latin word that means 'to turn'. Most vertebrates can bend and straighten their backbones by turning their vertebrae slightly.

Many things make vertebrates different from other animals. Most have a bony case to protect their BRAIN, ribs to protect their HEART, LUNGS and other delicate parts, and one or two pairs of limbs. And most vertebrates have a SKELETON made of BONE.

There are seven main groups of vertebrates. The simplest group includes the lampreys. Lampreys are eel-like fish with no jaw. They have a spine but no skeleton. Next come SHARKS and skates, which have a skeleton of cartilage. All other vertebrates have bones. They are the bony FISH, AMPHIBIANS, REPTILES, BIRDS and MAMMALS.

Victoria, Queen

Queen Victoria (1819–1901) ruled Great Britain for 64 years, longer than any other British monarch. During her reign, the nation grew richer and its empire larger than ever before. She was the queen of many countries, including Australia, New Zealand, Canada and South Africa, and she was the empress of India.

Victoria was the daughter of Edward, Duke of Kent. GEORGE III was her grandfather. She was just 18 when she inherited the throne from her uncle, William IV. Two years later she married her German cousin, Prince Albert. They had four sons and five daughters. Prince Albert died of typhoid fever in 1861. His death left the Queen deeply unhappy. For many years she wore only black clothes to show her grief. She also stopped going to public ceremonies.

Victoria was very popular with her people. In 1887, she had been queen for 50 years. All over the British Empire there were huge parades and parties to celebrate this Golden Jubilee. In 1897, there were more celebrations for her Diamond Jubilee. Her reign is known as the Victorian age.

▲ *A portrait of Queen Victoria.*

Video

A video is a recording of moving pictures and sound. It is usually made on a videotape, but there are also videodiscs, which are like large versions of compact discs.

You play a videotape in a video recorder that is connected to a television set. You see the video on the television screen. A video recorder can record television programmes on tape. Old programmes can be erased and new ones recorded on the same tape. You can also make your own videos if you have a videocamera. Electric signals from the camera or from a television programme are recorded on magnetic tape. The main difference from a music cassette recorder is that the record and replay heads in a video recorder spin round as the tape passes. This allows the head to move over the surface of the tape at high speed, giving the high recording speed needed to record picture signals.

Most of the programmes you see on television are video recordings.

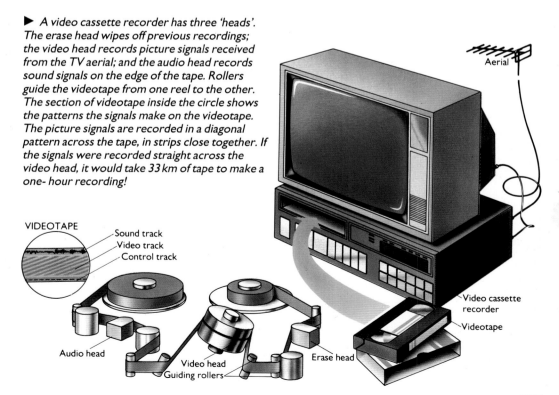

▶ A video cassette recorder has three 'heads'. The erase head wipes off previous recordings; the video head records picture signals received from the TV aerial; and the audio head records sound signals on the edge of the tape. Rollers guide the videotape from one reel to the other. The section of videotape inside the circle shows the patterns the signals make on the videotape. The picture signals are recorded in a diagonal pattern across the tape, in strips close together. If the signals were recorded straight across the video head, it would take 33 km of tape to make a one- hour recording!

VIDEOTAPE
Sound track
Video track
Control track

Aerial

Video cassette recorder

Videotape

Audio head

Video head
Guiding rollers

Erase head

VIETNAM

Government: Communist
Capital: Hanoi
Area: 329,556 sq km
Population: 66,710,000
Languages: Vietnamese, French, English
Currency: Dong

Vietnam

Vietnam is a country in SOUTH-EAST ASIA. It is a little smaller than England and only 55 km wide in some parts. Vietnam is a hot, damp country.

Vietnam was once ruled by France as part of Indochina. After World War II, it was divided into two countries, North Vietnam and South Vietnam. Hanoi was the main city in the north and Saigon (now called Ho Chi Minh City) the capital of the south. From the 1950s until 1975, the two countries were at war. South Vietnam was supported by the United States. North Vietnam was communist. Now the whole country is communist.

The Vikings

The age of the Vikings lasted from about AD 800 to AD 1100. The Vikings came from Scandinavia (Norway, Denmark and Sweden). They were originally farmers, but to find new lands to settle they crossed the seas in swift sailing ships with carved dragon prows.

The Vikings earned a reputation for being blood-thirsty warriors, and were feared throughout western Europe. Vikings raided the coasts of England from the year 789 and eventually controlled the eastern part of the country.

However, the Vikings were not only raiders and pirates. They were superb seamen, braving the Atlantic Ocean to explore Greenland and even North America.

YGGDRASIL'S ASH TREE

The Vikings had a myth about a huge world tree called Yggdrasil's Ash. Its branches held up the sky. Beneath the tree was Asgarth, the home of the gods. Long roots spread out from the base of the trunk. One covered Midgarth, the world of men. Another root covered the realm of the terrible Frost Giants. A third root covered Hel, the world of the dead. Also among the roots were two wells. A drink of water from the well of the wise god Mimir gave knowledge. Beside the other well, the Well of Fate, lived the three Norns. They were called Past, Present and Future. They wove a cloth. Every thread represented the life of a person. When they cut a thread, that person died.

▶ *The Oseberg ship is a Viking ship dug up on a farm in Norway in 1904.*

VIKING HISTORY		
AD	789	First Viking attacks on England
	800	Beginning of the Viking Age
	830s	Vikings found the city of Dublin
	850	Swedes begin to settle in East Baltic and Russia
	860	Discovery of Iceland
		Harald Fairhair becomes the first king of all Norway, and many Norwegians settle in Britain
	874	First settlers in Iceland
	876	Norwegian Healfdene rules Northumbria
	886	King Alfred defeats Guthrum
		Danes allowed to settle in the Danelaw in eastern England
	911	Scandinavians settle in Normandy
	930	The first meeting of the Althing, the national assembly in Iceland
	982	Eric the Red discovers Greenland
	986	Coast of North America sighted by Bjarni Herjolfsson
	1000	Iceland becomes a Christian land
	1003	Leif Ericsson lands in North America
	1030	King Olaf of Norway killed at Battle of Stiklastad.
	1047	Harald Hardrada becomes king of Norway
	1066	Harald Hardrada killed at Battle of Stamford Bridge in England, by King Harold of England. Duke William of Normandy defeats Harold to become king of England
	1100	End of Viking Age

▲ The head of a Viking warrior (bottom right) is carved from a piece of elk horn and forms the handle of a stick. The god Thor is often shown in Viking art. This silver amulet (top right) is made in the shape of the god's hammer, decorated with a face with large, staring eyes. The Viking spear is richly decorated with engraving.

They traded as far to the east as Russia and Constantinople. They had their own laws and a parliament. They were also skilled artists.

Virus

Viruses are very small living things that cause diseases in plants and animals. They are smaller than BACTERIA and can be seen only with a very powerful electron MICROSCOPE.

You can be infected with viruses by swallowing them or breathing them in. Some insects carry viruses, which they pass on when they bite you. Once inside the body, a virus travels around in the bloodstream. It gets inside a living CELL where it produces more viruses. Sometimes the cell is entirely destroyed by the viruses.

Diseases caused by viruses include measles, chicken pox, mumps, AIDS, influenza, and colds. Viruses are very hard to kill. INOCULATION helps to prevent some of these diseases.

When a virus enters the body, the blood produces substances called *antibodies*. After a while there are usually enough antibodies to kill all the viruses and the patient recovers.

MINERAL SALTS

Calcium and **phosphorus** are found in milk and cheese. They help to build healthy bones and teeth.

Iron, found in meat, liver and spinach, is needed by the red blood cells.

Sodium and **potassium** are needed by the nerves, in body fluids and in nearly all cells. We can get sodium from sodium chloride – table salt.

Iodine is found in fish. It is needed for growth and helps the thyroid gland function properly.

Fluoride helps to prevent tooth decay.

Copper, cobalt and **manganese** are also required in very small quantities.

All these minerals are contained in a normal balanced diet.

SOURCES AND USES OF VITAMINS

Vitamin	Found in	Needed for
A	Milk, butter, eggs, green vegetables, fish oil, liver, carrots	Fighting disease and seeing in the dark
B₁ (thiamine)	Yeast and wheatgerm (whole wheat bread)	All 'B' vitamins needed for healthy appetite, energy production and healthy nerves and skin
B₂ 9 other 'B' vitamins	Yeast Milk, meat and green vegetables	
C	Oranges, lemons, tomatoes and fresh vegetables	Healthy blood and gums, healing, protection against colds
D	Cod-liver oil, cream, egg yolks (and with sunlight, fat below the skin forms vit. D)	Strong bones and teeth
E	Whole wheat bread, brown rice and butter	Not fully understood
K	Green vegetables, liver	Clotting blood

Vitamins and Minerals

Vitamins are chemicals that our bodies need to stay healthy. They are found in different kinds of food. Scientists call the six kinds of vitamins A, B, C, D, E and K. Vitamin B is really a group of vitamins.

The first people to realize that certain kinds of food were important to health were sailors. On long voyages they got a disease called *scurvy* if they could not eat fresh fruit and vegetables. These contain vitamin C. From the 1700s, English sailors were given limes to eat to prevent scurvy. This is why they were nicknamed 'limeys' by the Americans.

No one food has all the vitamins we need. That is why it is important to eat a mixture of things. Some people take their vitamins in pills. No one really needs pills if they eat well. Very old people, young babies and women expecting babies all need more vitamins than usual. But too much of some kinds of vitamins, such as vitamin A, can be bad for you.

We also need minerals in small amounts. Calcium is an important part of BONES and TEETH. We get it from milk and cheese. Iron is needed for haemoglobin, the part of red blood cells that carries oxygen from your lungs to tissues. Other minerals needed are iodine, phosphorus, sodium, and potassium. We get sodium from sodium chloride – table salt.

Four vitamins – A, D, E and K – can be stored in the body's fat. These vitamins, therefore, do not have to be consumed every day. The other vitamins – the B vitamins and vitamin C – cannot be stored in the body in this way, so we should have some of them every day.

Volcano

A volcano is an opening in the surface of the Earth. Burning gas, boiling rocks and ash escape from this opening. Sometimes they trickle out, sometimes they explode. An explosion is called an *eruption*.

Some volcanoes are gently sloping mountains with cracks, or fissures, in them. Hot liquid rock called *lava* flows out through the fissures. Other volcanoes are steep-sided mountains with a large hole at the top. These are called cone volcanoes. They are the kind that explode.

Erupting volcanoes can do a lot of damage. The city of POMPEII was destroyed by Vesuvius in AD 79. In 1883 Krakatoa, a volcano in Indonesia, erupted, causing a tidal wave that killed 36,000 people. Volcanoes can also make new land. An island called Surtsey, south of Iceland, was made by a volcano erupting under the sea in 1963.

If you look at where volcanoes are found around the world, they make a pattern of long chains. These chains mark the edges of the huge 'plates' that form the Earth's surface. They are the weakest part of the Earth's crust. One chain, called 'the ring of fire', goes right round the Pacific Ocean. Earthquakes, geysers and hot springs are all found in the same area as volcanoes.

▼ A simple section through a volcanic region. Magma from the underground chamber (1) rises up the central vent (2) or side vent (3). During eruptions, ash (4) may shoot into the air and lava (5) flows out of the vent.

Volume

The volume of an object is the amount of space it takes up. You can find out the volume of a rectangular solid by measuring its height, width and depth and multiplying the figures together. So a block with equal sides, each 10cm long, has a volume of 1000 cubic cm (1000cc): that is, 10cm × 10cm × 10cm.

It is easy to find out the volume of boxes or bricks or anything with straight edges. Measuring the volume of something with an irregular shape is more difficult. A very simple method was discovered by ARCHIMEDES, the Greek scientist. A story told about him says that he was getting into his bath, which was full to the brim, and water spilled over the side. He suddenly realized that the volume of water that had spilled over must be exactly the same as the volume of his body. This means that any irregular object can be measured by plunging it into water and measuring the rise in the water level.

Vulture

Vultures are large birds of prey. They live in the hot, dry parts of the world. The largest land bird in North America is a type of vulture. This is the California condor. When its wings are spread out, they measure up to 3 metres from tip to tip.

Vultures do not hunt for their food. They live on carrion, the rotting bodies of dead animals. Sometimes vultures have to wait for their dinner until a large hunter such as a lion has made a kill. When the lion has eaten its fill, wild dogs and hyenas gorge on the remains. Then it is the vulture's turn.

Most vultures have bald heads and necks. This stops their feathers getting messy when they plunge their heads into large carcases. They have very good eyesight and can spot dead or dying animals from far away. They also have a keen sense of smell. Some vultures use tools, for example, the lammergeyer drops bones onto rocks to break them open so it can eat the marrow inside.

Griffon vulture

Egyptian vulture

◄ *These vultures are usually found around mountains. The Egyptian vulture will drop stones onto eggs to break them open so it can eat the insides.*

Wales

Wales is part of the United Kingdom of Great Britain and Northern Ireland. It lies to the west of England and is a country of low mountains and green valleys. The highest mountain is Snowdon and Cardiff is the capital city.

The Welsh are descended from the Celts. English is their main language today, but about a quarter of the people still speak Welsh. Many Welsh people are striving passionately to keep their language alive.

South Wales is a traditional coal-mining region but there are now few mines left. Most of the people live in industrial towns like Swansea and Cardiff. Steel is another important industry. In the mountains of north and mid-Wales many people are sheep farmers. Wool is one of Wales' main exports.

WALES

Area: 20,761 sq km
Population: 2,857,000
Capital: Cardiff
Languages: Welsh, English
Highest point: Snowdon, 1085 m
  above sea level
Chief products: Coal, steel, wool,
  paper, textiles
Agricultural products: Barley, hay,
  oats, potatoes, turnips

Walrus

The walrus belongs to the SEAL family. Its enormous canine teeth look like two tusks. These tusks can be up to a metre long. The walrus uses them to scrape up the clams and shellfish it eats. It also uses its tusks to fight, and even polar bears keep away from fully grown walruses.

The Atlantic and the Pacific walrus both live in the cold ARCTIC. They are big animals. The male Atlantic walrus measures up to 4 metres and weighs as much as 1800 kg.

In the 1930s walruses almost disappeared through being hunted for their tusks and skins. Now there are laws against hunting them and their numbers are slowly increasing.

The title 'Prince of Wales' is given only to the eldest son of an English sovereign. Prince Charles is the 21st Prince of Wales. The first was Edward, son of Edward I, who was given the title in 1301.

◀ The walrus swims in shallow Arctic seas. It has flippers but no tail. Clumsy on land, the walrus can swim at speeds of about 24 km/h.

▲ *George Washington began his career as a surveyor and mapmaker.*

Washington, George

George Washington (1732–1799) was the first PRESI-DENT of the United States of America. He commanded the victorious colonial troops in the Revolutionary War against the British. One of his officers said this about him in a speech to Congress: 'He was first in war, first in peace, and first in the hearts of his countrymen.'

George Washington was born on a farm in Westmoreland County, Virginia. In 1752, he inherited an estate called Mount Vernon. In 1760, just married, he went to live there. For a while he farmed his land. Then, in 1775, the Revolutionary War broke out. Washington was chosen to be commander-in-chief of the American troops. Despite many problems, the American colonies won their independence from Britain.

He tried to return to farming, but in 1787 he was asked to help in drawing up the Constitution. In the first election, he became president. Altogether, he held office from 1789–1797. When he finally withdrew from public life, Washington retired to his beloved Mount Vernon, where he died two years later.

▼ *The chemical formula for water is H_2O. This means that each molecule of water is made up of two atoms of hydrogen and one atom of oxygen. By using two electrodes to pass electricity through water (shown above), it can be separated into hydrogen and oxygen gas. This process is known as electrolysis.*

Water

Water is the most common substance on Earth. Seven-tenths of the world's surface is covered by water. Water is also the most important substance on Earth. Without it life would be impossible. Life first started in water, and the bodies of all living things are mostly water. Water helps to remove body wastes in the form of the waste liquid, urine. Water is also the main component of blood.

There is no such thing as 'pure water'. Water contains MINERALS, which it has picked up from the surrounding earth and rocks. Water is made of the ELEMENTS hydrogen and oxygen.

Water exists in three forms. At 0°C it freezes into solid ice. At 100°C it boils into steam. Normal air takes up water easily, and CLOUDS are huge collections of water particles. At any time, clouds contain millions of tonnes of water, which falls back to Earth as RAIN. Some of this water stays in the soil or underground for years, but most of it returns to the oceans.

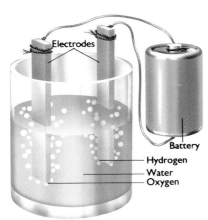

Electrodes

Battery
Hydrogen
Water
Oxygen

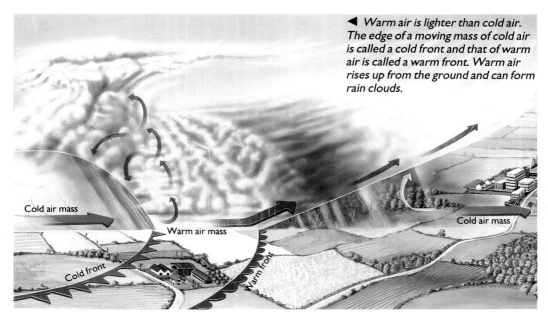

◀ Warm air is lighter than cold air. The edge of a moving mass of cold air is called a cold front and that of warm air is called a warm front. Warm air rises up from the ground and can form rain clouds.

Cold air mass

Warm air mass

Cold front

Warm front

Cold air mass

Weather

The weather – sunshine, fog, RAIN, CLOUDS, WIND, heat, cold – is always changing in most parts of the world. These changes are caused by what happens in the atmosphere, the layer of air above the Earth.

The atmosphere is always moving, driven by the Sun's heat. Near the EQUATOR the Sun's strong rays heat the air. At the North and South poles the Sun's rays are weaker and the air is colder. This uneven heating means the atmosphere is never still. Huge masses of warm and cold air flow round and round between the tropics and the polar regions. As these wandering air masses meet, rise and fall, heat and cool, they cause weather.

When cold and warm masses meet, the air whirls inward in a giant spiral called a *depression*. Depressions bring clouds, wind, rain and summer thunderstorms. They can also cause violent tornadoes and HURRICANES.

The meeting line between two air masses is called a *front*. When cold air pushes up behind warm air, it forms a *cold front*; when a warm air mass catches up with a cold mass, it creates a *warm front*. An *occluded front* is formed when a cold front overtakes a warm front. Weathermen expect rain and snow ahead of a warm front. Showers usually form along a cold front.

▼ Anemometers measure wind speeds; vanes show direction. The psychrometer, a kind of hygrometer, measures humidity. Thermometers record air temperatures and barographs record changing air pressure.

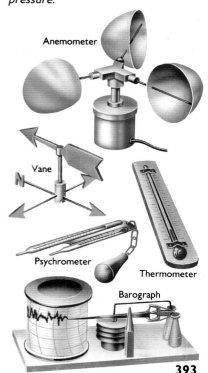

Anemometer

Vane

Psychrometer

Thermometer

Barograph

One man can easily operate 20 of today's fully automatic looms. If a thread breaks, the power is cut off automatically and the machine stops. Some machines use compressed air to blow the weft through the warp.

Weaving

Curtains and sheets, shirts and carpets, towels and suits are just some of the many useful articles made by weaving. In weaving, threads are joined together in a criss-cross pattern to make cloth.

People have been weaving cloth to make clothes since the STONE AGE. The oldest fabric we know of was woven nearly 8000 years ago in what is now Turkey. These first weavers learned to make linen from *flax*. By 2000 BC the Chinese were weaving cloth from SILK. In India, people learned to use fibres from the COTTON plant. Meanwhile *nomads* (travellers) from the deserts and mountains of Asia discovered how to weave WOOL.

For thousands of years, making cloth was slow work. First, the fibres were drawn out and twisted into a long thread. This process is known as spinning. Then, rows of threads were stretched lengthwise, side by side, on a frame called a *loom*. These threads made up the *warp*. A crosswise thread, the *weft*, was then passed through from one side of the loom to the other, going over and under the warp threads. A *shuttle*, like a large needle, was used to feed the weft through the warp.

Spinning wheels and looms were worked by hand until the 1700s. Then, machines were invented for spinning and weaving. These machines worked far faster than hand looms, and cloth became cheap and plentiful. Today most woven fabrics are made by machine. However, special silks and woollen materials are still woven by hand.

▼ Cloth is made by weaving two different types of thread together on a loom. During weaving, the heddle creates a gap by raising and lowering different warp threads. Then the shuttle moves the weft thread through the gaps, going over some of the warp threads and under others, to make the cloth.

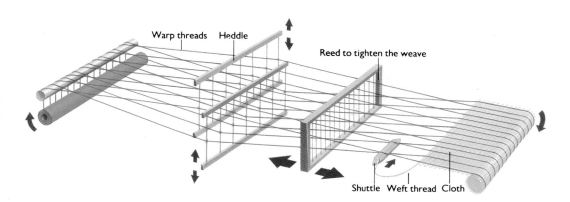

Warp threads   Heddle

Reed to tighten the weave

Shuttle   Weft thread   Cloth

Weights and Measures

Weights and measures are used to work out the size of things. The two main kinds of measurement are weight and length. 'How many?', 'How far?' 'How big?' are all questions to do with weights and measures. People first needed units of measurement when they began to build towns and to trade goods. The ancient Egyptians, for example, based their measurements on the proportions of the body. Our word 'mile' comes from the Roman *mille* which meant '1000 paces'.

Most countries now use the metric system for measuring lengths, distances and so on. The metric system is a decimal system (based on 10) and was first used in France in the late 1700s. Another system was used for a long time in Britain and is still used in the United States. It is known as the imperial system. The table below gives some common units of measurement in both systems, and some useful conversion factors.

WEIGHTS AND MEASURES

Length
Metric units
millimetre (mm)
10 mm = 1 centimetre (cm)
100 cm = 1 metre (m)
1000 m = 1 kilometre (km)

Imperial units
inch (in)
12 in = 1 foot (ft)
3 ft = 1 yard (yd)
1760 yd = 1 mile = 5280 ft

Area
Metric units
square millimetre (mm²)
100 mm² = 1 square centimetre (cm²)
10,000 cm² = 1 square metre (m²)
100 m² = 1 are (a) = 1 square decametre
100 a = 1 hectare (ha)
100 ha = 1 square kilometre (km²)

Imperial units
square inch (in²)
144 in² = 1 square foot (ft²)
9 ft² = 1 square yard (yd²)
4840 yd² = 1 acre
640 acres = 1 square mile (mile²)

Volume
Metric units
cubic millimetre (mm³)
1000 mm³ = 1 cubic centimetre (cm³)
1000 cm³ = 1 cubic decimetre (dm³) = 1 litre
1000 dm³ = 1 cubic metre (m³)

Imperial units
cubic inch (in³)
1728 in³ = 1 cubic foot (ft³)
27 ft³ = 1 cubic yard (yd³)

Capacity
Metric units
millilitre (ml)
1000 ml = 1 litre (l)
100 l = 1 hectolitre (hl)

Imperial units
gill
4 gills = 1 pint
2 pints = 1 quart
4 quarts = 1 gallon = 277.274 in³
Apothecaries' fluid
minim (min)
60 min = fluid drachm (fl dr)
8 fl dr = 1 fluid ounce (fl oz)
5 fl oz = 1 gill
20 fl oz = 1 pint

US units
1 US gallon (liquid) = 0.8327 gallon (imp)
1 US gallon (dry) = 0.9689 gallon (imp)
1 fluid oz (US) = 1.0408 fl oz (apoth)
16 fl oz (US) = 1 US pint

Weight
Metric units
milligram (mg)
1000 mg = 1 gram (g)
1000 g = 1 kilogram (kg)
100 kg = 1 quintal (q)
1000 kg = 1 metric ton, or tonne (t)

Imperial units (Avoirdupois)
ounce (oz)
16 oz = 1 lb
14 lb = 1 stone
112 lb = 1 hundredweight (cwt)
20 cwt = 1 (long) ton = 2240 lb
2000 lb = 1 short ton (US)

Nautical Measurement
1 fathom = 6 ft
1 nautical mile (international) = 1.151 statute mile (= 1852 metres)
60 nautical miles = 1 degree
1 knot = 1 nautical mile per hour

▶ *During the 1700s, pirates working from bases in the West Indies attacked many Spanish ships sailing through the Caribbean Sea. These ships often carried treasures collected from Spanish colonies in Central and South America.*

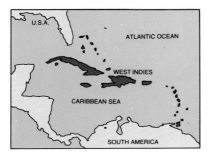

When Columbus discovered the West Indies he claimed all the islands for Spain. But, as Spanish power weakened in the 1600s, pirates of many countries began to sail the Caribbean. The English government employed the fierce buccaneer Henry Morgan to attack the Spaniards, and in 1674 he was knighted for his services.

The blubber under the skin of large whales can be up to half a metre thick. For hundreds of years, whales have been killed for this blubber. Oil was taken from it and used to make soap and margarine.

West Indies

This chain of tropical islands stretches from Florida in the United States to Venezuela in South America. On one side lies the Caribbean Sea, on the other stretches the Atlantic Ocean. The islands are really the tops of a drowned range of mountains. Palm trees and tropical grasses grow here, where it is almost always warm. But fierce autumn hurricanes often destroy trees and houses.

The thousands of islands are divided into more than 20 countries. CUBA, JAMAICA, Haiti, and the Dominican Republic are among the largest.

Whale

Whales are big sea MAMMALS well built for living in the water. A thick layer of fat called blubber keeps out the cold. A whale's body is shaped for easy swimming. Its front limbs are shaped as flippers. It also has a broad tail flattened from top to bottom, not from side to side like a fish tail.

Unlike fishes, whales must swim to the surface to breathe. Before breathing in, they blow out stale air through a *blowhole*, or two slits on top of the head. Baby whales are born in water. As soon as they are born they swim up to take a breath.

There are two groups of whales. Toothed whales like the DOLPHIN mostly catch fish. But killer whales are toothed whales that attack seals, penguins and other whales.

Baleen whales are the other main group of whales. Baleen whales include the gigantic blue whale, the largest animal on Earth.

Wheel

Wheels are one of man's most useful inventions. This is because a wheel turning on an axle is a very good way to move loads. It is easier to move a heavy load with wheels than it is to lift the load or drag it on the ground.

STONE AGE people may have learned to roll loads along on logs. But Bronze Age people first invented the wheel about 5000 years ago. The oldest known wheels looked like slices cut across a log. But each solid disc was made of three parts.

At first, the wheels were fixed on the axle, and it was the axle that turned in holes in the cart frame. Later, the axle was fixed and the wheels revolved on its ends.

Then people learned that a wheel with spokes was just as strong as a solid wheel, but much lighter. Today the wheels of cars and planes have hollow rubber tyres filled with air to make them springy.

Ball bearings keep wheel hubs turning easily on their axles. Wheels with notched edges turn one another in the gears that help to work all kinds of machinery.

William the Conqueror

William the Conqueror (1027–1087) was William I of England, and England's first Norman king. Before that he was Duke of Normandy in northern France, the most powerful lord in that land. (Normandy was named after the Normans or Northmen, also called VIKINGS.)

When William visited England in 1050, his relative EDWARD the Confessor may have promised him the throne of England. In 1064 William forced Edward's brother-in-law Harold to agree to help to make William king. But when Edward died in 1066, Harold had himself crowned king of England.

William quickly set about invading England to seize it for himself. His Norman army sailed across the English Channel in open boats. There were about 7000 troops, including knights who brought

▼ Sumerians made solid wheels from tree trunks about 5000 years ago.

▲ People started using wheels to make pottery around 3250 BC.

▼ During the Middle Ages, water-mill wheels were used to drive simple machines.

► This is a modern motorcycle wheel. It is made of metal and has an air-filled rubber tyre.

their war horses. William defeated Harold's ANGLO-SAXON army at the Battle of HASTINGS, fought in Sussex near where the town of Battle stands today.

William spent three years winning all England. He built many castles, from which his knights rode out to crush their Anglo-Saxon enemies.

By 1069 the Normans had conquered a third of England, and William had become the most powerful king in western Europe. He claimed all the land in England as his, but he lent some to his Norman nobles. In return, the nobles supplied soldiers for William's army. William's descendants ruled England for many years.

When William the Conqueror conquered England in 1066, he and his nobles brought over their own language – Norman French. For many years the words that the common people used were still old English, while the words of the wealthy and ruling classes were largely French. The common people tended 'sheep'. When the sheep was cooked and put on the ruling class table it became the French 'mutton'. In the same way, old English 'cow' became the French 'beef', 'hog' became 'pork' and so on. Modern English contains these and many other words that came from Norman French.

Wind

Wind is moving air. Slow winds are gentle breezes. Fast winds are gales. You can see the speed of the wind by its effect on trees and buildings.

Wind blows because some air masses become warmer than others. In warm air, the tiny particles of air spread out. So a mass of warm air is lighter than a mass of cold air that fills the same amount of space. Because warm air is light it rises. As warm air rises, cool air flows in to take its place. This causes the steady trade winds that blow over tropical oceans. CLIMATE and WEATHER largely depend on the wind.

A scale of wind speeds was worked out in 1805 by Admiral Sir Francis Beaufort. It is called the Beaufort Scale. In it the force of the wind is shown by numbers from 0 to 12. The number 0 shows that there is a calm in which smoke rises straight up. At 1 smoke drifts slowly. By the time we get to 4 we have a breeze in which small branches are moving and flags flap. At force 7 whole trees are moving and it is difficult to walk against the wind. Force 12 is something few of us will ever see. It is a full hurricane, with terrible damage to ships at sea and houses on land.

Wind power describes the way in which the ENERGY of the wind can be used to make electricity. A windmill uses wind power. For many years in the NETHERLANDS, people have used windmills to grind corn or pump water. They were used in Asia as early as the AD 600s. Nowadays, people are trying to make better windmills as a way of generating electricity.

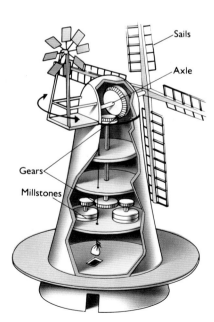

Sails

Axle

Gears

Millstones

▲ This traditional windmill was used to grind corn. As the wind blew, the axle turned the millstones that ground the corn.

Wolf

These CARNIVORES include the red wolf of South America, and the grey wolf of the world's northern forests. Grey wolves have thick fur, long legs, and powerful jaws. A pack of wolves can chase and kill a sick or injured deer much larger than themselves. When grey wolves are hunting, they howl to signal to each other where they are. Each spring a she-wolf has four to six pups.

Throughout history there have been stories of wolves raising human children from infancy. The most famous story is that of Romulus and Remus, the twin brothers who founded Rome. More recently, there is a story from India of a child raised by a wolf until she was about nine years old.

Women's Rights

'Women's rights' means the right of women to be full citizens, equal to men in every way. Until this century, women did not have these rights. In some countries today they still have very few rights.

At the beginning of the 20th century, women did not have a vote, so they were powerless to get changes through parliament. In 1903, Mrs Emmeline Pankhurst and her daughter Christabel started the Women's Social and Political Union, fighting for women's right to vote. These suffragettes addressed crowds, chained themselves to railings, broke windows and set fire to pillar boxes. Again and again they were put in prison, but they kept on protesting. It was not until 1928 that the voting law for women became the same as that for men in Britain.

▲ Emmeline Pankhurst fought for the British woman's right to vote. She died in 1928, the year that women finally won equal voting rights.

Wood

Wood is one of the most valuable materials that people use. It can be sawn, carved and worked.

Thick timber is used for buildings and boats, while roughly cut logs and boughs are used as fuel for fires. Planks are made into furniture, barrels and boxes. Seasoned pieces can be shaped into musical instruments and delicate ornaments.

The wood we use is the tough inner material of trees and shrubs. It is protected by a thin layer of bark. It is very strong, and can support many times its own weight. The wood of a TREE is made up of thick fibres that give it strength.

Softwood, from pines and firs, is used mostly as pulp to make paper. Some is used for building. Hardwood is used to make furniture.

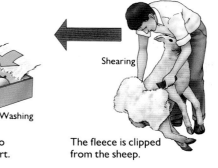

Squeezing

Shearing

Washing

The wool is washed to remove grease and dirt.

The fleece is clipped from the sheep.

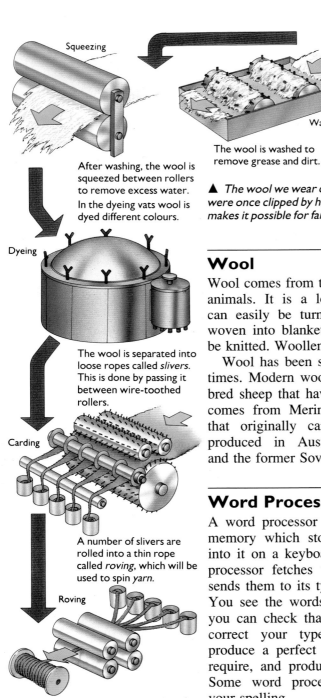

After washing, the wool is squeezed between rollers to remove excess water.
In the dyeing vats wool is dyed different colours.

Dyeing

The wool is separated into loose ropes called *slivers*. This is done by passing it between wire-toothed rollers.

Carding

A number of slivers are rolled into a thin rope called *roving*, which will be used to spin *yarn*.

Roving

▲ *The wool we wear comes from the fleece of sheep. Sheep were once clipped by hand, but the invention of electric shears makes it possible for farmers to clip over 200 sheep a day.*

Wool

Wool comes from the fleece of SHEEP and some other animals. It is a long and thick kind of hair that can easily be turned into yarn. The yarn may be woven into blankets, carpets and clothing, or it can be knitted. Woollen cloth is heavy and warm.

Wool has been spun and woven since STONE AGE times. Modern wool, however, comes from specially bred sheep that have good fine wool. The best wool comes from Merino sheep. These are white sheep that originally came from Spain. Most wool is produced in Australia, New Zealand, Argentina and the former Soviet Union.

Word Processor

A word processor is a kind of COMPUTER. It has a memory which stores all the words that you type into it on a keyboard. Then, whenever required, the processor fetches the words from its memory and sends them to its typing unit to be typed onto paper. You see the words you have typed on a screen, so you can check that there are no mistakes. You can correct your type and the processor will then produce a perfect letter or whatever document you require, and produce as many copies as you want. Some word processing programs can also check your spelling.

German soldier

British soldier

World War I

Between 1914 and 1918 Europe, the United States and much of the Middle East were locked in the first struggle that could be called a world war. On one side were Germany, Austria-Hungary and Turkey. On the other were France, the British Empire, the United States and Russia.

The battle soon became a stalemate in the west. The two sides spent four years in trenches in northern France, fighting over the same patch of ground. But in the east, Germany had better luck. The Germans attacked Russia so strongly that by 1917 Russia withdrew from the war.

After the United States joined the war in 1917, the Allied armies slowly pushed the Germans back. In November 1918 peace was declared.

US soldier

▲ Uniforms of American, British and German infantrymen during World War I. The opposing sides were often in trenches only a few hundred metres apart.

World War II

World War II cost between 35 and 60 million lives. The German dictator, Adolf Hitler, dreamed of world domination. Germany was supported by Italy. In Asia, Japan also had ambitions to control its neighbours. The so-called Axis powers (Germany, Italy and Japan) were opposed by the Allies (Britain, France, Russia, the United States and other nations). Important war leaders were Winston Churchill (Britain), Franklin D. Roosevelt (USA) and Joseph Stalin (Russia).

The war was fought on land, on sea and in the air. Civilians suffered as much as soldiers, especially from bombing of towns and cities. On land, there were huge tank BATTLES in Russia and North Africa, while at sea submarines sank many merchant ships. In great naval battles fought in the Pacific, aircraft carriers proved to be more effective than battleships. It was a scientific war, with new inventions such as radar and the V2 rocket.

When the Allied armies invaded Germany, ending the war in Europe, people were shocked by the horrors of the Nazi concentration camps in which millions of Jews had been killed. The war in Europe ended in May 1945. In the East, Japan fought on until August 1945, when the Americans dropped the first atomic bombs on the Japanese cities of Hiroshima and Nagasaki. Only then did Japan finally surrender, bringing World War II to an end.

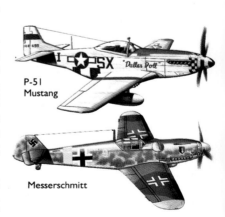

P-51 Mustang

Messerschmitt

▲ The German Messerschmitt (above) was involved in the Battle of Britain in 1940 against the British Spitfire. The American P-51 Mustang (top) was one of the most successful warplanes ever.

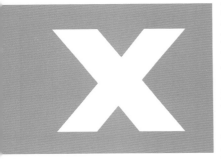

X-ray

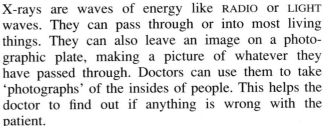

X-rays are waves of energy like RADIO or LIGHT waves. They can pass through or into most living things. They can also leave an image on a photographic plate, making a picture of whatever they have passed through. Doctors can use them to take 'photographs' of the insides of people. This helps the doctor to find out if anything is wrong with the patient.

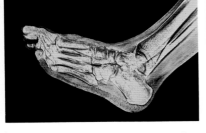

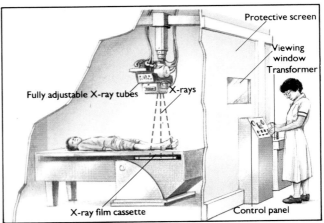

▶ A radiographer takes an X-ray of a child's foot. The resulting 'photograph' (above) has been coloured to show the foot and ankle bones more clearly.

X-rays are produced inside a glass tube that has no air or other gases in it. Inside the tube, at opposite ends, are a *cathode* that gives off electrons and an *anode*, or target. When the cathode is heated, electrons fly off and strike the anode, producing X-rays.

Wilhelm Roentgen, a German scientist, discovered X-rays by accident in 1895 while he was passing electricity through a gas. For this work, Roentgen received the first Nobel prize for Physics in 1901.

▼ The xylophone is used in orchestras and bands. Resonators, metal tubes below each bar, help to amplify the sound.

Xylophone

The xylophone is an odd-looking MUSICAL INSTRUMENT that produces a crisp, bell-like sound when played.

A xylophone has rows of solid wooden or metal bars fixed to a frame. Each bar is a different length and produces a different sound when struck. An electric version of the xylophone, called a *vibraphone*, is sometimes used.

Yangtze River (Chang Jiang)

The Yangtze is the longest, most important river in CHINA. From its beginnings, high in the mountains of Tibet, it flows 6342km across the centre of China, pouring into the Yellow Sea near Shanghai.

The river takes its name from the ancient kingdom of Yang, which grew up along its banks 3000 years ago. Today, the Yangtze is still one of the main trade routes in China. Big ships can sail up it as far as Hankow, nearly 1125km inland. Smaller boats can reach I-Ch'ang, which is 1600km from the sea.

Millions of people live and work on the Yangtze. Some live on the river itself in wooden sailing boats called *junks*.

Yeast

Yeast is a plant which is also a kind of FUNGUS. The whole plant consists of just one CELL. It is so tiny that you cannot see it without a microscope. It is very useful because it turns sugar into alcohol and carbon dioxide gas. This process is called fermentation. Yeast plants do this because they do not produce their own food. They live on sugar instead. Today yeast is grown in huge vats. It is then pressed into cakes or small pellets, ready to be sold.

Yugoslavia

Yugoslavia is a country in south-east EUROPE. Most of it lies in the BALKANS. It is a rugged, mountainous country. In the west, the mountains sweep down to the Adriatic Sea. Inland, the country is mostly scrubby and poor. Around the river Danube in the north, the land is fertile. Most of the country's farming goes on around here. Farmers grow wheat, barley, plums, olives and grapes, and keep cattle.

Yugoslavia's 24 million people come from different nations and speak many different languages. Most of them are Serbs, but there are also Croats, Slovenes, Albanians and Macedonians. They also follow different religions. In 1991 the republics of Slovenia and Croatia declared their independence. Fighting between Croats and Serbs intensified and continued into 1992 despite international efforts to arrange a cease-fire.

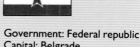

Government: Federal republic
Capital: Belgrade
Area: 255,804 sq km
Population: 23,898,000
Languages: Serbo-Croatian,
    Macedonian, Slovenian, Albanian
Currency: Dinar

Zaire

Zaire is a huge, hot and rainy country that sprawls across the heart of AFRICA. It includes most of the vast Zaire River, once called the Congo. This river is the second longest in Africa – only the Nile is longer – and one of the longest in the world. The Zaire is an important means of communication for the people of central Africa.

Much of Zaire is covered with thick jungle. There are lakes and highlands in the east and south. Copper, cobalt, and diamonds are mined here. But most of Zaire's 35 million inhabitants are farmers. They grow tea, coffee, cocoa, and cotton.

Government: Republic
Capital: Kinshasa
Area: 2,345,409 sq km
Population: 35,562,000
Languages: Bantu, French
Currency: Zaire

Zambia

Zambia is a country in southern AFRICA. It is entirely surrounded by land. Zaire, Tanzania, Malawi, Mozambique, Botswana, Zimbabwe, Namibia and Angola all share borders with Zambia.

The name Zambia comes from the Zambezi River. This runs across the western part of the country along the border with ZIMBABWE. Zambia was the British protectorate of Northern Rhodesia until it became an independent republic in 1964.

Much of the country is rolling, highland plains. The majority of Zambians are farmers. But most of the country's wealth comes from its copper mines. In the 1980s severe drought caused famine, and in 1990 Zambia suffered its worst violence since 1964.

Government: Republic
Capital: Lusaka
Area: 752,614 sq km
Population: 8,073,000
Languages: Bantu, English
Currency: Kwacha

Zebra

Zebras belong to the HORSE family. They live in the open grasslands of Africa to the south of the Sahara Desert. Zebras have creamy white coats covered with black or dark brown stripes. Each animal has its own special pattern of stripes. Burchell's zebra is the most common type of zebra found in East Africa. It has wide brownish-black or black stripes.

Zebras live in herds. They feed on grass and are often found roaming the grasslands with herds of antelope. Although zebras can run very fast, they are often hunted by lions, leopards and hyenas. People also used to hunt them for their attractive skins and tasty meat.

Zimbabwe

ZIMBABWE

Zimbabwe is a small country in southern AFRICA. It lies inland, about 240 km from the Indian Ocean. About 97 out of every 100 people are black Africans; the others are mostly white.

Zimbabwe is bordered by the Zambezi River in the north. The Zambezi is famous for the Victoria Falls and the Kariba Dam. The Kariba Dam is part of a great hydroelectric operation that supplies power to both Zimbabwe and its neighbour ZAMBIA.

Until 1965, Zimbabwe was the British colony of Southern Rhodesia. In that year, it declared itself the independent country of Rhodesia. Britain, however, did not recognize the new nation's existence. During the next 15 years, growing unrest and guerrilla warfare caused many problems. In 1980 the country became independent, under a black-majority government, as Zimbabwe.

Government: Parliamentary democracy
Capital: Harare
Area: 390,580 sq km
Population: 9,369,000
Languages: English, Shona, Sindebele
Currency: Zimbabwe dollar

Zoo

Zoos are places where wild animals are kept. They are cared for, bred, studied and sometimes saved from dying out. There are now more than 330 zoos in the world.

The first zoos were in ancient Egypt. Queen Hatshepsut kept a zoo in 1500 BC. More than 3000 years ago, the emperors of China kept animals, birds and fish in natural gardens where they would feel at home.

> The world's zoos range in size from small, privately owned collections to large public zoos. Berlin Zoo houses more than 2000 different species of animals, more than any other zoo in the world.

◀ This painting of the Broad Walk with elephants at Regent's Park Zoo in London was done at the turn of the century. The zoo was founded in the 1820s by the Zoological Society of London, though today it is more generally known as the London Zoo.

About Your Index

No encyclopedia can have entries on every subject, so there is a vast amount of information that can only be found by looking in the Index. There is no entry on the atmosphere, for example, but if you look in the Index you will find lots of information and pictures under **Acid rain**, **Air**, **Climate**, **Cloud**, **Greenhouse effect**, **Ozone layer** and **Weather**.

Take the index entry on Tokyo for example:
Tokyo 25, *199*, **368–369**
The main entry on the capital of Japan is on pages 368 and 369. On page 29, under the entry on **Asia** there is a picture of Tokyo's modern buildings. The entry on **Japan** on page 199 shows us a photograph of the city's busy overhead railway.

Page numbers in **boldface type** (heavy and dark) indicate where the main reference to the subject can be found. Page numbers in *italic type* (slanting) refer to pages on which illustrations will be found.

INDEX

INDEX

INDEX

INDEX

Acknowledgements

The publishers would like to thank the following for kindly supplying photographs for this book:

Page 9 Heather Angel; 14 Sonia Halliday; 23 Michael Holford (top right) Bridgeman Art Library (top left) Tate Gallery (bottom); 28 Istanbul University; 32 Frank Spooner (top) Zoe Dominic (bottom); 43 Mansell Collection; 53 Dennis Gilbert/Grisewood & Dempsey Ltd; 57 M. Kroenlein; 69 Giraudon; 70 Mansell Collection; 71 Science Photo Library; 75 Kobal Collection; 82 Science Photo Library; 116 NASA; 123 Science Photo Library; 135 Metropolitan Police; 139 Hulton Picture Company; 141 Allsport; 151 Popperfoto; 152 Jane Burton/Bruce Coleman; 156 Courtesy, Royal Brierly Crystal; 169 Simon Bruty/Allsport; 170 National Portrait Gallery (top), British Museum (bottom); 174 SCALA; 185 Science Photo Library; 198 N.H.P.A.; 200 National Gallery; 205 Allsport; 207 Science Photo Library; 210 Bridgeman Art Library; 212 SCALA; 227 Science Photo Library; 229 Science Photo Library; 231 N.H.P.A.; 247 National Gallery of Art, Washington D.C.; 259 Shell Photographic Library; 265 Westermann Foto; 267 Courtesy, English Chamber Orchestra; 271 The Hutchinson Library (left); 275 South American Pictures; 277 Ontario Science Centre; 283 Mary Evans Picture Library; 290 The Hutchinson Library; 292 Mary Evans Picture Library; 296 Science Photo Library; 299 Science Photo Library; 300 Science Photo Library; 306 Michael Holford (right), SCALA (left); 307 Heather Angel; 311 Picturepoint; 320 Science Photo Library; 325 Science Photo Library; 327 National Portrait Gallery; 334 Peter Newark's Western Americana; 337 Picturepoint; 342 The Hutchinson Library (top); 364 Picturepoint; 365 The Hutchinson Library; 371 Peter Newark's Western Americana; 377 Science Photo Library; 384 National Portrait Gallery; 386 Spectrum; 405 Mary Evans Picture Library.